Michael Rossum's book is phenomenal. I have known a great deal about his life, but I was riveted to each page and every chapter. The way he writes takes me to every moment he mentions, every person I knew, every color and feeling and painful experience he recants or that he spoke about with me previously. He is a masterful writer about his truth. His book must be read, because it is rare insight into a man who never gives in or gives up. He has outlived everyone and keeps me going, too.

—Betty Ann Judah, MS, Educational Specialist and Consultant, The Dyslexia & Learning Disability Center, Inc.

For those of us who experienced - and more importantly - participated in any of the upheavals of the 60s and 70s and 80s will relate and enjoy Michael Rossum's amazing adventures and journey of self-discovery in Touchstones.

From the early days of the Haight Asbury, later hitchhiking through Europe, behind the iron curtain, and following the Hippie route through Iran, Afghanistan, India, and the Middle East, he was a witness to global changes of the period. From camel caravans and the atmosphere of pre-Taliban Afghanistan to the villages of Nepal and the beaches of Goa, he captures the time where the world was open to those who experienced the freedom of that time. Jump to the glory days of the gay scene in New York and San Francisco and the devastation and loss during the AIDS epidemic - Michael has seen it all.

—Anne Ross, Writer

This book is an amazing romp! It's almost as though ten lives have been lived in one, here for us to explore vicariously through this writing. It is the story of a young man claiming his identity, traveling the world, and finding spirituality, told through his relationships along the way - his "Touchstones". Add to that the historical context of this life well lived, and I couldn't put it down. Definitely a life affirming read. Hopefully it will find it's way to the big screen one day.

—Lynn Taff

Touchstones

A Survivor's Story

Michael Rossum

Touchstones - *A Survivor's Story*

Copyright © 2019 by Michael Rossum

All rights reserved under the International and Pan-American Copyright Conventions. No part of this book may be reproduced or transmitted in any form or by any means, electronic or mechanical including photocopying, recording, or by any information storage and retrieval system, without permission in writing from the publisher.

The scanning, uploading and distribution of this book via the Internet or via any other means without the permission of the publisher is illegal, and punishable by law. Please purchase only authorized electronic editions, and do not participate in or encourage the electronic piracy of copyrighted materials. Your support of the author's rights is appreciated.

This is a work of nonfiction. Names, individuals, places and incidents were known personally to or by the author or were personally experienced by the author and not created as fiction—though limited by the author's memory and recall in exactitude.

Ruby Red Slippers Publishing
131 Red Hawk Court
Brisbane, CA 94005

Cover Art © 2019 by Michael Rossum

Edited by William Greenleaf

Trade Paperback ISBN: 978-1-7331694-0-0
eBook ISBN: 978-1-7331694-1-7

First Edition • June 2019

Production by Ruby Red Slippers Publishing

Printed in the United States of America

This book is dedicated to Robin, Adele, and Mark, and to an entire generation of my peers who taught me what true courage looks like, and who died too young.

Table of Contents

Chapter 1 Man in the Mirror 1

Chapter 2 Gene 5

Chapter 3 The Ramirez Family-Mexico 35

Chapter 4 The Ramirez Family 41

Chapter 5 Michael and Graham-LSD and the Spiritual Path 53

Chapter 6 Robin 1971 63

Chapter 7 Easter Break-Meeting the "In laws" 69

Chapter 8 Michael Hampshire House 77

Chapter 9 European Tour-London to Paris 85

Chapter 10 Journey to the East-The Silk Road
  Rome-September 1972 125

Chapter 11 Delhi 155

Chapter 12 India—January 1973 177

Chapter 13 Bombay 199

Chapter 14 Brescia, Italy 205

Chapter 15 Bill Tester 217

Chapter 16 Barry McKinley 237

Chapter 17 India 267

Chapter 18 New York, New York 273

Chapter 19 Michael Strater 295

Chapter 20 Mark 309

Chapter 21 The Epidemic 327

Chapter 22 Steve Matejka 349

Chapter 23 Adrian 367

Chapter 24 Christmas 1989 381

Chapter 25 Eli—Path to Freedom 427

Epilogue 435

Photographic Table of Contents

1. Adele, 1922 13
2. Michael and Gene, 1955 17
3. Arthur and Adele, 1942 33
4. Robin, 1971 62
5. Hampshire House, the author, 1971 76
6. The walls of Jerusalem 109
7. Jaffa Gate Market 110
8. Boy playing soccer, on the walls graffiti from the Intifada riots 111
9. Jerusalem, busy archways run underground 112
10. The heart of Muslim Jerusalem taken from the back terrace of Ibrahim's house; the schoolteacher who gave us refuge in his house during our near escape from Israeli Defense Forces 113
11. Smuggled painting – Vaclav Popoff, Hungary, 1971 120
12. Robin and Michael in Katmandu Valley, in the village of Swayambhunath, and the famous Monkey Temple in the background 161
13. Tibetan refugees from China, 1972 168
14. Tibetan refugees spinning wool into balls for our landlords 170
15. Nepalese landlord's wife, Faye, Faye's mother with Faye's older daughter and children 172
16. Clementino, to right of Robin, leaving village for India 174
17. Robin – Epitaph 215

18. Bill Tester 216
19. Barry McKinley, Fire Island, 1974 236
20. Fire Island, sunning around Barry's pool, Barry in the middle and model "Baby Bob" taken from my journal 1974 248
21. Paul Meyers 287
22. Limousine leaving New York with Paul Meyers, 1976 292
23. Michael Strater 294
24. Mark 308
25. Mark, 1983, Laguna Beach our first weekend together 325
26. Richard Chamberlin 341
27. Loy, professional bodybuilder 342
28. Jerry Alvarnez 343
29. Ad for publication, on Gay Men's books; Muscling into the Mainstream Gay Books 344
30. Alex Desy, owner of Prima Facie Salon on Castro Street; I had my first exhibition of photographs at his opening that launched my career, and he created his dream of opening the salon 345
31. Christian Ashman center with twin sister Ingrid, their mother smuggled them out of East Berlin to West Berlin in 1948 each in a suitcase. Christian escaped Communism but he couldn't escape AIDS 346
32. AIDS Quilt tells the story of the immense loss of life to the Epidemic 347
33. Steve Matejka 348
34. The Three Musketeers; Doll Boys, Australia, 1993 364
35. Adrian 366
36. Fog lifted from the Irrawaddy displaying majestic Burmese temples 395
37. Travelling companions Sue and Stewart on top of temple in Pagan valley at sunset 398

38. Thousands of skulls piled three stories high in memorial to 2 million murdered in the Killing Fields, Cambodia 402
39. Tortured and mutilated Cambodians strive to live after Pol Pot Regime's terror.. 404
40. Adrian and Michael in Angkor Tom, Cambodia 1994........... 405
41. Crossing the frozen Neva River, St. Petersburg, Russia 407
42. New Year's Eve shoppers line up at Kiosks, St. Petersburg........ 410
43. Park between Admiralty and Neva River, St. Petersburg, New Year's Day 411
44. Adrian and Michael frozen on the Palace Bridge with the Winter Palace and the Neva River in the background... 412
45. Street Vendors, Man selling hot roasted garlic 413
46. Hindu priest driving out evil spirits on beach in Bali after September nightclub terrorist bombing 418
47. Offerings at the Mother Temple after the Bali Bombings...... 421
48. My Teachers, Eli and Gangaji... 433

Chapter One

Man in the Mirror

I am a survivor. HIV has killed most of my friends, many acquaintances, and every lover I ever had. Who could have imagined a plague the scope of the Black Death in 1981? Now, no longer detectable in the blood, thanks to the HIV cocktail, it hides in the cells of the body waiting for the immune system to become compromised. Then it sends out its deadly message to attack the body, to invade and wring the life out of the ones we love. One cannot comprehend what it's like to lose so many people at once. The grief is overwhelming.

Long-term survivors always wonder how they survived. We feel a combination of angst, guilt that we survived, and gratitude that we have had so much more time on the planet. I was diagnosed with HIV in 1984. The doctor who diagnosed me died in 1985. None of us had any idea how much time we had. With no drugs to fight it, time was precious, and we didn't want to waste a minute.

Back then, our bodies were so fit, Adrian and I looked like Greek gods. When we danced together at the clubs, stripped down to our Levi's, the sweat dripping down our backs, it was as if we were all alone. Men would break us apart and start dancing with us, hoping for a chance they might take us home.

Now we're lucky to get out of bed. When we wake in the morning, the silence is deafening. Words cannot express the pain, limitations, and loss our bodies and minds have sustained. I always try to greet Adrian with my eyes, to let him know I'm there. He wakes but never speaks. His eyes say it all. He's worn out.

Our lives kept spiraling downward. There was never a plateau in which we were capable of coasting. First, we got neuropathy in our feet. It was so bad I could barely walk. Then I started limping due to pain in my hip joint. It turned out to be an HIV-related arthritis in which calcium crystals destroyed the joint until there was no cartilage left. I had to have my right hip replaced. Some months later, the left hip followed suit, then there was back surgery a month later for a disc herniation. It took a year out of my life to recover. Adrian, meanwhile, was complaining about a lack of energy and was diagnosed with HIV fatigue. It was one thing after another, and it never let up. I had cancer that shook me to my core. I'd had so much vitality and was so strong. I had lived with HIV for well over two decades and showed no side effects. I was six foot three with eighteen-inch arms and weighed 230 pounds. I was in the prime of my life. Cancer was something that happened to other people.

I had a lump in my neck and had to have it biopsied. After the surgery, they told me the tumor was malignant. I had Kaposi's sarcoma cancer. As I began to put on a fresh gown following the surgery, I couldn't raise my arm above my shoulder. It turned out that the doctor who performed the biopsy had cut the accessory nerve that runs from the shoulder to the brain. Fortunately for me, a brilliant neurosurgeon sewed it back together. I regained the use of my shoulder and was able to return to the gym. Somehow, I felt that by working out, I could create a protective shield. It was denial but buried so deep that when I had to face it, I cracked.

My first visit to the oncologist was a humbling experience. I never realized how many people have it. I was alone that day. All around me were people in various stages of cancer treatment. We sat in silence in the waiting room. Each had his own story. We all had loved ones praying for our recovery, hoping that this time it would work, the tumor would shrink, and our lives would be prolonged, maybe even saved.

After four infusions of chemotherapy and with five more to go, I stood at the sink and looked at myself in the mirror. My eyelashes were gone. My cheeks were sunken. My muscled body had begun to atrophy. The sight jolted me like a shock wave. I ran my hands through my thinning hair and told myself, "You'll get through it." Yet I found myself mourning for a body in decay, even bitter. Such a dichotomy. I knew it was going to happen. I just thought I had more time.

As I stared at the man in the mirror, I began to look back on my life, and a smile came across my face. I thought of all the amazing things I'd accomplished, and the equally amazing people who'd touched me to my depths. I began to laugh, realizing that every decision I'd ever made had led me to this place and the man I'd become. How could I betray myself now at the end? For I had lived a blessed life.

Chapter Two

Mazel Tov

I was born in Manhattan on May 30, 1949, Memorial Day, on the Upper West Side. Since it was a holiday, a lot of people were out of town, including most of my relatives. My father had been through three false alarms. He put my mother in a cab to the hospital around five in the morning and went back to sleep. My mother's water broke on the way, and I was almost born in a Checker cab.

My aunt Emma, who was still in town and had gone to meet my mother at the hospital, called my father to tell him to come immediately. "You have a son! Mazel tov."

You could say my old man and I were off to a rocky start, and we hadn't even met.

The Barbary Coast

I grew up in the San Francisco Bay Area in the 1950s and '60s. Ferries crisscrossed the bay to the ferry building, where the planks would drop, and a steady stream of cars would empty onto Market Street. It was the age of innocence. In the living room was a television screen about six inches wide, which sat on a three-foot-high box with a speaker in it. *Howdy Doody* was on, and all the kids from the neighborhood huddled together to watch.

It was a magical time to grow up in America: no wars, plenty of opportunities, and a growing middle class. My dad got a public relations job in San Francisco, and we lived downtown in what's now called the Tenderloin. Back then it was an area of apartment houses and stores that jutted angularly into Market Street. Later in the '60s, when we'd moved to the Berkeley area, it would become crime-ridden and its name synonymous with pimps, prostitutes, and petty crime.

Oddly, I can't remember much about my childhood. I can honestly say I never lacked for anything. I had a roof over my head, food on the table, and plenty of love. I knew my parents weren't well-off, but what I didn't know was how much they were borrowing to stay afloat.

When I was six, I didn't know a whole lot about the world except that sometimes it could be cruel. I was the new kid on the block, and Jewish, in a gentile neighborhood. Coming home from school was a bit like maneuvering through an asphalt jungle. I'd avoid certain streets where I knew I'd meet trouble.

I saw some boys playing tetherball in my neighborhood one day, and I innocently asked if I could play.

The biggest of the three approached me, stared for a moment, then said, "Look here, Jew boy, you can't play with us. You killed Christ."

I was in shock. I had nothing to say. If I denied it, there would only be more condemnation. I'd heard slurs against Jews before, but never directed at me. My head hung down, I walked home, confused and hurt.

I relayed the story to my mom, who'd experienced anti-Semitism firsthand on the Lower Eastside in New York. The ignorance, cruelty, and prejudice that parents pass to their offspring was something we'd discussed before. I think she'd been preparing me for this day.

"They said I killed Christ, Mom."

Seeing that I was wounded, she said with her dry sense of humor, "Well, you go back out there and tell those boys you never even knew him."

"I can't do that," I said.

We looked at each other quizzically for a moment, and then began laughing uncontrollably.

She was my island of refuge, where I could receive communion, a spiritual reservoir in which I could grow as if in a cocoon, someday to spread my wings and fly. She told me I was unique—which is to say, through her intervention, a little sibling rivalry, and perhaps a father who wished I'd been aborted—that I was somehow different from the rest of them.

Adele was a tall woman with long, wavy hair and beautiful blue eyes—not like the sky, more like the sea on a calm day. A Renaissance woman who, though she had all the riches in the world, at her core remained a proletariat.

Raised in New York City by immigrant parents, she spoke eloquently with an accent that betrayed her humble beginnings. She was Bohemian, having grown up with aunts who were suffragettes, and remained Bohemian in that way for the rest of her life. People were always complimenting her on her necklace of Russian amber, antique Rajasthani necklace of silver with jade droplets that her father gifted her, and her Native American jewelry and such. Her mother, also a suffragette and a founder of the Socialist Labor Party in America, had learned English from a dictionary. Her father was to become the first Jewish vice president of the American Thread Company.

She was a socialist, dedicated to ending the class struggle. One could see in her face the determination that only comes from belief in oneself. She and my father were determined to make the American Dream come true, for everyone.

One day she had some friends over for a weekly bridge game, and a woman from Texas joined them to make a foursome. I was eating a sandwich in the kitchen while watching them play and listening to their conversation.

When Adele played the deuce of spades, the Texan said, in a heavy southern accent, "Well, down in Texas when you play a deuce of spades like that, we call that nigger bridge."

There was a long silence.

Adele fought back the urge to throttle this ignorant woman. In true fashion, she held out a bowl instead and said, "Nuts, anyone?"

Upon picking out the largest Brazil nut and taking a bite, the Texan exclaimed, "Down in Texas, we call these nigger toes."

Unable to control her anger, the veins in her neck bulging from holding her breath, Adele finally had enough. "Well then, remind me never to go to Texas!" she said. The Texan clammed up real quick.

My parents belonged to the Socialist Labor Party of America. So not only was I on the fringes of society politically as a Commie Red, I also had evidently killed Christ. I was the son of two immigrant families from Russia, the Rosumovskys on my father's side and the Zimmermans on my mother's. Being of Russian ancestry in the midst of the Cold War only added to my disdain for the life my parents had chosen for me, as I desperately wanted to fit in. Why couldn't we be like everybody else?

I mean, don't get me wrong. I loved my parents for being nonconformists who wanted to see the whole world living with dignity and enough to eat. But my status in the herd was already spiraling downward. I'd just entered the first grade.

Still, I'd have to say the sixth grade was my real undoing. We'd moved to Hayward, south of Berkeley. That was a mistake. It was 1960, and the presidential elections were in full swing. It was Nixon and Kennedy going head-to-head, and secretly I wanted JFK to win.

My teacher at the time, Mr. O'Neal, asked the class how many of us would vote for Nixon and how many for Kennedy. He wanted a show of hands, which he counted. There were thirty-one students and only thirty votes, so he asked, "Who didn't vote?"

I raised my hand reluctantly.

"Why didn't you vote, Michael?" he asked.

"Voting for Nixon or voting for Kennedy would be like voting for Tweedledee or Tweedledumb," I replied.

There was complete silence. No one seemed to get it, not even Mr. O'Neal.

"Well, for whom would you vote then?" he asked.

Somehow knowing that my life would change forever, but wanting to keep true to the principles I grew up with, I said with some trepidation, "Eric Hass of the Socialist Labor Party."

There was a huge collective gasp, then a moan of disbelief, at which point the students began speaking to one another in hushed sounds. Then the noise began to sound like buzzing bees. The buzzing grew louder and louder until I was saved by the bell and class was dismissed. My social life was on life support.

On Sundays, my brother, Gene, and I would have to help our parents pass out Socialist Labor Party leaflets in the parking lot of suburban Southland Mall. This was their way of trying to inform the working class about the party and that there was an alternative to the Tweedledee and Tweedledumb governance. But not everyone saw it that way.

One Sunday as I was sticking leaflets under the wiper blades of cars, a man approached me. He pulled the leaflet off his windshield, looked at it, and read a few lines.

"You little Commie brat!" he screamed, vengeance in his voice.

Dad looked around to see what all the fuss was about, and the two men made eye contact. Dad then turned back to the business of passing out leaflets.

I felt apprehensive and looked to Gene, who was six years older than I.

"Don't worry, Mick," he said. "He'll be okay."

The man approached my father, screaming, "You goddamned Commie bastard!" He knocked the huge stack of leaflets from my father's arm.

Dad calmly picked up the leaflets and continued to distribute them. When the man approached him again and again knocked the leaflets from his hands, I saw something I could never have imagined. My father, the pillar of nonviolence, punched the man right in the face. He went down like a ton of bricks and lay there groaning while my father picked up the leaflets and continued distributing them.

This was the conviction my parents held toward changing the society we lived in. My dad made me feel proud, and I'll never forget that day. He really was an inspiration. Someone who believes in something so strongly that nothing will shake his resolve is a person with real conviction and integrity. I continued to pass out my leaflets because I believed the future my parents envisioned was a just cause.

Adele

Adele wore her hair up off her long face and neck, which gave her a certain kind of elegance. She had natural beauty and wore little makeup unless she went out. But when she did get dressed up, I'd watch her transform from the mom who cleaned my room and picked up my dirty socks into an elegant woman.

One night when my father was waiting for her to come out of her dressing room, he said to me, "Mick, women are always late." He shouted to her, "Come on, we're going to be late."

But when she made her entrance in the strapless turquoise evening gown and matching silk shawl, all I could say was, "Wow, Mom, you look like a movie star," and she did.

My mother taught me how to love by example. She showed my father warmth and affection. Equally, she showed my brother and me the same love, affectionately playing with us when we were young, always cuddling me. While holding me, she'd ask, "Do you know how much I love you?" and I'd respond, "How much?" No matter how many times I asked, it was always the same answer: "More than words can say."

Adele also taught us what it meant to be compassionate and to treat others with kindness. If I'd point out someone with a disability, she'd say, "There but for the grace of God go I." I knew intuitively what she meant. She was so ahead of her time, an idealist and revolutionary on so many levels, ready to upset the status quo, whether dealing with problems my friends were having with their parents or setting out to change the government and the world.

Adele's early years were shaped by family and the Socialist Labor Party, with family always coming first. She was so understanding. I used to complain about my father's absence. I was hurt by his lack of attention. When he had a free day, he'd go golfing with his buddies. She'd explain to me in her warm, soothing way that Dad was working hard to give us the life we were living and he needed some time to recover from the stress of work. Then she'd say, "Let's do something nice for him."

"What?" I'd ask.

"Want to help me make him a chocolate cake?"

That was how she defused confrontations—with an enlightened heart and a kindness that came from within. I think she must have been a Buddhist in another lifetime, for she had compassion for all living things—except for flies. She kept the flyswatter by the stove and used it regularly.

Adele was a beautiful woman and an awakened spirit. She loved her family unconditionally, and she strove for something much larger than herself. Her goal was to change the social order for Americans living in poverty, who suffered at the hands of the capitalist class. She hoped one day to see a system of governance with a human face. As far as she was concerned, my brother and I were here to work toward that end, showing compassion to the millions who lived below the poverty line by fighting for socialism. In that way we'd work to ensure American workers had fair-wage jobs, and that would protect the growing middle class and make America a prosperous country. She believed that a country should be judged by the poorest of its people. She knew this from her own experience growing up in New York City.

Adele's personal experience with poverty would mold her ideas of a classless society for the rest of her life. She worked tirelessly to end racism, which she believed was due to the captains of industry separating the working class and preventing the unity of people—black, white, and other people of color. She was a nonconformist and a social reformer. Those are the people willing to take a stand for their ideals because they feel morally obligated. Adele saw firsthand the overcrowded streets of the Lower East Side and Harlem, where she lived as a girl.

Later, she lived in the brownstones of the Upper East Side. Her father became the first Jewish vice president of a gentile firm called the American Thread Company, though he never forgot his humble beginnings. He was one of the founders of the Socialist Labor Party in America.

She was appalled by the difference in her life after her father's good fortune, so much so that when the family chauffeur drove by the bread lines of the '30s, she'd duck down to the floor because she felt guilty that her family was doing so well when so many millions were suffering. She got involved with the Socialist Labor Party in her teens and made a lifelong commitment that as long as she drew breath, she'd fight for the working class.

You'd think that a woman like that growing up in the '20s would have been interested in boys, fancy cars, and the Charleston, and you'd be right. She was. But she struck a harmonious balance between having fun and putting America's growing poverty and inequality first.

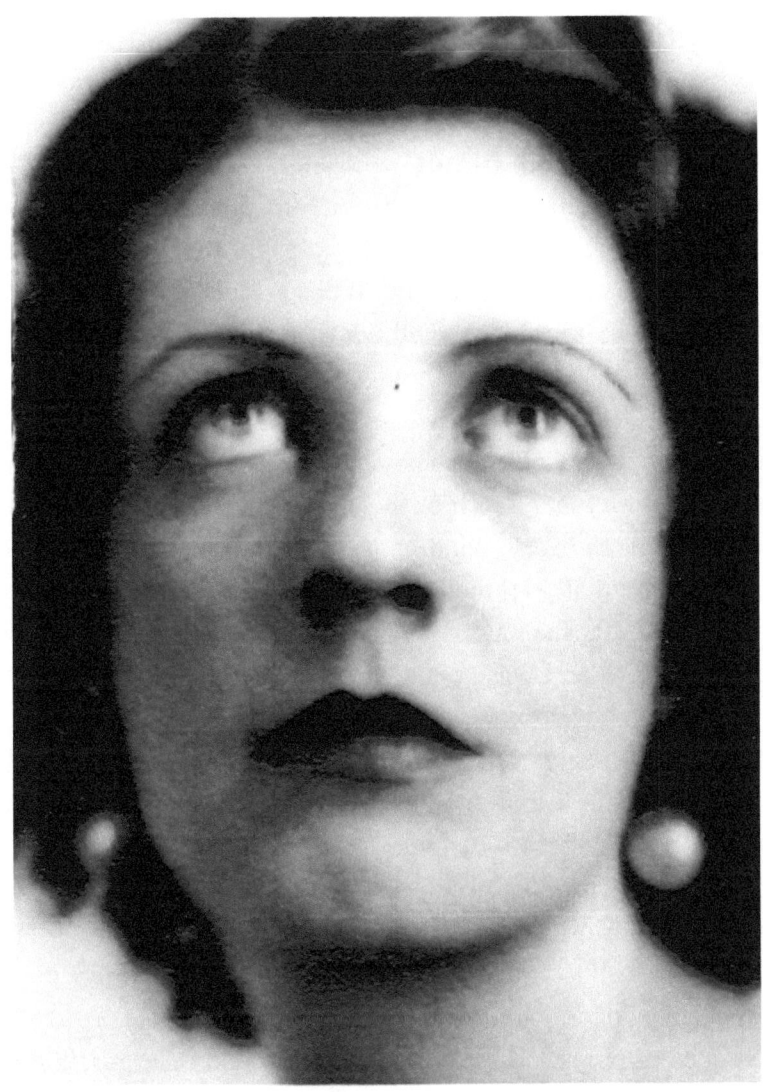

Adele, 1922

Beyond her ideals, Adele suffered the same things all middle class families suffer growing up with teenage boys—not enough money, and an authoritarian husband who always admitted that she wore the pants in the family, which was the truth. We were as dysfunctional as any other family, but we were lucky to have two parents who loved one another unconditionally and who encouraged us to speak our minds and talk about our problems. Perhaps so much so that they became our friends' counselors, as many of them found it easy to talk to them, while it was quite the opposite with their own parents. They'd say, "You're so lucky to have such great parents."

But in every family dynamic, there are always problems. We knew they were right, but we had our own private issues.

Adele also had some household management troubles. She lacked domestic skills when she married, as there was always someone there to do the work previously. She was a horrible cook at first. Sometimes she'd forget that the chicken's innards were wrapped in plastic inside the bird, and we'd wind up eating TV dinners instead. To her credit, she eventually learned to cook, and her homemade chopped liver was the best. She taught me how to draw, to paint, and to speak a little French when I was young.

I truly believe that parents who are aware of a child's needs and abilities in those early years can have a huge impact on an individual's talents. Case in point: I got my BA, majoring in Spanish and minoring in art. I speak a couple of languages and was able to learn conversational Chinese, Hindi, and Arabic when I traveled. I love art and dabbled in lots of media and took photographs professionally. I owe this all to Adele, as it was she, with loving kindness, who infused those talents into me at a young age. It also was Adele who encouraged me to reach for the goals I never thought possible. She nurtured me so that my roots grew deep and I had a solid framework. She understood the human condition and knew that I'd wind up someday suffering as she had in her lifetime. She hoped that by being well rooted, I'd weather the storms and the challenges that life would present.

When my father died of a heart attack in 1982 while my parents were visiting relatives in New York City, I went there to bring them home. A friend of mine, a gay flight attendant, had arranged first-class seating, and he took care of me on the flight. I didn't realize how much I'd loved my father and what a profound effect he had on my life. I cried myself to sleep, and in the morning, we arrived.

The next day, my mother and I were the only ones to sit with him. Mother in all her protectiveness didn't want me to go down to the funeral home where he lay. Perhaps she wanted to be alone with him to tell him how much she loved him and so on. But I, too, had my goodbyes to make. You only get one chance. I was torn apart inside, but I held it together for her.

We flew home that night, mostly in silence. When we arrived at the apartment where they'd spent so many years together, I looked around and knew she had to leave. There, she'd be consumed by my father's ghost. We sat at the dining table, and I produced the small package of cocaine that had been fueling my comatose body.

"Give me some of that," she said.

"Mom, are you sure?"

"Why not? If you're going to be up half the night, so will I."

I laid the lines out, and with a rolled-up dollar bill, we snorted the white powder. We talked all night, looked at pictures, and spoke about all the things that were just beneath the surface and had never been touched upon.

"From here on out," she said, "don't you ever keep any secrets from me. I want to know everything, good and bad." She hugged me.

I promised, as tears fell and we embraced, neither of us wanting to let go until we'd cried all our tears.

After my father's death, our relationship grew stronger. Adele told me about the affair my father had. She had a lot of thoughts she'd never shared with anyone. Now they came pouring out. It was cathartic for both of us. I had a new lover, Mark, and she became an integral part of our life together. My friends came to love her. They called her Adele, and she was their friend. She was mine too.

When she contracted lymphoma in April 1994, she was almost eighty-two. Adele came to live with me and my lover, Adrian, and to die with us. She'd be the hardest to let go of out of all those who preceded her. I used to come to her room, which was on the main floor of our Victorian on Grove Street, and put my head on her swollen belly and beg her not to leave me. I know it was selfish of me, but that's how deep the connection went with us. It was on a cellular level, and I was losing where I'd come from. I felt like the umbilical cord had been cut and I was orphaned, floating in space.

It was heartbreaking when she left us, but she didn't suffer. She left me knowing that I was in good hands with Adrian, who loved me unconditionally. She died on a hot day in August. I woke that morning and went to her room. Her ocean-blue eyes were open, staring up at the ceiling, peaceful. Her spirit gone had left its shell behind. No more suffering. I hugged her one last time before the medics came to take her away. I went to our garden, which was our refuge, and cried for the remainder of the day, and mourned her for years afterward.

Gene

When we were growing up, my brother and I were like the characters Wally and the Beaver from the TV series *Leave It to Beaver*. Gene was older and, of course, taller, as handsome as they come, with broad cheekbones and hazel-green eyes. His hair was the color of obsidian, jet black and shiny. He was my protector, and I wanted to be just like him.

Michael and Gene, 1955

When I was in the first grade, he was in the sixth. He made my breakfast in the morning, helped me get dressed, and walked me to school. I used to climb the fence behind my homeroom class just to watch him play at recess. I guess I idolized him. He was mathematically inclined and athletic too. He knew how to play the game with my parents. He was a model kid. He seemed to me to be everything I wanted to be and wasn't.

He had a wry sense of humor. Once when I went on a trip to New York with my mother, we called home and he answered. I'd left my prize ducklings, two mallards I'd won in the Alameda County Fair, in his care.

"Hi, Gene," I said. "How are the ducks?"

"Your ducks are dead!" he replied in a loud voice, knowing full well I'd fall apart.

I started crying immediately, and then he assured me that they weren't. I came to appreciate his unpredictable and sarcastic sense of humor as I grew older.

He was promoted to advanced classes in mathematics, played varsity basketball for Arroyo High School, played the clarinet in the band, and was hugely popular with both guys and girls. When he discovered Bob Dylan's "Blowin' in the Wind," he taught himself to play the harmonica, the guitar, and the bongos, which he played all at once.

More than his talents, he was the apple of our father's eye. I knew I couldn't take his place with Dad, and I never wanted to. I loved my brother because of who he was—one of the most generous, funny, and intelligent human beings I'd ever met. It would be some twenty years later that I'd learn he was envious of my dance abilities, my artwork, and my language skills.

On his graduation picture, he wrote, *Michael, try to remember to work harder than I did so you can make Mom and Dad a little prouder. We all want you to be successful in life. Our wishes and hopes for the future are with you. Your loving brother, Gene.*

He'd learned well. I was the rebel, the one who disobeyed and gave my father hell for not being there for me. Now, in my infinite wisdom, I can see how difficult it must have been for Dad, who wanted to be a writer and was saddled with a job he hated and two kids to support. My brother was different. He knew how to please him, and they genuinely had a special relationship.

Gene got a scholarship to the University of California at Berkeley to pursue his dreams—right inside the hailstorm of People's Park, Joan Baez, Bob Dylan, Mario Savio and the Free Speech Movement, LSD, and Timothy Leary.

When I was a senior in high school, I went to Berkeley during the People's Park riots to visit my brother. He was living in a dorm not far from the campus on Dwight Way. Everyone in the Bay Area knew what was happening in Berkeley. The university and the city had become the conscience of America.

First there was Mario Savio and the Free Speech Movement, which ignited campuses across the country. Students wanted to be able to speak freely on all subjects and be able to disagree with what was written in their textbooks or spoken from a lectern. This brought out all the activists, including celebrities like Joan Baez, Bob Dylan, and Angela Davis marching down Telegraph Avenue, the main thoroughfare to Sather Gate, the entrance to the university. Arm in arm, they faced off with a police tactical squad in full riot gear. That's how scared Big Brother was of the Free Speech Movement.

People's Park was a small plot of land owned by the university. It had lain vacant for years. Now there was talk of building a parking lot on it. The people, both students and locals, wanted to see it developed into a park where everyone could meet and congregate. The thought of another concrete parking lot was abhorrent. The students took it over, tents went up, and people started to build a park with their bare hands. They even laid sod. It was considered a "free space," and lots of musicians would come and play. The flowers were blooming, and the people of Berkeley had gained a new park.

This peaceful use went on for a few weeks until one day, the bulldozers showed up to tear it all down. The space was surrounded by hundreds of people, and then there was a call to arms. More people showed up until there were thousands. That was the day I arrived, the day the riots began.

My brother and I went to the park with some of his friends to give our support. Shortly after arriving, we encountered the armed tactical squad. Officers descended on the crowd with billy clubs and tear gas. We started running for Sather Gate and the refuge of the university. As we ran, they ran after us, chasing hundreds of people and beating them brutally.

The university would be no safe haven. As we ran into the student union, they threw tear gas canisters inside. We hid in the bathrooms for a while until the tear gas forced us out.

When the news got out about what had happened at Berkeley at a peaceful protest, the People's Park movement grew overnight. The next day, there were even more people. As the days passed and the riots continued, cat-and-mouse battles took place in the streets. We learned to bring wet handkerchiefs to wrap around our faces and avoid breathing in the tear gas. For the brave and courageous ones who were able to pick up a canister and throw it back at the police, we cheered.

A curfew was called, and people had to be off the streets by 6:00 p.m. It was getting difficult to move around after curfew. The National Guard was called out, and soldiers stood on every major street corner, rifles drawn. Just before curfew one night, girls appeared on the streets carrying baskets of oranges. They were passing them out to the soldiers in an attempt, we thought, to show good will and let them know we were no threat. Then the news came out on every pole and billboard that there was to be no fraternizing between the locals and guardsmen. Seems that the oranges had been injected with LSD, and over a hundred guardsmen had to be hospitalized. The fraternizing had allowed many of us, including my brother and me, to get back home after curfew.

Soon after this, another plot of land on University Avenue, the Annex, was taken. Gene and I were there, and when we looked down the long avenue toward the freeway, we saw armored trucks rolling up that main avenue with more guardsmen. Ordinary housewives and citizens came out of their homes and lined the streets. Berkeley was besieged. Now the crowds were mixed—not just students anymore—and they were outraged at what was happening.

The guardsmen jumped down out of the trucks and ran toward the crowd, now in the middle of the lawn on the Annex, with bayonets fixed. I'd be lying if I told you we weren't scared to death.

I stayed close to Gene. "I can't believe it," we both said at the same time, as did some of the citizens.

I think the few thousand people or so in the crowd were either numb with fear or just defiant, but no one moved as the soldiers jumped down. When they faced us, they began to march in a line, slowly and cautiously moving toward us with bayonets fixed. They came right up to us with their bayonets, and they couldn't do it. They faced us, and we stared at each other for a minute or two before they stood down. A roar came up from the crowd and then a sigh. It had finally come to an end. At least for that day.

After People's Park, the age difference between Gene and me was no longer an issue, and we were becoming friends as much as brothers. I was so proud of him at Berkeley.

When Timothy Leary came to Berkeley, I was back in high school. He told the students at the university about the wonders of a new drug called LSD that was mind-altering. He told them to "turn on, tune out, and drop out." My parents and I had no idea that Gene had done just that, and that he had dropped out of school and was experimenting with LSD daily with Leary and others down in Lake Chapala, Mexico. Then one day we got a call that he was in jail in San Diego on possession of marijuana and LSD. That was when things started to spiral downward.

While in the custody of my parents, Gene would have terrible arguments with them over their world view on socialism and his on bypassing the social system and going directly to LSD. Gene said it would open society up to its own humanity much faster. This created a schism between them that was irreparable, one that would cause me to see the failure of my father to realize the depth of Gene's mental instability. My father, steadfastly standing on his principles, would argue rationally with Gene as if he was able to understand his argument, but Gene was hardly able to comprehend what was going on. My father's lack of understanding of how sick Gene was would haunt him to the end of his days.

My father was arguing with a son who believed LSD was the answer to the world's problems. On some level, I believed my brother was right. LSD could open people up to being in the world without their egos and enable them to meet one another without expectations or fear, just as they are. But the truth was, it was unrealistic, and my brother couldn't see that. His mind wasn't completely rational. He was sick. Gene became violent, something I'd never seen before in my otherwise perfect brother.

One day I came home to find my mother completely distraught. She'd found a stash of his marijuana, which she thought was contributing to his mental malaise. She flushed it down the toilet. He began to look for it, and when he couldn't find it, he became enraged. By the time he was done looking, the house had been trashed, the TV was a hulk of electronics on the kitchen floor, and he'd put his hand through the vanity mirror in my parents' bedroom. I'd never seen him like that. We both feared for our safety. We were so frightened that we fled the house to call my father. It was terrifying to see my poor brother like a tortured animal. He was out of his mind with rage.

Later, when he volunteered to commit himself to Napa State Hospital for observation, he confided in me that his thoughts were coming into his head as fast as flipping through the pages of a phone book. He asked me, "Michael, do you love?"

"Yes, I love you, and Mom, and Dad."

"I don't love anybody."

His response chilled me to the bone.

After the Napa Hospital experience, I believe he was deathly afraid that he was as crazy as some of the other patients there, who sat all day in a stupor, or who broke out in song, or who became extremely agitated. He was diagnosed at Napa with adult schizophrenia, a disease that attacks young people in their twenties.

As a family, we were in uncharted territory, torn between trying to love him at home or be brave and leave him in an institution until we could get a handle on what was happening. We chose the latter, and that resulted in his first suicide attempt. He cut his wrists in a lavatory and had to be rushed to emergency. My parents, desperately trying to find someone to help him, heard of a group of doctors who were dealing with young patients, all of whom had experimented with LSD. The patients found their way to a mental facility at Mendocino State Hospital. The doctors there were using B12 injections to treat them, and had found some success. Gene was transferred there in February 1968. He had just turned twenty-four in October.

He started to show a positive response to the treatment and had met a young girl there. We were ecstatic. Then in April of that same year, I was home alone when the sheriff of Mendocino called with the news that Gene was missing from the hospital. I couldn't imagine what that meant. My mind kept swirling in the darkness of my thoughts. Then a few minutes later, the sheriff called to tell me they'd found Gene hanging from a tree on the grounds of the hospital.

I dropped the phone. "No, no, no!" I screamed.

I lost my mind that night. My big brother hanging from a tree? The grief of a beloved brother who finally lost the battle was unthinkable. I threw myself on the floor and wailed from my gut. I couldn't stop. It just kept coming. I wailed and wailed, pounding the floor with my fists. It came like an avalanche, destroying everything in its path, guilt that I hadn't gone to see him the last time my parents went to the hospital, blame for my father's inability to embrace Gene even if he didn't agree with him, anger that Gene didn't love me enough to stay. It just kept coming, this avalanche of gut-wrenching wailing that covered all my thoughts in a blanket of sorrow. My brother was dead.

My parents came home from shopping and found me there. One look said it all. They dropped their grocery bags, cans and jars crashing to the floor in a crescendo of broken hearts. The three of us held one another and wailed like wild animals.

My flesh and blood was hanging from a tree on a cord from a Venetian blind that he'd smuggled out of the hospital. My protector no more, dangling, cold and blue.

Arthur

Dad wasn't around much when I was young, but he was warm. He used to hug me, and we'd play, and he'd roughhouse with me. The intensity of his roughhousing seemed to become a bone of contention between him and Mom, and arguments ensued that I was too young for him to be boxing with me. Mom tried to reason with him, but he always justified his actions.

Something changed when I was about six or seven. He just stopped participating with me. My older brother got all the attention. That pretty much set the stage for how I'd wind up coming between them for the rest of my childhood, as she always rose to my defense.

My father worked long hours, and when he finally came home, he settled down on his bed with his usual scotch and soda and the *Sports Illustrated*, which left little time for the two of us. There was a friction between us that I never understood, until much later, when my mother told me how much he wanted to continue his writing. He'd been at RKO Pictures, long before they were married. The more responsibilities he had, the less chance he had of fulfilling his dreams. But as an eight-year-old, this was difficult for me to understand.

Granted, I was a willful child. An example of his authoritarianism occurred when I was about seven or eight. My parents and Gene would gather around the television, all nice and comfy on the sofa at eight-thirty to watch *The Ed Sullivan Show*. I never got to watch it with them because my father insisted that I go to bed at eight-thirty, no exceptions. I was rebellious and felt that if they all could watch it, why couldn't I?

One evening after they all settled in and the first performer was onstage, I snuck out of my bedroom and down the hall to the living room. They were all curled up on the sofa, engrossed in the show and laughing at some comedian, when I suddenly ran into the front room and jumped in front of the television set. Blocking their view and screaming like a wild banshee, I tore off my pajamas and danced naked in front of them, gyrating back and forth. "Now see how much you like watching *The Ed Sullivan Show*," the little beast in me said. "I want equal time."

Taken by surprise, the three of them laughed hysterically. That night was a turning point. I sat with them from that evening on and watched *The Ed Sullivan Show*.

As I grew older, my father and I battled over control. I wanted to control my own life. He saw it differently. One night I asked him if I could stay overnight at a friend's house. My mother was the one who made all decisions regarding my brother and me early in our lives. Then when I turned thirteen, the control shifted to my father. My mom was upset with his lack of participation in our lives, and in an effort to share parental control, he was now suddenly in charge of us. Both my brother and I saw this as a major blunder on her part.

"Mom," I asked, "can I go over to Mike's house after dinner?"

"Go ask your father," she said as she continued making dinner in the kitchen.

I went into his bedroom after he got home and noticed he had a highball in a glass by his bed. He was reading *Sports Illustrated* and didn't look up when I entered the room.

"Dad," I called out to him.

He looked over the top of his magazine. "Yes?" he answered.

"Can I go over to Mike Rose's house after dinner?"

"Did you finish your homework?"

"Yes."

"No, you can't," he said, without even bothering to look up from his magazine.

"But why not?"

"Because I said so."

What upset me most was his lack of concern for what I wanted, my needs and desires, and the heavy-handedness of his reply with no real explanation. With that, I stormed out of the house and went to Mike's house anyway.

My mother saw me leaving and cried out, "Where are you going?" but I kept going and never looked back. I guess you could call that rebellious, but without a reasonable answer, I lost respect for my father's judgment. This would be the beginning of my rebellion.

When I came home, he was waiting for me. He'd lost his temper and ran after me down the hall to the bedrooms. I ducked into the bathroom and slammed the door, just in time to see his foot come through it. That was it. I knew he was losing it. I unscrewed the screen on the bathroom window in the shower and wiggled out to the backyard. I waited for him to cool down and then returned for his retribution. I was on restriction for two weeks, which would last only two days. I felt sorry that we were both so disconnected from one another, but I reasoned that if he wouldn't be just, I'd make his life miserable. I became the rebel of the family, while my older brother was the shining apple—which was what my father expected from him, but not necessarily voluntary on his part.

My relationship with my father deteriorated after that, and I seemed to always be upsetting him. But I was not trying to be deliberate. Adolescence is such a difficult time anyway, but I seemed to have a particularly bad case of it. One weekend, while mowing the lawn, I managed to throw a sprinkler head I found through the bottom pane of the family room door. Arthur, an avid sports fan, was inside watching the World Series.

When he opened the door, I could see steam coming out of his ears. Dressed in his pajamas and night robe, he ran for me. I knew I'd have to flee if I wanted to live. As he continued the chase, I climbed the neighbor's fence and dropped over it just as I heard him say, "You'd better not come back!"

The next day, I broke the glove compartment door on his brand-new 1964 Chevrolet Impala. That Sunday, I clogged the plumbing through the entire house when I flushed a litter of stillborn rabbits that my pet rabbit bore the day before down the toilet. I'd reasoned it would be easier just to flush them than to dispose of them some other way.

My mother was washing dishes at the time and screamed, "Arthur come quick! There's blood and guts coming up through the sink."

As the weekend ended, I heard my father say to my mother, "Do you think this is a phase he's going through? Because I can't afford him."

By high school, I had a best friend, Kent, who worked at a Dairy Queen. I'd swing by around closing time, and we'd go see Marti, a girlfriend of mine, and hang out and talk for hours at her house. Kent was secretly attracted to Marti, but she only saw him as a friend, and this went on for quite some time. Sue, Marti's friend, sometimes tagged along.

Then one night in the summer of 1966, before we started our senior year, I bought a matchbox of marijuana. This would be the beginning of my undoing. Afterward, I tried the whole laundry list of illegal drugs over time. I grew my hair long and became a bona fide hippie during the Summer of Love.

Back in those days, they sold marijuana in small five-dollar matchboxes, the kind that held matches you'd use to light a fire. I called Kent and Marti that night and told them I'd purchased some and would bring it with me. We were all excited about finally trying it, but all of us were slightly apprehensive. I don't know why I decided to buy some. Maybe it was just time. I knew my brother was smoking it, and certainly Bob Dylan and Joan Baez were smoking it. The Doors and the Beatles were singing about it. I guess I was tired of being in the dark and living in a small Bay Area town where nothing of much interest went on.

When Kent got off work, I picked him up, and the four of us went up to the university, which had a great view of San Francisco and the bay. We listened to music while I rolled my first joint. By the time I was through, it looked like a banana. We smoked until we'd fogged the windows. Then, realizing how late it was, we started to drive home.

"I don't feel a thing," Kent said.

"I do," Marti said. "Look at all the headlights."

We looked at the streetlights and they began to distort and look like stars. By the time my friends dropped me off at home, it was after midnight. My curfew was eleven, and I was feeling good. Now I had a secret: I was high for the first time. I couldn't wait to tell Gene.

This euphoria came crashing down the moment I opened the front door. There he was, my father in his night robe, sitting in the living room with just one light on. The fear that he'd waited up for me kicked in. The adrenalin raced through my body. I was higher than a kite.

"Where the hell were you until after midnight? We were worried you got into an accident."

I was frozen. I wanted to speak, but nothing came out. I just stared at him.

"Well?"

I managed a thought. "I was at Kent's, and we drove up to the university to hang out."

I stared at him while he spoke, not hearing a word, just watching his mouth move. He looked like a strange animal.

Finally, I heard, "Just go to bed. We'll talk about it in the morning." He left the room.

I was numb, realizing how high I was. Marijuana was a powerful drug. Then I felt hungry and went to the fridge. I felt like I wanted to eat everything I saw. I started with some leftover pumpkin pie and then moved on to several slices of toast with peanut butter and jelly and a couple of glasses of milk. Then I went to bed. Around three in the morning I got up, went to the bathroom, and threw up.

My brother awoke and saw me over the toilet bowl. "Mick, are you all right?"

"No, I'm not. I'm high. I smoked some marijuana tonight."

"Wow, cool, little brother," he said as he helped me up.

"You won't tell Mom and Dad, will you?"

He promised he wouldn't, and for the first time, I felt like we were becoming friends.

After graduation in 1967, I moved to the city to go to San Francisco State. It was the Summer of Love. My brother was already living in the Haight-Ashbury, and my life was about to change dramatically. My relationship with my father was in a state of limbo. We spoke on the phone, but he always seemed to be upset with me or disappointed in my choices.

When I told him I was majoring in a foreign language with a minor in art, he asked, "So how will you make a living with those two subjects?"

I said I could teach, but I could tell by his voice he was disappointed. It appeared I never could make him happy, and I so wanted him to be proud of me. Even though there was distance between us, I always knew that he loved me. That was the dichotomy. He never seemed to be able to show it, but underneath the veneer of disapproval was a deep and abiding love.

Some years later, when I was working as a struggling photographer and living with a woman by the name of Lorrie, we invited my parents over for dinner. Lorrie prepared an incredible meal and during dinner had gone into the kitchen to fetch some wine. When she returned, she sat down in the flimsy director's chairs we used and flew right over, chair and all. She'd gotten dressed for the occasion, and her petticoat and dress flew over her head until all you could see was a pair of legs in panties and high heels sticking straight up out of the petticoat. It looked hysterical but was nothing to laugh about. My father made an unkind remark, and it threw me into a tirade.

All the years of listening to his authoritarian edicts pushed me over the edge. All the rage that had built up spilled out, and I shouted, "How could you insult Lorrie like that? You're a sorry man. Just because you're my father doesn't mean you can treat me with disrespect. I'm thirty years old. I'm a grown man, and you can't control me anymore. If I make poor decisions, they'll be mine and mine alone. I'm an adult, and if you can't treat me as such, then I'd just as soon let you go. You've made my mother's life miserable all these years. You put me in the back seat of the car as an observer of life instead of a participant, and you are responsible for my brother's death."

He jumped up from the table. "Adele, if you're not waiting for me outside in five minutes, I'm leaving without you." Then he walked out the door to his car.

Extremely distraught, my mother sat there in tears. "That wasn't fair, Michael. You know he had nothing to do with Gene's suicide."

I knew I'd hit a raw nerve. I was sorry for it and wanted to apologize, but he was gone. There was truth in what I said, but it came out like a volcano exploding in such a hurtful way, and I knew I had to make peace with him. I went outside to the car, which was parked on Eighteenth Street, a steep hill running up to Twin Peaks. My mother followed me, as did Lorrie.

My dad rolled down the window and yelled at my mother to get in the car.

"I'm not leaving like this," she said. "Come inside."

I got down on my knees on the asphalt and clung to the open window. I begged him to please come in and talk with me. "Dad, I'm so sorry," I said. "What I said about Gene was unfair, and I want to talk to you."

He drove off with me still clutching the open window frame, my knees dragging along the asphalt until I had to let go. I fell off and lay in the street sobbing. Lorrie and Mom helped me up, and we went back inside. The three of us sat around the table and talked.

"He's a nice man, but he never should have had kids," I said. "Mom, you know I've always been between the two of you. I think he's jealous of me."

"Don't be silly," she said. "He loves you just the same."

There was truth in what I'd deduced, but even so, she was in denial. Family dynamics are so complicated. The truth was he was living a life he'd lost to circumstances. Writing was what he wanted to do, and beneath that loss was anger toward me for somehow causing it.

Some time had gone by since he'd driven off, and we all waited, each of us thinking, *Where is he? Is he okay? Is he coming back?*

It wasn't until after my father died that Mom told me the truth. What was the truth? I was longing to hear it.

"Well," she said, "when I got pregnant with you, your father wanted me to have an abortion. He insisted, but back in the '40s, it was illegal and very dangerous, and I wanted you with all my heart. I refused. You see, he was already struggling with work and taking care of Gene, and he saw you as another mouth to feed."

This totally made sense, considering the way he treated me. I knew it all my life. I could feel it, but I could never put my finger on it. Because what kid wants to know that a parent never wanted him? It's almost unthinkable, so you deny it.

Ten minutes later, there was a knock at the door. It was Dad. "Would you please come out to the car so we can talk alone?"

"Yes, of course," I said.

Lorrie and Mom looked out the upstairs front window. I was so glad he was okay, and a major shift in our relationship was about to take place. It would be one of those "ah-ha" moments, when everything is clear for the first time in your life.

"Son, I'm sorry for what I said to Lorrie. It was a joke and in bad taste. I know things haven't been the best between us, and I know that a good part of it is my fault. I'd like to make it up to you. Let's talk further about how we can make it better. Kid, you know how much I love you." He reached over to me to give me a hug, which I returned. Then he kissed me and hugged me tightly, the way I'd always wanted to be hugged by him.

I was still in shock. I never thought the day would come, and I cried in his arms as I did when I was a youngster. I'd rebelled against him, and stood up for the man I was. In the process, my father regained a son and I regained a father. He only lived for five years after that night, but we were the closest we'd ever been since I was a baby, and that was the gift we gave each other.

"Tell your mom to come down," he said. "It's time for us to go. I'll call you next week."

As they drove off, I held Lorrie in my arms, and we watched their Lincoln fade down Eighteenth Street. All was good again in Oz.

We became the best of friends in those last years of my dad's life. We grew to love each other and had a deep and abiding respect for one another. He'd call and ask me for my opinion. He also shared with me how sorry he was for not being the father I needed when I was growing up. He told me he was proud of the man I'd become.

My father taught me that a man's word is his honor. He showed me by example to believe in something greater than yourself, and that what benefitted others was true compassion. His dedication to socialism was the greatest gift he gave to me. I am thankful, for it has always made me feel humble in the face of those less fortunate. Both my parents were instrumental in guiding me along the journey of self-inquiry to a place of humility, love, and compassion.

In November 1984, I sent the two of them on a trip to New York City for my mother's birthday to visit relatives. They had a family reunion and dinner in a nice bistro on Bleecker Street. My father was happy to be in the company of his family and in the city of his childhood. I was so glad I could make it happen for him.

Arthur and Adele, 1942

After dinner, the men of the family walked home. The women took a taxi. They finally arrived on Mercer Street, where they'd all gathered for a nightcap. My father entered the doorway of his cousin Ira's apartment and called out to Mother. She came to him and realized something was seriously wrong. He'd had a massive heart attack. She held him as he slid down the side of the wall, never to regain consciousness. That's how he passed—surrounded by his family and the woman he adored.

In the end, we'd found one another. As dysfunctional and convoluted a relationship as it was, he was a pillar of strength for his daunting determination to make this world a better place.

Chapter Three

The Ramirez Family—Mexico

In the summer of 1965, we arrived at the border at Mexicali to catch a train to Mexico City in a sweltering 120-degree heat wave. From one side of the border to the other was a stark contrast. I'd never seen such poverty, even in the worst slums in America.

The corrugated roof of the railway station captured all the torridness and turned the station into a pressure cooker. Hundreds of people waited for the train, sitting on their haunches, in some cases with all their earthly belongings surrounding them. In the heat of the desert, the perspiration trickled down their brown faces, their white shirts and blouses stained from it.

What first caught my eye were the peasants—poor Indians. The women had babies slung over their backs and wore colorful shawls and hand-embroidered dresses. The men were in white pants, straw hats, and huarache sandals, carrying serapes, their hands tough like leather from hard labor. The faces of these people, etched in sandstone like the parched Sonoran Desert, told a story of survival. Their belongings, tied up in cardboard boxes, sat on the floor in front of them while they snacked on fried pork rinds.

How did I find myself on this sweltering platform in Mexicali in the middle of June? A year prior, at the beginning of my sophomore year of high school, I had to take a foreign language. It was required to enter a four-year college. Since California had a large Hispanic population, Spanish seemed the obvious choice. After my first semester, my teacher approached me with a proposition to study at the University of Morelos in Cuernavaca. She thought it would be a great experience for me. Who knew what an enormous effect Mexico and my host family would have on my future?

My mother and father agreed after much cajoling and reminders from me that I had enough funds to pay for the trip from a small trust, due to an accident on a faulty skateboard I had when I was young. But the trust was contingent on my being eighteen years old to withdraw it. They were reluctant, as I was only sixteen, but eventually gave in.

I left San Francisco on a Greyhound bus with thirty other students from the Bay Area who were in the same program. On the way down, I met up with two great gals, Judy and Linda, from Belmont on the peninsula south of San Francisco. We would become great friends. Judy was effervescent, with long blond hair and blue eyes. She reminded me of a cheerleader, but she was much worldlier than I expected. Linda was a hot redhead who was wild, with a great sense of humor and a kind heart. We clicked.

I was grateful to have met them, being so far from home and starting a new adventure. The three of us sat on the platform on our haunches, eating tacos while we waited for the ticket office to open. We bought our Pullman tickets and waited in the crowded station for the eight-thirty train to Guadalajara.

"I've never been out of the county before," I said.

"You know, now that you mention it, neither have I," Judy said. Her eyes contradicted her soft smile. She saw the poverty and the misery all about her but chose not to speak of it.

We were all excited about the chance to study abroad and looked forward to meeting our host families. I don't think we were prepared to see the immense poverty we encountered from the first moment we stepped off the bus and headed to the train station. Nothing could have prepared us for the scene on the platform. What must we have looked like to them? Rich and privileged comes to mind.

Between the open platforms, I saw the sun begin to set over the desert landscape, the colors red like blood, pastel salmon, and dark blue. I made a mental note of how intense it was. The train arrived, and the mass of humanity picked up its belongings and headed for the platform. It was chaotic, with people pushing and shoving. Our Spanish wasn't that good, and no one could direct us to our car. They waved their hands in the air to show they didn't understand and queued up at every doorway of the long line of coaches. In the massive rush to get on the train, it was everyone for himself.

I walked up to a conductor, the girls standing behind me, and asked him in Spanish where our car was. He directed us to the front of the train.

We found our seats, and they were quite comfortable. They were '40s Pullman cars that the United States had sold off to the Mexican National Railway. We were about an hour out of Mexicali when the porter asked me if he could make up our beds. The two seats we were sitting in, when pushed together, made up a bed, and the top bunk lowered from the ceiling.

Our group filled three-quarters of the coach. It was like a high school sleepover with everyone in their pajamas. I took the top bunk, and Judy took the lower one.

She climbed up to say good night. "Can you believe we're finally on our way?" she asked. "I was so scared when the train pulled in that we'd be trampled by the crowd. Did you see all those poor Indians? I felt so sorry for them."

"I know," I said. "But did you also see how strong and proud a people they are? We've got so much to look forward to once we get to Cuernavaca and our families. A whole year in Mexico. Wow!"

"Yeah, I'm excited," she said. "Well, good night then. See you in the morning in the dining car for breakfast."

"*Buenas noches*," I replied. As I settled back in my berth and closed my eyes, I could feel the rhythm of the train swaying slightly back and forth and the sound of the metal wheels on the tracks. To the sounds of *clickety-clack, clickety-clack*, I drifted off to sleep.

The next morning, the train stopped in Benjamin Hill, a small town surrounded by desert, where the dining car was put on between first class and second. I got dressed and met Judy in the dining car. It was so hot—120 degrees according to the thermometer on the wall, and only the fans in the ceiling to cool us. They weren't enough.

"Hey, Judy," I said.

"Hi, Michael. Come sit with me." Judy motioned with her hand on the seat next to her.

I sat down and wiped the sweat from my forehead.

"It's hot as hell in here, isn't it?" she asked.

"What happened to the air conditioning?"

"They said it would be fixed in an hour as soon as we get moving."

With the heat, I'd almost lost my appetite.

"Did you sleep well?" she asked.

"Oh yes, like a baby."

Just then the train started to roll, the whistle blew, and the steam from the engine flowed briefly by the window.

"Oh, finally there's the air conditioning!" Judy exclaimed, rolling her eyes.

While we sat waiting to be served, I looked out the window in amazement. All the people from second class who had gotten off for coffee and food at the taco stands panicked and began running en masse back to their seats. It was that herd mentality that resides in us all. Did they think the train would leave hundreds of people stranded in the Sonoran Desert? All this passed through my head before breakfast was served. I'd never experienced such a class separation.

When we stopped in Hermosillo, the capital of Sonora, to take on water, we passed one rusted, abandoned train car after another in the desert. People dwelled in them, trying to scratch out a living in the inhospitable environment. Little children in only T-shirts, naked from the waist down, brown bellies distended from malnutrition, covered in dust of the same color, stared back at us blankly from the old cars. I looked on in shock as the train rolled passed them. There must have been at least twenty or so. They seemed like part of the landscape, like a still life. Unable to comprehend such desperation, my mind simply captured the image like a photograph.

When the train came to a stop, Judy and I decided to stretch our legs and began walking from one car to the next. When we reached second class, the heat hit us like a wave after the coolness of our now air-conditioned coach. People were so sick from the heat that they were vomiting out the windows. Babies lay on the floor asleep or in their mother's arms, too hot to remain awake. The people stared at us from their wooden benches, their clothes soaked with perspiration. Their eyes followed us as we passed by them, wondering why we were there.

I looked into their faces, and all I could see was their despair and suffering. The smell of rotting food permeated the coach. The aisles were so messy that cleaning crews were mopping them up, and the bathrooms reeked of urine.

Judy put her hand over her mouth and nose.

"Let's go," I said. "This is beyond anything I could have imagined."

Numb, the two of us went back to our seats, and no words passed between us. As we sat in our comfortable cushioned cabin, I could hear the voices of the other kids in the background, laughing and playing board games with one another, without a clue about how the rest of the passengers were faring.

Judy and I bonded that day. We were just two naïve kids from the Bay Area who woke up one day and found we'd lost our innocence. The real world was nothing like the one we'd been living in.

By the time I arrived in Mexico City, I'd already spent four arduous days traversing the Sonoran Desert from the semiarid states of Sinaloa and Michoacán to Guadalajara, where we passed huge *maguey* plantations that stretched as far as the eye could see. Maguey is a cactus plant that, when pressed, releases a white milk called *pulque*. When distilled, it becomes tequila. The weather had changed from the stifling heat of the desert to more mild temperatures with humidity. It was bearable. The train then began to wind and switch back and forth up the Sierra Madres to the summit and down into the Valley of Mexico.

The poverty continued to shake me. When we passed the old box cars and saw the people living in them, I understood why my parents had been fighting for socialism for so long. Anyone with a heart would have felt that desperation. All those years of talking about socialism with my parents and their friends in the Socialist Labor Party could not have prepared me for Mexico.

I was met at the train station by Raul Camacho, the only son of the family I'd been assigned to. Judy and Linda met their families on the platform too. We all hugged each other, and then Raul and I left. We made our way out of the Valley of Mexico back up into the mountains and down into Cuernavaca.

Chapter Four

The Ramirez Family

Something was off with the Camacho family from the beginning. They introduced themselves with smiling faces and were nice enough, but behind the facade, I sensed a darkness. They argued a lot when I was out of the room. Señora Camacho's son, Raul, was still living with them and attending university, which seemed a little odd as he was in his thirties and unmarried. I also noticed that the maids, Margarita, and the younger one, Concha, seemed almost frightened. Maybe it was me, I thought, and I just needed time to settle in.

The house on Calle Madero was pleasant and comfortable enough. I had my own room, with a view of the Sierra Madres, and I could see Popocatépetl, the snowcapped volcano.

Cuernavaca was the playground of the rich from Mexico City. Many of my friends were placed in wealthy homes with tennis courts and swimming pools, the lucky tarts. My house, on the other hand, was rather mundane. It sat on a hill that ran parallel to the highway. The living room was centered around a mostly untended patio. Terracotta pots lacked care. The one attractive part was a wall filled with purple bougainvillea.

In the center of the house stood the kitchen. The table there was the center of activity. Señora Camacho was not what I'd call a good cook. Everything tasted of too much chili, so at first my meals shrank to soup and buttered tortillas. Besides the food, the pea-green walls in the kitchen were most unappetizing.

The rest of the house had white plaster walls with wood beams. It was a lower-middle-class home with furnishings that needed updating, but it was Señora Camacho's attitude that made me notice that something was wrong.

Cuernavaca was called the City of Eternal Spring. I read that Montezuma built his summer palace there because the climate was so agreeable. To the Aztecs, the whole valley that lay before it became a place to worship the gods, with many small pyramids connecting the city. Hernán Cortés destroyed the temple complex, taking away much evidence that the great Aztec warrior ever existed. He then used the same stones to build El Palacio de Cortés, which overlooked the valley, and he became Cuernavaca's new governor.

He enslaved the men, forcing them to work in the fields or the mines. But the women were free to come and go. Mexico was becoming a matriarchal society, where the women had more power than the men. The men internalized their anger, and this gave birth to machismo.

My first few days in Cuernavaca taking in the history and applying it to the people was mind blowing. I was learning so much. I started school the week after arriving at the Camachos', and I loved my classes and my teachers. Everything was taught in Spanish, so I had a learning curve. But after a few weeks immersed in the language, it started to come, and I was dreaming in Spanish. I couldn't believe it. It was flowing out of me without even having to think about it.

As I mentioned earlier, the Camachos fed me food with hot chilies, something I wasn't used to at home, and it was just too hot for me. I lost weight, and the kids at school began calling me *Flaco*. It was all in fun, but I was skinny, so I knew I was going to have to break down and start eating the chicken *mole*—a chocolate and chili sauce.

The university we attended had been set up by a famous Dutch anthropologist by the name of Lini De Vries. Lini had studied the linguistics of indigenous Mexican tribes for most of her life. She also worked on important archeological sites, including Monte Albán, near Oaxaca, for twenty-five years before she opened the extension program. She spoke Mayan from the Yucatan, and Nahuatl, the language of the Aztecs. She spoke Zapotec and Mixtec languages from Oaxaca and dialects of the tribes on the Gulf Coast. She was an amazing, enigmatic personality who was so in touch with herself and the work she was doing that she lit up a room with her enthusiasm. Then in her early seventies, she wore a Mayan dress and her white hair piled up on her head, held in place by several tortoiseshell combs inlaid with silver and turquoise. Silver bracelets decorated her arms, and Mexican earrings swung side to side as she enthusiastically taught us the history of the country.

She was inspired to start an extension program out of the University of Morelos for foreign students, sharing Mexican culture and the Spanish language with Americans. My curriculum consisted of Spanish, anthropology, archeology, Mexican culture, and history.

The school was in an old monastery with a huge courtyard in the middle. Things were going well for me there and I loved it. But my home life was not what I'd hoped it would be. The señora was controlling, and one day I caught her cornering the maids and taking money from them that I'd given them for doing my laundry. The maids were two Indian girls in their teens. They exuded such kindness and warmth, and there was a sense of innocence in how they saw the world. I asked them how much the señora paid them, and they told me a dollar a day to cook and clean, and to iron and fold the laundry. I couldn't believe it was so little. I found Señora Camacho to be a despicable, manipulative, and mean-spirited person. I confronted her with the issue of the laundry and the girls, and she told me it was her house and she did what she wanted. I knew I couldn't in good faith stay in her house any longer. I was looking for a loving family where I would be included as a son, and hers wasn't it.

I went to talk to Lini about a change in families, but saw Judy first. She told me her host family's relatives lived in the downstairs duplex and wanted me to stay with them. I was ecstatic. I'd visited Judy and had lunch with her family, and had met the Ramirez family downstairs weeks prior. It was perfect. I moved the next day.

In our host families, Judy's father was the cousin of my father-to-be. He'd married an ambitious woman by the name of Pilar. She was arrogant and believed herself a class above the relatives downstairs. Judy would have me over to lunch, and Pilar would put on airs about how well-off they were compared to the relatives below. She served three-course meals in a European style. Mexican was not on the menu. If you asked her, she'd tell you she was Spanish, not Mexican. She said some awful things about her in-laws, my future family-to-be, that weren't true. It bred contempt from everyone downstairs, as well as from Judy, Linda, and myself. The truth was that Pilar was trapped in a bad marriage with two children who were spoiled, and she was unhappy with her life.

When I finally met the family downstairs—Elvira, her husband, and their four kids: Raul, Margo, Ernesto, and Maria; along with the father's mother, whom we called *Abuelita*, Little Grandmother, because she was so small—I knew I was in the right place. They were warm and loving, the salt of the earth.

Abuelita used to like to drink *pulque*, the unfermented juice of the maguey, or tequila plant. She said it was for medicinal purposes, but I knew she was having a nip now and then. She'd tell me stories and then take a swig of the pulque and continue.

They were an honest, hardworking, lower-middle-class family struggling to make ends meet, but they had heart. Raul was studying architecture at the university I attended while Margo studied economics at the University of Mexico City and was home on weekends. The two youngest members of the family attended grade school.

My host mother, Elvira, was a silversmith. Every Wednesday, she took the bus to the city of Taxco, two hours away. Taxco was the "Silver City," well-known for its mines since the days of the Spanish. She'd buy silver and onyx, abalone shells and turquoise. It was an all-day affair, and on those days, it was my responsibility to pick up Ernesto and Maria from their elementary school, take them home, and look after them while I did my homework.

Elvira was a beautiful Indian woman, *mestizo*, half Indian and half white, with a creamy brown complexion and long black hair.

Every morning she brushed it with a mixture of tomato and water, an old Aztec ritual that made her hair glisten and stay together much like a pomade would. I'd watch her in awe in the mornings as she sat in front of the mirror. I asked her why she put the mixture in her hair, and she told me it was healthy for the hair and kept it from breaking. There were so many things I was learning in Mexico. Every day was an adventure.

We were a working family. Everybody had their tasks. One day, Elvira sent me out to get tortillas, with a basket and a cloth to cover them so they'd stay warm. It wasn't like going to a market in the States and picking up a loaf of bread. I waited in the *tortilleria* as the tortillas were made by hand right in front of me. When my order was ready, they filled the basket.

After I left the shop, a black car cruised alongside me for a while. When it stopped, two *federales*, Mexican police, got out. They asked for my papers.

"What papers?" I asked in Spanish.

"Do you have an identification card or passport?" they asked.

"Why do you want them?"

"We believe you might be a suspect in a robbery of a bank downtown," they replied in an accusatory manor.

"A robbery suspect carrying a basket of tortillas?"

"Give us five hundred pesos and you can go," the tall one said.

"I will not," I said, becoming agitated. "I wouldn't give you one peso. You have the wrong person. I live right down the street. I'm a foreign exchange student. Would you like to talk to my mother? She's at home."

The tall one said to the short one, "*Vamos*, Pablo. Let's go."

I couldn't believe a sixteen-year-old kid was getting shaken down for a bribe by the police. I went home and told Elvira.

"I wondered why you were so late," she said. "Those pigs. The whole country is corrupt."

That was when I stopped looking to the police for help and started looking at them as most likely on the take.

Everything was fresh in Mexico. I went shopping with Elvira daily at the *mercados*. I loved listening to her haggle if the price was too high, and I loved looking at all the Indians with their colorful baskets full of yams, papayas, mangos, and cabbages. The only part of shopping I despised was when we had to buy meat or chickens. The meat hung on hooks outdoors and had flies buzzing around it. The chickens were live, and the merchant killed them on the spot. I'd always avert my eyes. Americans aren't used to confronting our meals in that style. But after watching the butchers in Mexico, I certainly could appreciate those packages of hermetically sealed meat at the supermarket.

Elvira set up shop in the basement of the house in a large room that had a view of the ravine. We called it *La Barranca*, and it was a shantytown of homeless who had built houses on government land out of corrugated metal, bricks, and sometimes cardboard across the river from us. That was our view, a window to the poorest of Cuernavaca's citizens, who weren't hidden behind great walls with swimming pools and tennis courts like the wealthy class of the city.

Two other silversmiths would come to work with Elvira to create beautiful jewelry. They made bracelets and chains, earrings and rings, all inlaid. Then she sent them to her husband, Raul Sr., at his shop in Tijuana. He lived there six months of the year, and it was a big strain on the family when he was gone. Elvira was a strong woman, and she was the head of the household. She made the decisions in his absence.

For the first six months of my stay, I never got a chance to meet my host father. Then one day in the middle of the term, he came home. It was such a joyous occasion. I could tell that he was much loved, missed, and appreciated.

Elvira became my mother very quickly. We grew to love one another, and I was accepted unequivocally as her son. She even called me *hijo*, which means son. It was odd to be accepted into this new family without all the baggage I'd acquired from my own.

I grew to love them, too, and the simple life we led. I'd wake up to a breakfast of tortoise eggs, calf brains (which I had serious second thoughts about), tortillas and beans, fresh orange juice, and a *torta*, a roll with jam and butter. The tortoise eggs didn't have a shell, only a membrane, but tasted just like chicken eggs. Elvira would mix the eggs and brains together in a frying pan much the same as you might cook hash, and it had a similar flavor. After breakfast, I'd drop off the two youngest at school and go on to my classes at the university. It felt good being part of a new family, in a new city and a new country.

Abuelita told me the story one night of how the family came to wind up in Cuernavaca. "My family," she said, "lived in Mexico City at the time when Zapata laid siege to the city. The fighting was fierce as the government forces tried to hold on to the capital. We lived not far from the main cathedral, which was in the center of the city. Zapata's forces came in from the west side, and the only other road leading out of the valley was the *camino* to Cuernavaca and Puebla, the cities south and to the east." She reached down into the pocket of her dress, pulled out a bottle of pulque, and took a swig. "My husband had horses. So the whole family, twelve of us, rode out on horseback across the valley and then the Sierra Madre. We were starving. There was no food in the city." She took another swig and paused.

I begged her to continue. I was getting a better lesson in Mexican history at home than I could have ever received in school.

"Where did I leave off?" she asked.

"The part where you were all on horseback and fleeing the city."

"Oh yes. Bandits tried to steal our horses, but my father had a gun and shot one of them. When we finally got out of the city, we headed for Cuernavaca, but in those days, it was a thirteen-day ride."

"It took you thirteen days?"

"Oh yes," she replied, "and I hadn't ridden a horse before. We found people along the way in the smaller villages and bought food from them. Then one day, we rounded the crest of the mountain outside town, and there was Cuernavaca."

The crest she spoke of was a panoramic view of the whole valley, including the towns of Tepoztlan, Cuautla, Lake Tequesquitengo, and El Salto.

"It was beautiful, and we've been here ever since," she said. "My father bought the land that this house sits on and all the land to the south." She waved her hand in the direction of La Barranca. "We had a big farm in those days." She yawned, rested back in her rocking chair, pulled her shawl over her head, and drifted off to sleep.

I became fluent in Spanish after two months, and that was an achievement. I fell in love with the language. I finally knew what I wanted to do after college: I'd become a teacher.

My brother Raul and I were close. We shared a room. He was my confidant. He'd ask me all about the United States, and I'd ask him all about Mexico. We were both interested in history, books, architecture, and girls—at least I thought I was at the time.

Raul took me out on my first date at the university. Cristina was her name. She was tall and pretty, and we complemented one another. Her aunt had to go with us because she had to be chaperoned. I'd never heard of such a custom and found it strange and confining. She'd be just out of earshot, but always there.

Cristina really liked me, and I liked her, too, but it was awkward. Whenever her aunt wasn't looking, she'd steal a kiss and would put her hands on me. I was shocked and pleased at the same time. However, it never seemed appropriate, and I felt like a thief in the night, always fearful of being caught.

School was going well, and Easter was approaching, which in Mexico is a big deal because of the religious doctrine of the Catholic Church. The entire country genuflected when passing a church. I thought it bizarre, having been brought up a Jew and a socialist, but I respected the culture. The Indians had been forced into it, and so their style of Catholicism was a mixture of pagan rituals and Catholic it. What Judy didn't tell her mother was that Alejandro was coming with us. They were in love for real. I watched as their relationship grew. I was happy for her, and we all shared the secret.

We skipped the Pyramid of the Sun for an unescorted vacation to the capital of fun. Ah, Acapulco. We arrived at three in the morning, and the humidity was so heavy we felt high. We had no hotel room. We got off the bus with our suitcases and headed straight for the deserted beach, immediately walking into a string of empty hammocks in front of a high-rise hotel. What luck! We threw our bags into the hammocks and ourselves into the ocean. It was marvelous. We went to sleep that night clutching our suitcases and hanging in the warm sea breeze.

～～～

My year in Mexico was nearing its end. I'd seen and learned much on my journey. My classmates were struggling to stay in school and get an education. Many were needed at home by their families to work in the fields and businesses, or to find jobs to help make ends meet. They knew their relatives were sacrificing their own immediate happiness so they could get an education and improve their lives.

I was going back to a life in the States that I no longer could relate to. For kids in my area, school was a chore they were forced to do, not a privilege. Most of my friends were uninterested. They paid no attention in class and always looked to the future, when they could get out, if they didn't just drop out. I couldn't go back to getting drunk on six-packs of Budweiser behind the railroad tracks with the boys, hanging out at the local McDonald's, toilet papering the principal's house, or trying to get into some cheerleader's underwear. I was so far from that life now that I didn't even recognize it. It was all so juvenile and repulsive.

I had learned that an education is a privilege and comes at a price. My Mexican brothers and sisters taught me that. Abuelita taught me about real struggle and revolution, and the price that's doctrine, colorful and steeped in mysticism. I'd go to Sunday Mass sometimes just to hear the mariachi play.

I loved going to El Mercado Central, the big market on the river where the Indians from all over the valley brought their goods to sell. They had really nifty stuff like guitars and talking parrots, live reptiles, beautiful textiles and baskets. It was a kid's fantasy, the Indians all dressed up in their tribal clothes, from so many different tribes. I especially liked *El Brujo*, as he was called. He was the medicine man and carried anything and everything for what ails you. Magic mushrooms, herbs for fevers, he had it all. He also was a wise and enlightened human being. Some Mexican people were afraid of him because of his profound powers, but I was totally fascinated by him, and he liked me. He showed me an herb to make me potent.

Wow, that's far out, I thought.

The school took an Easter break, and Lini De Vries organized an anthropological excursion to Monte Albán, the site of a magnificent ancient Zapotec city built on the convergence of the Sierra Madre Occidental and the Sierra Madre Oriental on what the Zapotecs called the "Roof of the World."

My world had become so rich with colors and smells, accents and language that I never would have been awakened to in the Bay Area. I came alive in Mexico. Before, I looked at high school as something I had to do to get to college, where I'd honed dodging bullies in the halls. Here, I was suddenly free, no baggage, and I was loving it.

The girls and I had become best friends, and Judy now had a boyfriend, so we were being a lot more social. His name was Alejandro Polanco. He was a tall, handsome Mexican student at the University of Mexico City, but he came from Cuernavaca and was home on weekends.

Lini had organized another excursion, this time to Teotihuacan. Our plan was to tell everyone we were going and then get on a first-class bus for Acapulco. Judy told Pilar, her Mexican mother, that she was going on it. I lied to Elvira too. I knew she'd never allow

49

paid for freedom. Elvira taught me that no matter how hard things get in life, we always have one another. Raul, my host father, taught me that you do what you must to provide for your family, that there's no sacrifice greater than love of family. Lini De Vries taught me to love the Mexican culture and to embrace the Spanish language as a force of communication with twenty-three other countries. It was now my second language. She taught me to inquire about everything and to be fascinated with the world.

When the school term concluded, my host family took me to the train station in Mexico City. It was time to say goodbye—goodbye to a year that was life-transforming, a year in which I'd fallen in love with my adoptive family and country. There were no words expressed. When the train pulled into the station, we all knew we might never see each other again. We hugged on the platform, and everyone had tears in their eyes.

I'd changed their lives, too. I stood in between the cars and looked down on them as they stood silently staring up at me. Elvira tried to give me a smile to show me the joy I'd brought them. Then the train whistled and began to move, and they all began moving too. With tears flowing, they ran after the train as it gained speed, all the way to the end of the platform, and then we all waved.

I could still see them waving when they were tiny specks on the horizon. Then they were gone.

Chapter Five

Michael and Graham—LSD and the Spiritual Path

The first time I took a psychedelic, I was seventeen years old. It was 1966, the beginning of my senior year. I'd just returned from studying in Mexico. My two best friends from school, Graham and Michael, had convinced me that we should go to Mazatlán for Easter break. After my studies in Mexico, I relished the idea of returning. I felt like Mexico was a part of me.

Graham and Michael were totally different from my other friends. Michael had read Kahlil Gibran and George Gurdjieff, two enlightened prophets, one Sufi, and the other a Christian mystic. Both expounded the idea of no separation: everything was one, and connected.

Graham and Michael were both seekers who opened me up to searching for my true self, unlike my other friends, who were in the pursuit of pleasure and not much else. My year in Mexico had shown me a side of myself I'd never experienced. I was maturing, my values were changing, and it wasn't just fate that brought the three of us together. I was evolving enough to know that there was more to life than chasing pleasure, and Graham and Michael had already come to this realization by the time we met.

Graham was a year older than I and had been held back due to a learning disability. He was slow to grasp ideas, but once he did, he understood perfectly. He was blond and muscular. The nicest thing about Graham was the kindness that permeated everything he did. I was drawn to him on several different levels.

Michael was my peer, and extremely well read for a boy of seventeen. He really was a philosopher, and both Graham and I gravitated toward the light he shed on so many subjects. We were in awe, and knew there was truth in what he said.

We started our Easter break trip by hitchhiking to the border at Tijuana. We managed to get as far as Salinas, then got picked up by migrant workers in the valley and rode in the back of their truck. We passed miles of green artichokes and lettuce in neat furrows. The truck left us in San Luis Obispo. We stuck our thumbs out again and got a ride all the way to Ventura.

By then, night had fallen, and the three of us wondered if we'd make the border by midnight, or if we'd sleep by the side of the road. Just then, a white '67 Chevy Impala drove past us onto the shoulder, leaving us in a dust cloud. The driver motioned for us to get in.

"Hi, how far are you going?" Michael asked the well-dressed man.

"Los Angeles," he said. "Get in."

Michael jumped in the front seat, and Graham and I got in back. Michael did most of the talking. Once the driver began to speak, we knew something was wrong. His manner of dress was odd, too. His white polo shirt accented his dark tan, and his blond hair looked dyed. He wore a pink belt and white khakis with white slip-on Dockers. When he talked, he slurred his words.

A little later, the car began to swerve, coming close to hitting the dividing wall. Graham and I yelled from the back seat, "Slow down!" but he continued driving erratically.

Graham and I felt so vulnerable that we put our sleeping bags between us and the front seat, in case the driver did collide with something. Every now and then, Michael looked back at us with a raised eyebrow, but we all believed we were in grave danger. Then the driver asked Michael to look down in front of him for a bottle on the floor of the passenger side. Michael pulled up a bottle of Jack Daniels whiskey and handed it to him. He took a swig as Graham and I looked on in horror.

Michael saw what was happening and encouraged Troy to drink. When the bottle was finished, Troy asked Michael to stop for another. He finally passed out somewhere between Santa Monica and Pacific Palisades, and then suddenly we passed Los Angeles.

"Michael, we passed LA," I said. "Where are you going?"

"San Diego," he said matter-of-factly.

Graham and I looked at one another, our eyes wide, and began to laugh. Michael was a master manipulator. Then Michael joined in, and we laughed all the way to Coronado Beach, where we abandoned Troy and his car at six in the morning. We wondered when he woke up what he'd think—parked in the Coronado Beach Club parking lot with a view of the Pacific Ocean. Maybe he wouldn't remember how he got there.

After we left Troy, we crossed the border into Tijuana. We bought second-class bus seats for Mazatlán and grew more excited about our little adventure. Ahead was warm weather, sultry seas, and a place on the beach with our names written all over it.

Our blessed adventure went terribly wrong where the border of the two states of Baja California and Sonora meet. Seems one didn't need a visa for Baja, but to enter Sonora, Mexico, proper, we needed something called a tourist visa, and it was obvious to the *federales* that we were lacking papers.

They dragged us off the bus into a beat-up Toyota truck and drove us to a remote part of the Sonoran Desert. While they laughed, they strip-searched us and slashed our sleeping bags looking for possible drugs, making them almost unusable. "Ha, ha, ha." They sounded like scary Zapatan banditos from a bad movie. They seemed to relish tormenting us. When they saw we had nothing to offer them, we were driven to the Mexican border town of Sonoita and deported.

As we crossed the white line in the asphalt that separated the two countries, a far cry from today's militarized walls, we turned to face them. In my best Mexican slang, I told them, "*Mexico*," gesturing with my hand around my fist where they could put it.

"Pull the car over," I said urgently. "I want to get out."

Graham echoed the sentiment.

Michael the manipulator said to the driver, "Hey, Troy, why don't you let me drive you to Los Angeles, and you could sit back and drink in comfort? What do you say?"

"Why, that's very nice of you, Michael," he said, slurring the last couple of syllables. They changed places.

Graham and I were relieved, and relaxed back in our seats. Michael could charm a snake.

They talked in the front seat for a while, and then the man turned to me.

"Where you from, handsome?"

"San Francisco," I said.

"How old are you?"

"Seventeen."

"Um . . . tasty."

I moved closer to Graham, and we looked at one another inquisitively. "He's queer, isn't he?" I whispered.

"Yes, I think so," Graham said with a Cheshire cat grin, "and I think he likes you."

The man continued to drink, and Michael kept him occupied with conversation, but his hand wandered over the back seat to my knee. I threw his hand back again and then again, but each time he tried again, moving closer to my crotch. Maybe he knew something I didn't, but I was frightened by his advances.

He looked over the back seat at us, and then he stared at me with a glassy look that only comes from too much booze. "I like you, handsome Michael," he slurred.

Graham came to my defense. "Hey, Troy, keep your hands to yourself."

As I look back on it now, I wonder if somehow Troy knew something that would take me years to find out—that I was gay. I'd never met a gay person before, but I hoped they weren't all like Troy.

They lost it and rushed toward us, but by then we were in the hands of our own. Touché.

We found ourselves in the hotbed of conservatism, Arizona, something I'd never experienced before. The people and the land were inhospitable. We were in the middle of the vast Sonoran Desert with only cacti for companions. We tried to hitch a ride north to Ajo, but no one would pick us up. Quite the opposite. They tried to run us down and screamed epithets: "Dirty hippies! Cut your hair!" And worse.

An Arizona Highway Patrol car stopped and told us to keep on moving. Then by chance, a group of teenagers in an old model Chevy four-door, probably coming back from Mexico, slammed on their brakes. "Where you all goin'?" they cried out.

A guy and a girl sat in the front seat, and a couple sat in the back. Turned up full blast, the radio played "Purple Haze" by Jimi Hendrix. These were my kind of people.

"We're going to Ajo," we replied.

"Get in. We'll take you there."

The smell of marijuana permeated the car.

"Do you want to smoke a joint?" asked the driver, a young kid with long, scraggly locks.

"It's great stuff," said his girlfriend, who wore too much makeup for a girl her age.

Graham answered for all of us. "For sure."

After what had happened in Mexico and the less-than-friendly treatment by our own government, I was ready to get high. "Can we do this somewhere secluded?" I asked. "We don't want Smokey the Cop catching us smoking in the car."

"Sure, we can go down by the reservoir," said the young girl in the back seat.

"That sounds perfect," I said. "Some tranquility, just what we need." I told the story of the nightmare we'd endured.

We all sat on the reservoir, our feet dangling over the brown water while we passed around the joint.

"You've got some nasty Highway Patrol in these parts," I said.

"Yeah, they're like that down here," the driver said.

"How do you manage to have a good time in this kind of atmosphere?" Graham asked.

"Oh, we know how to avoid them," the driver responded. "We take the back roads."

It was interesting. Here we were in the middle of the Arizona desert, and there was a cultural revolution going on all over the country. Born in the Haight-Ashbury district in San Francisco out of a need for change in society, it had spread all over the country, even to little Ajo, Arizona. We felt like we were among brothers. Younger though they might be, there was a comradery established immediately, and they came to our aid and went to great lengths to keep us safe. This was the unspoken code of what would later be called the hippie generation.

We asked our young rescuers about Ajo and what we could expect there.

"Oh, Ajo's got the county fair going on right now," said the young driver. "It's fun, rides, and cotton candy. You won't be noticed."

Our eyes opened wide at the thought of having some fun, and of course, we were high, which made the fair all the more attractive.

"That sounds great," Michael said. "Let's go."

We all agreed.

Our friends dropped us at the fair and bade us farewell. They were lifesavers in the desert.

When the three of us walked in, the Ferris wheel was running, and I begged both Graham and Michael to go up in it. The three of us got into one seat with Graham in the middle. As we went up, the vista of the desert came into view, and it was spectacular. The sun's rays—red, yellow and orange—fell on the never-ending cacti and tumbleweed that covered the desert floor. As the sun began to set, the horizon stretched as far as the eye could see.

We went on to the bumper cars, and I took a beating from both my friends as they crashed their cars into me repeatedly. Laughing uproariously, eating our cotton candy, we left the fair. Our hearts were light as we headed for the outskirts of town.

Still clutching our cotton candy, we stuck our thumbs out again, this time for Gila Bend and the highway to Colorado and the resort town of Boulder. By then it was dark.

A car approached, its headlights blinding us, and we stuck our thumbs out for a ride. It was the Highway Patrol again. With a loudspeaker, the officer told us to keep walking out of town or he'd arrest us.

As we walked, he drove right behind us at five miles per hour with his headlights on. We walked in silence, in disbelief that this was how people were treated outside the safety of our little cocoon in San Francisco, which we'd naively believed was like the rest of the country. After about two miles of this treatment, I started to laugh. I mean, it *was* laughable. Was he going to walk us all the way to Gila Bend?

Our laughter grew, and soon all of us were hysterical as well as high. I started goose-stepping, and Michael broke into song as we goose-stepped, the three of us singing, "Springtime for Hitler and Germany."

I guess that embarrassed the highway patrolman. After all, we were just teenagers. He finally left, and we cheered.

A few minutes later, another set of headlights appeared, and we stuck our thumbs out again for Gila Bend. As the car came closer, we could see the outline of a white Chevy Impala. It was our friends. They were back. They'd been watching us when we left the fair and saw the Highway Patrol car pull out after us. What luck! Everyone had a good laugh, and they drove us all the way to Flagstaff.

The next day, we got a ride from Flagstaff to Gallup, New Mexico, in a VW van. The side doors were open, giving us an unobstructed view, as if in a movie. I watched Navajo boys riding bareback, herding their sheep. Indian women in velvet blue and purple blouses with long skirts and covered in silver and turquoise tended their gardens and wove blankets in front of their hogans, homes made from wood and covered with sheep hides. I was discovering the indigenous side of America. I knew one day I'd have to come back to this place of beauty.

We spent the next week trying to get back to San Francisco on very little money, having been separated from most of it by the Mexican cops. One night we found ourselves in Big Sur camping out when one of the hippies from the next encampment invited us to share their hearth and something they called LSD.

I don't know where the hours went. Big Sur Creek sounded like music, and the tree trunk I was perched on seemed to breathe in and out. Somehow, I wasn't freaked out, but rather saw the subtlety of a living tree that was alive, but in a way I'd never experienced before. I was like a child of illusion discovering the world for the first time. What a revelation, a reality that exists without ego.

Michael and Graham and I weren't separate from one another. Neither was the forest, nor the creek, nor the rocks. We sat around the campfire discussing this revelation, the light reflecting in our wide eyes. We began to see the world as made up of integral parts that were all interdependent, connected and one. We would never be the same. We'd had a glimpse of our true nature. It was love. And thus, my spiritual journey was conceived.

Michael Rossum

Robin, 1971

Chapter Six

Robin

Robin was a mystic who played a silver flute and conjured a vision of swamis, cobras swaying to and fro in baskets, and Pygmies who smoked pot. She was a healer, and she knew exactly what to say to soothe the aching heart. She was my best friend.

It was her eyes I noticed when we first smiled at one another, dark brown with just a hint of gold as they glistened in the autumn sun. She was beautiful and seemed shy, I thought at first, but I could see she was letting me in a little deeper with each glance. Her long blond hair and peach-like complexion shone on that cold fall day. We smiled as though we'd known one another forever. Yet in the unspoken silence, there was a deeper conversation going on.

She was a real New Yorker, with a heavy but soft accent. I watched her every movement. She was wearing a suede vest over a tight brown nylon top, large exotic silver earrings, and a leather shoulder bag. Her cotton dress flowed to the ground.

She turned toward me. "Hi, I'm Robin," she said, breaking the silence. "You're Jewish, right?"

I hesitated, wondering how obvious that must have seemed to her. "Yes, I am. And you too?"

"Yes, I am." She smiled. "I'm from New York, and I'm finishing my master's in political science."

"I'm a language major," I replied. My thoughts were still on her original question. I don't know what it is about Jewish people, but we always must ask that question of one another. Perhaps it's a sense of belonging, or looking for kinship, of having something in common outside the larger society that's always segregated us.

I fell in love with Robin almost overnight. She was the kind of woman who always had your back, whoever you were, even if homeless on the streets. It took no time to discover the depth of her love for mankind, and once you did, you realized it was her strength. She possessed a soul of intuition and warmth that would encompass you, and a sense of humor that would take you by surprise. She was sensitive, with a smile that was irresistible and a laugh that was infectious. I think that's why I fell in love with her. Saying goodbye to her would be one of the hardest things I ever had to do.

We met in September 1969 in the commons at San Francisco State. The war continued to rage in Vietnam. Nixon was raining bombs on Cambodia. Students nationwide were standing up for an end to the war, their demonstrations by then weekly events. In San Francisco, the Summer of Love was over. Bell-bottoms and paisley shirts were the style, and Elton John's "Your Song" was our song.

Robin and I really hadn't talked much. It was all glances and body language. It was intriguing, yet it made me hunger to know more. Who was this woman from the East? She was obviously very bright. A year younger than I, she'd already finished her BA and was working on her master's. She'd skipped a year of college as well. I wondered what her interest was in me. Was it purely sexual, or was there more?

"Would you like to get together later for lunch?" she asked.

"Sure. Noon?"

"Groovy. See you then." She kept looking at me out of the corner of her eye while she held court with the others around her.

My interest was piqued. I looked back, and she did too as I trailed off to class.

I saw her a few times after that first encounter. We'd sit in her "illegal" in-law apartment on San Jose Avenue and talk for hours about everything—politics, the world, books, and music. The ceilings there were less than eight feet high, which gave it a warm, cave-like feel. It was dark, since it was below ground level. She'd laid down a huge Persian carpet in front of the fireplace with big Rajasthani pillows. It served as our lounging spot for reading the newspaper, smoking pot, meditating, and eating dinner. We basically lived our lives cross-legged on that carpet. It was a charmed, Bedouin life.

The more I grew to know her, the more I was drawn to her physically, and we slowly became romantically involved. She was vulnerable. She'd been through a lot of sadness for a girl of nineteen. Sadness and tragedy hadn't been a stranger to either one of us, so it was a common thread that bonded us. She was an emotional woman of great strength, but when she broke, I felt like I needed to protect her.

It was there with the fire crackling in our Bedouin cave that the stories of her journey came to life. She told me about her privileged life in Woodmere, New York, one of the Five Towns on the western edge of Long Island. Every house was enormous, three stories with shuttered windows, usually painted white with black trim, atop expansive lawns that couldn't be ignored. The circular driveways leading to the front doors, flanked by lions-in-waiting, only betrayed their owners' newly acquired wealth. Had it been anything but the late '60s, I would have expected lawn jockeys.

No one was farther from this lifestyle than Robin. Her father died when she was fourteen. He'd been her mentor. He came from modest means and never forgot that the only important thing in life was family. Henrietta, Robin's mother, was like a Stepford wife. She wanted the clothes, the house, the social life, and all the pretentiousness that came along with newly acquired wealth and life in the Five Towns. In her defense, she had a good heart and she was generous, but you wouldn't find that on the surface.

Robin told me she'd used heroin at the age of fourteen, which shocked me at first. Then I realized she was trying to tell me something. She'd been out there in the world in a way that most fourteen-year olds at the time could never imagine. Not only was she unique, but she'd lived life on the edge, and had survived. When you live your life on the razor's edge, you are free. Freedom for us both was paramount. We made a pact to stay true to ourselves, to speak the truth, no lies, not even in the face of our own fears.

She hung out in the East Village with the jazz and music scene. She knew so many people. We'd go to the Fillmore East, where she turned me on to all kinds of music, not just rock. Robin was so ahead of her time. She conversed as if she had the wisdom of a sadhu while interjecting her unique style of humor, half self-deprecation and spontaneous. She was real, and her laughter would hook you. She knew many performers and even introduced me to the great jazz singer Taj Mahal. Robin loved Elton John and Laura Nyro, and introduced me to their music. She bought tickets to see Elton at the Fillmore East, and he wore his red shoes and glasses. You know how songs define a moment or a period in your life? Well, Elton John's "Your Song" embraced all that I felt about Robin. I believe it was mutual.

Maybe another factor that drew us together was wisdom: her worldly wisdom and my political wisdom as a socialist. The combination gave us the ability to see the world from a fresh perspective.

We sat smoking pot before class as she told me story after story of exotic trips to Morocco and Algeria and other parts of Africa. She'd crossed the Indian Ocean to Bombay from Mombasa, Kenya. She'd seen the Taj Mahal in India and had explored all the mystical places I'd only dreamed about. She told me about the people and cultures of all these exotic lands. I was mesmerized like a cobra in a basket.

She went on to tell me about how she and her friend Paul had gone into the deepest jungles of Uganda, where the Pygmies lived, in search of an African gray parrot. She described the Pygmies as very small Africans with big hearts. She sat with the women and smoked a marijuana joint the size of a cigar. Evidently, the Pygmies saw the benefits of opening their minds with marijuana to explore their world, and what was even greater, their souls.

Paul and Robin were in the jungles for three days with the Pygmy tribesmen and slept in the bush until they'd finally found and captured the perfect young parrot. I'm sorry to say that after bringing the parrot out of Africa and having it in quarantine for six months, poor Paul lost the bird. Somewhere between Omaha and Winnemucca on his way out to see us in California, he forgot to roll down the windows of the car, and the bird roasted to death in ninety-degree heat.

She called me Mick, and she was the only one I allowed to call me by my nickname.

She told me of a cruise down the coast of Malaysia in a sailboat with two friends she'd met in Thailand. "Mick, these guys were so nice, and so knowable. They asked me if I wanted to sail down the Malay coast to Penang with them. Well, what could I say but yes?"

Subsequently, after leaving Thailand, they found themselves on the sailboat lost in the midst of a freak hurricane. They ended up pitching water from the boat all night long with buckets just to stay afloat, as the waves splashed over the sides. Sunrise gave way to calm and the storm finally subsided. They finally arrived in Penang, an island off the Malay Peninsula, exhausted, shaky, and happy to be alive.

Robin stirred in me a desire to see the world, and not just any place, but the far reaches of the globe, the places most hadn't traveled. I couldn't get enough of the tales, her wonderful smile, her amazing intuition, and the laughter that filled the room. To my surprise, within a week or two, we were living together. She'd become my mentor and lover.

Chapter Seven

Easter Break—Meeting the "In-Laws"

When Easter break came, Robin asked me to go back to New York to meet her family. I was hesitant, but she assured me it would be okay. She wanted me to meet her friends, the people she'd grown up with, whom I'd heard so many stories about through all the wonderful discussions in front of the fireplace.

Suddenly, the characters I'd heard about had faces. There was the beautiful doctor's daughter, Rosalind, from Cedarhurst, and Bobby Riddell and Ross Isenberg from Far Rockaway. I met her best friend, Eve Eisenstein, and her African traveling buddy, Paul Schwartz. There was Kenny Gutterman, her gay friend, who was in love with her ex-boyfriend Bobby, who turned out to be gay too. It was a little like an episode out of a soap: *Lives in the Five Towns*.

Her older sister, Susan, was following in her mother's footsteps. She was an editor at Dell Books in Manhattan, and she wanted the house and the car, the clothes and the apartment on the East Side. Robin's sister was classy. She knew how to dress conservatively and still let the guys know she was available. But she was a good girl. She held out for the wedding ring. So when her boyfriend, David, proposed, it was no surprise. With one marriage in the making, Robin's grandmother, who turned out to be a real piece of work, was ready to begin working on Robin.

The grandmother had narrowly escaped Hitler's death camps. She left Warsaw just before war broke out in Europe. Her sister wasn't so lucky. She was sent to Auschwitz. I met her later in Israel, but that's another story.

In her heavy Yiddish accent, Robin's grandmother told her, "You should find a man, and if he doesn't look like a monkey and has a nose in the middle of his face and he has two eyes—marry him."

"Marry Michael?" Robin asked. "But, Grandma, I'm not ready to get married, and I'm sure Michael isn't either. We just met."

"He's a good Jewish boy," her grandmother said. "He's tall and good-looking, and I can tell he has a crush on you."

"Oh, Granny, it's too early to tell," Robin said.

"Ah, too early to tell. I got married when I was sixteen years old. I hardly knew your grandfather, but I knew he was a good man."

They were charming people in their East Coast way, a little neurotic and dysfunctional, but whose family isn't? Even Henrietta, with her bouffant hairdo, Capri pants, and loads of costume jewelry, came out from behind the wall that she'd built up to protect herself to show me some kindness, and let her guard down long enough for me to get a glimpse inside.

It was Easter, but it was also Passover. That was the real reason Robin had to go home. I'd have to prepare myself for my first formal Seder dinner. I was brought up Jewish culturally, but knew nothing of the religion. Socialism, the proletariat, and the capitalist class were my catechism growing up.

The table in the formal dining room looked like it was set for visiting royalty, with massive silver candelabras and fine china for fifteen. Suddenly, I wasn't just visiting as Robin's friend from school. I was a potential suitor, and what's more, I was Jewish, a prerequisite.

Robin had no interest in this charade. But she was performing her duties as a good daughter so her mother wouldn't cut off the flow of money. If she stayed in college and married a nice Jewish boy, the cash would still flow. After all, this was the "island of Jewish princesses."

Suddenly, the doorbell rang. Her nouveau riche Republican family descended on Passover dinner like Ramses at the Red Sea. I was introduced as Robin's friend from school in California, but that's where the polite conversation stopped. Over the bitter herbs and unleavened bread came a barrage of questions intent on finding out just who I was. Knowing Robin's history, they were suspect. Robin was, after all, the black sheep of the family. She didn't care about the status quo or the Republican Party. What now, she's brought a hippie to Seder dinner?

Robin's uncle Saul began. "Why is this night different from all others?"

I was way out of my comfort zone. I thought this could only end badly.

After the questions and prayers were over, her uncle smiled at me. "So, Michael, Henrietta tells me you're Jewish and your family comes from New York originally," he bellowed from his end of the table.

"Yes," I said. "Uptown—Seventy-Ninth Street. But I grew up in California."

"So, you like it out there in San Francisco with all those hippies and radicals?" Uncle Saul cried out.

Uncle Jacob chimed in too. "What side are you on, the North or the South?"

"What side?" I replied. "If you mean, am I against the war in Vietnam, then yes, I guess I am a radical."

They shook their heads in disbelief. Was I way out of line standing up for my beliefs during Passover, one of the holiest days in the Jewish calendar?

"Don't you think President Nixon is saving us from communism?" Saul asked. "I mean after all, if Vietnam falls, Southeast Asia will fall like dominos to the communists."

I explained my view, that the war in Vietnam was a civil war between the North and the South. The only reason we were there was to protect capitalist interests in those markets.

There was silence at the table. The uncles and aunts all smiled at one another in collective acknowledgement that they'd uncovered a subversive. They wanted to expose me for everything they were not.

We were revolutionaries. We saw the world differently, in a loving way, with compassion even for our enemies. We wanted to change the world—to bring down the Iron Curtain and open Fidel's Cuba for dialogue and trade. Stopping the war was our main objective.

As heated as the discussion grew, they were respectful of my position.

From there the conversation took a racist twist, which I found ironic in a group of people who were celebrating their freedom from slavery. Suddenly it was, "The Schwartzes did this," and, "The Schwartzes did that." It was the blacks who were causing so much trouble.

We battled it out over three long, arduous hours, and when it was over and the leftover matzo crumbs were brushed from the table, Robin's uncle Saul came and hugged me. He said, "You know, Michael, I don't agree with you, but I like a man who stands on his principles. You know socialism in this country will never work."

"How do you know? It's never been tried."

"I like you, boy. You've got *chutzpah*. It was nice meeting you."

A few days later, on Easter Sunday, Robin and her good friends Rosalind and Eve Eisenstein asked me if I wanted to go to the Easter Be-In in Central Park and drop acid. I was jazzed and agreed without hesitation. She told me that half a million people were expected, and Jefferson Airplane would be playing at the bandstand, along with Richie Havens and Cream. We all jumped into Roz's Volkswagen Bug and took off on the Long Island Expressway for the city. We arrived at the midtown tunnel in no time, and before I knew it, we were in Central Park.

We got there just as people were finding their places in front of the stage. There were so many "heads" there, hippies from all over the world. It was an overwhelming feeling of being part of a much larger phenomenon, a gathering of the people who would change the course of American history, and the icons who sang our songs of liberation.

We threw down our blanket and knapsacks near the bandstand and got settled in as thousands of people filed in behind us. The bandstand ran down the east side of the park, which had huge, expansive lawn areas with the occasional shade tree. There were several bandstands, but the largest center one could hold the staging and equipment for three separate bands. The stages had backdrops in black cloth and huge towers of speakers on the sides. Eventually, half a million people would show up. The crowds surrounded the stages from all directions, with the city skyscrapers from the West Side rising out of the greenery.

Before the bands began to play, the crowds entertained themselves. There were jugglers and people on stilts. There were circles of people who had all come together like tribes with their headbands and long hair. Our hair defined us. We knew we could trust a brother with long hair to share a ride or a joint, and we looked to one another for support and a helping hand. Of course, there were the oddballs who weren't trustworthy, but they were few and far between.

It was about love and brotherhood. It was about changing the status quo. It was about revolution. We thought that acid was the vehicle to bring us there because it broke down the boundaries of the ego. It allowed us to experience the here and now with open hearts, in the present moment. It was so strong it didn't allow you to think in the past or the future, just the now, what was happening in this moment, moment to moment.

The music began, and circles of people began to dance. The jugglers and clowns walked through the crowds. It was festive and joyous, and Robin and I danced, our arms raised high to the heavens in bliss and love—for one another, for the crowd, and for the moment.

When it was time to leave, we walked through the crowd, and suddenly I began to have what they call a bad trip. Everything became exaggerated. People's laughter became sinister. I passed junkies shooting up heroin right in front of me. Some people were drunk, and their drunkenness was horribly depressing. I saw prostitutes looking for tricks. The crowd became ugly, and I started to see all the things in society, in the big city, that were dark and unsavory.

As we walked through the crowd, Robin could see that something was wrong. "Hey, Mick, what's happening?" she asked. "You look uneasy."

I related as best I could what was happening.

"Look, honey, there are lots of things that are bad in our society," she said. "We don't know why we're here, but we're here, and you have a choice. You can either accept it and be here, or cut yourself off from it."

"Good. Then I want to cut myself off from it."

She looked shocked by my answer. She knew then that they had to get me home as soon as possible. She could feel my paranoia as I contracted and withdrew.

I got in the car, and there was complete silence. Everyone was aware of what was happening to me. The Volkswagen Bug seemed as like a bubble streaming through the canyons of New York. I was sure they were taking me to a hospital on Long Island, but suddenly we were in front of Robin's house. She took me upstairs to our bedroom and gave me a lot of space, but nothing would stop the journey I was on. Tears rolled down my cheeks, and I began to cry. I realized I was crying for Gene, my poor brother who'd hung himself, silenced forever. I'd never again feel that fraternal hug and laughter and beautiful energy from such a fine man.

All the memories began pouring out. All the grief that I still hadn't fully and completely experienced was staring me in the face. I'd lost my innocence in the Big Apple at the Easter Be-In. That was what I was experiencing, and it tore me at the core. I wanted to cut myself off from it all. If this was what the real world was like, I wanted no part of it. It was all so painful.

Fortunately, the acid began to wear off, and I fell into a deep sleep.

Michael Rossum

Hampshire House, the author, 1971

Chapter Eight

Hampshire House

Back in San Francisco, we decided to move to a larger place. We found a house for rent in a neighborhood on a beautiful hillside overlooking downtown and the bay. We asked Bobby Riddell, Robin's friend, whom I'd met at Easter and who had come home to Far Rockaway for the holiday also, if he'd share it with us, and he agreed. We called it Hampshire House, and it became a focal point for people in the neighborhood to hang out. It was an old Victorian built in the 1880s in a section of the city called Bernal Heights. Around the corner from us, where the freeway passed a rocky hill, was a cul-de-sac. All the neighbors on the cul-de-sac knew one another. Some were second-generation.

The stairs that led to the front door were high, so we had a commanding view of the city. Inside, there was a large living room with pocket doors that opened to the dining room. Across the center hall was a huge kitchen with stairs on one side that led to the attic. There were two bedrooms at opposite ends of the attic. Behind the kitchen was a sunroom where I grew our pot plants. The gas heater was in the living room and had to be lit with a three-foot-long piece of bamboo where we placed the match so as not to burn all the hair off our arms.

It was a rundown rental with a slum landlord, but we were happy there because we all had one another. Bobby played drums, so some nights it was like a jam session. With musicians and locals all partaking in the spontaneous coming together of the neighborhood, Hampshire House rocked. Robin and I lived upstairs in one of the attic bedrooms. It was furnished in the style of the time. Cinder blocks with wooden shelves held all our records. Bobby took the larger front bedroom, which he shared with his drums.

These were some of the happiest days of my life. We were a family. None of us had a pot to piss in, and we were all on food stamps. I used to make enchiladas for dinner, and anybody who was over would eat with us. Later, we acquired another roommate, Woody Woodruff, also a student at SF State studying drama, who would succeed in becoming a first-class director off Broadway. He rounded out the house in the bedroom across from us in the attic.

Hampshire House began to take on the look of a commune. It was just that. We communally shared everything, and it was in that sharing that there was great humanity and compassion for our house, our neighborhood, and the world outside.

Robin's mother, Henrietta, and her grandmother came out for Robin's graduation from her master's program in political science in June. We invited them for dinner, along with my parents. In our dining room we had an old Persian rug, and for a table, we used an AT&T wooden spool that had once held coiled wire. Now cut in half, it stood in the middle of the rug. All around the table were large Rajasthani pillows that we sat on instead of chairs.

We made a beautiful broiled salmon for dinner with potatoes au gratin and fresh broccoli. Henrietta brought flowers for the table but had no idea what she was getting into. When they all began to figure out how they'd sit on the floor, I watched as Robin's grandmother maneuvered. Without saying a word, the seventy-five-year-old Holocaust survivor made herself comfortable with no complaints, wanting to let Robin know how proud she was of her.

The walls were painted a dark blue and were highlighted by beautiful gold-framed gemstone paintings from India. It was an amazingly creative space. Now we were all together on the floor, eating around the table hippie-style, celebrating Robin's achievement. It was quite a picture, but that was Hampshire House, a little rough around the edges, but classy.

At school, the focal point was the Vietnam War, which was still raging. SF State had become the center stage for protests, as well as a focal point for the Free Speech Movement, which had spread from Berkeley. Free speech now engulfed the campus and the nation with a new meaning. Our generation wanted to think for itself. People began to protest the school's hard line on what was being taught. They wanted ethnic studies, and the right to disagree with a teacher or administrator without being penalized with bad grades or expulsion.

One day, a truck backed up onto the campus at lunchtime. The students wanted to talk about these issues. A few speakers began to explain the reason for the strike and why others should join it. S. I. Hayakawa, the president of the university, decided that he'd have none of the antics of Berkeley's People's Park on his campus. He climbed up on the truck while the student was talking and proceeded to tear out the speaker wires from the generator.

People stood up in shock, abandoning their lunches. He'd enraged us so that a hail of sandwiches and milk containers rained down on him until his Yves Saint Laurent suit looked like a salad bar. Once the media picked up on what was happening, everything escalated.

That was the beginning of the San Francisco State boycott. It started as a protest, but it grew in strength to include the ROTC on campus, which recruited young men—most of whom had little knowledge of what was going on in Vietnam—with promises of how they could see the world and get careers in the army. We felt that if they wanted to recruit men for the war, they should do it someplace where they weren't so accessible. It was like we were accomplices.

As the protests grew daily, more and more students boycotted classes, and the crowds in the commons grew larger and louder. Hayakawa thought if he could throw enough scare into us with the tactical squad and tear gas, we'd go away. But when that failed, he brought out the big guns.

Robin had to finish her master's or she'd be cut off by her family, so she continued to go to class. My best friend, Fausto, and I would go to our Spanish classes, and we'd debate the merits of the boycott.

We finally recruited our teacher, Mr. Williams, to join the strike. He was a young professor from the Midwest, smart, and he could think outside the box. He was our Spanish literature professor, but that day we weren't reading Cervantes. Instead, we'd invited him to cut class and take a trip to Mount Tamalpais to take a real trip, on mushrooms. That's how it was back then. We were all discovering ourselves, professor and student alike.

A few weeks into the strike, Nineteenth Avenue saw tanks and the National Guard rolling toward the school as if there was war raging. Robin and I had been protesting that day in front of the ROTC office on campus. Around two hundred people were holding down the building that housed the ROTC. We wanted ROTC off campus.

Amid a barrage of tactical squad and tear gas, we were encircled. We watched as the tanks surrounded the entire campus. The average San Franciscan was awestruck by the force that was being used. Everyone made a run for wherever they could find safe ground. The film footage went worldwide, and for the first time, we felt the iron fist of the United States on our backs. We knew we'd struck a raw nerve.

Fausto and I passed by the library, which looked on to the Commons, and noticed all the straight conservative kids standing and gazing (with their noses pressed against the windows) out from its security.

Fausto said, "Look at those assholes. It's as if they were watching a circus performance while we get teargassed and beaten up."

"I've got an idea," I said. "What if we went up to the fifth floor administrators' offices where the corridors are empty and brake a fire alarm, and force them all out into the Commons so they can get a taste of what it's like to be teargassed and beaten with billy clubs. Maybe then they'll realize that they have a stake in the Boycott and what's going on in our struggle and how passionate we are about achieving our goals."

The tactical squad finally got to where we were. We knew there was no way out except through the front doors, which were being held down by mounted police in tactical gear. They came from the back entrance inside the building in the small corridors, beating everyone in their paths. I saw them grab a young girl by her ponytail as she ran for the front, and they smashed her in the face with a baton.

"We have to get out! Stay close to me!" I told Robin as we made a run for the front doors and the exit. I threw the doors open, and people began running out, trying to dodge the officers on horseback as they swung their rubber batons. I saw a trash can nearby, and picked it up and threw it at the two officers guarding the exit. Their horses reared up, and the police were caught off-guard long enough for most of us to escape.

By the time it was over, the resistance had been crushed, the president, who hadn't been seen on campus in four years, was walking the grounds unhindered, and all the teachers who'd taken part in the protests were purged, including Mr. Williams. It was graduation day, 1971.

The Draft

Graduation Day was over. I didn't even go to my commencement ceremonies. When I went home to Hampshire House, my induction notice for Vietnam was waiting for me. I was frozen. Have you ever felt like you were about to be annihilated? That's what it felt like to me—a mixture of fear and anger. Anger that someone else had a rein on my life, and fear I no longer had control of my own destiny. I was a victim, one who must obey.

They wanted me to kill innocent people who were fighting a civil war. I saw the news about My Lai. Take up arms and "kill the gooks." That's what they called the Vietnamese. They were just "gooks." It's easier to kill people if you see them as objects. As a Jew growing up in America, I knew what names like gook meant. They meant hate.

I'd known it was coming, but I wasn't prepared, and probably never would have been. I'd evaded the draft for nearly five years on school deferments, and now the war was at my doorstep. *Oh fuck*, I thought. It was me they wanted to grind up and send to Vietnam. It was me that would be used as fodder for their war.

Robin couldn't console me. We discussed leaving the country, but that felt like a cop-out.

For a brief period in the summer of 1970, I'd worked at Letterman General Hospital as a night janitor. I saw the casualties of Vietnam firsthand. I saw the plastic body bags going down to the morgue, the guys with no arms and legs being wheeled down the halls, and others with post-traumatic stress disorder who looked vacant. They were so lost.

I was determined I wouldn't go to Vietnam.

My dad said when I started college that the war would be over by the time I graduated. But it was still raging. I came home after receiving the notice and asked, "What should I do, Dad? They want to send me to Vietnam."

"I don't know, son. But we'll support you whatever you choose to do."

For the first time in my life, my daddy couldn't save me. I could see it in his eyes. He felt helpless and impotent. Going to Canada was out of the question. My cousin had fled the year before to Edmonton, Alberta, and wrote how unhappy he was and how much he missed his family and the country he loved, which he'd never be able to return to.

I consulted some activist groups. They suggested I see a psychiatrist who was helping young men like me get deferments on medical grounds. I decided to see him. There was 80 percent draft evasion in San Francisco, the highest in the nation. That meant that out of every ten guys, eight refused to go. Before I knew it, I was reporting to the Oakland Induction Center.

The protesters outside screamed as we filed off the bus. "Don't go! Don't go!"

If we refused, the government would put us behind bars. So I tried to fail. Every test they gave me, I failed. I poured sugar in my urine sample. They passed me. I flunked the math test. They passed me. The last test was for people who had psychological problems. I found myself standing in underwear and cowboy boots, waiting for the medical officer.

An officious man entered the room. "What's your problem, son?" he asked.

"Sir, if I have to go to Vietnam, I will commit suicide," I said. I handed him the letter from the doctor confirming that I was unfit for duty.

The officer looked up at me and spoke four words: "Follow the yellow line."

It led right out the front door. Yee-haw, I was discharged. I did it. I'd fought my personal battle with the Vietnam War, and I'd won. I was free to try to end it here rather than there.

card allowing me access to the National Health Service. That way, I could go to the hospital when I needed my stitches removed and the cast replaced.

A brilliant doctor from Jamaica helped remove the stitches. The doctor from Long Island had put in one continuous spiral metal strip, which was a new technology being used by doctors in the States to close wounds of that type. One look at it, and the Jamaican doctor was floored, as was I. Not sure about how to remove it, he consulted his colleagues. They finally figured it out. They'd cut each spiral as it came out the wound, and pull out the metal stitches. It took a while, but it was done. I was so impressed by the professionalism and dedication of the young doctors, and I thanked them profusely. We in the States complained about national health care. Poppycock. It didn't cost me a dime, and I wasn't even a British citizen.

Some of Robin's friends were in an avant-garde theater group called the Theater in the Round. I saw them give a brilliant performance of *The Taming of the Shrew*. We were surrounded by all these smart, witty Brits, some of whom we shared the house with, and there was always an amusing story about the royal family or some scandal regarding a rock star.

I went to London Bridge. I saw the Queen's Guard, the British Museum, the Tate, and Westminster Abbey, so spectacular. This was my first experience in a church of its size, age, and history. Seeing all these attractions gave me a different perspective on my own country, which had fought a war to rid itself of this kind of pomp and ceremony. Yet the grandeur of it all could not be negated.

Hampstead Heath on acid. Wow. Tripping in the park, with its manicured gardens and green lawns, was so surreal, so peaceful and calming. We spent hours there. We met a couple of English heads who asked us if we wanted to smoke a joint, and we exchanged stories. I told them we were tripping. What began as a smile on their faces slowly turned into an all-knowing grin. We talked for quite some time, or at least it seemed. There were no barriers. We laughed and carried on. Even though our cultures were different, our

Chapter Nine

European Tour—London to Paris

School and my brush with the army were over. Robin and I had graduated. She received her master's degree in political science, and I got my bachelor's degree in Spanish. Robin invited me to go with her to Europe in the summer of 1971, but I told her I couldn't afford the trip.

"Mick," she said, "I've got this all figured out. My mother needs her house painted, and we could paint it and stay with her until it's finished, and then go to Europe. Then you'd have enough to make it. I found tickets for one hundred and fifty dollars on a Lloyd's of London charter. What do you think?"

"Robin, her house is enormous," I said.

"I'll help you."

It was just too tempting for me to say no. I went back to Woodmere to paint her mother's house in order to have enough cash to make the trip. Two-thirds of the way through the job, while painting the third story, I fell to the second-story sun deck and broke my elbow. Henrietta rescued me and had a great Long Island orthopedist operate and stitch me up. She paid me what she owed me and even had me sue her for the insurance money. It was through a cousin who was a lawyer, so it stayed in the family. When I was paid, it was assumed that I'd share it with Robin. That was the deal.

I went on my first trip to the Continent in a plaster cast. That wasn't quite how I'd imagined it.

Robin had friends everywhere. We stayed with some friends of hers in Highgate Hill in North London. They even helped me get a humanity was the same. Our exchanges brought us closer to understanding their culture. They were completely open with us, and we were likewise. It felt like we'd known one another longer than a few hours.

Hampstead Heath was nothing compared with my first encounter with some Scotsmen in a pub in London. It was unnerving, since I thought we were all speaking English, and their brogue was so heavy. I sat down at a table and said, "Excuse me, is this chair occupied?"

The three Scotts cried out in unison, "No, it's not. Have a seat. It's yours now."

"Where are you from, eh?" asked a chubby red-haired man.

"From the colonies," I said.

"Which ones?" chimed the other three.

We all had a good laugh.

"You're a Yank, eh?"

"Yes."

"Well, sit down and have a pint with us. King George may have lost that colony, but you've gained three Scotsmen."

I already liked them. That did it. They kept buying me pints. We talked for hours, but I didn't understand a word they said. I asked them if they could repeat themselves so many times that I finally stopped and just nodded and smiled through the remainder of the conversation.

I learned about the Scotts and the Welsh, the cockneys from London, and the Irish. It reminded me of the States with all our different accents, from Brooklynese to Cajun. Many times, we don't understand one another either.

Finally, Robin arrived. I introduced them to her, and she talked awhile with them.

On our way out, I asked her, "Did you understand them?"

"No," she replied.

"But you carried on with them for so long."

"I was just being polite."

"Well, you really rocked their boat for someone who didn't understand a word they said."

Her smile would have rocked anyone's boat.

The Continent

France was calling us. It was time to move on. We strapped on our knapsacks, grabbed a train at Victoria Station for Ramsgate, and headed for the hover port on our way to Calais and the Continent. I was jazzed. London was great, but Paris? Ooh la la.

A mixture of a helicopter and a ferry, the hovercraft slid up on the beach at Calais like a giant jellyfish. The next thing I knew, I was walking on sand to the street just off the beach. I was in Normandy. My first thought was *D-day*, that it was here we fought to end Hitler's hold on Europe. At the risk of sounding maudlin, it felt like sacred ground.

We made our way to a typical French café with lace curtains in the windows. We could see the establishment was quite full. When I opened the door, its bells announced our arrival. The owner of the café, a beautiful woman in her forties, looked up at us. She wore a plain gray skirt with a burgundy cardigan and a low-cut blouse. The floors were made of wooden planks that had seen many days. Burgundy café chairs sat next to the tables, which were covered with white tablecloths and held African violets in small vases. I ordered two cafés au lait. The coffee came in a large bowl, and I drank in deeply my first taste of France.

It was there that I had the first encounter of many to follow with European toilets, or WC. "*Mademoiselle, s'il vous plaît, toilette?*" I was practicing my French.

She understood me and directed me to the water closet.

I opened the door and stood there in a stupor. *What the hell is this?* I thought. Had there been some mistake? "Excuse me, madam," I said in French, "the one for the men, please."

"That's it," she replied.

Okay, that's it, so get in there and figure it out, I thought. There were two foot pads and a hole with a string hanging down to flush it. I was so sure this was the women's bathroom. I looked up when I was finished. *Where's the toilet paper?* I saw the string hanging to one side, grabbed it, and pulled. The water came swirling up around my shoes and the bottoms of my pants. "Welcome to France," I muttered.

In Calais, we stuck our thumbs out for Paris and got a ride to Boulogne. Halfway there, we were thrown out in the middle of wheat fields by a pervert from the Peugeot factory that was just north of there. He was trying to cop a feel up Robin's skirt. I'd threatened him with my cast, but he was a big man in factory overalls, and I was no match for him. So there we were as the sun set, without a ride and little prospect for another. Fortunately, I'd purchased a bottle of wine, some great brie, and a fresh loaf of bread in Calais. Our first night on the Continent, and the stars were our celestial ceiling and the wheat fields a soft bed where we lay our heads.

The next day, we entered Paris. Our ride dropped us off in front of the Paris Opera House near the Rue des Italiens. I got out of the car to see a French gigolo walking around with a baby ocelot amid the sidewalk cafés. Waiters in black uniforms, with white towels over their arms, carried trays of beverages. I was so ready for a drink. Wow, Paris, and we were finally there.

We sat down, and I hailed a waiter. "*Monsieur, s'il vous plait,* two Cokes please."

I sat there in awe in the shadow of the Opera House, sipping my Coke, as if it were a dream. Then the bill came, and I snapped out of it. Ten dollars for two Cokes.

I fell in love with Paris. The Marais, with its cobblestoned streets and the eleventh- and twelfth-century edifices, Notre Dame with its gargoyles, Île de la Cité like a jewel in the Seine, the Louvre and the D'Orsay. Robin and I climbed the Eiffel Tower, using the stairs all the way to the top, as the elevator wasn't in service and we weren't going to miss the view. The City of Lights was the most beautiful city I'd ever seen.

Robin spoke French, and with her gregarious personality, she drew people to her, and they gave her insights into the many places we visited. Then she'd tell me the history of the sights. She was knowledgeable about so many things. From her narration in front of the Palais du Justice, I could imagine the people in the courtyard waiting to see the execution of Marie Antoinette. With so much history in Paris, my head was swimming.

"There's Balzac's house, and this is the Hôtel de Ville," she pointed out.

At the Arc de Triomphe, I pictured the now-infamous photos of the Nazis entering a fallen Paris, a city under occupation. While in the historic district of Marais, I felt the Jews. I saw Hasidim in their shops, mothers picking up their children at the synagogue from school, people in the outdoor cafés in conversation, men walking to the ritual baths. I wondered how it must have been for them, trapped in this beautiful city, betrayed by their neighbors and their government, and shipped off to concentration camps for the Final Solution. There was a placard in the Marais, a memorial to those deported to the Drancy concentration camp. It was painful to see firsthand, as one-third of my family died at the hands of the Nazis. I couldn't get these feelings out of my head.

I could have spent more time in Paris, but we had to meet Robin's relatives in Israel sometime in July. So we stuck our thumbs out for the South of France.

We had an invitation to the Running of the Bulls in Pamplona from my literature professor, Señor Maleon, and had to meet him before July 6, the day of the patron saint San Fermin. That meant crossing the Pyrenees, and we only had a few days to make it.

We got lucky. With our backpacks in tow, we headed out for Bordeaux and were picked up by a most unusual ride. A finely dressed man in a Mercedes stopped and told us he was going as far as the Bordeaux area. We developed a chemistry between us that went deep. Just because he wore a suit and drove a Mercedes didn't mean he couldn't be open to common ideals. Our conversations about politics, Eastern philosophy, and the war indicated a mutual understanding. He liked us, and I think he genuinely wanted to go out of his way to share with us a little of the exciting journey we were on.

By the time we reached Bordeaux, it was night. He invited us to stay with him in his chateau on the outskirts of town, taste his wines, and share an intimate dinner with him. It was more than we could have hoped for. We woke to a beautiful *petit dejeuner*: croissants, cheese, marmalade, and café au lait. We thanked him for his generosity to such strangers, just travelers on the road.

"*De rien*," he responded. "It was nothing."

We were back on the road again, waiting for another unlikely ride. Hills with row upon row of grapevines filled the Bordeaux countryside. A pair of Portuguese laborers, returning from stints as guest workers in Germany, picked us up in a Volkswagen Bug. We hopped into the back seat, which was full of all sorts of appliances they were taking back to their families in Lisbon.

Both men had big mustaches, dark skin weathered by the sun, and hands that had seen hard labor. They reminded me of the Marx Brothers. They were trying to read a map and seemed to be berating one another. Confused, almost to the point of slapstick, they at times read the map upside down. It was like watching clowns.

"What are they doing?" I kept whispering to Robin. "What are they doing?"

"I don't know," she said. "I don't know."

They asked me every few kilometers, "What does the sign say?"

"Twenty kilometers to Irun," I said. "Bear to the left." I finally realized they were illiterate. That's why they'd picked us up.

We traveled for some time through the Basque country on the French side before winding our way up through the Pyrenees, a mountain range of exquisite granite peaks jutting up like knives into the heavens. Hannibal crossed it on elephants. Only it wasn't the elephants I feared at the crossing, but La Guardia Civil of the Franco regime. The last Fascist dictator left in Western Europe from World War II was still in power, and he retained an iron grip on the Spanish people.

Irun is one of the few passes that cross this rugged mountain range. It's a beautiful town built from the same gray granite. As we neared it, I could see the border and the Spanish flags above the customs house.

We were all ordered out of the car, and two officers approached wearing the Civil Guard uniform, black with a red stripe running down the pant legs and an odd seventeenth-century triangular hat called a tricorne. They looked stern and menacing as they came closer and spoke to me in Spanish. They told me they wanted to see my papers. Then they told me that they'd have to saw off my cast. "*Quitate la casta*," they said.

I was furious. What did they mean, saw off my cast? Were they out of their minds? I did my essay for my bachelor's on the Spanish Civil War, and my contempt was growing by the minute. "What are you looking for?" I asked.

"Contraband."

I told them in Spanish that they'd have to saw off my arm if they wanted the cast. They looked up at me, disgusted by my lack of cooperation and frustrated at my language skills and attitude. They took a cursory look at both ends of the cast. Tired of us, they waved us on.

Franco's Spain

Traveling in Europe was like a dream for me, but after studying four years of Spanish language and history, I was really fulfilling my dream by going to Spain and meeting Señor Maleon for the Running of the Bulls in Pamplona. Hemingway's *The Sun Also Rises* was the first time I'd read about the Running of the Bulls. The Festival of San Fermin dates to the times of the Romans. I wanted to watch those crazy Spaniards running in front of the bulls like they did in the days of the Colosseum.

We met up with Señor Maleon in Pamplona. This was Basque country, and he was fiercely Basque, and he fell in love with Robin immediately. He'd been paramount in teaching me the Spanish classics and the history of the Spanish Civil War through the poetry and stories of Federico Garcia Lorca. He was part of the Spanish Inteligencia before he came to the States and a youngster during the Spanish Civil War when Garcia Lorca was murdered and thrown into a ditch in an unmarked grave. But his family fought against Franco. He was an amazing man as well as a remarkable teacher. He invited me to Spain still in the hands of Franco. It was as if I was getting and education in literature and history that was still going on, not in the past but in the present. I only realized this much later.

He took us straightaway to the Plaza Central, where people had already started gathering for the all-night party that preceded the morning's Running of the Bulls. Everyone wore white with red scarves around their necks. The plaza was a sea of humanity, undulating red hot underneath the Spanish sun.

I took off my shirt and stuck it in the back of my Levi's. It was ninety degrees, and the sweat poured down my back. I looked to the right and saw two Civil Guards approaching us. *What now?* I thought. *Don't these guys ever go away?*

"*Ponte su camisa o te vas para la carcel,*" they ordered. "Put on your shirt or we'll take you to jail."

"This is one repressed nation," I said under my breath.

The good professor Maleon motioned to me to put it on, and I apologized to them, explaining that I was from the States and didn't know the laws.

After they left, he turned to me and said, "Michael, they are not to fool around with. Take their threats very seriously. This is how they have maintained power all these years."

There was my lesson in totalitarianism at work. I'd return to a different Spain many years later.

Robin was such a great traveler, so easygoing, always with a song. Nothing got her down. Everything was an adventure. "Mick, I can't imagine you in a Spanish jail cell. You'd cause a revolution." She laughed.

She was right. I was a hotheaded hippie idealist.

We got up early the next morning to watch the bulls being paraded into the central plaza. One gate on the plaza opened on to one long street, where they'd be herded out by gauchos on horseback when they were ready to be released. We walked halfway down the crowded barricades to watch. We found a place looking through to an empty street, save for the thousands of people shouting for the bulls to be released. The gauchos opened the gates, and the stampede of angry bulls began.

Then we saw the throng of men with red handkerchiefs around their necks running for their lives. Most had been up all night drinking, which would make sense, as you'd have to be drunk or crazy to run in front of a ton of live beef with horns pointed at you. With the first pass of the bulls, we saw some men trampled, others picked up and tossed like rag dolls, and the remainder jumping up and clinging to the barricades.

"Oh, this is horrible!" Robin cried. "Mick, I can't watch anymore." She'd seen enough and asked if we could go. I, too, had seen an eyeful. I don't like to pass judgment, but it was barbaric. It was a two-thousand-year-old tradition, but it felt archaic. Our naïveté about how gory it could get had escaped us in all the fanfare. We expected that more men would cling to barricades rather than run right in front of bulls.

Later that day, we met up with Señor Maleon and some of his friends for drinks in the plaza. It was time to say goodbye. The Spanish are a warm people, and Señor Maleon gave me a big hug that I returned in kind. We thanked him for his invitation, shook hands, and walked from the bar on the plaza toward the train station.

We were off for Barcelona and Cataluña. As fate would have it, I'd never see the delightful professor again.

I had no idea that the $2,000 I started this journey with would take me all the way to the Middle East and back. We hitchhiked our way from Barcelona to Marseilles, to the ancient papal city of Avignon, and over Roman bridges to Caen and Nice on the French Riviera. Provence was a special place, and I knew one day I'd return.

Now I got an up-close glimpse of how the rich lived. The beaches of the Riviera were beautiful, but the people were so full of themselves, the European upper classes flashing their wealth in the most ostentatious ways. Well-to-do matrons under the shelter of beach umbrellas, sporting expensive designer bathing suits and covered in Bain du Soleil. Robin and I just looked at one another and laughed. No words needed to be exchanged as we watched a matron with too much makeup sharing licks of her ice cream cone with her poodle. It was like that with Robin. We read one another's thoughts.

Monte Carlo

Back on the road again, we got a ride to Monte Carlo. Our ride dropped us off right in front of the Casino Royale—the casino made even more famous by the marriage of Grace Kelly, the American movie star, to Prince Rainier, the blue blood of Monaco. As I looked up the steps, I couldn't help but notice the Belle Epoque gilded bronze awning and above it the Herculean statues, one holding the flag of Monaco and the other the flag of France.

The casino was beautiful. As we walked through the colonnaded lobby toward the grand hall, we were awestruck by the splendor of the glass dome and the multitude of crystal chandeliers that surrounded it. We checked our knapsacks with the coat check while admiring the ornate sculptures, frescoes, mirrors, and the marbled walls. We felt like we were in a grand palace.

I couldn't believe that this little kid from San Francisco was playing craps at the Casino Royale, hobnobbing with Europe's elite, dressed in tuxedos and evening gowns and the glint of diamonds. This was no ordinary casino. I was in complete awe.

I went to the craps table and ordered a drink from the waitress.

"*Oui, Monsieur,*" the croupier said. "Your bet?"

"Oh yes," I said and put ten francs on the line.

The man at the head of the table threw the dice.

The croupier shouted out, "Eight."

They paid the line, and I came out with twenty francs.

Robin and I took my winnings and went for lunch.

An Italian truck driver picked us up outside of Monte Carlo on his way to Milan that night. Halfway there, he asked us to sing him a song in Italian, so Robin and I broke into a line from a Dean Martin song. "When the moon hits your eye like a big pizza pie, that's amore."

I'm sure he understood "pizza" and "amore," but that was about it. I realized later he was bored with us.

Shortly after that, around midnight, he said it was time to go to sleep. He slept in his cab, while we bunked down by the side of the road. In the morning, we were going to Milan. We got all comfortable in our sleeping bags, with our backpacks for pillows, when suddenly we were suffocated by a plume of diesel gas as the driver sped off with the two of us neatly tucked away for the night. We started laughing at our naiveté.

There we lay on the highway, and Robin, as if nothing had happened, put her head back down on her knapsack. "Michael, look up," she said. "It's the Milky Way."

Milan's Duomo was magnificent. The fortress that protected the city was intact and an architectural wonder. I was really seeing the world for the first time with my eyes wide open, savoring all the flavors, scents, different cultures, languages, and customs that gave me a glimpse into history I'd only read about. Now I could touch it, smell it, and feel it.

I think I knew how lucky I was to be with Robin on the journey. It wasn't just a summer vacation in Europe. I'd gathered so much information about the world. I was sucking it up like a sponge, and growing. The journey was becoming more like an odyssey. I realized about this time how sheltered I'd been growing up with my parents in middle-class America. But the cocoon was cracking, and the more I saw of the world, the more I wanted to know. There was a spiritual side of me that was evolving too. I felt like there was no separation between the countries and the people I met, only boundaries that were made up in our minds and on our maps, boundaries that divided us.

Yugoslavia and the Balkans

When we arrived in Trieste, near the former Yugoslavia, now part of Croatia, I started to feel a shift in the European landscape. Horse-driven carts filled with hay rolled by. I noted the colorful peasant women dressed in balloon pajamas in ornate designs, with matching blouses and scarves over their heads. The men wore tunics, pitchforks in hand, as the carts tossed from side to side on the cobblestoned streets. Their sunbaked faces were expressionless.

Croatia, Serbia, Bosnia, Kosovo, Macedonia, and Montenegro, in a loosely aligned confederation called Yugoslavia under the leadership of the Soviet-backed dictator Tito, had been carved up after the war. It was the area formerly called the Balkans. I'd never been to a communist country, and the differences were stark. I never would have thought that these same people—Serb, Croat, and Muslim—would be killing one another in little more than twenty-five years. Tito had done so well to keep the hostilities between them below the surface.

As luck would have it, I was good at communicating and relating to the people despite my absence of language skills. I cornered a young guy on the bus and asked him if he could help me with some simple phrases in Yugoslav—like "How are you?" "Thank you," and "please."

Robin bought us first-class tickets on a bus to Dubrovnik, an eleventh-century walled city, a World Heritage site. It was magnificent, built above the cliffs overlooking the Adriatic coast.

The bus made a stop early the next morning in Split. Robin was asleep, and I didn't want to wake her when I got off to buy us a couple of Cokes. I'd brought just enough money for my purchase and some sweetbread. As I was making change, I heard the engine of the bus start, and before I knew it, the bus was pulling away from the curb. I started running, a Coke in each hand. As I ran, the Coke came streaming up and then down both my arms. I ran faster, screaming, "Stop, stop!" But as I reached the corner, the bus rounded it and headed up a steep hill and out of the city. I was in shock. I stood perfectly still while the Coke dripped down my arms.

People who saw what had happened came up to me, and as best I could tell from their tone and body language, tried to console me, telling me it was all right, not to worry.

Who's worried? I mused. *I've got two Cokes to my name.* I sat there on the curb for a moment. I drank one bottle of Coke, and downed the other in complete disbelief. Then I surrendered to my fate.

I walked back to the ticket kiosk, frightened that I'd be lost for God knows how long in Yugoslavia, with no coat, passport, bus ticket, or money. There was a hole in the window where people spoke to the ticket master. I stuck my whole head through it. "Comrade," I said, "please help me."

He was so impressed with my language efforts that he put me on a second-class bus for Dubrovnik. I could only hope I'd be able to find Robin there.

Two hours later, my bus pulled into a rest stop. Next to it was another bus. I looked over to see Robin just as the bus was about to pull out on the road. I jumped off and hailed the driver. As I climbed on board, everyone cheered. I saw Robin's laughing face, filled with joy. It seems she awoke sometime during the journey, after the bus had left Split. Much to her dismay, she found a Yugoslav in my seat instead of me. We were reunited again.

Dubrovnik was delightful. The people were gracious, and the Adriatic was one of the finest coasts I'd seen, next to our own in California. We'd just finished dinner and were on our way back to our hotel through the main square when we came upon a group of freaks who were partying and smoking hashish. They asked if we'd join them, and of course, we didn't refuse.

"Where'd you get the hash?" I asked.

"From those merchant marines over there in the square," one of them whispered.

There they were, Turkish sailors. Robin and I approached them and asked if we could buy some hashish. They were most agreeable, and we finally got a little stash for the trip.

After Dubrovnik, we flew on Yugoslav Airlines to a dusty city called Skopje, the capital of Macedonia, where we caught a midnight train to Athens. We only had a few weeks in Athens as we had a flight to catch to Tel Aviv to meet Robin's aunt and uncle in Haifa.

Greece

Syntagma Square in Athens was home to the American Express office, the Grand Central Station for most of eastbound hippiedom. It was where we collected our mail, changed money, sent for money, bought traveler's checks, and hung out. That was where I met Egidia, Pelito, Joanie, and Giancarlo—on the steps of American Express.

Egidia was from Milan. She was traveling with her Argentine boyfriend, Pelito, a major fashion model from the runways of Milan and Paris. He was a real good-looker, with high cheekbones and big green eyes and long eyelashes. Joanie was a blond dressed in a sheepskin coat from Turkey, wearing bangles and pajama pants from India held up by a silver Rajasthani belt. She was an American Jewish girl from my hometown of San Francisco, and her boyfriend, Giancarlo, was an artist from Italy. Eventually, by sheer coincidence, we'd all wind up living a few blocks from one another in the Haight-Ashbury.

I met them independently of Robin. She was still out on the island of Serifos, from where I'd just arrived. We needed cash, so I returned to Athens early.

The island of Serifos was exquisite, quiet, and remote. There were hardly any tourists there, so we had the island to ourselves.

Most people in those days were going to Mykonos to party. We wanted to get away from all that and really see Greece.

We slept out on the beach for two weeks, and the Greeks would come down and offer us *retsina* and *ouzo* and play the guitar and sing for us late into the night. The town was perched on the rocky crags above the beach and the port below, and the townspeople often invited us in for meals. They never locked their doors, and the only way up the mountain was by donkey or by foot. It was that kind of place, from a different time. We were always made to feel welcome even though there was a language barrier. We ate fresh sardines and cod, dry goat's cheese, delicious brown bread, and of course, olives. Such kindness from strangers was culture shock.

Upon Robin's return to Athens, I introduced her to everyone. We hit it off brilliantly. Even though Egidia wasn't fluent in English, I was able to communicate with Pelito in Spanish, and he'd in turn translate our conversation into Italian. Pelito relayed the story of their journey to India overland through the Middle East. As he told us of these exotic places, he began to paint beautiful pictures of colorful women in silk saris and men wearing turbans while riding camels, of exotic temples, the green jungle with teak forests, and the golden temple of Varanasi on the banks of the sacred Ganges, where the devout Hindus prayed, bathed, and later were cremated. Their stories made me hunger to travel there.

They talked of wild monkeys and elephants, and trained bears. I was intoxicated by the possibility of going. They invited us to join them, but Robin said we were too short on money for that long a trip, so we proceeded as planned to the Promised Land. But Egidia and Joanie had planted the seed, and I'd one day find myself on the Silk Road to India, and beyond.

Israel: The Promised Land

The Arab-Israeli conflict was at its height. It was July 1971, and there was talk of war. Things were so bad that we had to fly to Cyprus to get into Israel, as the Arabs wouldn't let our El Al flight fly over their airspace. We arrived in Tel Aviv after there had been a bombing. People had been killed and injured, so the Israelis weren't taking any chances. We were met in front of a makeshift arrival lounge of cyclone fencing corralling us in. It looked like a war zone. The ominous ceiling panels dangling in midair gave us an idea of the power of the blast, and the grave loss of life that had taken place there just a few days prior.

The female immigrations officer asked me questions. "Where are you from? Are you carrying any bombs?"

"No, I'm Jewish," I said. "Why would I carry a bomb?"

"Are you carrying any bombs?" she repeated.

"No."

She searched everything, even my ballpoint pens. Officials were nervous and extremely uptight, determined to avoid another attack.

Tel Aviv was everything I imagined it would be. It had been built in stages. The old Arab city had been taken over by the British, and there was a colonial feel to it, especially at high tea at the King David Hotel. It was modern, and it was one of the few cities that had skyscrapers. Ben Gurion Street was the main shopping area. The tree-lined streets reminded me of the new Israel, as there was evidence of building going on everywhere.

We immediately made our way to the bus station in Tel Aviv, traveling to the northern city of Haifa. We'd been invited by Sala Greenspan, Robin's aunt, to stay for two weeks. She and her husband, Angel, were survivors of the Holocaust. She'd been in Auschwitz, and he in Bergen-Belsen. They met in a relocation camp in Sweden. While there, she had to be put in a full body cast from her neck to her feet, as her bones were so weak from malnutrition. A walking skeleton, she'd lost all her hair and teeth.

Sala spoke almost no English and had trouble speaking Hebrew, even though half her life was spent in Israel, and so we spoke in Yiddish. I'd never met a Holocaust survivor before, and I was in awe of this phenomenal little woman. I kept looking at the numbers tattooed on her arm, mesmerized by the cruelty and depravity, the complete lack of empathy that the Nazi machine inflicted on my people.

As she shared her story one morning over boiled eggs, toast, tomatoes, and fresh cheese, it was evident that her life itself was a testimony to raw courage. She related how they'd come to her village and taken every member of her family. Soldiers loaded them on a train to Auschwitz, where they were sent to the gas chambers. She was forced into slave labor, working in an ammunitions factory making bullets. She told us of sixteen-hour-a-day work shifts with just some salt water and a little potato once a day to sustain them. She said she started to fall asleep on the assembly line, when the SS came and told her, "*Du schlafen, und du kaput,*" or "You sleep, and you're finished."

Her neighbor down the street in Israel, whom I also met while there, was credited with saving her life by keeping her awake until liberation. The odd thing about that conversation about the concentration camp was that it came up every morning when Sala served breakfast.

She'd say in Yiddish, "I worked in an ammunitions factory and the SS would come and say, 'You sleep, and you're finished.'"

I began to see how damaged she was, and indulged her each morning as though it were the first time I was hearing it. I watched the two of them in awe, she and Angel, as they managed their daily lives. They were married in Israel in 1947, and they gave birth to Hanna a year later. We also met Hanna, who was serving in the army and stationed near Haifa. I kept thinking how they'd defied the Nazis by surviving, then went on to have an entire life filled with even the joy of a child. I felt honored to meet them and share the time we had together. Their generosity, warmth, and love was undeniable.

Hanna was a *sabra*, a cactus known for its tenacity and strength while growing in harsh conditions. She was part of this new generation in Israel that had grown up without discrimination, never being looked down upon or made to feel less than any other human. I drew strength from her, having been discriminated against myself by those was proud to tell me that no rockets had since hit Tel Dan, which reassured us.

After a few beautiful days on the Tel Dan, we head headed back to Haifa.

On the way, we stopped at a kibbutz on the Lebanese border called Kiryat Shmona, which two days prior had been hit by rocket fire. What was interesting about this kibbutz was that all the Jews in it were black, many of whom had been saved in a raid on Entebbe, Ethiopia. I'd never seen black Jews. As we walked the main street, we found the incredible silverwork they're known for. Robin bought a few pieces, and I felt honored to meet the people.

After Haifa, Robin and I bonded like never before. Shortly after the Golan Heights and the raid on the beach, we left. They had a war to fight. I must say, I never felt my Jewish roots as deeply as on this trip. All the people we met were like one large family. Yet we were still tourists, and I wanted to see Jerusalem. That day we went down to the Haifa bus station and waited in line to buy tickets to the Holy City.

It was a long line that moved at a snail's pace, slow enough that a Hasidic rabbi picked me out for a conversation. "Are you Jewish?" he asked.

I couldn't lie. "Jewish, not really Jewish," I said.

He replied in a heavy Yiddish accent, "You either are or you aren't."

"Well, not really," I said again.

"Were you born of a Jewish mother?" he asked.

"Yes," I said.

"Then you're Jewish!" he exclaimed. "Now repeat after me." He put a yarmulke on my head while he tied a prayer in a leather box called a *tefillin* up my arm.

Everything was happening so quickly. I barely had time to realize I was being proselytized.

Robin grinned at me like a Cheshire cat, knowing I still had no idea what was happening. She kept quiet out of respect for the rabbi, but I was a captive.

same anti-Semitic forces our parents had experienced. It was like a feeling of a lack of self-worth, as though you were born that way, a little like discriminatory DNA.

One day we were at the beach swimming when two Israeli jets strafed the sand. Instantly, sirens blared, and everyone on the entire beach got up and left. Being tourists, we weren't sure what to do, so we headed home, too, and found that our living room had been turned into a nursery. A twenty-four-hour alert had been called, and parents dropped off their children at Sala's and went to their posts. An entire country was standing by to defend itself against war, and everyone had a job to do, even Sala and Angel Greenspan. I'd never experienced such a show of solidarity, patriotism, and strength.

The Golan Heights

Hanna and Angel told us about a beautiful resort in the Golan Heights called Tel Dan on the Tel Dan River. It was located on land taken by the Israelis in the 1967 Yom Kippur War. On the road leading up to Tel Dan, we passed through the city of Kunetra. All along the road, there were burned-out Syrian tanks. When we reached the city, it was destroyed, a virtual ghost town. I looked up at one of the ruined apartment complexes on the fourth floor and saw a dining room cut in half. The table and chairs were still standing, and there were pictures on the walls. It was so eerie. The destruction was devastating. I'd never seen a war zone. With the PLO firing *katusha* rockets into Northern Israel at any time, it was frightening. The Israelis took the Golan because the Syrians were firing on the towns and cities below in Israel with rockets, and the vantage point was deadly.

As we passed through the city to the outskirts, trees appeared, and we ventured deeper into the pine forest. Then the Tel Dan River appeared. It was winding through campgrounds that resembled a *kibbutz*. There were many people there, including the Israeli army. The next day I met a tank commander by the name of Moshe. He described the terrible battle that had taken place there to gain the Heights. Now they were protecting that border from the Syrians. He

Next, he threw a prayer shawl called a *tallith* over me, and I began reciting from the Torah, part of the Jewish Bible, in Hebrew. It was so awkward when we finally got to the ticket window. I apologized, telling him I had a bus to catch, and he let me go. When I looked back over my shoulder in his direction, he was already looking for his next prospect. I was shocked at how little I knew about my own people.

In Jerusalem, we found great accommodations in the Christian Quarter. Jerusalem is holy to just about two-thirds of the world. Everyone wanted a piece of the pie, each making their claim on it, justified by their own righteous God. I've never seen a city in which the people went more out of their way to show how separate they are from the rest of humanity.

Jerusalem was an extraordinary contradiction. It was captivating and ancient, but it was also pious and extremely conservative, breathtakingly inspirational, yet narrow-minded and often dangerous. It was at odds with itself. Even for me, the nonbeliever, there was a glimmer, a tug at the heartstrings that these were my roots.

The magnificent walls that surrounded the city and the Tower of David were architecturally superb. When we went to part of the Jewish Quarter, which had been blown up by the Jordanians during the 1948 War of Independence, we discovered another city beneath the one we were in—the city of Aelia Capitolina, built on the ruins of Jerusalem when it was destroyed in 70 AD. Amazingly, below the city of Capitolina, they found the original city of Jerusalem. There was a thirteen-room villa with ritual baths and mosaic tile. The walls were painted, and there was evidence of fire when the Romans destroyed it. The *amphoras* filled with grain and olive oil were found broken open and lay exactly as they'd been left that fateful day. It was a city within a city within a city.

Robin wanted to score some hashish our first day there. I was frightened by the prospect after seeing how officious immigrations had been upon our arrival in Tel Aviv, but I could see she was determined. We walked to the Arab market near the Jaffa Gate. I had no idea where she was going, and I don't think she knew either, but as we leaned against a wall, there opposite us on the other side of the street was a young man staring at us. Robin smiled, and he smiled back.

Nonchalantly, she approached him and asked, "Do you know where we can get some hashish, a small piece?" With her fingers, she made it clear what size she wanted.

He smiled and nodded, motioning for us to follow him.

He seemed trustworthy, so we went with our instincts. We followed him through the narrow streets of antiquity, limestone-colored with the yellow hue of the sun gleaming on the surface of the rough stone.

"Wait here," he said. He stepped into a shop and came out minutes later with a big black chunk of it.

The man's name was Ibrahim, and he turned out to be an elementary school teacher. Robin invited him to smoke some with us, and he took us to a place on the old wall where we could look out over the City of David. He produced a small pipe from his coat pocket and filled it with the hashish we had just purchased. He lit it and passed it to Robin, then to me, and I passed it back to him. Suddenly he looked down the wall and noticed an Israeli Defense patrol coming toward us.

When they saw what we were doing, they began to pursue us.

"Follow me," Ibrahim said in a frightened voice.

I looked back and saw the patrol trying to get around the tourists and devout Jews who were praying between us and who obstructed their pursuit. I saw their machine guns, and we began to run.

Once off the wall, we ran up steps and down steps, past archways that led to alleys, and still they were in hot pursuit. We ran through people's courtyards, up steps and then more steps and alleys, until finally Ibrahim burst into a private home and slammed the doors behind us. He put his finger over his lips to silence us as he listened at the front door.

Two little girls and a woman covered by a veil stood behind an interior door huddled in silence. *Where are we?* I wondered. *Whose house is this?*

Ibrahim stood by the door a little longer to make certain the danger had passed, while visions of my life in an Israeli prison passed through my mind. With his hands, he gave us the sign to relax, then motioned for us to sit down on the carpet. We lowered ourselves to the floor, and he introduced us to his wife and children.

I could still feel the terror and the sweat dripping between my shoulder blades when he asked his wife to bring us tea. It was then I saw the two worlds that separated Jerusalem. I knew there were always two sides to every story, and grace had given me the opportunity to see it up close and personal. I could have never taken one side or the other in the Arab-Israeli conflict after that. I'd seen the Jews and the Holocaust victims who claimed Jerusalem on the one hand, and the Arab Palestinians on the other. Both had legitimate claims. The tea was served, and when we had finished and it was safe, we slipped back out to the streets.

The following day, I was shocked to run into Helen Liebowitz, a girlfriend of mine who had been an art major at San Francisco State. Now she was selling lambskin coats in the Arab bazaar.

"Helen, hi, what are you doing here?" I asked.

"Well, I have an Arab boyfriend here, and I'm living with him. I arrived about three months ago."

I wanted to know more, but she felt uncomfortable talking to me there. She asked if I'd meet her for dinner at a restaurant in the Muslim Quarter. When I asked Robin if she'd join me, she declined, so I went alone.

Helen was there at a big table with mostly young Arab men. She stood up and introduced me to all of them. One of them was her boyfriend.

"How do his parents feel about you being Jewish?" I asked her.

"They don't know," she said.

I wondered how long the relationship would last. I also wondered if somehow Helen was working with, and had fallen in love with, the Palestinian Liberation group Al-Fatah via her boyfriend. I ate some hummus and a little falafel while Helen filled me in on her life.

She'd met her boyfriend at school in San Francisco and came back with him at the beginning of summer.

I stayed and talked for a while, but my ear was tuned toward another conversation going on at the table, one that included Yasser Arafat and Al-Fatah, and a secret stash of grenades. It could have been all talk, but it made me uncomfortable.

I stood up. "Shalom, Helen, I really must go," I said, excusing myself. I shook hands with all the young men I'd met, a little fearful of what Helen may have fallen into. I wished her the best of luck.

On the road back to the hostel where Robin and I were staying, a young Arab man on a motorcycle came up from behind. He kept calling out to me, "Hey, Abraham, hey, David."

I turned to him as he drove up next to me and said, "I'm not David or Abraham."

Just then a switchblade flipped out from under his leather jacket. "Give me your money," he said.

Like an idiot, I said, "I've only got travelers' checks." I dug into my pocket.

"Give me everything you've got, and the watch." And with that, he sped off on the motorcycle with my travelers' checks, watch, and even a topaz ring my mother had given me for high school graduation.

I was speechless. Jerusalem was turning out to be much more dangerous than I could have imagined.

When I got back to the hostel, I told Robin, "You'll never believe what happened to me."

But she could, and she laughed uncontrollably. As always, my horizons with Robin were growing daily. We were discovering ourselves and the world. How could I possibly have known that a chance meeting at San Francisco State would have led to all these incredible experiences I was having? Robin and I were two free spirits in the moment, letting it dictate where and how we'd be challenged and where this journey would take us.

The walls of Jerusalem

Michael Rossum

Jaffa Gate Market

Boy playing soccer, on the walls graffiti from the Intifada riots

Michael Rossum

Jerusalem, busy archways run underground

The heart of Muslim Jerusalem taken from the back terrace
of Ibrahim's house; the schoolteacher who gave us refuge in his house
during our near escape from Israeli Defense Forces

Michael Rossum

Istanbul to Hungary

I talked Robin into going to Istanbul. We had to fly to Cyprus from Tel Aviv because of the no-fly zone. I was sorry to leave Israel. I felt a deep attachment I wasn't prepared for, and an emotional tie I hadn't experienced in the other countries we'd visited. I felt my roots in Israel. It was such a conflicted experience.

Istanbul was beautiful, with a European flavor. Cafés lined the small streets and alleys that led to the main bazaar, and Middle Eastern cuisine was as prevalent as French bistros. The setting had a history that dated to Troy, the crossroads of the Middle East. The people were a mixture of the East and West. Huge mosques rose up everywhere, including the Hagia Sophia, which was originally a Byzantine church built by the Roman emperor Constantine. The mosques were a definite reminder that the city held a certain mysticism unlike any other in the Middle East. The calls to prayer from all the different mosques were like a Middle Eastern symphony.

I bought tickets on what I'd later find out was the tattered Orient Express from Istanbul to Budapest, via Bulgaria and Serbia, deep behind the Iron Curtain.

On our way through Bulgaria, the train stopped in Sophia, the capital, for two hours for lunch. We had no local currency, and we were hungry. We went to the dining room in the train station, only to find that local currency was all they accepted. We rose to leave when the news of our predicament got around to the dining room's clientele, most likely through our waiter. He came back and pushed us back into our seats. Though I couldn't understand him, two plates of steaming hot goulash appeared on our table moments later.

We were so surprised and grateful that we sat for a moment in disbelief. As we looked around the dining room, everyone was smiling at us. Lunch was on the Bulgarians. We smiled back and nodded our thanks. I can't imagine that happening in Grand Central Terminal. We had seen so much kindness on our journey, it reinforced our belief that mankind was basically good. I left a couple of US dollars under the plate for the waiter. At least it was a reciprocal gesture on our part, even if they were useless.

We purchased our tickets in Belgrade for the journey to Hungary. The train station manager told us we could get our visas on the train for Budapest. I bought a watermelon from the nearby marketplace. I figured if we got hungry, we'd have plenty to eat.

Around three in the morning, we passed through the Iron Curtain, and our sleep was abruptly disturbed. The door to our compartment was suddenly thrust open, and two Hungarian immigration officers stood among the six of us. Robin and I were traveling with a Polish family headed to Warsaw.

One of the officers flicked on the bright bare lightbulb, flooding the dark compartment where we slept. "Passport control!" he shouted. "Papers, papers."

We all scrambled for our documents.

He took mine and Robin's and surveyed them for an extremely long time. Then he mumbled something to his partner and said, "You two come with me."

We grabbed our knapsacks, and I grabbed the watermelon, unsure where we were going.

"You Zurich a Beograde," he said.

We were being deported. Both of us were frightened. "What's wrong?" we asked. What would they do with us?

They motioned with their machine guns for us to get up and then pushed us down the corridor with the butt ends of their guns while everyone looked on in shock. *What could two Americans with the watermelon have done?* they must have wondered.

As the guards escorted us off the train, we noticed other people also were getting off at the stop. Then we were taken to the other side of the tracks to another platform, the whole time being prodded by the machine guns when we didn't move fast enough. We weren't alone. Another man was being deported as well, an Arab.

We sat on the platform for hours, guarded by two soldiers with machine guns and two German shepherds in tow. I was tired and hungry, so I broke the watermelon in half with my pocketknife. I carved out some slices, and the Arab man took one. I offered one to the soldiers, but they refused, shaking their heads and not showing any emotion, their rifles still fixed on us.

So there we sat, eating our watermelon until the next train back to Belgrade arrived. We were escorted onto it, the doors closed, and we were heading back to Yugoslavia. We found out you had to obtain a visa for Hungary in Belgrade from the embassy. The information given at the train station was incorrect and may have been given to us purposely. We didn't know for sure.

Back in Belgrade, we managed to get to the Hungarian consulate, photos in hand. We'd taken them in one of those automatic machines in the train station. We got our visas and were back on the train that night headed for Budapest.

We made it as far as the Yugoslav border before our conductor from the ride before came to examine our tickets again. He demanded that we pay for our own deportation. Robin was adamant that we wouldn't since they'd given us false information. So again, we were escorted off the train, this time by Yugoslavian soldiers.

Robin was furious, and as it happened, spoke German, which the Hungarians understood. When she got to the stationmaster's office, she told him the whole story plus relayed how the conductor had flipped her off. We were on the train that night for Budapest.

While we waited, I recognized a man standing nearby as having been on the train with us the day before. I made polite conversation with him in the little German I knew, which was actually Yiddish.

"You're going to Budapest?" I asked.

He answered me in German. "*Ja, kommen sie mit mir zu das heim von mein kommerad,*" or, "Yes, you come with me to the house of my comrade."

I looked at Robin and said, "*Ja, danke.* Yes, thanks."

I believe he saw our predicament and reached out to us. Such generosity from strangers again was overwhelming.

As we neared the border, I saw the fence, with just enough room for the train to pass through. It really was an iron curtain. Outside each town we passed, we saw Russian tanks, with the omnipresent red sickle and hammer flapping from their antennas.

The man we met in the train station offered to put us up with an artist friend of his in Budapest. His friend, Vaclav, had a studio that we could stay in. The man was a real enigma, finely dressed, unlike most Hungarians who wore blue flood pants and jackets to match. Maybe he knew what Robin and I represented, coming from the West, a new way of thinking about the world that he shared but could not speak about in public. He said foreigners had to register with the police twenty-four hours after arrival or be subject to jail.

Budapest is divided by the Danube. The train pulled into Pest, and our companion introduced us to Vaclav. Vaclav shook our hands with both of his with vibrancy and a grin. His effervescence was obvious.

At that point, it was time to say goodbye to the man who'd shown such incredible kindness. *"Danke schoen, mein freund. Du bist ein guter Mensch,"* I said in my best mix of German and Yiddish.

"Das macht nichts," he said, shaking my hand as our eyes met. "It's nothing."

He and Vaclav walked toward a budding apple tree, exchanging quiet words. Then the mystery man turned the corner and disappeared. He'd never given us his name, and Vaclav never told us.

Vaclav took us by bus to be registered. Because he was underage, his father should have signed for us, but Vaclav forged his father's name. Hours later, there was a knock at the door. It was the police, come to arrest him when the signature didn't match his father's—a policing of citizens that was unimaginable in the States. Mr. Popov, Vaclav's father, tried to cover for him by explaining that because of his hours working in a water reclamation plant, Vaclav wouldn't know when he'd be home.

The police asked us, "Where are you from?"

Robin replied in German, "California, the United States."

"And is it true you will be staying with the family for two weeks?"

"Yes," we replied.

We were shocked that they'd be so gracious, though we had no intention of staying that long. Vaclav must have filled in that portion and guessed. We couldn't imagine living under the dogma of a totalitarian state like that. It was obvious that the Hungarians felt oppressed under the Russian occupation. At the time of our visit, the Hungarian Revolt of 1956 was fresh in the minds of the Hungarian Stasi, the counterpart of the Russian KGB.

Vaclav was a painter, and he lived and worked in his studio. The studio was a white stucco structure, round with a thatched roof, which his father had built. At one time, it must have stored grain. The main house was thatched as well. It looked like a Hungarian farmhouse. Vaclav painted political paintings that if seen in public would have landed him in jail. Chairman Mao was painted with red stars in place of his eyes. Little Hungarian villages were painted with ghostlike spirits flying through the streets and over the rooftops—hearing everything that was being said behind the walls. They were marvelous—dark and eerie. They left us with a chill.

At night we sat around a small TV, watching the news of wheat being harvested and the announcer telling the viewer what great advances had been made in production.

"Communist propaganda," I said.

At that they turned off the TV and turned on Radio Free Europe. The whole family chimed in with "American propaganda."

We all had a good laugh. Robin and I realized the extent to which the two blocs would go to win hearts and minds, and neither one was winning.

The city of Budapest was spectacular. Not one iota of neon could be found anywhere. It was untouched by commercialism. You could still see the bullets left in the buildings from the 1956 uprising. The Hapsburg Palace on the banks of the Danube was home to the Austrian-Hungarian Empire. The onion-shaped domes of the churches and the spires of the parliament building gave it all a fairy-tale feel.

After two weeks exploring Budapest, it was time to say goodbye. We'd become very close. I don't think Vaclav and his family ever expected to share their home with two Americans. Nor did we expect the generosity of our Hungarian hosts. It was obvious to me now that the well-dressed man who drove us to meet Vaclav at the station in his Mercedes wanted us to meet Vaclav and his family. I never knew his name, and we never saw him again.

When you look back on your life, there are certain moments that are life-changing. This was one of them. Vaclav came to me and asked me to smuggle one of his paintings to the West. He told me that he wanted the people there to see what life was like under Russian domination.

Without even a moment of thought about how dangerous it would be, I said I'd take it. I wondered if this was the objective of the well-dressed man from the train all along, to help Vaclav get one of his paintings out of Hungary to the West. Or maybe it was the extraordinary relationship we had with Vaclav and his family that made him feel comfortable enough to ask.

That night he prepared the painting for travel. He took it off the stretching bars and coiled it neatly, and we pulled it through a hollow cardboard roll, stuffing the ends with newspaper. I knew it was illegal to take it out of the country, so I knew there was risk involved, jail time, I assumed. Should I be caught, the authorities also would discover the painting's origins. Vaclav must have taken that into consideration. When you're young, you think you're going to live forever, and you put yourself out on a limb, never thinking the branch might break.

We left for Austria the next morning. It was an emotional goodbye. We'd probably never see them again. Vaclav's mother gave Robin a beautiful old hand-painted wooden box, thrusting it into her hands. We hugged her when we left.

Smuggled painting – Vaclav Popoff, Hungary, 1971

We were ordered back on the bus. My knees were still shaking when I looked down at the poor man who'd been arrested. As we passed through the border gates, I looked up to see a sign: *Welcome to Austria.* I'd never felt such relief.

Carmine—August 1972

Back in San Francisco, Robin and I were already working to put money together for a trip to India. Egidia and Joanie had inspired us with their exotic tales of Bombay, opium dens, and the acceptance in the Himalayas of the many faiths living side by side. Daoists, Buddhists, and Hindus lived in peace with mutual respect in Kathmandu. The hippies were accepted too. There also was a small group of Europeans, Canadians, and Americans living there.

Our experiment at Hampshire House was coming to an end. I'd stay on for the summer while Robin went home to Long Island, and we'd meet up in NYC in September.

I think I always knew I was gay, but with an authoritarian father, coming out just wasn't possible. I'd been holding back my feelings for so long. I knew I had to take the opportunity to see if they were a part of who I was. I'd have to take the plunge into gay life. Leaving Robin didn't even enter my mind. As far as I was concerned, it was an experiment. I'd have to trust myself to find the truth.

I'd heard about The Stud, a gay bar in the South of Market area on Folsom Street, so I went down and walked in. The place was packed. I made my way to the bar and asked for a vodka tonic. I went to the back of the bar where there was a little more space. The truth is I felt awkward. There were some very attractive guys in there, but I wasn't connecting. I started to check out what they were wearing—mostly leather jackets, flannel shirts or tight T-shirts, bell-bottom jeans, and tennis shoes, some boots.

As I panned the room, a handsome man stuck out from all the rest. He caught my eye, and evidently, I caught his. He had thick, jet-black hair and big blue eyes. His lips were full, his neck was thick, and I could see his Adam's apple above his white T-shirt,

When we reached the end of the street, we turned back and waved goodbye. I stared at the surrounding buildings, dark from years of gathering soot and dirt. Their little house with its apple tree in the front yard stuck out like daylight. They waved until we rounded the corner.

Robin and I didn't speak as we walked to the station and the train that would take us to the West. We were amazed by what we'd experienced in Hungary. We walked through the tree-lined streets hand in hand, smiling, and reflected on what Vaclav and his family had given us—a real view behind the Iron Curtain, unbiased and full of love. Did I think the government was horrid? Yes. But again, the people were the same as we'd encountered everywhere: good.

When we reached the Austrian border, I was surprised to see the electric fence. It stretched in both directions as far as the eye could see. What had I gotten myself into?

There were four watchtowers, two to three stories high, and five hundred yards apart. Inside were men with submachine guns. The full impact of my decision to smuggle the painting came over me in a rush of adrenalin. My heart was pounding. My hands were sweating.

"Passport control!" shouted an officious guard as he climbed onto the bus at the border. The guard unfastened the panels in the ceiling, looking for people trying to escape. Scary German shepherd dogs were waiting as we filed off the bus one by one, passports in hand.

I felt goose bumps on my arms and fear racing through me. I looked at Robin. I could tell she felt the same way.

The guards searched my knapsack for what seemed like forever. I'd put some dirty socks and such on top to discourage them, but it didn't work. They dug and dug. I was sure they'd find the painting. But finally they stopped and waved me on with a cold nod. Then they found some written material hidden in the coat of another man. They confiscated it and took him away.

which stuck out from under his blue-and-white flannel shirt. He wore a leather bomber jacket and blue jeans, and he was moving through the crowd straight for me.

"Hi, my name is Carmine," he said with a wistful smile.

"Michael," I said. "Nice to meet you." We shook hands.

His strong grip felt good. We talked. I can't tell you about what. I didn't say too much, as my eyes were transfixed on his eyes and mouth.

"Would you like to go back to my place?" he asked.

I was stricken with panic, mixed with excitement. Adrenalin raced through me, and my heart pounded. "Yes, that would be nice," I said, barely able to get the words out without stuttering.

As soon as the door to his apartment shut behind us, our hands were all over each other. My hands couldn't unbutton his fly fast enough. Making love with Carmine was hot and passionate, tender and intimate. It was exquisite, like nothing I'd ever experienced. We were two life forces coming together sexually. He lay on top of me, and I felt the weight and force of a man. It was so different from lying with Robin. We kissed, and he made love to me in a way I'd never known. When I found myself back in my car later, I was euphoric. Carmine had opened me up to myself. I was gay.

I fell in love with him over the summer. Carmine was Italian, and he was a hairdresser on Polk Street. He was from somewhere back East, near Philly, I think.

I told him about Robin. He was supportive and kind, two qualities I'll always be thankful for. As I eased into love with him, I knew it was right. Even if I wouldn't be with him forever, at least I knew I was gay. I had to tell Robin, but how?

The night before I left for New York, Carmine had me over for dinner. I think he knew it was over, but we knew we'd shared something special. We made love most of the night with such passion. In the morning, he drove me home to Hampshire House, and in his hand was a present. I opened it and found the most amazing cloisonné bronze bell with a handle. It was from India. Carmine was so sensitive. It was his way of saying goodbye. I've kept it all these years to remind me of my first love.

A few years later, I saw Carmine on Castro Street, gaunt, HIV wasting his body, so thin and fragile. His beautiful blue eyes were still alive, looking out of this shell that had become his body. I hugged him and kissed him on the cheek and told him how grand it was to see him again. All I felt inside was sorrow, but I wouldn't let it out for his sake. I didn't see him again, but I read his obituary in the *Bay Area Reporter*, a gay newspaper. He'd become another statistic in the CDC's list of those people who died of the AIDS epidemic in San Francisco in 1981.

I knew how much our trip meant to Robin, and I still loved her. I was torn between hurting her and being true to myself. Yet I finally knew which world I belonged in. I decided I'd go with Robin to Nepal as planned. When the time was right and when we were alone, in a quiet place, I'd let her know what I think she already knew. If I'd been straight, I would have married her in a minute. But I had to think about her happiness and mine. The truth will set you free, but it can hurt like hell. So, with that in mind, I'd tell her what I knew would break both our hearts. I'd already decided that I was going overland to India alone. I needed time by myself.

Robin was fine with this and understood my need. We'd meet in Delhi in December.

Chapter Ten

Journey to the East—The Silk Road
Rome—September 1972

My Pan Am flight touched down at Ciampino Airport in September in the middle of a transportation strike led by the Communist Party in Rome. I didn't know this until I was on the ground and an angry mob met us. Red banners stretched the length of the arrival lounge, but I couldn't decipher the writing on them. Once I got outside, taxi drivers approached in droves asking exorbitant prices for a ride into central Rome.

It was there that a pleasant and unassuming young woman approached me, carrying what looked like a piece of luggage from the '40s. Though she spoke perfect English, her accent was foreign. She asked if I wouldn't mind sharing a cab into Rome, and I readily agreed.

As we rode, she told me her name was Helen Bernstein. She'd just arrived in Rome, and everything she owned was in that odd suitcase. She'd been a political prisoner in South Africa, and only a week earlier had finally obtained her passport after ten years of being denied travel outside the county. Helen came from a well-to-do Jewish family. The policy of apartheid had separated her from her freedom. Caught in public with a black activist, trying to end apartheid, she was sent to jail for a year, and her passport was confiscated for ten years. All the while, her thoughts were of leaving the country. The week before I met her was the day she planned her trip. She packed only one bag for a stay abroad so as not to alarm the authorities, kissed her parents goodbye, and left the country overland.

When I asked her where she'd go, she told me she'd likely seek political asylum somewhere in Europe. "Freedom feels so good," she said. "It's so new. It will take some time to decide." She asked me why I'd come to Rome.

"I'm actually not staying in Italy," I told her. "I'm on a journey to the East, to India and the Himalayas, not too unlike yours, in search of freedom."

She smiled at me, then reached down on the seat of the taxi and grasped my hand, squeezing it slightly. We shared our stories. Then she asked me, since I was alone in Rome for one night and she was as well, if I'd like to dine with her. I really believed this was no chance meeting and accepted.

I called on her that night. We went out to some quaint little place in Trastevere down by the Tiber River, and we talked for hours. She was such a courageous woman. She'd taken on the South African government, and she'd paid a high price for her ideals. It takes that kind of courage to change the world.

"Hey, I saw an ad as I was coming here advertising a midnight tour of Rome," I said. "Since we both only have twenty-four hours here and it's our first time, would you like to go?"

She agreed without hesitation. We toured Rome together until dawn, in awe of the city and of one another, as we shared our dreams of the future. Then I left on a flight to Istanbul, and Helen began a life of freedom outside South Africa.

Istanbul

I looked out my window as we neared Istanbul. In the distance, the minarets of the Hagia Sophia, the Blue Mosque, and all the other mosques rose up from the city like spires to the heavens. We were flying straight in from the Mediterranean over the city, right into Istanbul, the crossroads of the Muslim world. I had no idea where this journey would take me, but in that moment, it seemed surreal—magic carpets, men on camels wearing turbans, exotic veiled women. It was *The Arabian Nights* for sure. I'd been there with Robin the year before, but I'd never seen it from the air, and it looked so exotic, this mixture of East and West.

I was met by a 1955 Chevrolet with no brakes. The driver, a short man with large hands and a big Pancho Villa mustache, would coast down the hills so as not to waste gas, but clearly he knew what he was doing. I arrived at the ferry shaken, but in one piece.

Istanbul has two sides, separated by the Bosporus. One is European, and the other is Asian, the gateway to the Middle East. As I crossed the river, I looked around to find a reassuring face. I realized then I might have overestimated the number of Westerners making the journey to the East. I was the only Westerner on the boat. The Turks stared back, trying to size me up, hundreds of dark-haired, dark-eyed faces staring at me. I felt alone.

I represented to them something foreign. Who were these strange, long-haired hippies from the West who wore blue jeans with patches and colorful beads around their necks, with headbands and straw-like cowboy hats? The men wore beards and mustaches, and the women, they complained, wore nothing at all. They didn't cover themselves and were indecent. Why were they in Turkey, and where were they going?

The ferry landed, and I made my way to the train station. It was there that I saw other Europeans on the platform. I assumed we were all waiting for the same train. Seeing them in the station was reassuring, just knowing there were others like me who were making the journey to the East eased my angst.

I purchased a second-class unreserved ticket from Istanbul to Erzurum on the Iranian border. The cabin was an old European train that the Turks had commissioned from the British, God knows when. World War I, by the looks of it. It seated eight people in the compartment, with a sliding glass door into the main hallway.

The last to get seated, I threw my gear up on a luggage rack and sat down by the doors. As I looked around, it was bloody well depressing. I was sitting with a group of Turks who looked like they were ready to separate me from my belongings, so I kept a close watch. With my very limited command of the Turkish language, I tried to make conversation to break the ice, and we had a few laughs at the start. But then I had to go to the bathroom.

Two Turks followed me there. It was at the end of the car behind us. I pulled back the drape that covered it and found a toilet, with no paper, just water to clean up with. In the midst of relieving myself, a man took his pants down and tried to hump me from the back. The other grabbed my hands to enable him. We struggled. I freed myself and pushed one man down behind me and raised my fists to the other. We had some words, but I didn't understand what was said. I was pissed off, but who could I make a complaint to? The conductor spoke no English.

I returned to my seat in the compartment to find that my backpack had been riffled through. The camera was missing as well as my cigarettes and ten hits of windowpane acid that had been tucked inside one of the cigarette packs. I was furious, especially about the acid. That was my stash for the trip. I imagined myself high on the Ganges in Varanasi, having a spiritual moment on acid, or up in the Himalayas near Mount Everest.

I was genuinely infuriated, and the thieves were frightened at first. Then they became indignant, as though this was common practice. The final straw came when they held me down and took off my Hush Puppies and slid their dirty plastic slip-ons over to me. It seemed like a fair deal to them. I was so enraged by their behavior that I threw the one I suspected was behind it out of the compartment, slammed the door shut, and kept it closed with my foot. The other Turks began laughing, but it was no joke. I finally grabbed my gear and left the compartment, looking for another seat for the twelve-hour journey to Erzurum.

I stumbled into the first-class area, and found it deserted except for two lonely-looking Westerners sitting rows apart from one another. I passed them both, then turned around. Facing two perfect strangers, I asked them if they'd help me. After I relayed the whole story of the Huns back in second class, their faces changed from interested to horrified, wondering if they'd be next. They invited me to stay, and we introduced ourselves.

The first was a round, jovial Englishmen by the name of Timothy Adams, a civil servant from Newcastle who'd just quit his job. He was perhaps the most unlikely fellow to be making such a journey. The other was a long-haired guy, a Swiss-German by the name of Hendrik from Geneva. Quiet and reserved, he didn't have an occupation. We were all headed in the same direction, east for the subcontinent along the Silk Road. We were an odd threesome, but we found refuge in one another, three strangers in a strange land.

We arrived in Erzurum the next day and made our way for the nearby Iranian border, but there was a snag. It seemed they didn't need visas for Iran, but as an American, I did. To make it worse, there was no visa office in that remote part of Turkey. The closest one was in Trabzon on the Black Sea. My traveling companions were kind, especially considering we'd just met. I didn't want to hold them up, but they decided to spend two nights in Erzurum to wait for me to make the journey over the frozen mountains and down to Trabzon.

I left the following day for a six-hour jog by bus over the rugged, snowcapped Gumushane Mountains. I'd left my backpack with the boys and traveled light with just my passport. As we descended out of the mountains, I could see the Black Sea as far as the horizon. When we arrived, I found a big city with a Slavic look to it. It had shuttered windows, yellow-orange walls, and red tile roofs, along with palm trees and humidity. It was a welcome change from the dark, frozen towns of Turkey on the other side of the mountains. I went to the Iranian consulate "tout suite," as the boys were waiting for me. I got my visa, checked into a hotel, and caught the first bus back to Erzurum the next morning.

The mountains were beautiful. Nestled into the mountainside were small villages made of stone, smoke rising from the chimneys. Little old women sat by the roadside in Muslim headscarves, selling bread. We had to stop several times for goat herders to move their livestock off the road. It was the picture of winter—granite mountains, crystal-clear rivers, gorges, and a frozen gray landscape with pine forests.

Back in Erzurum, the guys were happy to see me, and I was ecstatic to see them. I could feel the unspoken bonds that had developed between us and knew I'd made two new friends.

"Let's go celebrate," Tim said. "Let's go to the *hammam*." The hammam was a local bathhouse that offered massages and steam baths.

"That sounds like a terrific idea," I replied. After the trip, I needed one.

The baths cost about a dollar to enter. Before we knew it, we were wrapped in what I'd describe as a washcloth, bathing ourselves before the massage. The main room was filled with steam and men washing themselves with fresh water that flowed into stone basins attached to the walls. While they washed, they stared at the three of us. We must have been an oddity to them, or maybe they were just interested. We all started bathing, but when I went to wash my private parts, I took off the towel I was wearing. Before I could finish, the manager came in screaming at me. When I didn't understand him, he tied my towel around me in a knot and left. Everyone was staring at me.

"These guys are really repressed," I said to the boys. "Mustn't give them any ideas or they might come unhinged with lust."

"I think it has something to do with their religion," Tim said.

"Allah said wash your privates in private?" I asked.

We were definitely strangers in a strange land. So I washed my privates underneath the towel of Muslim morality.

Iran

Mohammad Reza Pahlavi became shah of Iran in 1941. However, during a period of conflict, he was forced to leave the country. He was reinstated as the supreme leader of the country following a CIA-backed coup in 1953, and the democratically elected prime minister was jailed. The shah was in power when I passed through in October 1972. His regime ruled with an iron fist. He had death squads called the *SAVAK* that maintained fear among the lower classes while enabling the upper classes to pursue their desire to become the most Western country in the Middle East.

As we crossed the border, a gentleman stood and addressed the whole bus. He was a doctor who'd made the border crossing previously. He told us the Iranians would force us to take large doses of antibiotics, and it would lower our resistance to other infections. He said we should hold the pills in our mouths until we got back on the bus, then spit them out. I found it kind of alarming, and there was some apprehension among everyone on the bus.

Armed Iranians with machine guns boarded the bus, had a look around, and asked us some questions. Then they ordered everyone off the bus and into white tents off to the side of the road. Once inside, we saw officious-looking nurses who asked for our names and wrote them down, along with our passport numbers. We were then forced to take red-and-white capsules, an antibiotic. Those who refused would be sent back to Turkey.

We remained quiet, and no one contested the edict. We exited the other end of the tent and got back on the bus, whereupon most of us immediately spat out the pills, until the floor was covered in red-and-white capsules. When the bus cleared the border, there were cheers, for we'd already become rebellious against the tyranny that would eventually topple the shah's regime.

Our first stop was Tabriz, where I noticed young men in designer suits walking down dusty roads to the center of town. I hadn't seen that kind of fashion statement since leaving Rome. In a country where most of the people were have-nots, it was a stark contrast.

Tabriz was beautiful, provincial, and built out of stone. It was picturesque with its snowcapped mountains and mosques with gold and turquoise domes. Though our encounter with Iranian authorities had been less than cordial, I was impressed by the beauty of this small town.

Tehran was another story. I entered the city through the Azadi Monument to the Martyrs, a fifteen-story gateway in the middle of a roundabout. It dwarfed our bus as we passed into central Tehran. There was lots of traffic and quite a few beautiful women who weren't wearing the traditional *chador*. Up until then, the chador or the *burqa* had hidden the women we'd seen from public view. Suddenly, women were in high heels and miniskirts. They'd be caught in the middle of the street traffic in their six-inch heels, and no one would stop. Of course, there were women in traditional Muslim clothing and men as well, but by and large, the upper classes were dressed in Western fashions. It was as though we were in London or Paris. I was taken aback by how Western it felt compared to the rest of the Middle East.

Talking to the average guy in the street, I found a deep distrust of the West. I noticed the move toward some liberalization on a superficial level with all things Western, but this westernization wasn't going unnoticed by most people. They thought the country was moving too fast in a liberal direction, and they wanted to retain their deep Muslim way of life. The people I spoke with in the market felt that the shah represented this push to westernize the country by force. They spoke of people who disappeared and were never seen again. There was hatred of the regime and even more for the SAVAK. Even in 1972, I felt there was enough unrest that I wasn't surprised when the revolution finally came.

I found that the Iranians were insulted if you described them as Arabic. They'd tell you they were Persian and spoke Farsi. For three hundred years, they said, it was against the law to speak Farsi, after they were invaded by the Arabs in the seventh century. The Iranians were Persian to the core and fiercely proud of that distinction. I found that many middle-class Iranians spoke English, as most were sent abroad for college in England and the States.

As Tim, Hendrik, and I entered the railway station, we were confronted with a huge photograph of the shah and the empress, Farah, taken when he was crowned after his father's death. The photograph was three stories high, floor to ceiling. Even if you didn't like the royal couple, you had to take notice of this propaganda tool.

We left Tehran to go to Persepolis. I was told not to miss it if I had a chance. It was the seat of power for the Persian Empire. Emperor Darius had built a monumental city there with architecture that rivaled any world capital of the time. It was impressive. Now I understood their fierce Persian nationalism. I stood in the shadows of the colonnades of the temples and reliefs with Persian kings on gate entrances. On one was the bearded king Cyrus, who freed the Jews from bondage in Babylon. Being Jewish only added to my interest and love affair with the ancient world. I could just imagine this city full of life and how majestic it must have been.

A few days later, the boys and I caught a train going east to Mashhad. It was a beautiful city built of extraordinary blue tiles and home to the finest turquoise in the world. It turned out to be the religious center of Iran. Very few people wore Western clothing, and most of the women wore the chador. It was here that I started to see a mixture of people from the East. There were Mongolians, Tajiks, Uzbeks, Baluchis, and Afghans. You could feel a certain sense of intrinsic spirituality in Mashhad. It had an undeniable draw on the people, something I'd missed in Tehran. The people were much more conservative than in the other cities we'd visited. Then I heard the call to prayer that came from several mosques in the area. "*Allahu akbar*" rang out in all directions. "God is great."

Afghanistan

Nothing could have prepared me for Afghanistan. Upon leaving Mashhad, we hopped into a minivan in Eslam Qal'eh that would drive us across the border to Herat. Tim and Hendrik were in the back seat, and the driver indicated I should sit in the front seat, which already had two occupants. They scooted over for me. I'd noticed since leaving Europe that it was a common custom, giving space to a stranger. The men wore magnificent turbans piled high on their heads. They were very friendly and smiled at me.

I smiled back and climbed in. I looked at my traveling companions and remarked how friendly the men were.

"That's nice," they said. "Now look down at their hands."

I looked down and found that the men were handcuffed to one another. They were Afghan bandits being deported. We'd been warned that the Afghans basically belonged to five tribes of bandits, and that the current bandits in power were now governing it. We also were aware that Afghanistan was the poorest country in the world.

When we crossed the border, I took off my sweater to change my shirt. I turned around and found the sweater missing. It came as no shock. I just didn't think it would happen quite so quickly. I'd been robbed already, right under my very nose. A few minutes later, to my surprise, an Afghan immigration officer was wearing it. He even had his shirt collar neatly pulled out over the neckline of the sweater.

Very smart, I thought. But I was miffed.

"Hey, that's my sweater," I snarled. I had a long winter ahead of me, and I'd need its warmth. When confronted, the guard politely took off the sweater and gave it back to me as though nothing had happened. Was that a hint of what was to come?

Herat, Afghanistan

When we arrived in Herat, at the frontier of Afghanistan, it was the beginning of November and the ground was covered in frost. The bus was half full with Western Europeans by the time it arrived. The closer we got to the subcontinent, the more hippies filled the transports going to the East. I talked with a few of them—a couple from Verona and his lady, who were making the journey for the first time and had no idea what to expect, and another from London and his lady from Spain. Some had made the journey before and were quite comfortable in their knowledge of the crossing, as well as their overall feeling that all would go well.

I asked about the border crossing through the Khyber Pass. The crossing from Afghanistan into Pakistan, the Spanish lady told me, was no problem. When I asked about the crossing between Pakistan and India, I got the same response, only louder and more confident.

"No problem" was a phrase used to describe every situation. Even the shopkeepers and the little beggar boys used it. The more I heard it, the more problems there seemed to be.

When the bus pulled into the station, we were mobbed by young boys jumping up at the bus windows, where we sat mesmerized. They were swinging pieces of black hashish the size of cow patties in front of us. We all thought we'd died and gone to heaven. We knew hashish was illegal, but there they were in broad daylight pushing it in our faces. They were so nonchalant. People began exchanging afghani right out the windows for the black gold. A hash patty that size cost us eighty cents. In the States, it would have sold for at least a hundred dollars.

"Wow, Michael, can you believe this?" Hendrik asked as he stuffed a five-thousand afghani note into the hand of a boy about ten years old, covered in dust and barefoot.

"Hendrik, can I share that with you?" I asked.

"Sure," he said. "It's so black and huge, we'll share it."

We looked for taxis, but there were none to be found. The only mode of transportation was the *tonga*, a beautifully ornamented horse-driven carriage. Now this was pretty laid-back. I was starting to feel at home. The tongas were pulled by magnificent-looking horses and topped with ornaments of woven wool with bells attached. The horses even had bells around their feet, so all you could hear was the chiming of bells, *cling-cling, cling-cling* as the carriages ran through the streets.

In search of a hotel, we all mounted a carriage. As if transported to another place and time, we felt like *pashas* riding to the sound of those bells going up and down the streets. It reminded me of a scene out of *Doctor Zhivago*. We spent two weeks in Herat.

Music wafted through the marketplace as women dressed in tribal fashion, adorned with silver jewelry, coins, and valuables sewn into the front of their dresses, went about the daily chore of buying food for their evening meals.

Hordes of little kids in threadbare pajamas, with dirt on their faces and unkempt hair, followed behind us, pulling on our sleeves. "You have one bakshish for me?"

Even though I knew this was a business for them, I couldn't help myself. I carried hard candies in my pockets at all times and pulled them out to give to the kids. The looks on their faces when they saw the sweets was pure joy.

We passed shops of all kinds. Everywhere we heard, "Come to my shop, Habib, my friend. I have very good deal for you." Occasionally there would be something that grabbed my attention. "Come, sit down," the owner would say, and we'd sit on a rug of extraordinary beauty while they'd try to part us from our money. No one was better at this than the Afghans. "Mint tea?" the man would ask. Then a hookah pipe laden with hashish would arrive with the mint tea, and the bargaining would begin.

Herat was an ancient city. It seemed like time had passed it by. It sat on the edge of a desert with mountains on all sides, and in the middle of town stood the Herat Citadel. Made of red sandstone, its outside walls were at least five stories high, with turrets. Inside, its courtyards and living spaces were exquisite. I could see it from the back window of my hotel room.

The castle was there when Alexander's armies swept over Afghanistan in 320 BC. The town had four main streets of commerce, and the housing, mostly made of mud brick, stretched for miles to the snowcapped mountains in the distance. The city was filled with Afghans wearing huge turbans and bandoliers of bullets across their chests, carrying long rifles over their shoulders. The women were covered head to toe in blue burqas and children in multicolored pajamas. The nomad camel caravans would come in off the desert to sell their rugs. It reminded me of a Wild West frontier town. In most ways, there was no rule of law. Tim and Hendrik were just as overwhelmed as I was by the enormous freedom we felt. We stood there in the street in the shadow of the castle for a few moments and took it all in.

My hotel room had hardwood floors and a nice rug that took up the space in front of a crude stone fireplace that was the room's only heat source. A pile of sticks lay by the fireplace. The front window looked onto the street below, and the back window, covered with lace curtains, onto Herat Citadel and the mountains.

The guys and I sat in my room, smoked hash, and talked about the world. We shared our experiences and got to know one another. Hendrik was from Geneva. He'd gone to college and, like me, wanted to explore the world. He was a little reserved, as Swiss-Germans were known to be. But once he opened up, he had a great sense of humor, though dry, and his warmth shone through.

Tim had grown up in Newcastle and worked for the government ever since he'd graduated from the university. Now he was walking away from that whole life to discover who he was. He was a round-figured, jovial type and seemed the least likely of the three of us to be making this kind of journey. His commentary was always interesting, as he tried to compare our Western civilization with that of Afghan culture and customs.

We were all discovering ourselves, and what better place to do that than in Afghanistan, where nothing was familiar? We were all on shaky ground. We literally felt as though we'd gone back in time. It was like discovering a new land with no blueprint or landmarks. There were no printed travel books on Afghanistan, no Lonely Planet guide on the best places to stay in Kandahar and Kabul, or where to find cheap eats in Jalalabad and Bamiyan. We were on our own, in what would turn out to be one of the most dangerous countries in the world.

The inhabitants were kind. I made friends with a shopkeeper who sold rugs and textiles. Ahmed was his name. I visited his shop almost daily, and whether I bought something or not, he welcomed me. We'd talk for at least an hour or more over mint tea and a hookah, and then I'd have to excuse myself. Otherwise, we'd have talked all day. He was so intelligent. I learned so much about Afghanistan through him. We talked about customs, and he told me how Afghan men had to buy a wife, or they couldn't marry. Then it dawned on me how many men were having sex with other men, as I'd find out personally on my trip to Kabul. He told me why the women wore the burqa. When they reached thirteen, girls were considered women and could no longer mix with boys or go out of the house without a male relative. Once they were in the safety of their homes, the burqa came off.

"Ahmed, why do the women have to fear other men who aren't their relatives?"

"The burqa keeps adolescents from meeting with each other before their arranged marriage," he said, "and married women from men that are not their husbands."

This was such a stark difference from Western culture, but I respected the tradition, and I tried to understand it. I couldn't help but feel that women were like property. This was foreign to me, but I also didn't know much about Islam at the time. It was hard to pass judgment.

He told me about the turbans that I admired so much. He said they were three meters long and that certain colors were worn by certain tribes. He let me try one on. You can't imagine what three meters of heavy cotton or silk feels like when piled on top of your head. One look in the mirror and you feel like an exotic sheik. I didn't want to take it off. He told me about the camel caravans that came from Baluchistan on the full moon to sell their carpets and jewelry. He was full of so much information, and our exchanges were a joy. He asked me on one of those visits, "Why are Afghanis so poor and Europeans so rich?"

I took a deep breath. I didn't know how to tell him, but I responded as simply as I could. "Because Afghanistan has no resources to offer other than the best hashish, heroin poppies, and rugs in the world."

He looked at me in silence, taking it all in, and though he understood, there was still that look of bewilderment. "How could these be the only products Afghans have to offer?" he asked.

I couldn't blame him. "Ahmed, you have no industry, and the government isn't helping to provide any."

"This is true," he said.

I'd never seen such poverty. It wasn't that the people were lazy. Far from it. They were industrious, hardworking farmers, and, like everyone else, wanted nothing more than to take care of their families.

The question of poverty would haunt me all through Asia. How long would it take for the world community to respond to it? For the moment, it was a daunting thought, and maybe the answer was never.

I noticed something strange while in Herat. Russians stood out like sore thumbs. It was obvious they didn't fit into the landscape. The shopkeepers complained they never bought anything, even when the Afghans came down in price. They seemed to be all men, no women or children that I saw. What were they doing there? It seemed strange. Such a poor country hardly seemed their style, and Russians weren't usually granted travel visas outside the Eastern Bloc. In hindsight, maybe it was no accident they were there. Afghanistan was ripe for a revolution. The people were discontented. The rest is history.

One night, I foolishly decided to take some acid that Hendrik had brought from Switzerland. I went to the outskirts of town to watch the camel caravans of the Baluchi tribal nomads come in off the desert into Herat, as Ahmed said they would. People said it was a magnificent sight. Sometimes as many as two hundred camels would arrive. The owners came to sell their wares—handmade rugs and rug bags—in the market. They arrived only once a month, during the full moon.

As I made my way down the dusty streets, past sparse lampposts, the streets became darker and darker and the sky more and more brilliant. The universe seemed to have suddenly been turned on like a light switch, and the full moon shone down bright on the dark and vacant streets. Maybe it was my heightened state of awareness, but for whatever reason, as I reached the edge of town, there in the darkened street I saw two figures, their turbans silhouetted. They drew something from their sides, and there was a flash of light as the moonlight hit what I suddenly realized were the blades of their daggers.

I stopped dead in my tracks. I knew my life was in danger. I was about to be murdered! I ran with the speed of adrenalin pushing me faster and faster. When I finally looked back, I had a good lead on them and saw they'd stopped running. When I was safely back in my hotel room, it finally dawned on me how dangerous Afghanistan really was.

The next day we were in a chai shop having tea with a couple we'd just met, people who were passing through Herat on their way back from India to the States.

"These two Afghans last night pulled their knives on me," I said. "It looked like they were going to kill me."

"You didn't hear about the two guys who were killed on the road to Kandahar yesterday?" the young woman asked.

"No, we didn't," I said.

"They were camped out by the road and stabbed in their sleeping bags. All their belongings were stolen."

A chill ran down my spine.

Days later, we were all again congregated in my room with the fire burning. Now very cold in Herat, it was lightly snowing outside, but we were warm and cozy. Sitting on the floor crossed-legged, having a smoke, we were talking about our plans when we heard some strange chanting outside in the street. We pulled back the lace curtains and saw some kids all dressed in school clothes—boys in white shirts and blue pants and girls in blue skirts and bobby socks. They were carrying a banner in English and Pashto, a protest over the recent increase in the price of bread. At the time, General Daoud was in power, leading a corrupt regime.

We looked down the street in the other direction and saw an army lorry drive up. It parked just underneath our window. To our amazement, the soldiers jumped down from the vehicle, lined up across the street, and fired into the crowd. The first line of kids fell. Most were bleeding, some profusely. The remainder of the crowd scattered down the street, screaming. When all was quiet, the army officers picked up the dead and wounded. They loaded them on the truck and left.

We stepped back from the window in horror, unable to verbalize what we'd witnessed.

"Jesus Christ, Jesus Christ, they just killed those kids in cold blood," Henrik finally said. "What are we going to do? Shit, I can't believe it. Those dirty bastards. They just killed them."

Tim was still so scared he couldn't speak. No one could believe it.

"Who knows what's going on in other parts of the country?" I finally asked. "Maybe this is more widespread than we thought. We have to leave tonight."

We all agreed. I lowered the curtains, and we began to pack.

Kandahar

I realized after the shooting and my near-death experience that my friends and I were in uncharted waters. Afghanistan was as dangerous as it was captivating. We purchased tickets to Kandahar, which had a reputation of being a lawless kind of place in the heartland of the Pashtun, in Helmand Province. Later, these same men we saw on the streets of Kandahar, carrying bandoliers and rifles, bearing faces of stone with a commanding presence and an air of arrogance, would call themselves the Taliban.

The bus we boarded that day had icicles hanging from the ceiling. We couldn't understand why there would be icicles inside the bus, even if it *was* cold outside. A man wearing a black turban and carrying a rifle ordered us to the back of the bus, and then we understood—the back window was missing. It was no wonder there were icicles. It was freezing. I'd purchased an Afghan sheepskin hat and an Afghan shawl, which I wore over my navy pea coat to keep out the cold. The bus was filled with Afghans. My friends and I were glad to be sitting together and huddled against one another for warmth as we settled in for the long ride.

Halfway through the trip in the middle of nowhere, on the only paved road that crosses the entire country—a road built by the

Russians—we broke down. We had a flat tire and no spare. We'd have to wait for reinforcements, which would be the next bus to pass, hours away. While we waited, I saw a dark cloud on the horizon. It looked like a dust storm. When I mentioned it to the boys, they thought it might be a vehicle, but it wasn't on the road.

As the dark mass neared, we could begin to make out the figures. To our joy and astonishment, it turned out to be a two-hundred-camel caravan of Kuchi tribespeople crossing the road a hundred meters from our bus. What a sight to behold as they moved with lightning speed across the desert. In the lead were young men and women, their camels loaded with large multicolored handwoven rug bags thrown over their humps, huge saddlebags. These held everything they owned: their tents and rugs, and rugs to sell, cooking pots, and food. Afghanistan is one of the few places left where nomadic tribes still roam the land.

What a sense of freedom they possessed. You could feel it as they galloped past. The young children would hold on to the sides of the rug bags and pick up their feet for a while, then run alongside for a few yards, then repeat the whole process all over again. The old men and women and the youngest of the tribe trailed behind, as is the way in nomadic tribal communities: the strongest in front and the weakest bringing up the rear, followed by their herd of goats.

They took no notice of us, but I looked at them. The men and the women in the front of the caravan were so full of life, intent on survival and bringing the tribe to safety. In seconds, they'd disappeared into the vast desert as if they'd been swallowed up, just like a mirage.

I was becoming a seasoned traveler, and Afghanistan would either make or break me. I was glad I'd decided to go without Robin. It gave me an opportunity going overland to truly be by myself and to discover the depths of who I was. Spending time with the boys gave me the opportunity to be with people if I chose, which was nice. They'd covered my back a few times, so I was grateful to have met them. To understand the pain and suffering, to empathize with the Afghan people, and to know I wasn't separate from them came easily. I chalked it up to the love in my home growing up with my socialist parents. This was a turning point. I met myself on the road to Kandahar. I liked who I was and was beginning to feel comfortable in my own skin.

We passed walled villages made of mud bricks, two and three stories high. Terraced up the mountainsides, they melded into the landscape. The walls surrounding the villages were covered in a mud plaster, so they looked smooth against the sunlit blue sky and the arid brown and red mountains on the horizon. It appeared as if they rose straight up from the earth of the same color, man and his environment blending into perfect harmony. Usually there was only one entrance, guarded by huge and ferocious mastiffs, dogs that were chained to the walls at all times. The gates made of huge wooden beams were massive and surely meant to keep their inhabitants safe. If you were an intruder or an outsider, the whole village knew of your approach before you reached the gates. The towns resembled fortresses, with spots along the walls for lookouts. Not all the villages were this elaborate, but you could tell some were old.

We'd brought sandwiches of fresh chicken with hummus on the bus, and the three of us were starving, so we pulled them from the brown bags and began to eat. After a couple of bites, several of the Pashtun stood up. They were fierce-looking, with black turbans and bandoliers of bullets crisscrossing their chests, baggy harem pants, sandals, and long rifles.

One of them pointed his rifle at us and motioned for us to put away the food. We didn't know what was going on, but we quickly shoved our sandwiches back into their bags. It finally dawned on us that it was a holy day called Ashura, a day of fasting from sunrise to sunset, and we'd broken Sharia law. I wouldn't have thought that as nonbelievers we'd be held to these laws, but that was one of the enigmas that plagued me while in the Middle East. The laws and Islam on some levels seemed so dogmatic. Things were either black or white. There was no gray.

As I looked out the window of the bus, I could see that Kandahar was much larger than Herat. The capital of Helmand Province, it was built in a large valley surrounded by mountains. It was a fertile area with much agriculture. The houses were the same color as the earth and were built of mud bricks. The streets were wider than in Herat and crowded with shoppers.

Women in blue and black burqas lined the streets, chaperoned by male relatives wearing large turbans, vests over their shirts, and ballooned pajama pants. They carried guns and bandoliers over their shoulders. Every once in a while, we'd see a nomadic Kuchi or Baluchi woman covered by a black shawl with a magenta design around the edges, depending on their tribe. Their blouses had a distinct hand-embroidered square patch in the center up to the neckline. They wore exotic jewelry: pierced earrings with chains that ran through the nostrils on either side, studded with occasional semiprecious stones like lapis and carnelian. They wore silver belts around their waists. It was a relief from the endless line of burqas.

However, as we entered the city that rain-soaked November day, the poverty overwhelmed me. The unpaved streets had turned to mud.

We traipsed through the streets and found a restaurant. We pushed open the doors to reveal a room full of men sitting cross-legged on rugs, eating at communal tables. They looked up, startled, and then resumed eating. We were shown to an empty space at the tables and had to order with no menus and only my little knowledge of Pashtun. As I sat there with all these men in turbans, their rifles against the walls, I felt as if I'd been transported hundreds of years into the past. Other than the rifles, there was nothing to remind me of the twentieth century.

As we sat cross-legged, the three of us nodded politely at the two friendly bearded men across from us, not sure whether we were truly safe. Our food arrived, shish kebab and rice. Since we had no utensils, we dug in with our fingers cupped together to form a sort of spoon.

it back on his thigh. He was a handsome man, well-built, with beautiful dark skin and green eyes and jet-black wavy hair. I didn't put his hand back because I wasn't interested. I put it back because I was afraid the boys would find out I was gay and that it would change our relationship. He tried several times more, then finally gave up.

By the time we arrived in Kabul, we were all sporting beards and mustaches and wearing sheepskin hats, Afghan shawls, and worn-out blue jeans. Tim had cast off his English 007 raincoat for a sheepskin coat, and with the beard, you never would have recognized the civil servant from Newcastle. He was in complete transformation, and I liked the new Tim. The old Tim never would have been unkempt or taken chances. We looked like we'd been on the road for years. We had enough of the language down that we could converse a little and order food.

We checked into the hotel. I got my key and told the boys I would meet them downstairs for dinner in an hour. I got into my room, threw my bag down, and heard a knock on the door. I opened it, and there, to my surprise and delight, stood the Afghan army officer. Before I could say a word, he came in and started kissing me and feeling my chest. It was mutual, and we began tearing each other's clothes off. We made love and then he got dressed, thanked me in Arabic, and left.

Was I to be forever thankful for his attention and once again surprised by the Arab world and its hypocrisy? For even I knew that sex between two men was a serious crime that carried the death penalty. Being gay was a hanging offense. Most Western heterosexuals don't even think about the risk these men in the Middle East take every time they share their bodies with another man, that which comes only natural to us all, love.

Kabul was the capital, and though it was an ancient city, it had much to offer after the backward cities we'd come from. Chicken Street was where the Westerners congregated. It was off the main street in Kabul near the blue-domed mosque and a park in the center of the city. Though it was stark that time of year, we felt at home.

Later that night, as we walked shoulder to shoulder, we joked about the seriousness of our companions at dinner. Somehow as we tried to find our hotel with almost no light save that of the moon, we lost Tim. He'd fallen into a huge open latrine. Such latrines aren't uncommon for third world countries, but usually they're covered. It was only when we heard him moan that we realized he was missing. It was so dark we couldn't figure out where he'd disappeared. Then we heard another moan. Poor Tim had fallen into you-know-what. We had a time getting him out while we all laughed uncontrollably. We pulled him from the mire and stood a few feet away.

"You stink, man," I said.

"Ja," Hendrik said.

We made our way back to the hotel, walking upwind from Tim. We realized it was too dangerous to hang out in Kandahar, so we decided to head to the capital, Kabul, the following day. There were few streetlights, and, as foreigners, it was hard to know whether our lives were at risk. This was the center of what later became the bastion of the Taliban.

Kabul

On the bus from Kandahar to Kabul, the boys took seats in front of me, and I rode solo. It was a long trip, and I was hoping I'd meet someone interesting. The bus filled up, and I found myself sitting next to a captain in the Afghan army.

He spoke to me in Pashtun. "How are you?"

"Fine," I replied. "Nice to meet you." That was about all I knew of pleasantries in the language.

The boys looked back to check on me to make sure everything was all right. Surmising that all was good, they relaxed back in their seats for the ride. The captain introduced himself as Abdullah and proceeded to talk to me in Pashtun. I informed him that I didn't speak the language. Then things got quiet. His English was as bad as my Pashtun, so we smiled a lot. About a half hour into the journey, I felt his hand on my thigh. I smiled and took his hand off and placed

There, all of Western hippiedom seemed to cross paths, with those of us traversing the Khyber headed for India and those returning headed for Istanbul. It was called Chicken Street because most of the restaurants served a half-roasted chicken for around a dollar fifty. Its shops were filled with heavy woolen socks, hats, vests, and leather boots suited for the winter journey. It became our hangout, where people, mostly Europeans, drank mint tea, ate, and shared their stories. I was one of the few Americans on the road.

As we sat drinking our tea, I listened to the cacophony of languages that arose: Italian, French, German, Spanish, Portuguese, and even some Scandinavian tongues. The Europeans used broken English to communicate with the Afghanis. So we shared our stories.

The tales of the Silk Road ranged from the exotic reaches of the Himalayas, like Kathmandu and Pokhara, to the beaches and volcanoes of Bali and the temples of Bangkok to the spiritual centers in India, including Varanasi, Kashmir, Amritsar, and Dharmsala. People spoke of Agra, Jaipur, Pondicherry, and Portuguese Goa. I'd already heard about Goa and was planning to go there. It was on the Indian Ocean and boasted spectacular beaches with Portuguese fishing villages right on them, with houses for rent. It was also a place where Europeans and Americans gathered each month for a full-moon ceremony. One could only speculate what it was all about.

A woman with big beautiful silver earrings, long brown hair, and heavy black kohl under her eyes approached me in the café and sat down next to me. She wore a long skirt, boots, and a Rajasthani mirrored vest. "Are you going to India?" she asked with a strong Italian accent.

"Yes."

"Have you seen the Golden Temple at Amritsar?"

"No."

"Oh, it is beautiful. You must see it. It's so amazing."

That conversation must have stuck in my head, because when we got to Amritsar, I took the boys straight to the Golden Temple. It was conversations like this on the Silk Road that kept stoking the fires of imagination and opened us up to the world. We were like a family in Kabul. We shared danger, comradeship, hash, and a love of adventure. They called us hippies, but we were from every country in Europe and the Americas. We never thought of ourselves as hippies. We were travelers on the same road, brothers and sisters on a spiritual journey to the East, and Kabul was the crossroads.

Jalalabad and the Khyber Pass

The bus held a mixture of Afghans, Pakistanis, and Westerners on their way to the Khyber Pass. The pass is the only road out of Afghanistan over the Hindu Kush, the high mountain range that separates Afghanistan from Pakistan. We passed through the Kabul Gorge, where over the millennia the river had carved rock formations of exquisite beauty. The bus followed the gorge for miles. As we looked out our windows, we could see several thousand feet to the raging river below, spectacular and dangerous.

Afghan buses are piled high with goods, luggage, and sometimes people, so they're top-heavy. The road is barely large enough for two vehicles, and accidents are common. The lorries that didn't make it dotted the sides of the Gorge.

We arrived in Jalalabad too late to cross the Khyber. The sun was setting, and we were forced to spend the night. All of us were tired and a little cranky, and it was starting to show. We were two and a half months into our journey.

Everyone who had crossed it told us that the Khyber Pass was long and dangerous and that it took eight hours to pass. It was best not to travel alone, and never after sunset. When we came to the entrance of the pass, there were a few tribal men with guns watching the convoys going through ahead of us. A sign in English and in Urdu, the language of the Pakistanis, read: *You are entering the Khyber Pass. Do not take pictures of tribal women or pictures of military installations. Do not cross after sunset.*

As we passed the entrance, we began to climb slowly up the grade. I sat next to an Afghan, a Pashtun, who was going to visit family in Pakistan. He sat with his rifle resting on his chest, a bandolier of bullets over his shoulder. In Afghanistan, this was the way of life. The guys sat behind me.

As we made our ascent into this rocky, mountainous no man's land, an area neither country could control—a situation that still exists today—I noticed guns sticking out of the houses on the mountain directly across from the road. They were following us with their rifles as we made our way up the mountain. The grade became steeper and steeper and the bus slower and slower, until we were crawling. From time to time, we passed military forts that must have been built by the English in their war with the Afghans in the mid-1800s.

We passed the time playing cards and telling stories. At some point, we heard shouts from the back of the bus. Some German guy had photographed the forts, and the Pakistanis were in an uproar. They fought with the man until they'd subdued him, then opened his camera and tore out the film. We were slightly shocked, but after spending some time in Pakistan, I'd come to realize the country was consumed with paranoia about yet another unsubstantiated, imagined Indian invasion.

Pakistan

We came down out of the pass into Peshawar, Pakistan. I'd never seen a scarier town than this one. It was a frontier town, dusty and dirty. The sidewalks were made of wooden planks like in the Wild West. Guns, heavy weapons, and bandoliers of ammunition hung on hooks for sale, like in a meat market. The streets were crowded with a mix of Afghans, Pakistanis, and European hippies. The three of us kept looking at one another in astonishment that this kind of lawlessness could exist.

The next day, we found passage on a train to Rawalpindi. The name sounded so exotic, but names can be deceiving. It was a large city with no redeeming qualities. We spent the night in a fleabag hotel on straw mattresses. It was a dump. We couldn't wait to leave, and the next night we got tickets to Lahore.

We arrived at the train station early and were met by three Pakistani women. They were Hindus dressed in saris and had glass bangles jingling on their wrists.

The boys were getting all hot and bothered by the attention from the ladies. Tim said to me, "Did you see that? They're coming on to us."

They were excited to finally be able to see women's faces without a burqa or chador hiding them. I think it had been so long since anyone had gotten any sexual vibes on our journey that they came completely unhinged. I didn't want to rain on their parade, but the one thing that gave the women away was their five o'clock shadows growing out through their makeup. But they managed to pull the wool over Tim's and Hendrik's eyes.

"Yeah, now look at their beards," I said.

They were so embarrassed. "Oh no," Tim said.

Hendrik grew quiet as we walked away. Maybe I should have just left them with their fantasy. I didn't mean it negatively. After all, they were my brothers—or sisters, if you will.

We arrived in Lahore the following day. When we left the station, we were mobbed. A period of fasting had ended, and everyone was in a joyful mood. Tens of thousands of people had donned their best white shirts and were celebrating in the streets. For us, it was bedlam. It was all we could do to find a tonga and get to our hotel.

Already, I couldn't wait to get out of Pakistan. It was uncomfortable from the beginning. It felt like we'd gone from the frying pan into the fire. Lahore seemed chaotic compared to Afghanistan. We'd finally reached Asia, and it was filled with millions of people.

The next morning, we boarded a bus that would take us to the border with India. It climbed a big mountain pass, and we finally reached the summit, then started to descend. At that time, the two countries had just finished a war, and the border crossing was a nightmare. One thousand people had to walk across the dusty border that zigzagged past twenty-foot screens made of bamboo mats like a maze. First, we had to go through Pakistani immigrations, where world. The people radiated bliss in their smiles. All I could feel was joy.

For the first time since leaving Afghanistan, I felt free. The contrast with the Middle East was like day and night. I'd just come from a place where guns and bullets were part of the everyday dress and where I was considered an infidel, an outsider. Now I was in a place that seemed not to separate people, but to encourage inclusion of everyone, and where everyone had the potential to attain nirvana. Exotic, strange, and as foreign as it was, I felt completely at home.

It was time to say goodbye to my friends. It was hard to leave them. We'd shared the most difficult part of the journey to the East together, and we helped one another through it. As it turned out, I'd never see them again.

I was the first to leave. The platform was crowded with people sitting on their haunches, as everyone in Asia does. When the train to Delhi pulled into the station, there was chaos. The entire group on the platform stood up at once, a knee-jerk reaction. We did too.

I gave Tim and Hendrik a long embrace. "Goodbye, guys, it's been an incredible journey," I said, then thanked them once more.

I ran for one of the cars as the train was still moving and the steam from the engine was spewing out a thick fog. As I tried to board, the horde behind me literally pushed me into the car. I found a place next to a window facing the platform. People filled every inch of space until there was nowhere left to sit. People began sitting in front of me on the floor, on their bags. No sooner had everyone settled in than the train began to move. I stuck my hand out the window, frantically waving goodbye. The boys waved too. Then they were gone.

I sat back in my seat, alone for the first time in months. Sadness filled me for a moment, but in the next, it was all about the new journey. Faces looked up at me, curious and strange.

A gentleman sitting across from me asked, "*Saab*, what is the purpose of your mission here in India?"

I was dumbfounded. "I'm really not sure," I said. "I've come to find out who I am."

officials searched just about everyone. Then we faced the Indians, who did nothing more than copy down our names and passport numbers and wave us on. It took around eight hours.

As we passed the last screen, there to greet us, much to our delight, was an asphalt street lined with palm trees, complete with Sikh guardsmen in crisp green uniforms and red turbans, and a marching band playing music. There were even buses waiting to take us to the train station. What a dichotomy.

We gave a collective sigh of relief. We'd made it to the subcontinent, India. What exhilaration! Even though India was chaotic, a whole new sense of freedom filled the air. I was to meet Robin in Connaught Circus in Delhi in just a few days. I missed her.

The last part of the journey was concluding. So was my incredible friendship with my traveling buddies, Tim and Hendrik. Our trip would end in Delhi. Tim was going to Varanasi, and Hendrik was headed for Bombay. On our last night together, I asked them if they'd join me on a pilgrimage to the Golden Temple in Amritsar as a means of saying goodbye. I'd heard so much about it in Afghanistan. They agreed, so when the train pulled into Amritsar, we got off.

Amritsar, India

My first impressions of India were at the Golden Temple, the holiest shrine for the Hindu Sikhs. We entered through the main gates, removed our shoes, and followed the crowd into the main courtyard. The Golden Temple was surrounded by a lake with a long walkway that was the only entrance and exit. Around the lake were large white arcades with columns that could hold thousands of people. The gold temple dome glittered in the noonday sun, and the three of us marveled at its architecture. It was here that the journey took an unexpected turn.

I was taken aback by the sheer number of human beings in the place, the exotic garb of the women, and the colorful Sikh turbans. I felt the mysticism of a spiritual moment of bliss. That's how I'd describe it, a moment of bliss, a feeling of being at one with the

I don't think he understood fully, but he nodded his head in a swaying motion like a cobra, then said in Hindi, "*Achha, sahib.* Okay, sir."

During my travels, each time we neared a border, I'd corral a local from that country, sit him down, and pick his brain for local vocabulary. Because I spent so much time in India, I wound up learning enough of the language to communicate on a basic level.

My language lessons had just begun, and my thoughts began drifting to Robin. I was excited to see her and to tell her of my travels. I'd gained a certain confidence, and at twenty-three years of age, I felt I'd gained a little wisdom on my travels along the Silk Road.

Chapter Eleven

Delhi

I got out of the train in Delhi and made my way to the street, where I was besieged by twenty or so kids begging for money. "Saab, saab, you have one rupee for me?" they cried.

Completely overcome, I was saved by a taxi driver and jumped into his bemo, a three-wheeled motorcycle with a carriage. "Connaught Circus. Hotel Regency," I said.

Robin would be waiting for me there. I couldn't wait to see her. As my bemo pulled up to the beautiful colonial Victorian edifices that lined the circle, there she was. I didn't even pay the taxi driver. I just jumped out, and we embraced like we hadn't seen one another in years. It felt good to be close to the one I loved in such a captivating and exotic place.

Even though only two and a half months had passed since we'd left one another in NYC, she looked different. Her eyes were brighter than I remembered, and her smile coy, seductive, and happy—happy like I'd never seen her before. She was in her element in exotic, edgy, mystical India, where cobras came swaying out of baskets, *sadhus* lay down on beds of nails, and holy cows roamed the streets. I had so much to tell her about my journey to the East.

Her best friend, Eve Eisenstein, had accompanied her to Delhi. I'd met Eve briefly in Woodmere. Her father was a psychiatrist in the Five Towns, but oddly enough, he couldn't help his daughter. She was suffering from depression but had found relief from a guru made famous by the Beatles, the Maharishi. She was a disciple and had decided to come to India at the last moment with Robin on a pilgrimage.

I had no idea she was coming. When I met her in India, she'd donned a white sari and wore a necklace of beads with the guru's picture on it. Frankly, I thought she was in a cult. It felt like it, anyway. This devotion to the guru had consumed her life, and the woman I'd met in New York looked nothing like the one in Delhi. I tried to be Eve's friend, knowing how much she meant to Robin, but she wasn't responsive. I realized she was jealous of our relationship, so I tried extra hard to be kind to her.

The day after I arrived, the Maharishi was speaking to three thousand people sitting on the ground in the dusty polo fields near the Red Fort. Robin asked me to come. Eve was onstage with the other devotees, with garlands of marigolds around her neck and a red dot on her forehead that signified she'd been blessed that day by a holy man. I went along for the ride, not knowing exactly what to expect. But I was moved by this holy man.

He spoke in English, and there were many Western devotees in attendance. However, the majority were Indian from all over the country, and of necessity, they used English to speak to one another because of the differences among their fourteen languages. If he'd chosen to speak in one of the Indian languages, many would not have understood him.

I was moved by his ability to engage the people, helping them understand that the only way to freedom is through compassion, and that holding on to desire only brings suffering. Yet I still felt an inability to fully surrender. It felt like he could be a false guru. It was just a feeling I had, mostly because of Eve's devotion. At the same time, his words spoke the truth, and I was moved by them. This was my first encounter with a spiritual leader, and India would prove to be a great teacher. It gave me the experience I needed to recognize my true teachers later in life.

Kathmandu

I told Robin that I wanted to go to the Himalayas and to Kathmandu as we'd planned. It was a place neither of us had been before, a new adventure for us both. What I didn't know was that Eve had invited herself, and Robin had agreed. I was uncomfortable with the decision but went ahead with it. I was disappointed that we wouldn't be alone on the trip. I told her about my experiences in the Middle East, and she was wide-eyed as she listened. She realized I'd grown up somewhere between Rome and Delhi, and I think she was delighted. But there was something else about myself I hadn't revealed to her: I was gay.

The three of us left Delhi for Raxaul, an Indian city on the border of Nepal. Again, there was chaos at the station. There were people everywhere. While waiting on the Lucknow Express, I saw a man throw his bag on the top of the train. Then he climbed up the metal grab rails, which are used for maintenance. His wife handed him their little boy, then their little girl and another bag, and then she climbed up herself with the ease of a monkey. The top of the car was flat, and most people sat on top of their luggage. By the time the train left the station, most cars were full to the brim. In those days, the steam engines didn't travel at the speeds they travel today.

But now I was used to it. I was savvy. This time, we had porters who brought our knapsacks onto the train and held our seats until we could get on. I was learning fast. It was a long journey by rail, and the ride took two days. We first had to go to Allahabad and then to Lucknow, where we changed trains and headed north to where the subcontinent of India, flat as a pancake, meets the rising foothills of the giant Himalayas. The Himalayas were formed some seventy million years ago, when the subcontinent smacked up against the Eurasian plate. It was most evident as our steam engine chugged north.

I looked out the window at the flat rice fields, and the foothills for as far as the eye could see. In both directions, they stretched straight up, a thousand feet at first, then behind them the mountains rose up to two, three, four, and eight thousand feet. It was spectacular.

At Raxaul, we had to take an eight-hour trip through the mountains by bus, on a road that was described by everyone who'd taken it as extremely dangerous. In fact, years later, our friends Joanie and

Giancarlo would die when their bus careened off the same kind of road in Manali, India. Unless you had the money to fly, it was your only choice.

Robin and I sat together, and Eve was behind us next to a Nepali man. As the bus began its ascent, we saw lush jungle growing on the sides of the mountains. There were palm trees and mango groves. The landscape changed as we ascended. The mountains were steeped with rice fields, so green and lush it was like a postcard. Still higher, we encountered pine forests.

It was somewhere around here that we ran into trouble. There wasn't enough room for the bus coming down the hill to pass us. As Nepal had been under English rule, they drove on the left side of the road, and we were looking straight down a ravine some four thousand feet. We sat just over the back wheels, and as the driver backed up to make room, one of the wheels on our side was dangerously close to the edge of the shoulder. To make matters worse, I noticed the wreckage of a bus several hundred feet down the ravine, with jungle growing all through it.

Robin looked down and let out a gasp, and we all moved over to the center aisle to put the weight on the remaining back wheel still on the road.

"Don't worry, Robbie, it'll be fine," I said. "We didn't come all this way just to wind up in a ravine. The universe will provide."

She looked up and smiled.

The other bus passed, and after some effort, ours returned to the road in the direction of Kathmandu.

When we reached the top of the range, we looked down over a panoramic view of Kathmandu Valley. There lay a beautiful city like Shangri-La. Its three main temples rose out of the valley floor, which had a river running through it. The agriculture was a patchwork of rice fields, lush green fields, and fallow areas. The terraced rice fields rose up out of the valley. Behind the ten-thousand-foot mountains that ringed the valley floor were twenty-thousand-foot snowcaps in the background, gazing into Tibet and China. It was spectacular.

Kathmandu was beautiful, something out of a storybook. The three-story temples built of beams that were whole trees had side-by-side drums at the top that were as big as a living room. Men played them with drumsticks the size of baseball bats. You could hear their sound all over Kathmandu Valley, calling people to prayer. For so many years, this place had been difficult to reach, and people lived in relative safety and peace, developing their culture undisturbed.

I'd never seen such diversity of people or diversity of religions coexisting in one place: Tibetan Buddhists, Hindu, Nepali, and Chinese Daoists all living together. It was a true paradise, and everyone was welcome, even us.

Hash was legal. You could smoke it everywhere. You also could buy it anywhere, and we did. The first time I walked into a hashish shop, I was floored. Not only did they sell it, but they had grades at different prices. Wow! Where were we? It felt so unreal.

Swayambhunath

After we'd explored Kathmandu, we began to visit other cities in the valley. We went to Patna and the Great Stupa in Boudhanath, and then to the Monkey Temple at Swayambhunath. This temple has great significance in Buddhism. It's said that the Buddha gave his first sermon to the people after leaving India on this hilltop. The king of Nepal built a temple on it in 464 AD, and named it Swayambhunath, meaning "self-created." Mythology says the valley was once a lake and the hilltop was a lotus blossom. When the valley was drained, the blossom remained.

The village at the base of the hill was called Swayambhunath. It was quite small, maybe three hundred people. There was a well, which the whole village depended upon. The well was at the base of the entrance to the village, which was terraced up a hillside. Cobblestones marked the beginning of the path leading through the narrow streets into the village. On one side of the well was a small café run by a Nepalese family, and on the other was a small restaurant run by Tibetan monks from the temple. It was in this quaint village, three miles from Kathmandu, that Robin and I decided to take up residence.

At that time, there were maybe a dozen foreigners living there. As we climbed through the narrow streets, the villagers were quite friendly but thought it a little odd that we were so off-the-beaten track. They looked at us with a kind curiosity, though their smiles welcomed us.

We found a path that deviated from the main path and was no longer cobblestoned but that had a view of the whole valley. We could see the temples rising from the valley floor in Kathmandu, the river, and the magnificent twenty-thousand-foot snowcapped Himalayas in the background. We came to a complex of houses, and below us were terraced rice fields. We entered the courtyard where the Nepalese women were threshing rice on woven mats to loosen the grain from the stalks. They looked up in curiosity, stopped their work, and wiped their foreheads from the heat of the noonday sun.

No one spoke English, so I tried to let it be known in their language that we wanted to rent a house. There was much discussion among the women, and their demeanor took on a more serious look. One of the younger girls told us to wait while she fetched her father from the fields. When he came up, we introduced ourselves and asked him if he had a house to rent. He motioned for us to walk with him, and just down from the complex was a little house with small double doors that we had to duck down to enter.

An earthen-floor dwelling with a thatched roof and brick-and-plaster walls painted white, it had one large room with a ladder that led to a sleeping area with fresh straw. Through a small side window, we had a beautiful view of the Monkey Temple. It was perfect. We settled on four hundred rupees a month, around fifty dollars, and it was all ours, including the view out the front door of Kathmandu Valley and the mountains.

Robin and Michael in Katmandu Valley; in the village of Swayambhunath, and the famous Monkey Temple in the background.

We moved in just after the harvest. We were elated at first, but then reality sank in. We were living on mud floors with no running water. What about showers? And how about cooking? We had much to learn.

I was amazed that Robin, the Jewish princess from the Five Towns, was settling into a one-bedroom house in Nepal with earthen floors and a thatched roof. This was the woman who said spiders scared her and who used to jump up on a chair and scream or get behind me for protection, begging me to kill them. She was truly amazing. Once a week, she got on her hands and knees to help me take wet rags and smooth out the dirt floor and make it hard again. The first week, the floors were very hard. By the second, they were cracking up.

Water was a big problem. I went to the market and bought us three huge earthenware amphora vessels for holding water, one for drinking, and the other two for washing and cleaning. To be able to carry the water any distance, you had to wrap a thick cloth around your waist so that the vessel rested cushioned on your hip and across your body, with your one hand holding the bottom of the vessel and the other clutching the neck in the crook of your arm. Carrying water like this is part of indigenous life, and children are taught this from an early age. Western people aren't used to such manual labor, and knowing how heavy the vessels were, I was always amazed at how the aged managed it.

We were learning daily about living an indigenous life. The next big obstacle was bathing. After the first week of washing out of a bowl, I was ready to see what I could do about rigging up a shower. I went to the market, bought several pieces of sturdy bamboo, and set them up in tepee fashion, about six feet off the ground, just outside the house. I lashed the bamboo with local hemp and attached a hook at the center. I found a ten-gallon oil drum, pounded holes into the bottom, and used the metal handle to slide it over the hook. Voilà, a shower.

Robin was so proud of me. I filled the drum, and we had our first showers, with around two minutes to soap up and two to three minutes to rinse off. Robin was screaming and laughing as the ice-cold December Himalayan river runoff rained down on her. We were like children frolicking right in front of our little thatched house. The panoramic view of the rice fields went all the way to the river, then crossing the river were the temples rising out of the city.

Our Nepalese landlords came to see what all the noise was about, as they could see us from the complex above our house. There we were, the two of us soaking wet in our birthday suits, dancing under the shower with the whole neighborhood giggling and pointing fingers with their hands over their mouths. We were in heaven. Where else could we find such freedom?

As the nights grew colder, the normal method of keeping warm Nepalese-style, with the whole family sleeping upstairs together, wasn't working for our unaccustomed Western bodies. I had to figure something out, and fast. I kept looking at the huge earthen vessel that held our water, and I noticed that in the corner of the room was a square vent about five feet up from the floor and about the same distance from the second floor. I took a small screwdriver and began to chip away at the empty water vessel, right down the middle, so that I could reduce it into two halves. When it finally broke, I placed three very large flat stones, all of them roughly the same height and about two and a half feet in depth, in the corner by the vent. One fit perfectly square in the corner where the two walls came together. The others were laid next to each wall so that they comprised a triangle on which to lean the half-sided ceramic water jug, large end down, on the rocks with the thin neck at the top. I looked at it and thought it just might work. I called Robin in to look at my masterpiece, and she was impressed. I forged ahead.

I mixed up mud and rocks from around the rice fields with water. While Robin held the half vessel against the corner, where it sat on the two flat stones about two and a half feet above the dirt floor, I covered its sides with the rock-and-mud mixture until the whole thing was covered. Only the belly of the vessel wasn't mudded. I then attached aluminum metal tubing at the small end of the vessel's opening and took the tubing out the vent, several feet past the thatched roof and straight up. I plastered the space where the tubing and the vessel came together at the top and started a fire. It worked.

The fire cooked the wet mud mixture into a hardened mortar, and we were warm for the first time in weeks. What was even more remarkable was that we could cook on it too. The third large flat stone at the corner served as a place to put a cooking pot or frying pan. No more kerosene stove like the Nepalese used that filled the room with smoke. When the villagers heard about it, they all came down to see us cook. They'd gather in a group and sit on their haunches on the steps of the front door and watch.

Those were some happy days. Even Eve, who was somewhat distant when I was around, came down to eat with us. She'd taken a room with our landlords in the complex above our house.

Not long after we moved in, I got a knock at the door very early in the morning, before I was awake. I threw on my Nepalese shirt and blue jeans, made my way down the ladder from the sleeping quarters upstairs, and opened the door to find a Tibetan woman sitting on my steps.

She cried out in a low, drawn-out voice, "Ganja?" She confidently proceeded to show me all the different blends and styles of marijuana she bore in her dope-laden basket. "This one very strong."

That's how open the culture was about the use of marijuana. They'd used it for centuries for medicinal and psychological purposes, and there was no negativity to it. Now that hippies had come to the village, there was even more demand.

"*Namaste, didi,*" I said with my hands clasped in front of my face as if in prayer, which is the custom in India and Nepal. "How are you, little sister? *Kitna pisa?* How much is it?"

"Only twenty rupees," she said.

"I'll give you fifteen," I said.

She wrapped about a quarter of an ounce of the best ganja in Nepal into paper and passed it to me. From then on, I never went to Kathmandu to buy ganja. I had it delivered once a week.

By the third week in December, as we got closer to Christmas, the European enclave at Swayambhunath had grown larger. Two women from Wales arrived, Harriet and Philippa. They rented a couple of rooms in a Nepali house. Then an Englishman by the name of Thomas arrived with an Italian whose name was Clementino Pozzali. Clementino and I got on marvelously from the start. He was full of Italian charm and was extremely extroverted.

We met them all down at the well one day, and I invited them to a potluck dinner on Christmas Eve. Harriet was a Welsh girl from the town of Aberystwyth, with a dry sense of humor and a heavy accent. She was so much fun to be around. Phillipa was quieter. Thomas was a hippie from East London, an intelligent guy who knew a lot about Asia and was a good source of information about cultures, religion, and history. Clem was the heart and soul of all of us. He was so in touch with who he was, so confident, funny, and in the present. I loved being around him. His honesty and humor, so matter-of-fact, always had me in stitches.

Christmas Eve 1972

People began to arrive around four-thirty. It was crisp that day in Kathmandu Valley. The morning started out frozen, then by noon, the temperature was in the low sixties. Later, as the sun set below the tallest twenty-thousand-foot peaks that surrounded us, a chill came over the evening. I'd already stoked the fireplace to heat up the house and had laid the woven palm leaf mats on the floor and small pillows to lean on. Because we had no furniture, we did everything cross-legged on the floor.

Robin had finished wetting down the earthen floor for our guests, and I'd attempted to decorate the house with a few poinsettias that grew wild. I put them together on a ledge that was built into the house for storage, along with several Hindu leis of marigolds and an assortment of incense and candles. Centered among it all was a picture postcard of Krishna, the Hindu god who is always depicted with a blue face, to finish off our Hindu Nepalese Christmas altar.

Robin and I had some fun in Kathmandu the day before, preparing to make the dinner extra special since everyone would be thinking of home. We decided to buy a gift for each person, limiting it to two dollars. This came easily as there were so many beautiful handmade items that sold for under twenty rupees. We purchased silk scarves for Eve and the other girls, a little bronze statue of Ganesh the elephant god for Thomas, and a Sherpa woolen cap for Clem.

Eve arrived early to help Robin with the cooking, and brought her a picture of the guru for Christmas. They were making a big pot of chicken curry with potatoes and onions, cloves, and fresh chilies. Then the Welsh girls brought what looked like a delicious fruit salad. They hadn't seen the fireplace yet, and marveled at it.

"It's just amazing how you managed to figure it out, and it's artistic too," Harriet said. "With the belly of the water jug sticking out from the mudded rocks, it looks like a potbelly stove. It's lovely to be so warm and toasty on such a cold night. Thank you for inviting us. This is so nice."

They sat down with Eve on the woven mats and watched Robin making the rice in the fireplace.

"How wonderful that they can cook on it too," Harriet said to Eve.

"Yes," Eve said. "Michael is very talented."

I was in shock. Eve had never praised me for anything. Maybe she had a little love for me inside her breast after all.

There was a knock at the door. It was Thomas and Clem.

"Come in. Welcome to our humble abode, and I do mean humble."

"Wow, it's so warm in here," Clem said. "You lucky bustards. Merry Christmas, everyone. *Felice Natalie, tutti.*"

"Merry Christmas," everyone chimed back.

The room was full by then, and they sat down with the girls from Wales.

"Robin, what are you cooking there, my dear?" Clem asked in his cheeky Italian accent.

"Chicken curry and rice," she said. "I hope you like it."

They all began to talk, and as I looked around the room, I caught Robin's eyes. She smiled in that sweet way she had to let me know how proud she was of me, and then she let out that infectious laugh. I'll never forget how happy we all were to be sharing Christmas like a family, like a village, in the shadow of the Monkey Temple, which was what brought us all to the village in the first place.

If anyone had told me that this would be my life, that I'd be living in Shangri-La, surrounded by gentle people and breathtaking mountains, living my life simply in the moment, you'd have had to pinch me. It felt like a dream. Robin and I spent many nights sitting in front of our fire, like we used to sit in front of the fireplace in her little studio apartment in San Francisco, talking about the world.

In the middle of January, Tibetan refugees came down out of the high Himalayas, across the Chinese border, which was only four hours from Kathmandu Valley. They'd traveled the treacherous narrow pathways along the mountain passes to reach freedom, and there were more coming every day. This was the time of year they'd come, when the mountain passes were snowed in and the Chinese were less likely to follow them. I saw a group of maybe twelve, looking exhausted and hungry, arrive in the village carrying nothing but cooking utensils and sleeping rolls. They were magnificent. They reminded me of American Indians.

The leader was a tall man. He wore a blue tunic with brass buttons down one side and a high collar like the Chinese. His hair was long and in two braids that trailed halfway down his back. He wore earrings of turquoise, and around his neck was a large piece of turquoise flanked by two beautiful beads of coral. In the front, he wore an embroidered and woven loincloth and leather leggings, with leather moccasins.

There were women and children with them. As they made their way up the village path, they arrived at the complex of our landlords. There was discussion between the two men, as the women and

Michael Rossum

Tibetan refugees from China, 1972

children sat on their haunches awaiting the outcome. They looked exhausted from their journey, but they were safe now.

The next day, I saw them working for the landlord, rolling wool into twine and the twine into balls. Later that day, the landlord brought the leader of the Tibetans to us and asked if they could sleep under the eaves of our house. Robin and I agreed without hesitation, so that night, we gave them shelter. The leader, Tenzin, was a kind man.

Our time in Kathmandu had taught us one thing—the Tibetans were special people. They were kind and compassionate, and you could see it on the outside as well as on the inside. I hoped that when I left Nepal, I could take that compassion with me and try to live by it.

The Tibetans stayed for two weeks, until all the wool was finished, and then it was time to move on, as the landlord had no more work for them. As we parted, I gave Tenzin one of our wool blankets, and he gave me his necklace of turquoise and coral. I refused it, but he was quite serious. Robin and I shook his hand, and then the group wandered down the path toward the road to Kathmandu.

There were few roads in the mountainous jewel of a country, and that's probably what had kept it so pristine and difficult to conquer over the years. It allowed the world to pass it by while it slept undisturbed, nestled in the Himalayas, untouched by the twentieth century. Robin and I wanted to see Mount Everest, but it was expensive to go to the base camp. Instead, we trekked to Nagarkot, a village above Kathmandu Valley about ten thousand feet high. The trek began in Boudhanath, and then it was all by foot along the trekking paths that connected rural Nepal with the larger towns.

These trekking paths were usually no wider than the width of a man. A few could handle pack animals, but most were too steep even for them. We strapped our sleeping bags to our backpacks and began the climb. At first it was okay, but as we climbed higher and the air became thinner, we began to tire. The Sherpa and Gurkha villagers who were behind us, barefoot and carrying

Michael Rossum

Tibetan refugees spinning wool into balls for our landlords

hundred-pound rice sacks strapped to their heads, passed us. It was embarrassing.

We had to make it to the top of the mountain before the sun went down, or the cold would set in and we'd be finding our way in the dark. As we stopped for a rest, one of the Sherpa tribesmen called us over and pointed to the opposite side of the mountain pass. There in all its magnificence was a wild Nepalese tiger. What a sight.

Winded, we continued the trek, switchbacking back and forth, higher and higher above Kathmandu Valley. What an incredible view. But what we saw when we arrived at the summit was breathtaking, what the Tibetans call the "Roof of the World." The entire Himalayan range was visible for as far as the eye could see in every direction, snowcaps twenty to twenty-nine thousand feet high. As the sun set behind us, it lit up the entire range with a warm glow, and as we looked at the horizon, there was one peak far above the others—Mount Everest.

We stayed one night to be able to see a sunrise over Everest. Again, it was a moment of spirituality when the sunlight hit the top of Everest. It just took your breath away. I'd never forget the Himalayas; it was Shangri-La. We made our way down the mountain and back to the village, switch-backing all the way.

Because of the language barrier, we never exchanged names with the landlord's family. However, we made up names that described his family. For example, his wife was Faye, after Faye Dunaway, because she looked like her. The old grandmother was the Dame, and so on.

Nepalese landlord's wife, Faye, Faye's mother with
Faye's older daughter and children

One day the Dame came down to our house. She was hobbling and leaning on Faye's arm as she made her way to our doorstep.

"What's wrong?" I asked.

They sat on the steps and showed us the Dame's wound. She'd cut herself badly, and she'd tried to heal herself by stuffing the wound with newspaper. There was a black line from the newspaper print going down her leg, and it looked like gangrene might be setting in.

Robin and I brought her in. We boiled some water and tried to clean the wound as best we could. Then we tried to drain it, using hot compresses to draw out the infection. When the wound was fairly clean, we applied an antibiotic cream and bandaged it with clean gauze. She never flinched or expressed discomfort while we attended her. She returned the next day, and we repeated the process again and told her to stand on her leg as little as possible.

By the fourth day, she was healing. To show us thanks, she arrived at our door, still limping, with a vessel of water from the well. She let us know in body language how grateful she was. She set the amphora of water down, leaning it against the wall, then put her hands together and bowed. It warmed our hearts that we were able to make a difference. It was grace showing itself. From that point on, we forged a much closer relationship with the family.

My relationship with Clementino grew warmer and closer too. I'd finally figured out that he was gay. He didn't hide it. I was merely clueless. I believe he knew I was gay, too, but he never let on, and I didn't come out to him. I knew he felt affection for me, but I didn't feel the same way. He was so comfortable with himself. I'd watch him as he held court with all of us and brought us all closer to one another and made us laugh. He was flamboyant in his striped sweater, blue jeans, and Nepalese purse, his curly locks extending out from his Christmas Sherpa hat. And what intense blue eyes. He wasn't handsome, but he made up for any lack of physical appearance with heart.

One day he told me that he and Thomas were heading south, back to India. I guess I was a little surprised and could already feel the loss of his presence. This was a defining moment for me. When

Clementino, to right of Robin, leaving village for India

he and Thomas walked out of the village that day, Clem looked back and waved to us all. I knew then if a man like Clem was okay with himself, then I could be too.

~~~

Robin and I were good together. We loved one another, and I was glad we had that time together in Nepal. It's always hard to say goodbye to someone you cherish, but I knew it was time for me to tell her about my decision to leave. This would be the hardest talk I'd ever have with her. We'd shared so much, and it was because of her that I was becoming the man I was.

We sat down on the steps outside the house, which we often did in the early evenings, looking out on the valley that had been our home for these glorious months.

"Robin, there's something I've been wanting to tell you for so long, but because I love you, I couldn't find a way to say it. I'm gay." I was sure she knew it already, but it was time to tell the truth about it all. I told her about Carmine and our summer romance, when I finally realized I could no longer hide my conflict with the pain that sexually I wasn't being fulfilled.

She looked up at me with those sparkling brown eyes, so full of sadness at the thought, and we both cried. I tried to wipe the tears from her eyes, but it wasn't possible. The tears flowed like the holy River Ganges, whose beginnings start with a trickle and then rush to the delta, where they inundate everything. There was no stopping it.

She clasped her hands over her face. "Mick, somehow I knew this would come to pass. I just thought we could work through it. Now I know there's no hope. We shared so much together. I can't imagine what my life will be like without you there to share our thoughts and ideas and to follow our dreams and make them reality." The tears continued to roll down her cheeks. She spoke in a soft voice. "Were you ever in love with me?"

"Of course I was," I said. "From the beginning, you bewitched me, body and soul."

"Then when did you stop loving me?"

"I've never stopped loving you. I just realized I could no longer deny my feelings toward men, and it was Carmine who made me realize this. What I felt with him was like nothing I'd felt before. It was undeniably ecstatic, and I realized I could never go back to living in two worlds. I had to make a choice. I also realized it wasn't fair for either of us not to have a chance at love, in the true sense, fully. I'm so sorry I've caused you pain, and I don't want to lose your friendship.

"You're my confidante and the truest friend I have, but I must go for both our sakes. Not to be able to see you and share my thoughts with you is just as painful for me as it is for you. You've been a great force of good in my life, and I'll always be grateful. I wouldn't be standing in this earthen dwelling on a cliff below one of the holiest sites in Buddhism, looking out at Kathmandu, a Shangri-La surrounded by the Himalayas, had it not been for you. You are part of me now and always will be. Can you forgive me?"

She said nothing, but looked up at me with her beautiful eyes, wrapped her arms around me, snuggled up against my chest, and hugged me. Finally, she said, "I'll miss you, Mick, more than you know, but I do understand. What more can I say? Where will you go?"

"Back to India, probably Goa. And you?"

"I think I'll stay on here. Eve can share the house with me. That's as far ahead as I can think right now. When will you leave?"

"Tomorrow," I said as the tears rolled down her face. I kissed her, and then we hugged. She was my friend, my confidante, my lover, and finally, my teacher.

That night, we made love upstairs in our little house. In the morning, I left for India. It was hard looking back up at the house. It felt odd waving goodbye to my best friend. Knowing how my world would have been diminished had we not met was all I could hold on to, and there was fear, too, as I walked down the cobblestoned path toward the subcontinent and the unknown.

Chapter Twelve

India—January 1973

I traveled back through the mountain pass that led to India, filled with mixed emotions. I cried, I laughed, I missed Robin and the village I'd come to love. I was a bit frightened starting out on this new journey to find myself. Coming to terms with being gay was huge. At the same time, I felt like a free spirit. Returning to India made me feel like I was one of a million grains of sand, a speck in a sea of humanity that was the subcontinent. How would I manage on my own?

I'd heard about a place called Goa from Roberta, my girlfriend in LA. Small fishing villages on the coast of a former Portuguese colony, white sand beaches with warm water, palm trees, and banana pancakes—that's exactly what I needed, a break from the cold winter of Nepal, a jungle paradise.

I was sitting on the station platform in Delhi when the express train to Bombay arrived, and for the first time on the whole trip, I felt ill. I was feverish, with no explanation—the food maybe. There was the usual chaos, but I'd hired a porter this time to secure a seat on the thirty-six-hour train ride. As the train began to slow down at the platform, I saw my porter toss my backpack through an empty compartment window, and then he threw himself in too. I'd never seen such tenacity.

When I arrived at my seat, he was up in the luggage rack looking down at me, grinning like a Cheshire cat. "Saab," he said, "climb up."

"I can't sit up there," I told him.

"Saab, it is a very long journey," he said pedantically, with the usual swaying of the head. "You will be able to sleep here. Trust me."

My eyes lit up at the thought of sleeping for thirty-six hours. It was so inviting. I threw caution to the wind and climbed up. I laid out my sleeping bag, used my backpack for a pillow, and settled in for the long trip.

As the compartment swelled, I looked across to the other luggage rack and found a young mixed-race Indian man, very light-skinned, with blond hair, blue eyes, and freckles. He was dressed in Western clothes. He said hello, introduced himself, and told me he was traveling all the way from Calcutta to Bombay. I asked him if he was from Calcutta, and he said, "Yes, I'm going to Bombay to go shopping."

"That's an awfully long shopping trip," I said.

"Yes, I guess it is," he said, obviously not wanting to continue the conversation.

"What part of Europe are you from?" I asked, knowing full well he wasn't European.

He described himself as Calcutta-colored, which explained his appearance. It still seemed strange to me that someone would travel all that distance, some thousand miles by train, to go shopping, but I wasn't asking any more questions.

He saw that I was sick, and at several stops, he was kind and brought me tea and samosas from the platform vendors. Later, I woke from one of my fevers to find my luggage-rack mate shooting up heroin. His arm tied off with plastic tubing, he had one end clenched between his jaws. His right hand held the other end. With his left hand, he held the syringe. I looked over at him, and he smiled at me between his clenched jaws. I made no judgment. I felt sorry for him, that's all. I was too weak to do anything but roll over and sleep a while longer.

I looked out at the countryside as we passed through Rajasthan. The land was parched, and there were three-inch cracks in the earth everywhere. It was obvious there was a serious drought in this part of the country. By the time the train pulled into Jaipur, I was still sick. I noticed hundreds of people on the platform. As I looked down, I saw mostly women and children covered in dust and carrying cooking pots. These were the victims of the parched land I'd seen. They were going to Bombay for relief, fleeing the famine and the drought in third-class unreserved, no tickets. They filled the train to capacity, leaving standing room only, and most of the floor space had been taken up. As they sat on their haunches with their belongings, the look of despair on their faces was heartbreaking. This wasn't the India I was expecting. My heart was heavy. The problem was so overwhelming, and there was nothing to do but witness it.

I needed to use the toilet, but as I gazed down upon the mass of people below me, I wasn't sure how I could traverse through them to get to the WC. I finally lowered myself until my feet found space to stand on. As I made my way between the refugees, I found the line for the bathroom. It was long.

In line, an Indian businessman in a three-piece black suit, carrying a black attaché, smiled at me. "What is the purpose of your mission here in India?" he asked.

I looked around at all the misery beneath me. Was this somehow commonplace? I wondered where his humanity was, that such things as this could go on. I was outraged and asked in return, "What is the purpose of *your* mission here in India?"

"Ah, I see you make a joke," he said.

It was no joke, but what I did see was an Indian middle class with a distant moral compass. When I returned to the compartment, I found three Sikhs were sitting in my luggage rack, their legs dangling over the heads of the people seated beneath them. Shocked and feverish, I just stood there dumbfounded. My luggage rack-mate, seeing the situation and my lack of ability to deal with it, jumped down among all the people on the floor, and one by one, he ripped the Sikhs from the luggage rack. They fell into the crowd below, and then he admonished them. They took seats on the floor, and there was silence. Completely blown away, I thanked him and crawled up, lay down, and passed out.

The next thing I heard was the crowd on the floor rumbling as the conductor shouted out, "Bombay! Bombay! Bombay!"

Bombay

Bombay was a fascinating city, full of examples of colonial Indian architecture—Victoria Station, the House of Parliament, and the post office, to mention a few. The Gateway of India was a beautiful structure, like the Arc de Triomphe in Paris, only this arch had steps leading down to the Indian Ocean, as if welcoming all seafarers that pass through it.

I stayed at the Rex Hotel in Colaba, a section near the famous Taj Mahal Hotel. A Victorian hotel with balconies overlooking a tree-lined street, the Rex offered a view of the Indian Ocean. Its claim to fame was that Rudyard Kipling wrote there. Across the street was a lassi shop called Dipti Nivas that sold cold drinks made of yogurt and fresh fruits. It was the hip hangout for Westerners of every kind, but mostly hippies. After climbing the steps from the street, to my amazement, I came upon one whole wall made up of nothing but huge jars filled with every fruit imaginable, including some I'd never seen before, like *chiku*, which is native to India. It was round in shape, brown in color, and tasted like the sweetest pear I'd ever eaten.

The Rex Hotel clientele had changed since Kipling's days. The hotel was full of a mix of mild to unsavory guests. Most travelers were hip people on the road, checking out India. There were the occasional spiritual guests stopping off in Bombay before moving on to an ashram, and a few straight tourists, both European and Indian. But by and large, there were a lot of drug abusers holed up in the city, with access to heroin, morphine, and cocaine.

One day I was on my way out for breakfast when I found two police officers standing outside a room several doors down from me. I knew the occupants. I'd met them in the lobby. They were two Swiss guys who didn't seem at all like abusers—but then, who knows what goes on behind closed doors? As I passed by the room, I could see their bodies. It was gruesome. They had blood coming out of their eyes, ears, and mouths, and their syringes were still in their arms. They'd died instantly from an overdose of cocaine and heroin.

India, I was finding out, had some tragic stories, some of which I'd never forget, and others I had yet to experience. The duality of life, the bliss and the horror, was always present.

Another day, I heard a knock at my door. I opened it, and to my surprise, there was Roberta, the Italian beauty I'd met in Los Angeles through Egidia. Roberta had been in the States illegally and dancing topless on the Sunset Strip to make some cash in order to return to India. She'd invited me to come see her perform at the Classic Cat, and I'd agreed. From the beginning, we had an immediate connection, maybe like two souls who'd met in another life.

Her show was quite unusual for the type of place it was. Her performance echoed her experiences in India. She came out barefoot, wearing Indian harem pants, cymbals on her fingers, and a veil. She danced and exotically cast off her garments while using the veil to leave a little to the imagination. She was beautiful, unlike the other topless girls, who were kind of on the raunchy side. She'd told me she was going to Goa, but I never thought we'd run into one another. Sometimes the world is a small place.

"I'm looking for my friend Ricardo, and I find you instead." She'd wound up on the wrong floor and had rung my door by accident.

I don't think it was an accident, though. I think it was fate.

She threw her arms around me, and we shared a strong embrace. I was feeling lost. I knew no one in India, and this woman showed up to guide me. She gave me a soft place to land after leaving Robin.

I asked her to come in, lit up a chillum of hashish, and we talked. I told her about my journey across the Middle East, which she'd made before and knew well. Then I told her about Kathmandu and Robin and why I left her. I told her I was gay, and I was coming out. She understood well since she'd worked the runways of Milan and knew a lot of gay people in the fashion business. I can't tell you how much weight was taken off my back by having someone to talk to about it. She left to go find Ricardo, and I'd meet her later.

She invited me to go to Sukilachi Street that night, known for the Lucky Card Club, a notorious opium den. It was in the red-light district of Bombay. I'd never done opium, but I was open to at least trying it. I envisioned opium dens as plush rooms with Persian carpets and big pillows, with people lounging and smoking. That was not the Lucky Card Club.

Oh no, this club was a five-flight walk up a rickety staircase. Each floor was filled with prostitutes in colorful saris and too much eye makeup, beckoning to us. The club itself was nothing like I'd imagined. What a dump. It was just a cement floor with people lying on newspaper with their heads on blocks of wood.

When my attendant beckoned me to lie down on a crumpled-up piece of newspaper, I asked, "Could I please have a fresh piece of newspaper?"

"Oh yes, saab," he responded.

My vision of the opium den crumpled like the newspaper I was standing on.

Goa

Some days later, Roberta told me she was leaving on the next boat to Goa. I decided to join her. We met at the boat dock for the overnight journey to Panjim, the capital. She'd connected with her friends Ricardo, Maurizio, and Loretta, and made plans to meet them on the boat. We found them sitting at the back on the top deck. Ricardo lit up a chillum, a cylindrical earthen pipe filled with a mixture of hashish and tobacco with a wet rag wrapped around the bottom to cool the hot smoke as it was inhaled. We hung out on the top deck for most of the trip, talking and enjoying the fresh sea air. There were a few first-class cabins available, but we were all watching our rupees, so we slept third class, on deck in our sleeping bags.

Morning came as we headed into the Panjim River Delta. I saw the coast at either side filled with palm trees and white sand, just as it had been described to me. The boat turned into it and headed right down the middle of the river. There was heavy jungle on both sides for a few miles. Then on the right bank, the steeple towers of Our Lady of the Immaculate Conception rose out of the jungle and a Portuguese city with red terracotta roofs came into view. Portuguese Goa was founded by Saint Xavier, a Franciscan monk in the early 1500s. We could feel the excitement on board, and we couldn't wait to get to the beaches.

We docked and took a rusted-out ferry belching smoke from its diesel engine across the river from the city. It felt like a scene out of *The African Queen* with Humphrey Bogart and Katharine Hepburn. It was so remote. We were heading to the pristine fishing villages to the north, far away from the tourists, both European and Indian, as Goa was a destination for both.

Then we took a bus to the village of Calangute, where we said goodbye to Ricardo, who had a house on the northern beach of Vagator. Roberta, Maurizio, Loretta, and I lucked out and found a house to rent right on the beach. It was a Portuguese-style home with three bedrooms, a big terracotta veranda, and a view of the Indian Ocean. What more could we ask for? It cost us around fifty dollars a month.

We settled into the house by the sea and made it comfortable. Loretta and Maurizio shared one room. They'd lived in London for some time, and they spoke beautiful English. Maurizio had that English dry sense of humor and was delightfully funny, and Loretta was what Italians call "*la donna di la casa*," the lady of the house. She ruled, like the mother of us all. She kept us in line and made sure we kept up with our chores. I shopped and brought in the water from the well, Roberta and Loretta cooked, and Maurizio supervised and entertained us.

Roberta had found an orphan on the streets of Bombay, and being the compassionate woman she was, she took him in and brought him with us to Goa. He helped with the chores, got firewood, started the fire for the oven, and helped Loretta with whatever she needed.

One day the boy, Anchil, and I were at the well along with a group of five or six women waiting with their brass containers to drop them down the well and retrieve the only water available to our part of the village. Getting water was a big deal, because we all depended upon it. As we approached to get in line, they looked up at the boy and began to move away as though he had a disease. I couldn't figure out what was going on, but the boy lowered his eyes as he proceeded to draw the water. Somehow, he knew. They were saying things to him in Hindi, and I could tell by the tone and body language that they were upset and angry. Then it dawned on me: they were insulting him because they somehow knew he was an untouchable. What makes one man a Brahmin and another an untouchable? This was beyond me, but it was obvious the ancient caste system that the Indian government was trying so hard to abolish was alive and well in Goa.

Roberta was my confidante. I'd tell her everything that was going on inside me, and she'd reciprocate. She was a great support in those early days of coming out. She was like the sister I never had. She told me there was nothing to be ashamed about, that this was just my way of being in the world, and it was just different from the majority. "No big deal," she'd say. We'd walk down the beach and she'd spy a man she liked lying on the sand, and we'd comment on his physique and his eyes. Then we'd crack up because we both were attracted to him. She was so lighthearted and kind, and I loved her. In Milan and Europe, the stigma of being gay was nothing like what it was in the States. Remember, this was the early '70s.

Our day-to-day life consisted of swimming in the ocean, walking along the beach in the surf, enjoying long siestas on the veranda after our midday meals, shopping in the market for food (we had no refrigerator), getting water from the well, buying firewood, and in general, having fun in the sun and relaxing. The beach was literally seventy-five yards from the front door. At night, we could hear the pounding waves. Most of the houses were white plaster with verandas and terracotta tile roofs. It reminded me a lot of Mexico. Most of the Portuguese had left after independence in 1948, but there remained a legacy of colonization, culture, tradition, and mixed marriages that persisted despite the influx of Hindus from the north.

Most of the Goans spoke Konkani, while the national language was Hindi. Konkani was a cross between the native language and Portuguese. Their cooking was entirely different from the rest of India. They made Portuguese stews, fried fish, lobster, shellfish of all kinds, shark, French fries, and sumptuous banana pancakes with honey. They had a local liquor called *fenning*, very much like vodka, only stronger and made from cashew nuts. They celebrated saints' days. Even their style of dress was Western. For example, the local fishermen dressed in shorts and button-up short-sleeved shirts, and the women wore everyday A-line dresses with short sleeves. Even though the Goan population was dark-skinned, their features often were European, and many had blue-green eyes. They were a handsome people.

Everywhere we went in Goa, even in the middle of the jungles, we'd find white plaster churches with bell towers and terracotta roofs, churches served by priests. It was such a stark contrast to the India I'd come from, where Hindus dominated the landscape.

The Goans where outgoing and friendly towards the hippies who'd invaded their villages. They saw the advantages economically, and began to rent their homes to us. They'd either move in with relatives or build new houses for themselves. They transformed small houses on the beach into restaurants and were doing brisk business with the tourist trade.

Goa was the only state in India where alcohol was officially legal. The Christians, dominated by the Catholic Church for five hundred years, were a majority, though more and more Hindus from Bombay were migrating there. The gleaming white churches with tall belfries beckoned the faithful on Sundays. The village was a mix of Hindus, Sadhus, Christians, and hippies. Every now and then, some Indian tourists would stray off the beaten path and find their way to Calangute. To our amazement, they walked the beach in their black suits and ties, while still carrying their attaché cases. Arm in arm with their wives, who wore saris, they'd walk into the surf fully clothed. We knew they were conservative, but this was strange to us. We laughed, but they seemed to be having a great time.

The police also walked the beach every so often, almost as if it were an obligation, and then went back to their homes in Panjim at night. Access to the other northern beaches was so difficult that they didn't patrol them except on rare occasions when they hiked around the rocky points along the ocean to get to Anjuna Beach and Vagator. The communities on these beaches were a lot freer than at Calangute. They were considered nude beaches, and most tourists didn't venture past Calangute.

The village at Anjuna was the heart of the hippie enclave in Goa. There was the village, and then just in front of the beach was another whole community of vagabonds. All the displaced Europeans and Americans who had run out of money, were waiting for money, or were trying to save money had built a community out of palm leaves and bamboo. This city of tepees was built right on the beach in front of the fishing village. It was low-cost urban sprawl, if you will.

Some just preferred the indigenous life. We lived in a house in Calangute. Every month, there was a full moon party on the beach. They were spectacular events. We were like tribes of people: Italian, German, French, Argentinian, Peruvian, Spanish, and so on. People came from all over the world to congregate on this beach for two nights during the full moon.

We came to celebrate freedom of mind and body, expressed through music and dance. There was a freedom that existed nowhere else on the planet. We had to travel twelve thousand miles to find it. Where else could you dance for two days completely nude and then end the party by throwing yourself in the Indian Ocean, or watch the sunset from the beach with three to four hundred other people of like mind and never see a civil servant, not even a police officer?

Those of us in Goa from Anjuna Beach north were living an experiment in self-governance. Could a few hundred Europeans from all over the world live together in peace and respect while following an unwritten code of morals without killing one another? Those who robbed became outcasts. No one would take them in, and eventually they left the community on their own. Those who had drug problems were helped with food. Their problem was tolerated, but eventually they left, too, as most of us knew better than to feed their addiction. Heroin addicts were looked down upon as junkies.

Every Sunday, there was a flea market on the beach. People made and traded all kinds of artistic things, from shells found on the beach to gemstones from Rajasthan. The market gave people the opportunity to survive in the village, for years in some cases. Even the local Goans came to sell fruits and vegetables and fresh fish. Most people came and went by the end of winter, but more and more people were staying longer.

Anything could happen on Anjuna Beach. You were free to lose your mind or find it, have sex under the stars or be celibate, walk naked on the beach, smoke hash or not—it was all possible. Musicians with generators played all night. When the sun rose, they stopped. We'd all wander to the beach, sit, and watch another day in paradise begin, high on acid or just freedom.

The Goan fishermen were kind, and used to our Western ways. They'd get up at five in the morning and push their *dhows* into the Indian Ocean, lay their nets, and by 7:00 a.m., they were bringing in the catch, loaded right into the bottom of the boat. When the fishermen landed on the beach, their wives all came down with big straw baskets. They'd fill them with the catch, prop them on their heads, and walk to the market. It was beautiful to see the grace with which they trekked through the sand, balancing the heavy bounty on their heads.

On the full moon in February, all of us got dressed up and went to the full moon party. I put on my finest whites—an Indian *kurta,* or shirt with white cotton pants to match, a mirrored vest from Rajasthan, and my water buffalo sandals. Roberta wore a bikini top and balloon pants and a shawl. Maurizio and Loretta joined us, and we all took off our shoes and walked down the beach. The moon was already high, casting a white light on the ocean that glimmered as the waves rolled in and broke upon the sandy shore. We felt its warmth in the sand between our feet. Oh, glorious Goa!

We laughed and talked about how lucky we were to be in this paradise so far from home, where it was still winter and cold. We made our way to the point between Calangute and Anjuna Beach, where we waded across the Vaga River, and then climbed the rocky path along the point, past some fragrant cashew trees in bloom. All the while, the moon lit the way.

When we finally rounded the point, there was Anjuna, a half-moon-shaped beach. The sand glowed white in the light of the moon, and the palm trees swayed in the soft breeze. People already were gathering, and the music had begun. We danced all night to the music, melodious and seductive, and in the background, we could hear the surf pounding the beach. In the warm water, nude swimmers popped their heads up and down to the rhythm of the sea.

Small groups of people gathered in circles, passing chillums full of hashish. *"Boom Shiva Shankar"* rang out from the groups. "Hail, Shiva." They danced with their arms in the air as though praying to God. Smoking the chillum was like a rite of passage. We were free spirits. Anything was possible. We were separated by language, yet freedom has no language barrier.

We mixed from one group to another with a smile or a hug. *"Oui, si, ja,* yes," we cried out. "We are one."

The left side of our limbic brains was engaged, and there were no hard edges that defined the boundaries of our nations, nor our languages. The universe was ours.

When the first light of dawn came down through the palms, the music stopped. People gathered on the beach to watch the sunrise. Most sat in silence, in pure awareness of another day in paradise. We were children of illusion. It was a new day, and we were reborn too.

As the sun rose higher, people began to disrobe. Soon, most of us were swimming in the Indian Ocean. It was our baptism. Our sins washed from our hot, sweaty bodies, we were cleansed by the salt water. Some Indian women came down with fresh fruit, which we all took and broke our fast. Then little by little, the beach cleared, except for a few folks who lay out their *lungis* (Indian loincloths) and fell asleep in the warmth of the sun.

Roberta, Maurizio, Loretta, and I all made our way back to Calangute. We were full of joy, expansive. Our bare feet on the sandy earth reminded us of our connection to it. When we crossed the river, the fishermen were just back with a catch. There were dhows all down the beach, their crews pushing them onto the sand, the women already waiting with their baskets.

"Namaste," we cried as we walked past.

"Namaste," they shouted back as the crew threw their precious cargo from within the bowels of the boat: grouper, bass, shark, and dolphin.

The Goan world was precious and sweet. It was a simple life. The people lived off the land. Their families and their community thrived when they worked together to support one another. This was truly a communal life they lived.

We found a little restaurant that had just begun serving. Exhausted, we sat down.

"What will you have?" the waiter asked.

"Banana pancakes with honey, please," we cried in unison, then broke into laughter as we knew we were all on the same page. Ah! This was Goa.

Vagabond

When we arrived home, we were shocked to find we'd been robbed. The locked door had been broken open. Everything was gone—our clothes, cameras, money, jewelry, even our sleeping bags. That only wedding rings and religious objects remained gave the thieves away. Roberta put it together that the thieves weren't local Goans, but Europeans, in particular, Italians. She said Italians don't steal wedding rings and religious objects, as they're superstitious.

This narrowed it down to an Italian guy by the name of Lucho, whose romantic advances Roberta had refused. When we informed the police of our suspicions, they went to his house, only to find he'd left that morning for Bombay.

We were screwed. With no money to pay the rent, and it being the first of March, we had to vacate the house that day. We were in shock. Loretta and Maurizio returned to Bombay, as did Roberta and her French boyfriend. But I had nothing, and nowhere to go.

I was a vagabond, like the French heroin addicts I'd seen in the market begging for money. "Oh, *baba*, have you one rupee for me? I am cold and have no blanket."

I swore that wasn't going to be me, but I didn't know what to do, and I was in shock. I was dressed in my white pants and sandals and a Rajasthan vest—everything I owned. I'd been reduced to the life of the poorest Indian on the subcontinent, but with no survival skills. Nothing in my existence to that point had prepared me for what I was about to experience.

I sat on the beach in a yoga half-lotus position and meditated on my well-being for most of the day, then fell asleep in the sand. I woke before dawn, hungry and full of sand.

The locals knew of the robbery. It must have been five in the morning when one of the fishermen who'd lived behind our house tapped me on the shoulder. I recognized him. We'd always given one another good energy.

"Saab, can you help us push the boat into the water?" he asked.

I brushed myself off and helped the other four men push the boat into the surf. I didn't realize what a chore it was to move something that heavy off the sand. It needed all our combined strength.

Then he asked me, "Do you want to help us fish?"

"Yes, gladly," I said, but I had no idea what I was getting into. As we pushed off, the men helped me climb aboard.

The boat was about twenty feet long. Between the planks was a thick tar to keep the water out, but the bottom was still wet and smelled of fish. We stood on the netting, which kept our feet dry until we were out far enough to let the netting out for the catch. The boat was steered in a circular pattern, as we threw the net overboard with a buoy. When we'd made a complete circle and caught the light buoy from the beginning of the net, we began to pull the net in, catching any fish in it as the circle became tighter and tighter. Suddenly, I could feel the tug on the net and see them flipping madly as they tried to escape the nets: big snapper, bass, and groupers. We hauled them into the boat until they filled the bottom. We were stepping on live fish. It was a horrible experience, most unpleasant.

As I first slipped and slid all over them, I fell and ended up lying on top of them. The men had a good laugh at my expense, and of course, I had to join in. What an experience.

We got to the shore, and the women already were on the beach with their baskets, waiting for us. We all jumped into the surf and began pushing the boat onto the beach. With each wave, we got a little closer, until we were on dry land. The men smiled at me with approval, and then we got back in and began tossing the fish onto the beach. The women collected them and filled their baskets. When a woman's basket was full, she left for the market to sell the fish.

In return for my labor, Sebastian, the captain of the fishermen, gave me five large bass.

"For me?"

"Yes, you come tomorrow, okay?"

"Yes, I come tomorrow," I replied, and thanked him. As fate would have it, I'd become a fisherman.

I walked to the market. I knew most of the vendors, but now I was selling to them. I traded my fish for a knife, a woven mat to sleep on, a blanket, bananas, a papaya, and a candle. I still had one fish for dinner. Wow! Maybe I'd survive. I couldn't sleep on the beach in Calangute because of the police, so I headed with my bounty for Anjuna. Being robbed may have been the single most sobering moment of my life. I know now it was the freest I've ever been.

I found refuge in Anjuna. I laid my mat down just outside the tepee village, lit a fire on the beach, and roasted my fish while I ate a banana. The sun was setting, the moon was rising, and life was good. I really couldn't believe my situation. I pondered it, yet I wasn't frightened.

While I was cooking, a man I'd seen from time to time who lived on the beach approached my fire. In its glow, I recognized him, even though we'd never spoken.

"Hello," he said. "I am Umberto."

"My name is Michael. Where are you from?"

"South America. Uruguay."

I told him I spoke Spanish, and his eyes widened.

"*Es la verdad?*" he asked. "Is this true?"

"*Si, es cierto*, I said. "Yes, certainly."

I was surprised at how much we had in common. We had similar views on politics and spirituality, which we discussed at length. We were both from the Americas, the New World. We were free from ties to the kings and queens of Europe, and we were revolutionary in thought. I shared my fish with him. Then he broke out his chillum and some hashish, and we had a smoke. He told me he was waiting for money from home and that he'd help me make a tepee the following day.

"I have no money to pay you."

"*No es necesario. Somos hermanos*," he said. "It's not necessary. We are brothers." He explained that I was camped on the edge of the Spanish-speaking portion of the village. "We are all from Spain, Peru, Uruguay, Columbia, Argentina, and now the USA."

I didn't realize that even this micro village had sections. There were the Italians, the French, the Germans, the Swiss, and a smattering of Scandinavians as well, and now, the lone *Americano*.

Umberto came the next day as he promised, with several large pieces of bamboo, hemp, and six or seven woven palm leaves. He drove the bamboo poles into the sand with a hammer and anchored them with stakes. Then he tied them all together at the top with hemp. With the hemp, he attached the woven palm leaves to the bamboo structure. He added a flap of bamboo over the doorway, and voilà, I had a dwelling fit for Robinson Crusoe.

The tepee was built well. It could withstand the rain and the wind, should I be there that long. I laid the mats down inside. There was enough room to seat four comfortably and sleep two, just in case I had guests, which as it turned out, I did.

Aside from Umberto, a handsome young Moroccan man came to visit me one night. He spoke French, which I didn't. He knocked and came inside. He knew I was gay, but I didn't have a clue what his persuasion was. All I knew was that he was gorgeous, swarthy with blue eyes, long eyelashes, and full lips.

"*Voulez-vous coucher avec moi?*" he asked.

I had no idea what he meant. "I don't understand," I said. "Are you hungry?" He looked frustrated and left. I couldn't figure out what I'd said wrong.

It was days later that I spoke to Umberto, who was becoming my mentor. He was wise in the ways of the world, whereas I felt like a fledgling chick. I told Umberto that I felt alone because I was gay. There was no one for me romantically.

"Didn't you meet the Moroccan boy?" he asked in Spanish.

I nodded and told him what the man had said.

Umberto laughed. When he translated, I felt like a dunce. The Moroccan had asked if I'd wanted to go to bed with him, and I'd offered him something to eat. Finally, a chance at love, and I'd blown it. We eventually connected days before he returned to Morocco, and that night was one of the sweetest I spent in Goa—not in a five-star hotel but under the roof of my tepee.

I was considered part of the Spanish enclave on the beach. Few Europeans at that time spoke fluent English, so it was easier for me to blend in with them. A Peruvian couple living in the tepee next to me, Maria and Eduardo, were expecting their first baby in a month. I used to sit with her while she made beaded jewelry to sell in the Anjuna and Mapusa flea markets. Mapusa was the closest large town to all the beach communities. You were going far if you were going there. Panjim, on the other hand, took all day to reach. Maria told me about Lima and the Inca and Machu Pichu. I was fascinated. She made me a necklace of little conch and colored beads, which I still have to this day. She was courageous, and she believed in the freedom of the communal life we were experimenting with in Anjuna, as we all did.

Maria and Eduardo's story would be one of the saddest memories I'd take back from India. To this day, there's heaviness in my heart when I think of them. When the baby was due, Maria gave birth in their tepee. The proud parents came out holding the new infant. The whole village celebrated the birth. They played music and sang late into the night. What a beautiful day it was. We were celebrating a new member of our tribe.

Then that night, there were complications. Maria didn't have any breast milk, so they gave the baby goat's milk. Each day when I returned from Calangute from fishing with the fishermen, he was worse. On the third day, I heard wailing, and I knew the child was dead.

On the fourth day, Maria and Eduardo emerged from the tepee, their faces filled with grief, the infant wrapped in white cloth. The whole village took part in the cremation of their little boy. As the funeral pyre was lit and the smoke rose to the heavens, the gods cried. There wasn't a dry eye among us either.

It was obvious after a week in my teepee that I'd have to get word to my parents that I needed help. I borrowed a couple of rupees from Umberto for the bus ride to Panjim and back, but I had no money for a telegram. A kind couple from Luxembourg heard my story, and it touched them enough to give me three dollars to pay for it.

The telegram read: *Dear Mom and Dad stop I've been robbed stop Please send money to the Bank of Baroda Panjim Goa as soon as possible stop Michael*

I felt assured that in a few days the money would be wired, and I could leave Goa.

I wrote the couple from Luxemburg much later when everyone had returned from India, and they sent the most beautiful letter in response to my gratitude. I've held on to it all these years. If it hadn't been for their kindness, I might still be in India.

I was getting to know everyone in the village now, especially the Italians. Because of Roberta, I picked up a little Italian, but not enough. Then I met Danillo Fumagali and Maurizio Sarno. Danillo understood Spanish. We hit it off, and soon he was translating what I said to Maurizio. The three of us forged a wonderful relationship. After a while, I started to speak in a mixture of Spanish and Italian and then in Italian. Danillo was a real character, outrageous. I think he was gay and in the closet. Maurizio was warm, with a great sense of humor.

I met all kinds of crazy people. Bepe and Roberta were the king and queen of the Italian enclave, and they had a trained monkey. They used to hold court in a cabana on the beach and throw intimate parties. They were from Rome. They had money and servants and lived in one of the village houses behind the tepee town.

Then there was Rosa, who had a tattooed yin and yang symbol in the middle of her forehead. She had periodic blowups in which she upset many people, but they were tolerated. I also saw a kind side to her. She could be generous, but she was unpredictable.

Egidia was there, too, but I didn't see her much. She lived in Vagator, north of Anjuna. She invited me to her house once for lunch, but other than that, she couldn't offer me food, lodging, money, or help of any kind. I thought we were close friends and that she'd help me out, but she was coming from her own self-preservation and survival. I felt disappointed and abandoned, but I was surviving, and my friends in the village were supportive. I also started some friendships with the French, and so my vocabulary increased. I could at least be cordial. They were the most difficult group to get to know.

Four or five more days passed and I again made the all-day journey into Panjim to the Bank of Baroda. First I took the bus from Calangute to the river, then the ferry across it, then another bus to the bank. Mr. Gupta at the bank was genial and understanding, but said no check had arrived. I was disappointed, but I still felt that help was close at hand. I returned to Anjuna.

Another week passed with still no response. Then a letter arrived at the main post office addressed to Poste Restante, or General Delivery: *Got your telegram. Money has been sent to the bank.*

I returned a week later to still no check. I sent letters home saying: *Have not received the check yet.*

Two more weeks passed, then two more. By then, I was checking the bank once a month. The bank manager had tired of telling me, "I'm sorry, sir. There is no check for you today."

Could it be that I might not be leaving India anytime soon? Three months had passed since my telegram. I was going to need an act of God to get out of there.

One day I felt excruciating pain upon urination. *Oh no,* I thought, *I've got to get to a doctor.* I made the journey into Panjim to a clinic I was told helped the poor, and thought I'd check on the bank as well. The clinic was run by a church. When I entered the courtyard, I saw two lines, one for men and the other for women. Both were long. It looked like it would be an all-day affair.

People in Asia in general don't have a concept of personal space. They stand in a queue butt to butt. In India, everyone is in survival mode, so when a woman got in front of me with her male child, the men in the line started to push her around. I tried to intervene, but the cultural powers in India run deep, and they were much stronger than my protest. She was forced to the end of the line. Two hours later, I saw the doctor. He gave me a shot of penicillin but only enough for one day. I had to return for three more shots. The last one finally did the trick. Each day, I checked the bank. No money.

On the beach, I wore nothing but a loincloth. This was an accepted mode of dress in Goa in most beach communities. In town, Panjim, I had to dress in the only pair of pants I owned, my Rajasthani vest, and my buffalo sandals. My Afghan Baluchi rug bag served as a carryall. It was large enough to carry a change of clothing and served as a shopping bag for carrying fruit and any sundry goods back to my tepee.

I arrived at the bank after my last treatment at the clinic. As I approached, I saw the manager on the phone.

He looked up at me, and I heard him say, "Yes, madam, I think your son is here."

What were the chances? But there you have it.

He handed me the phone.

"Mom?"

When she heard my voice, she began to cry. When she composed herself, she told me she'd sent fifty dollars in a birthday card to Poste Restante in care of the main post office in Bombay. She said she and my dad also had wired five hundred dollars to the Bank of America. "Can you get to Bombay?" my mother asked.

Excited, I told her I could.

"We've sent check after check, but they never got to the bank from Bombay," she said. "When we investigated, we were told they were stolen by postal employees."

My mom's voice was comforting. After seven months on the road, I realized how much I missed my parents. I returned to Anjuna, smiling the whole way, almost giddy at the wonderful news.

I wouldn't understand the full depth of my experience in Goa until I returned home: eating out of abalone shells, cooking meals over an open fire, working with the fishermen, trading in the market; the beach, the full moon parties, the people of my village; Umberto, my wonderful teacher, who taught me I could survive by my wits and who gave me so much confidence.

It was over. An experiment in freedom was over, one I never could have planned or imagined.

I told Umberto first. He was happy for me, but I knew we'd miss one another. He gave me a hug, and then we had a smoke to celebrate. When I told Danillo and Maurizio, I asked if they could loan me five or six dollars to take the ferry to Bombay.

"Yes, yes," they said, to my surprise. "We are coming with you." I was delighted.

One by one, I told my friends in the village that I was leaving. Eduardo and Maria gave me a big hug. There were tears in Maria's eyes and mine, too, tears for their little boy and all the incredible days in her tepee listening to her stories. As the wind blew the palms in front of our little village and the waves we'd gotten so used to crashed on the beach fifty yards from us in the background, we talked. As the sun set on this speckled half-moon beach of paradise we called Anjuna, we cried. I said goodbye to the Italians, Bepe and Roberta. They gave me their address in Rome. I didn't see Egidia again until I returned to San Francisco. I was invited to the French stronghold as well. We smoked a chillum, and said our goodbyes.

"Bon voyage, bon chance!" they cried in unison as I left. "Have a great trip and good luck." I'd learned so much from them. I don't think they realized how much. I could converse comfortably in French now.

Finally, I packed my few belongings in my rug bag—my knife, the beads Maria had given me, and even the coconut I used as a cup—to remind me of where I'd been. I folded my loincloth and took it too. Then I opened the flap to my tepee, took one last look at what had been my home for four months, and abandoned it.

Maurizio and Danillo walked up the beach, each carrying a backpack. The three of us continued on in silence. We knew what we were leaving behind, but it was time to go. We began to climb the point, and all three of us took one last look at the village and waved to Umberto.

I could borrow from them, but I'd have to repay it when we got to Italy.

I went down to Chicken Street and passed a small shop selling handmade boots. I stared at them while the wheels in my mind spun. I had a crazy idea. I'd make a pair of boots with hash in them. I'd just walk across the Middle East and Europe. When I got back to Brescia where the boys lived in Italy, I'd sell the hashish to pay them back. Then I'd have enough money to get back to San Francisco.

When I entered the store, I was scared. *How do you go about asking a shopkeeper if he'll make a pair of boots with a kilo of hash inside them?* I thought. *Nah, this is Afghanistan. They'll make anything for you. But what if after he makes them for you, he turns you in to the police for a kickback?* Hell, I really needed to get out of Afghanistan, and I didn't have many other options.

"*As-Salaam-Alaikum, habibi,*" I said. "Hello, my friend." I waited until the shop was empty, then leaned over the counter and in a soft voice asked if he could make me a pair of boots with hashish in them.

"Oh yes," he replied with a reassuring nod, as if it were a common request.

Well, now, that wasn't so bad, I thought. *No going back now.* The kilo cost me fifty dollars. I had to go through with it. "So how much will it cost, my friend?" I asked.

"Twenty-five dollars."

"Twenty." We shook hands as we locked eyes. It was a deal.

"Tomorrow you bring the hashish, and I will measure you for the boots, yes?"

"How will you design them?" I asked.

"We will put the majority in the sole of the boot, and the rest will be in the heels and inside the lining."

"Have you done this before?"

"Oh, many times."

I guessed it wasn't so novel an idea after all.

He told me that they'd squeak a little.

Chapter Thirteen

Bombay

The ferry pulled up to the dock in Bombay. After Goa, everything seemed to move quickly—life, people, buses, oxen, and taxis all sharing the same flow. Maurizio, Danillo, and I were excited. I told them I'd treat them to a real dinner in a restaurant if the money was still in the birthday card as my mother had said. Postal employees had a habit of holding letters and cards from the States that might contain money up to the light, but I was hopeful.

I asked for mail under my name. An officious Indian employee sifted through all the *R*s, reading the names out loud. Miraculously, she produced a large envelope for me. I tore it open. Fifty dollars. For the first time in months, I was rich. I immediately went out and bought new whites and a pair of jeans for the journey back. Then I took the boys out for dinner at a Persian restaurant, and we ate like kings.

I got my money from the Bank of America the next day, and the boys got money from their bank too. My parents didn't have much money at the time, so $500 was all they could spare. I wasn't sure it would be enough to get me back to Rome. My Pan Am flight was still good for a year, and I had a few months left.

We left Bombay for Amritsar, then the border crossing with Pakistan to Lahore, the train to Rawalpindi, and the bus to Peshawar. We were making good time.

It was cool in April when we reached Afghanistan, and I was thankful I still had my pea coat. By the time we reached Kabul, I knew I didn't have enough money to get to Europe. The boys said

"Squeak a little? Oh great."

He explained that it would be one layer of hash and one of leather, with nothing to glue them together but the sewing. "No worry," he said. "You come tomorrow. I make them for you, no problem."

Every time I heard the words "no problem," there was a problem. They said it all over Asia as a mantra, but it usually came at a price. There could absolutely be *no problems* or I'd end up in an Afghan jail, or worse, a Turkish one. I said I'd meet him at the shop at twelve. He nodded, and I left with mixed emotions.

I was paranoid about Turkey and President Nixon. Nixon paid the Turkish government cold hard cash, and lots of it, to stop the illegal trafficking of hashish into the United States and Europe. The maximum sentence for a gram of hashish in Turkey was thirty years. Anything over that was a life sentence. But I kept telling myself it was that or languish in Afghanistan with no money. There weren't great prospects for calling my parents and asking for more. I'd just have to pray that I'd get through on my own intuition. My heart said yes, but my mind said no.

The next day I returned to the shop with the hash rolled up in newspaper, still a little wary of Farouk's proposition but filled with promise that he was solid and I'd be successful. I opened the door and walked in to find him in deep conversation with an army officer. *Oh shit,* I thought. *I'm going to get arrested right now.* I looked around for an escape. There was only one way out, the way I'd come in. *What am I doing here? I should run. I knew this was a bad idea. What a shmuck I am. I'm going to wind up in jail.* I had to find out for sure if it was safe.

I loitered, trying to avoid the two of them until the army officer left. He tipped his hat to me on the way out like he knew everything.

I approached Farouk. "Who was that guy?" I asked, trying hard to not show my paranoia. "He's in the army, isn't he? Is he the police?"

"No, no, no. He is my brother," he said reassuringly. "He hates the king too. You are not in any danger."

"Oh, what a relief," I said. I could barely breathe, and my face was flushed as the adrenalin sped through my body. I'd been sure I was headed for an Afghan jail. At that moment, I realized how serious the situation could be. I told no one, not even Danillo or Maurizio, what I was up to.

When the boots were ready, I stopped by the shop. Farouk was excited. He wanted to show me what a great job he'd done. I have to say, he was an artist. The boots were spotless. Handmade to fit.

"Try them on," he said.

I shed my buffalo-skin sandals from India for a pair of boots filled with black gold. I took a couple of turns in them.

Squeak, squeak, squeak.

They fit perfectly. I'd have to age them with a little mud, but there was plenty of that around. They'd have to look worn, or the Iranians might take notice.

We left Kabul and pressed back to Kandahar and Herat. We were enjoying Afghanistan immensely the second time around because we knew what to expect. It was all familiar. We sat back and watched the beautiful scenery pass by—villages, towns, cities, and the natural splendor of the snowcapped mountains, rivers, and gorges. We noted the camel caravans and the horse carts. Men in turbans slipped by us, smoking their hookah pipes in the shops. Women in blue burqas bought fresh vegetables in the market, somehow carrying on their lives with a view to the world through the mesh opening of their veils. I'd never return to this place—a country at the crossroads, caught between two worlds—fantastic and untamed, wild, and beautiful.

We boarded the bus, filled mostly with Europeans, and left all of that behind. I overheard conversations all around us. "I've got mine in my hat," one guy said. "Mine's in my vest," another said. Still another had sewn his into his belt. Everyone was smuggling hashish in their clothing. I kept quiet and didn't engage in conversation. It was dangerous, and I was frightened by the number of smugglers. With that many, someone surely would be discovered.

We passed through the border into Iran, and went through Mashhad, Tehran, and Tabriz. Finally, the driver told us we were nearing the Turkish border and to have our passports ready. I stood up to see the border. There were three buses ahead of us, and to the left was a compound enclosed by a wire fence. Then I saw them, the immigration officers. They had dogs on leashes. My heart began pounding.

Suddenly, hashish was flying out the windows left and right. I watched it litter the ground. Children ran after the pieces that had been tossed, collecting them, probably for resale.

I felt like a wild animal caught in a trap. Terror was all I could feel. It ran through every inch of my body. If I threw the boots out the window, they'd just find them and figure out it was me, the guy with no shoes. It was hopeless. I sat frozen with fear. I could see Maurizio's mouth moving, talking to me. His face was animated, his hands moving, but I heard no sound. In fact, as I looked around the bus, there was a lot of movement, but everything had become silent.

I watched as the first bus passed the checkpoint and drove out of sight. Then the second bus moved up, the dogs running around the perimeter, sniffing.

Fear still kept me from hearing anything but my own terrified voice inside my head. *You thought you were so smart. You thought you could beat the odds.*

Then, as if the trumpets sounded and the angels descended, I heard a whistle blow. I saw immigration officers taking the dogs into the wire-fenced compound to feed them. The angels were singing, "Hallelujah, hallelujah, hal-le-lu-jah."

Istanbul

After the border crossing, I told the boys what I had in my boots. They were shocked, but I was glad to unload. They knew what a close call I'd had. From then on, we kept extra near to one another. We still had a way to go to get to Italy.

When our train finally arrived on the Asian side of Istanbul, we boarded a ferry for the ride across the Bosporus. I'll never forget that ride. It was early in the morning, and the fog hovered over the whole area, a thick, white, watery mist that moved as we passed through it. Then, as if out of nowhere, the spires of the mosques of Istanbul rose out of the fog, and I knew it was over. It's like when the dream ends and everything becomes clear. I realized I'd had the journey of a lifetime and that I'd never felt such freedom before. Now that I was leaving, it became clear that perhaps I'd never know that freedom again.

Bulgaria

The boys and I shared a cabin on the train back to Italy. We were all asleep in a darkened cabin when suddenly the door was thrust open.

"Passport control!"

The light was switched on, and we awoke to harsh voices. There they were, two brown-shirted thugs of Bulgarian immigration. They were unbelievably rude. They tore passports from peoples' hands and returned them in the same manner.

The tall, dark-haired one looked at me distrustfully. "*Amerikanski.*"

"Yes," I said.

"How long will you be in Bulgaria?"

"One day."

No one actually got off in Bulgaria.

He stamped my passport. Then a stool was produced, and the other officer climbed up, took a screwdriver, and unfastened the panel in the ceiling, looking for escapees.

When we arrived in Sophia, the capital, there was hardly anyone on the platform. The people looked so dark. It was as though a cloud hung over them. It was in stark contrast to where I'd just come from. I'd had a case of melancholy ever since the ferry ride across the Bosporus.

Chapter Fourteen

Brescia, Italy

When the train pulled into Brescia, Maurizio and Danillo were excited to be home. But as I stepped off the train, I felt a pang of homesickness at their joy. My home was still so far away. I'd never been away for so long. Maurizio said he wanted to introduce me to his girlfriend and take me around to meet all his friends, but since he still lived with his mother, I went to stay with Danillo's family.

Danillo, for all his openness and Bohemian ways, changed when we got home, and it came as a bit of a shock. He introduced me to his mother, a homemaker, and his father, who owned Deli Fumagali downstairs under the apartment. It bore the family name and sold prosciutto, salami, ham, and cheese of all sorts. Everybody in this part of Brescia knew him. The family was quite well-off by Italian standards. Danillo had an older brother and a younger sister, who also lived with their parents and helped out in the deli while going to school.

The apartment above the deli was beautiful. It was really a house. The floors were terra-cotta, so brightly polished that you could see your face in the reflection. There was another floor above us where the family lived, but Danillo's room was on the second level, along with the living room, dining room, bathroom, and large kitchen. In the back of the house, there were big shuttered windows that opened onto a beautiful garden courtyard. I couldn't believe the opulence, such a contrast to my life in Goa.

As soon as we entered the house, Danillo motioned me to take off my boots and use the slippers that were lying by the front door. I thought that a bit strange, but this was Italy, not the States. I had to keep reminding myself of where we'd just come from. I didn't want to lose the bliss.

I shared Danillo's bedroom. He quickly threw his clothes onto the big terrazzo floor and motioned for me to do the same. Ah, a shower. What a luxury.

Danillo was very tall—as tall as me, over six feet. He had a slender build like a swimmer, with broad shoulders. I'd seen him nude before in Goa and thought nothing of it. I wasn't attracted to him, especially when he wore his clogs from Europe and a loincloth, which was his attire in Goa. But now he had a look on his face, and I couldn't quite read him. He got dressed quickly in a nice pair of slacks and a crisp starched white shirt. Then he slipped on a fine pair of Italian loafers with no socks, and he was finished.

I stared at him in disbelief. The water still dripping off my back, I held the towel to my face.

"Come on," he said. "We'll be late for dinner."

Oh yes, dinner, I thought as I threw on the same old dirty pair of patched jeans and a fresh T-shirt. I slicked my hair back in an effort to look presentable.

Dinner was served. First came a bowl of minestrone soup, followed by a plate of ravioli, followed by veal Milanese, a salad, and finally a cheese plate from the deli downstairs and fruit. I thought I would explode. My stomach wasn't used to all these rich dishes or to the quantity.

"*Andiamo per un giro*, Michael," he said. "Michael, let's go for a spin."

I gulped down my last piece of soft mozzarella.

"Go get your coat," he said. "It's cold."

By now I was pretty much communicating in Italian. When I couldn't find the appropriate word in Italian, I'd just throw in the Spanish one and everyone seemed to understand.

I got my coat and met him at the front door. I held my breath when I saw him. He was dressed in a full-length maxi coat to the floor. He looked like a Milanese fashion model. I couldn't believe the transformation. Was this the same guy I'd spent the past four months with?

We went downstairs and jumped in his red Alfa Romeo.

"*Andiamo per un cappuccino alle Castello,*" he said. "Let's go for a cappuccino at the castle."

"What castle?" I asked.

"Il Castello di Brescia," he responded.

Of course, I thought. *We're in Italy.* "Brescia has a castle?"

Brescia was an ancient Roman city. As we raced past what little was left of the ruins, we climbed a hill, and there at the top was a most enchanting castle. Danillo jumped out of the car and took me inside. From the coffee shop, we could see the whole town laid out at the base of the Alps. It was quite amazing, the terra-cotta roofs of the city contrasted against the green mountains.

After our coffees, we went to meet up with Maurizio in the center of town near the main piazza. It was here that I finally met the mysterious Maria Gracie, Maurizio's girlfriend that he had told me so much about. She was a potter who made beautiful pots and bowls, a real artist. We immediately hit it off. I was introduced to everyone: Queste e Giancarlo, Roberto, Paula, Daniela, Rosa, Carlos, and finally, Il Conde di Brescia, "the Count of Brescia," Sebastian.

"Wow! What a group of friends you have, and royalty as well," I said in Italian.

They all started to wail with laughter, including the count. Maurizio took me aside and whispered, "Everyone wants to buy hashish. Can you open your boot?"

"Well, not here," I said, "but tomorrow."

"We'll go tomorrow to the home of Sebastian, the Count of Brescia, and we'll party," he said excitedly. "He has a rock band and plays lead guitar. His parents are in the South of France, so the villa will be ours."

I brought the hash to the party and started weighing grams out like there was no tomorrow. Afghan hashish is the finest in the world, and that's because the pollen from the flowers is kneaded by hand until the oils break down and the substance becomes that much stronger.

As the count and his band rocked on, the palace filled with thick, heavy smoke, and I began to fill my pockets with Italian lira. Later during the week, I would go to the plaza and Maurizio would introduce me to his friends as we sat in the cafés and I sold the remainder of the hash in the sole of my boot to all the boys in Brescia. As the weeks passed by, I was well-known as the American with the Afghan.

The night before we went to the count's party, back in our bedroom, Danillo had helped me cut the boot open at the toe. And there it was, black as night, just as Farouk had promised. Nothing Farouk had done gave me pause to doubt his sincerity. I cut out a piece, and we weighed it.

"Twenty grams," Danillo said, patting me on the back. Then we got ready for bed. He undressed and climbed in on one side and I on the other. I wore my T-shirt. He wore nothing. Then his hand slid over my belly.

I stopped him at my chest. "*Cosa suchese?*" I said. "What are you doing?"

Before long, we were having incredibly passionate sex. Neither of us had had it in months. But then it dawned on me. This wasn't casual sex with a straight man. Danillo was gay, and in total denial.

We woke to a knock at the door. I started to jump out of the bed in case it was his mother, but he held me back.

"*Si, si, noi andiamo,*" he said. "Yes, yes, we are coming."

We showered, slipped on our clothes, and joined the rest of the family for breakfast. As I glanced up over my eggs cooked in red bell peppers, Danillo was silent. I realized that all Italian men were expected to marry women and have a family, whether they were straight or gay, so it came as no surprise that everything was hush-hush.

I didn't even tell Maurizio about the affair, so as not to damage their friendship. It seemed that nobody knew, including his family, unless all of them, including Maurizio, were in denial. Danillo was the big cheese in Brescia. I wondered where the man I'd met in Goa had gone. *What a dandy*, I thought to myself.

Danillo didn't work. We rode around in his Alfa Romeo from the castle to the piazza, drinking cappuccino and buying clothes. I finally got out of my dungarees and bought some new slacks suitable to wear back to the States.

After two weeks in Brescia, I'd paid the boys back for their help in getting me to Italy and sold enough hash to get me back home. I told Maurizio that I was going to Rome to catch my flight.

He said, "Yes, yes, but Maria Gracie and I we want to show you Umbria. You can't leave Italy without seeing Tuscany and Umbria. Then we will take you to Rome."

"Wow, that sounds super," I said. I could feel his warmth and Maria's. They were so right for each other. I couldn't think of a better way of saying goodbye.

The last stretch of the journey would be an adventure. The three of us would be heading off to Florence. They drove by Danillo's to pick me up. I'd said my goodbyes to all their friends I'd gotten to know over the length of my stay in Brescia at a party the night before. I gave Danillo a hug and told him, "If you ever get to the States, you must come and stay with me in San Francisco. Promise?"

He was more emotional than I expected. "*Si, certo*," he said, his eyes watering. "Yes, of course."

I guess I was emotional, too, as we both gave each other another hug. Then we drove off.

Maurizio took me to Lago di Garda before we made our way to Florence. The lake was fantastic, encircled by the Alps. "Majestic" comes to mind when I think of it. The ride around it was sublime. It was late May, and spring flowers littered the road. The villas along the lake were utterly beautiful, with docks leading out to the water, white birds overhead, and boats sailing. It was like a Monet painting. I was glad the two of them had asked me along.

When Maurizio said something I didn't understand in Italian, Maria explained in English. "Maurizio says, 'Now you will see the real Italy.'"

We all laughed as we glided out of the lake area onto the autostrada, headed for Florence. I'd never really seen Italy outside of Rome. I could still feel pangs of fear and homesickness.

Meanwhile, Florence was magical. We only had a few hours, so they took me to see the Duomo, the statue of David by Michelangelo, and the Palazzo Medici.

I had money again, after selling the hash I'd carried in my boot, so I stopped at a flea market and bought a beautiful hand-knitted sweater-jacket to spice up my look going through New York customs. I even got my long hair cut, two feet worth, like some rite of passage. I asked the barber for something stylish, and he gave me a shag haircut. I looked like Mick Jagger. I was moving on, but the hippie would always remain, no matter what I looked like on the outside.

They took me to Umbria next. I was enamored. Every hilltop had a castle on it, or the remnants of one, each more beautiful than the last. It was like a fairy tale, so easily imagined. What wasn't so easy to realize was that every hilltop represented power, and there had been many wars fought over the land.

When we entered Gubbio through the medieval main gate, I really felt like I'd been transported to medieval times. What a jewel. The streets were so narrow that only one car could pass through at a time. This was the town with the butcher, the baker, and the candlestick maker. I was determined to find a shoemaker who could sew my boot back up and make it look like new. After all, I couldn't look suspicious. I still had to get through customs in New York City. I found the shoemaker, a sweet old-timer. He fixed them while I waited and never asked questions.

We traveled to Assisi and Orvieto. We tasted wine, they taught me about cheese, and we ate like pigs. They were like family to me, and me to them. Then a sign pointed us to the Rome airport. I felt a pang in the pit of my stomach. The journey was coming to an end, and I'd have to say goodbye. I was nervous about customs in Rome.

I looked spiffy, aside from the haircut. I wore my beautiful wool sweater-coat from the flea market and my new pants from Milan. I was looking good—hopefully good enough to get through New York customs without a search. I'd been gone from home so long that

"What kinda job do you have that you can take that much time off?"

"I don't have a job."

"Well now, you've been to Iran and Afghanistan too," he said in a heavy Brooklynese accent. "Man, you've been all over the place. I'm gonna have to ask you to step over here for a moment and check your bags." He directed me to an area away from the customs booth. "Are these your bags?"

"Yes, sir," I said. *Keep it together*, I thought to myself. *This is just routine.*

"Could you open them?"

"Sure."

"Boy, you sure travel light. Ten months and two bags?"

"Yes, sir."

He went through one bag. He checked the sides, looked for a false bottom, turned it upside down, and shook it. He was sure I was carrying drugs or at least something illegal, and he was sure he'd find it. Then he looked disappointed. Finally, he began to politely return my belongings to the bag as best he could. "Welcome home, sir."

Welcome home? Oh my God, I've made it.

"Right out the sliding doors to your left," said the agent, motioning with his hand in the direction of the street.

I passed through the sliding doors, having an almost out-of-body experience. The cool breeze hit my face, and all I could I hear was a man shouting in a New York accent, "Cab to Brooklyn, fifteen dollars!"

my passport had an addendum that stretched to the floor when you opened it. Well, it was in the hands of the universe now.

While Maurizio got my bag from the boot, Maria Gracie gave me a hug. We were all friends. Maurizio threw his arms around me in that warm, loving way and kissed me on the side of the cheek like it would be the last time. We hugged and then hugged again. We'd shared something special. We were brothers on the Silk Road and would always remain so.

New York City

I'd cleared Rome customs. I was seated by a window, next to a couple, cordial American tourists on a Roman holiday. My mind drifted as I stared out the window, back to where it all began. I closed my eyes and saw the beach in Goa and the tepee village, Maria and Eduardo's son. I saw the fishermen, the fresh catch, the full moons, the sea, Umberto, Roberta, and Loretta. How would I remember this journey of freedom when I returned to my world? How could I keep myself open to the world and not shut down to protect myself? Would it be possible to be that free again?

I fell asleep, and when I woke, I could see the skyline of Manhattan out the window. I checked it all out mentally, took a deep breath, and said, "This is it. You're home."

It was May 1973, and I'd been gone almost ten months. The journey to the East was over.

Customs

"How long have you been out of the country?" The immigration officer opened my passport and the addendum fell to the floor, full of stamped pages and my headshot. He looked me square in the face.

I grew nervous. "Ten months," I said.

"Ten months. Jeez, that's a long time. Are you a student?"

Oh shit, here we go, I thought. *It's going to be the third degree.* "No," I replied.

"Okay, what was the purpose of your visit?"

"Tourism."

Epitaph

Epitaph

Robin returned to India in 1975. She'd gone up to Nepal, and she wrote that she'd fallen in love with a Frenchmen by the name of Bernard. That was our last communication. As fate would have it, we'd never see one another again. I've had a lot of losses in my life, but Robin's I feel every day.

Henrietta called me later that year to say Robin had been murdered in Paris after she'd returned there with Bernard. The Paris detectives were sure it was Simla, Bernard's jealous lover, who'd committed the murder with Bernard's help. But they were unable to find her body. I begged Henrietta to send me to Paris with a gun and that I would find out where she was, but she refused me. I think I could have killed Bernard, and I think she knew that.

This woman who gave me so much light had come to such a brutal end. My heart would be broken forever. I'm just turning seventy years old as I write these lines, and the light she gave still burns within me.

Robin – Epitaph

Michael Rossum

Bill Tester

Chapter Fifteen

Bill Tester

In 1967, San Francisco was referred to as "Mecca," or "Oz," or the "Emerald City." That's because it was. If you were a free spirit, if you had an open mind, then San Francisco was the only place to be.

I came here to start college at San Francisco State in 1967. It was the Summer of Love, and my brother was already living in the heart of the Haight. At the time, the area was run-down, and many of the shops had been boarded up. But the rent was cheap, and the old Victorians were large enough to support whole communes. It was hemmed in on one side by Golden Gate Park and on the other by the Panhandle. In the old days, it was quite an upscale part of town.

That summer saw the likes of Jimi Hendrix, Janis Joplin, Jefferson Starship, the Doors, and Country Joe McDonald playing free concerts in the park. Word of mouth or a blip on the local radio station meant several thousand people would show up spontaneously. Diggers, the local fish-and-chips store on Haight Street, would serve up a healthy portion for a few bucks.

They called us hippies. Like an infection, the size of the community grew until by the end of the summer it was so crowded that people were living on the beaches down by Fort Funston in caves carved into the cliffs. The *San Francisco Chronicle* estimated the number of people fourteen and older had reached upward of seventy-five thousand between the spring and summer of 1967. The hippies who were already here, going to school, moved north after graduation to Marin, Mendocino, and Humboldt counties, pushed out by the sheer numbers of newcomers.

The Summer of Love gave birth to the antiwar movement, free love, women's rights, black liberation, gay rights, and freedom to think outside the box. People were sharing their thoughts and their bodies, so the media called it free love. Free love was so liberating. We made love to one another, and that was how we met. Afterward, for the most part, we had a new friend. Or if we were lucky, we might have found our soulmate.

In 1968, I moved over the hill to a neighborhood known as "the Castro." I was living with two roommates from college and a sea otter in a large Victorian flat overlooking Noe Valley—the sea otter had the bathtub all to himself. Every day I'd walk down Castro Street to the Muni Metro station at Castro and Market, past young mothers with their strollers and elderly residents with grocery carts and men in black leather chaps. I really didn't think much about it for the longest time. I didn't realize I was living in the area that soon would become the gay mecca of the world.

I used to pass Toad Hall, the Midnight Sun, and the Elephant Walk on my way to school and never looked in at the clientele to see that the bars were full of men. Back then, the heart of the gay world was up on Polk Street, where people danced at Busby's, and Upper Grant at the Savoy Tivoli. But as time passed, the neighborhood began to change. Gay men were buying cheap property in the Castro and restoring old Victorians into the painted ladies you see today.

The main street began to take on the look of a village, with shops like the Obelisk, Does Your Mother Know, All American Boy, and Castro Camera, the now-famous camera store owned by Harvey Milk. The place was alive. At the Castro Theatre, a classic grand organ from the days of silent movies rose to the stage from below the floor, playing "San Francisco" to a crowd singing the words as if it were a national anthem. At other times, audiences enjoyed a Bette Davis movie, already knowing all of Bette's lines. "What a dump!" rang out in unison.

Like the Castro Theatre, the beautiful art deco Bank of America building, which now houses a Diesel Store, was another neighborhood landmark. After the bars closed at 2:00 a.m., the pizza parlor and the donut shop had lines down the street, with patrons waiting to soak up the malt with some greasy food or a cup of coffee. It made me feel like I finally belonged someplace, and that someplace was San Francisco. We were a village, and this was where I grew up.

I was coming home from school one day with a bag of groceries from Cala Foods, the local market, waiting for the 24-Divisadero bus, when I noticed a man on the opposite side of the street. In his thirties, dressed in a tight T-shirt, he stared at me with an intensity that to this day I'll never forget. My heart pounded with a mixture of fear and a strange sort of excitement. Without dropping his gaze for a moment, he began walking in my direction. I felt numb. I didn't make a move, just stood listening to the pounding of my heart.

"Can I give you a lift home?" he asked.

Dumbstruck, I muttered something like, "Yeah."

I can't remember his name. I called him a couple of times after that night, but when he found out that I was looking for more than just sex, he dropped me like a ton of bricks. I was hurt. It was my first time, and the experience was so positive—he was handsome, smart, charming, and sexy. I was so naïve to think he might be interested in me, when all he really wanted was to get laid. It took some time to get over him. Still, it was a step in the right direction for me, as I was moving closer to coming out.

Then I met someone in the summer of 1973 who did share those feelings. His name was Carmine. He was the first man I fell in love with.

The Cabaret

I met Bill Tester in the spring of 1973. I was looking for a job so I could earn some extra money and continue my travels. I was finishing my teaching credentials at San Francisco State at the time as well. Bill worked at a place called the Cabaret After Dark. It was on Montgomery Street and Broadway at the end of North Beach, the topless mecca of the world back then. The main feature was Carol Doda at the Condor Club and her forty-eight-inch breasts, sliding down a pole and dancing on top of a piano. I'd come to meet her years later in my photography class at the Art Institute, but that's another story.

I'd gone into the cabaret earlier in the day asking about work, and a handsome bartender who took a liking to me said, "Come back later tonight about seven p.m. and ask for Sally. Can you cocktail and wait tables?"

"Oh yeah, I can do that," I said as confidently as I could. The truth was I didn't know a Beefeater martini from a hamburger. Of course, being as green as I was to gay life, I was expecting my future boss to be a lady. But Sally was a man, as I'd awkwardly find out.

He took one look at me and said, "When can you start?"

"Tonight," I said, and that was that. I had a new job and was about to take on a new life.

As soon as I called in my first order, the bartender said, "You've never waited tables in your life. But don't worry. I won't give you away." His name was Bob, gorgeous Bob, and he taught me everything I know about liquor.

I'd been there for a few months when I met Bill Tester. He was a waiter in the dining room, below the cocktail lounge. Bill was drop-dead gorgeous and one of the kindest human beings I'd ever known. He had long dark hair, which he parted and wore with one side swept off his face, and he had the class of Cary Grant. We were destined to be best friends.

He took me aside one night and asked, "How would you like to work in the dining room where the tips are much better?" He said someone was leaving and Sally was looking for a replacement. He encouraged me to ask him about the opening.

Sally looked at me with some reluctance but finally agreed.

"Oh yeah," I told myself. I'd now don a tux jacket and bow tie and make some desperately needed cash.

I faced my first night with the dining crew with some trepidation, but I pushed back my fears and dove in.

The chef turned to me and said, "Tell Effy her order's up."

Bewildered, not having seen a woman on the dining staff, I asked, "Who's Effy?"

"That's Chuck," he growled.

"Oh, sure, I've got it." I walked up to Chuck and told him his order was up.

"Tell Mildred there's a table of five that just walked in," Chuck said.

"Who's Mildred?" I asked.

"Jim, the maître d'," he said, rolling his eyes as if annoyed.

Maybe this wasn't going to be so easy.

Back in the kitchen, Bill Tester hurried along with at least five hot entrées on both arms. In complete control, he said to me, "Tell Sissy table eight says his steak isn't rare."

"Who's Sissy?"

"Little Billy," he said as he swirled out of the kitchen like a magician with the plates.

Okay, this is too much to wrap my head around, I thought. I found Little Billy and gave him the message.

Then Mildred said, "Michael, you've got four people at table twelve. Bread and butter first, then get their salad orders. Billy's already got their drink orders."

Wow, my first table. I looked over at them, four queens in Hawaiian shirts with flower leis. I delivered the basket of bread. "Good evening, gentlemen. I see you've been to Hawaii," I said as I put the bread and butter on the table.

In silence, the four of them checked me out with their eyes.

"Nice basket," said the tall blond.

"Yes, the chef made them himself," I responded, referring to the basket of bread. "I'll come back with your salad orders." The busboys delivered water to the table. As I turned to walk away, I heard a roar of laughter, which I knew was due to an inside joke directed at me. When I made it back to the kitchen, I cornered Billy and relayed the story in fast order.

He put his hand over his mouth and broke out laughing.

"What? What's wrong?"

He looked at me. "Michael, they were commenting on your crotch. We need to talk later." With that, he was back on the dining room floor, serving.

I stood there for a moment feeling a mixture of anger and embarrassment. Was I ever going to fit in to gay life?

Years later, I ran into Effy (Chuck) at a restaurant where he was waiting tables. I was on a first date, which is always a little awkward, getting to know one another. As Chuck took our order and started to leave, I said, "Chuck, did you ever have a camp name for me at the cabaret? Because everyone called me Michael."

He turned back over his shoulder and said, "Of course not, Gisele."

I cracked up, realizing all these years I'd been referred to as Gisele behind my back. However, I wasn't too put off. I thought Gisele had kind of an international flare.

One night after work, I walked home down Montgomery Street toward Market Street with Bill, as we lived in the same neighborhood. We boarded the bus and sat down together.

"Bill, why does everybody have a girl's name in the dining room?" I asked.

"It's just our campy way of having fun while slinging food."

"What's your name?" I asked.

"Dandelion," he said, without batting an eye, and we both started laughing.

After a few months, I finally got used to the names, but it was always awkward for me. As time passed, Bill and I became the best of friends. He became my confidant. He showed me gay life and taught me the ways of the world of men, the tools I'd need to survive, and everything about drag queens. But the truth was I never did fit in. They all knew it, too, so when a position opened in the cabaret doing the lights and sound for the shows up in the light booth, the

They turned out to be the elite corps of the vice squad, those who arrest hookers, drunks, and drag queens. They netted me with two-tenths of a joint, but at that time in 1973, it was a felony. I was photographed and fingerprinted, had every orifice checked, and was booked on felony possession of marijuana and resisting arrest. I was taken to a large holding area that had four cells that opened onto a communal eating area. The jailer opened one of the four cells and, just like in the movies, pushed me in and locked the door. I was in jail with bank robbers and people who'd attempted murder, assault, and battery.

There were five other men looking at me from their bunks. "So what's your beef?" asked a big burly blond guy who looked like a truck driver.

"What's my beef? I don't understand."

"What are you in here for?" a Latino man called out as he looked over the magazine he was reading.

"I was arrested for a joint, and not even a whole one."

Even these hardened criminals were dumbfounded that the SFPD would pick up someone like me. "That's all?" They began laughing.

There was only one free bed available, and it was a top bunk, so I took it. The rest of the men in my cell weren't too talkative, which was fine by me. I was scared shitless. A rougher bunch of people you couldn't find. I lay there for a while as I replayed the whole story in my mind, over and over. If I'd just had enough time to take the joint out of the cardboard, they'd have had nothing on me.

Then I realized it was Friday night and the courts wouldn't open until Monday, when I had to be at work at Balboa High School to teach my first-period Spanish class. I was finishing my secondary teaching credential at Balboa, one of the toughest high schools in the city. Now my career was over in a flash. With a felony on my record, I wouldn't be able to go back to teaching, something I'd trained for years to do, and loved. I'd probably never teach again, my dream since my studies in Mexico at the University of Morelos in Cuernavaca.

"Michael Rossum?" I heard my name called out. A jailer came into the main room.

"Yes," I said.

"You can make a phone call. Do you want to make one?"

I tried to think. My father had caught me in my bedroom smoking pot when I was home for a weekend visit while in college. "Just don't call me when you're arrested," he'd said, then slammed the door. Of course, I had to call him. Who else could help me post bail?

"Yes," I blurted out after the long pause.

They took me to a room, and I called and woke up my parents. "Hello, Dad. It's Michael. I've been arrested for possession of marijuana."

He was angry, but much to my surprise also supportive.

I relayed the story of how it had gone down.

"We'll call John Garamendi," he said. John was a lawyer and a family friend. "We'll be there on Monday for your hearing."

"Thanks, Dad. I'm so sorry I've disappointed you."

I was returned to my jail cell. Just as they closed the door, the main one opened and in walked a friend of mine from the cabaret in handcuffs.

As soon as he saw me, he called out, "Michael."

"Gary? What are you in for?"

"Having sex in a bathroom with an undercover officer, but it's entrapment. He came on to me first."

Oh great, I thought, *just what the nice men in my jail cell want to hear, that I'm gay.*

Just as I figured, when lights were out, the big blond truck driver type jumped up on my bunk. "So how about giving me a blow job? I've been in here for sixty-one days with no sex."

"Hell no," I said. "Look at me. Do I look like a guy who wants to have sex?" I pointed to the bandage over my right eye.

"Okay, okay," he said. "I've just been in here a long time."

"Look, buddy," I said, "I've got troubles of my own."

He jumped down and returned to his bunk. I realize I probably disappointed half the gay community by my refusal, as it's every gay man's fantasy to have sex with a straight man in jail. But, trust me, it's not all it's cracked up to be.

When Monday rolled around, I'd spent the longest three days of my life at 850 Bryant. I saw my parents, my lawyer got my bail, and I was released on my own recognizance. I walked out of the building, and the first thing I saw was the blue sky and freedom. I swore that day I'd never wind up in prison again.

I had to tell the school and the head of the language department why I hadn't shown up for work on Monday with no call and no excuse. My charge was a federal offense, and they'd eventually be contacted by the police. My career as a teacher ruined, I'd lost my job and my self-esteem. The only person I could think of to call to console me was Bill Tester.

As I relayed the story, he asked, "Michael, do you want to come over?"

When I got there, we talked and talked. He was in total disbelief about what happened and that the vice squad would go to such lengths over a silly roach. Fortunately, it was a Monday, and neither of us had to work that night.

"Well, at least you still have one job," he said. "So much for fantasies about sex and prison."

We both laughed, which was exactly what I needed. That was Bill. No matter how bad the story, he could always find something to laugh about. I miss that, and the late-night phone calls. We were each other's confidants.

Bill had grown up on a pineapple plantation in Maui. His father was Portuguese and his mother a fair-skinned and blue-eyed Caucasian. She'd actually been born on the island. Their lifestyle seemed like something Michener could have written. They were quite well-off, as Bill described them. Big dinners on the pineapple plantation were a ritual. He described a receiving line where Bill and his parents and brothers wore white gloves. All the ladies wore

Hawaiian dresses with trains attached to them, with one end of the train fastened to their wrists, and they all wore exotic flowers in their hair. The men wore white tuxes and smoked cigars and drank brandy on the verandahs. They'd all dance outside as the trade winds blew.

Billy grew bored of the formalities of life on the plantation. When he wasn't attending parties, he was doing what he loved best: playing in the surf with his friends or hiking to one of his favorite places on the island, Haleakala, the big volcano. He had a degree in horticulture, and his apartment was filled with bromeliads from all over the world. A spectacular-looking man, he was swarthy with skin as smooth as silk and jet-black hair with green eyes. He had a swimmer's body, tall, lean and muscular. We worked out at the gym together. We also worked together, ate together, and went out partying together. The only thing we didn't do was sleep together.

Bill helped me pick up another shift at the cabaret, covering when people wanted time off. With the extra hours, I was able to stow away money for my return trip to India. I'd hoped to leave sometime in August. With my teaching career over, I had time to see more of the world. I was rooming with friends, so it would be easy for me to pick up and leave.

Bill was excited when I told him I was going back. He wanted to go, too, but he had a lot invested in San Francisco—an apartment, a well-paying job that gave him a lot of free time, and Jeff, his lover of five years. Bill was independent, and Jeff didn't mind when we'd drag ourselves back to the apartment at dawn, still high from the night before. He'd get up and make breakfast. It was an ideal open relationship. Bill came and went as he pleased, as did Jeffery.

Bill helped me maneuver through gay life. I almost needed a handbook. I'd learned what it meant to be "campy," and the nuances of "leather types," "cowboy western," "uniforms," "drag," "S and M," "porno," and "tranny." He showed me every bathhouse in town and every bar. Bill was an excellent guide. Coming out had a huge learning curve. I felt I'd met it, confident that I could hold my own in gay circles whatever their orientation because of Bill.

There was still something missing. Most of the information I'd gained was superficial, and the truth was, I'd had enough fooling around. I wanted to meet someone and settle down. But first I wanted to know myself better. The trip I'd made earlier to India overland from Istanbul to Nepal had opened me up to a world I still hadn't finished exploring.

Bill was happy for me, but I knew he was jealous. He wished he was going off to explore the world, too, but I was on a journey to find out who I was and what I really wanted. I'd miss his company greatly.

~~~

When I got to New York, I met a man by chance who changed my life. He was from Australia. I'll be saying a lot more about him later, but suffice it to say that I was excited at the prospect of falling in love. During a phone call, I told Bill I'd found true love, and I realized that I'd never really been in love before. I'd only had glimpses and infatuations. We stayed in touch over the next eight months while I became more involved with the Australian.

"Are you coming back to San Francisco?" Bill asked.

"No," I said, "I saved the money I was going to use for the trip to India when I knew I'd be staying in New York and put it into a savings account."

"Are you still going to India then?" he asked.

"Yes, I'm leaving in a few days. I need a break to see where this relationship is going."

When I arrived in India, I wrote Bill that I'd gone down to Goa on the coast. I'd been there before. I took a room in the main hotel on Calangute Beach. It was beautiful there, a sleepy little fishing village tucked away from the madding crowd on Forty-Second Street. I was glad I'd come because its peaceful environment gave me an opportunity to reflect on what had happened in New York.

Michael Rossum

~~~

I returned to New York and then on to San Francisco in 1976, almost a year later. I'd come back home to San Francisco with the money I'd saved, and began buying photography equipment. I now had a huge empty Victorian apartment with three bay windows and a roof deck. I devoted one of the bedrooms to a studio. I bought backdrop paper, a friend donated the lights, and I purchased a beautiful used Nikon SLR with several lenses.

I decided that I'd start shooting headshots for portfolios and see where it took me. Bill was one of my first shoots. I did the shoot in the tent room, which was my living room, decorated with silk saris I'd purchased in the thieves' market in Bombay. The saris trailed out from a Victorian rosette in the middle of the ceiling to where the wall and ceiling met, then fell straight down the walls to the floor. When I got to the bay windows, I turned the material into curtains. The room was octagon-shaped, which added to the elegance. I put in a low sofa and covered it with a rich Indian spread, placed a large Persian rug on the floor, and capped it off with lots of pillows to sit on. It was like a pasha's Bedouin tent. That was the backdrop for Bill's pictures. I wanted him nude because he had an exquisite body.

The pictures were spectacular, and from there I kept growing. Each shoot became an experiment with lighting and subject matter and background. Each shoot brought me closer to understanding the medium.

A wealthy friend of mine, Michael Strater, gave me the money to take classes at the Art Institute for a semester to hone my skills. That's where I met Carol Doda, the topless star of Broadway. She was in my class, and as things would have it, we were drawn to one another and became friends.

There's truth to the six degrees of separation people talk about. In a million years, I never could have seen our paths crossing. Yet when I got to know her, I found her to be an extremely intelligent woman with a lot of class and a great sense of humor. She'd had her breasts injected with silicone before implants were invented, and the first person they thought of was me. When I took the job, the dining staff was overjoyed to get rid of the greenhorn.

Tucked away above the cabaret lounge in my own little world of lights and sound, I prospered. I got to work with some fine musicians, singers (Sylvester, Grace Jones, and Dionne Warwick), comedians, and the most brilliant female impersonator, Jim Bailey. The sound booth was the most secluded and private part of the whole operation. I had visitors nightly, mostly people who'd knock on my door, just off the stairway that ran between the cabaret and the discotheque upstairs, to smoke a joint before their shift started or after it had ended. They were bartenders, waiters, kitchen staff, dancers, musicians. They all came there before the cabaret headliners began. When it was showtime, it was my space alone.

One night after work, Bill came up and asked me if I wanted to go home with him and Chuck. So we left the cabaret and started walking down Montgomery toward Market, where we'd each catch a bus.

Bill pulled a joint from his pocket and asked, "Should we smoke this on the way down?"

There was a universal sigh. "Yes," we answered.

As we smoked, we talked about work and our crazy colleagues. We reached the cable car turnaround on Powell Street and waited on Market Street for our buses. We continued to pass what was left of the joint; and then Bill pulled out a cardboard matchbook and tore the end of it off, rolling it up as a crutch for the last of the joint. He put the joint just inside the cardboard and rolled it up so as not to burn his lips. When Chuck and Bill's bus came, they handed the joint in the crutch to me, and we waved goodbye.

Seconds later as the bus pulled away from the street, three men in nylon parkas approached me and said, "San Francisco Police. You're under arrest."

I heard a voice in my mind say, *Swallow the joint, and then there's no evidence.*

I threw back the joint and tried to swallow it, but one of the officers grabbed me by the neck and tried to choke me. The second grabbed my head and smashed it against the pavement. As the two of them kept choking me, the third was handcuffing me. Unable to swallow the evidence, the cardboard and the miniscule roach dropped out of my mouth onto the sidewalk. Within seconds, a plastic bag appeared, and as I stared down at the evidence, it was swiftly scooped up. I was banged-up and had a bloody cut over my left eye that left a scar I still carry.

I couldn't believe that I was the highest priority on their list that night of pickpockets, pimps, and thieves that plague the Tenderloin. The cuffs were so tight I thought I'd lose both hands due to insufficient blood supply. I begged them to loosen them, but instead they decided in all their rage that they'd drag me by the handcuffs all the way to the police car ten feet away.

They read me my Miranda rights and began insulting me. "You fuck, I hurt my hand banging your head on the sidewalk," the officer complained. "What do you think you're doing smoking pot on the street, you little shit?"

I still had a little fight left in me. "This is San Francisco, or hadn't you noticed?"

They punched me in the stomach. "Smart guy, huh?"

"Don't you have anything better to do than pick on kids smoking pot?" I asked. "No heavier criminals on the street, or was it just a slow night?"

Another punch in the stomach.

I could hardly catch my breath. "What's the matter, you guys? Didn't you have your donuts today?"

They dragged me out of their car and threw me into a van loaded with other suspects headed for 850 Bryant Street, the city jail. It was cramped in there. The roof was so low we couldn't sit up straight. When the van was loaded with enough people—two transvestites, a prostitute, two drunks, and me—they took us to the dungeon in the basement of the jail.

gel would move freely in the soft tissue. She invited me over to her house once, and while I waited for her to get out of the shower, she told me that she had to wrap her breasts in a hot Turkish towel every morning so she could mold them back into shape from sleeping on her side.

I cracked up.

"That's the God's honest truth," she said.

She was so frank, and I loved her for that.

As time passed, Bill had ideas of his own for a business. He'd decided to open a shop on Haight Street selling bromeliads and other exotic plants. We were supporting one another in our prospective ventures, and life was full of promise.

Suddenly I started getting work by word of mouth, and the exposure of having worked with the famous photographer Barry McKinley in New York helped immensely. (You'll read a lot more about Barry in the next chapter.) People wanted head shots, portraits. I even started working for the *Advocate*, a local gay newspaper. I was getting offers for advertisements, fashion work for catalogs from Macy's, even an ad for Tiffany's. Then a friend of mine who worked for KTVU Channel 2 asked me if I'd take the still shots for Hugh Downs's *Over Easy* show, where I got the chance to meet and photograph Vivian Vance (Ethel Mertz) from *I Love Lucy* fame, Dina Merrill (*Operation Petticoat*, *Butterfield 8*, and *The Young Savages*), and Rita Moreno from *West Side Story*. I was excited.

My friend Alex Desy opened Prima Facie, a salon for facials on Castro Street. I'd asked him to come to Fire Island with me the summer before it opened, and we were invited to a party on Fire Island Boulevard. When we arrived, there were so many people in the house dancing. As we looked at the house sitting on its pilings in the sand, we noticed it was swaying back and forth to the music.

"I'm not going in there," I said.

"Me neither," Alex said. As we sat on the boardwalk smoking a joint, he turned to me. "You know, Michael, I'm thinking of opening a salon on Castro Street. I want to call it Prima Facie."

"Alex, that's fantastic," I said. "What does *prima facie* mean?"

"'The first look' in Latin," he said. "And I was thinking you could hold an opening of your photographs, you know, head shots of nothing but great-looking faces. What do you think?"

"Wow, that's great, Alex. I've never had a showing before, but to be honest, I'd be a little nervous."

"Your photos are great. I saw some of the head shots you took. I think they'd be perfect."

"Wow, my first show," I mused out loud.

Alex knew what he wanted, and he created the most beautiful space from a rundown Victorian flat upstairs on the second floor of a building on Castro Street, just as he'd planned. I set about finding the faces of some of the most beautiful men and women in San Francisco for the opening.

I began with Bill Tester, and I took a shot of Alex too. When I was finished, I had about twenty eleven-by-fourteen black-and-white head shots for the opening. I framed them in black, white, gray, and charcoal mats in Lucite frames. Nobody had seen them, not even Alex. A week before the opening, I started hanging them. There were four rooms, plus the entryway and the staircase going down to the street. I invited my parents to come, and Billy of course, and all the models. It was a champagne and cocktail affair, the likes of which Castro Street had never seen. Castro was becoming more upscale as young entrepreneurial gay men began introducing their ideas to the Village.

Alex's shop was a big success, and so was my show. It was September 1977. People loved the head shots—faces leaning on elbows, hands clasped, heads resting on them, all variety of positions. One thing they all had in common—I'd captured their essence, their souls, in black and white. Bill came to the opening, and he loved the pictures. My parents were impressed, and my dad's approval was important. So this was the beginning. Maybe I'd be a photographer.

It was Halloween. Bill called me. "Want to come to a pre-Halloween party at my house? We're getting dressed up as French maids, and then we're going to parade down Castro Street."

"Sure, why not? It'll get me out of the house."

When I arrived, it was chaos, the house full of men in varying degrees of undress. I watched ten hunky men with mustaches put on black fishnet stockings, and high heels, with little black blouses, white aprons, black bustiers, and elbow-length gloves. There were guys in pantyhose and high heels looking through a trunk of wigs. Another wore a wig and pantyhose and nothing else, a cigarette dangling from his mouth. Another was in a bustier and wig, sipping his cocktail. It was Bill's annual get-into-drag night, and they all did it so well. I saw Bill on my way out and told him how fabulous he looked—and he did—and that I'd be looking for them on Castro Street.

"You'd better," he said, laughing. "We'll be hard to miss."

"No kidding," I said.

When I saw them on the street, they were fabulous. People clustered around them. They were getting hit on left and right, and they were having so much fun. That was Bill: gay-hearted, anything goes, let your hair down, and let the good times roll.

When Gay Day came the following June on the anniversary of the Stonewall riots in New York City, we had a new enemy to combat. Homophobia from the right was mounting. As the evangelical right wing of the Republican Party began its evil campaign against gay people in Dade County in Miami, gays were thrown into the spotlight once more as immoral people who were recruiting children to be gay.

Anita Bryant introduced a bill that would make it illegal to hire a gay teacher. Teachers known to be gay were fired from their jobs and rooted out of the educational system. Bryant, the orange juice spokeswoman for Florida, was driving a campaign to strip gay people of the few civil rights they had. She wanted to send gay people back into the closet. Her McCarthy-era tactics of blacklisting teachers and others in the educational systems, as well as striking down fair hiring laws for gays, became paramount to the cause, and it was working. She won in Florida, and then took her campaign national. She hurt a lot of people.

When she dared to come to San Francisco, the "hotbed of breeding and recruiting heterosexuals," Bill and I joined a protest march. If she won in San Francisco, we'd be finished. It would take another twenty years to regain our civil rights. When she drove down Market Street, she was pelted with oranges. Everywhere she spoke, we picketed her lectures. San Francisco was the turning point. Gay people stood up to her and exposed her for the bigot that she was. Bill and I fought for gay rights, and eventually we won the battle. Wherever there was injustice—the Vietnam War, Tibetan refugees, gay rights, women's equality—Bill and I were there. Billy was a proud gay man. It was an honor standing with him.

By 1980, Bill had left Jeffery and was seeing Gary, his new beau. I invited the two of them up to my mother's house for dinners up in Diamond Heights from time to time. My mom loved Billy, and grew to love Gary too. In fact, Gary used to call my mom to get her advice on matters of the heart. We were like a family. Bill and Gary were in Maui when I sent my parents there for Dad's seventieth birthday. Bill had invited my parents while they were in Maui to let him show them Haleakala, one of his favorite places. When they flew into the island, he met them with a basketful of flowers and orchids, suntan lotion, and fresh fruit. Bill was so kind and classy. They were so taken aback by his love and generosity.

When he kissed them at the airport upon arrival, he threw leis over their heads and said, "Aloha. Welcome to Japan." He made their trip so special. That's the kind of friend he was.

Bill and I continued seeing one another in the mid-1980s from time to time for dinners and birthdays. And there were always the calls at night, when we confided in one another as we tried to make sense of our lives. We were best friends.

Then he met someone very special—Rob. They moved to the East Bay, where Rob had a fantastic home up in the Oakland Hills, and our visits became few and far between. Then one day around Christmas 1988, he called me and told me he'd been diagnosed with AIDS and he was dying.

I was crushed. "I really thought we were going to make it, Billy. I thought we were going to beat this thing."

"I'm gonna try," he said.

For two years, he struggled bravely and rarely complained, his humor unfailing. He ultimately lost the battle in June 1990. We were four months apart in age when he died at the age of forty. When I thought back on all the promise that life held for us both, how we'd come so far together, I felt robbed. He was one of the few people left who knew my story, and I his. With his death passed an era I'd never see again, one of shared history, memories, and dreams.

Life has never been the same since Billy passed. He was my link to my past, my last friend from a bygone era of freethinkers. We changed the world, and we opened minds and hearts. There is no one left to call and say, "Remember when?"

By the time Bill died, I'd lost over thirty friends. They were a whole generation of people just like me who had dreams—doctors, lawyers, waiters, ballet dancers, artists, cousins, small businessmen, construction workers, escorts, designers, and writers. In the blink of an eye, I looked around and I was the only one standing.

Two may talk together under the same
roof for many years, yet never really meet;
and two others at first speech are old friends.
Kahlil Gibran, The Prophet

Michael Rossum

Barry McKinley, Fire Island, 1974

Chapter Sixteen

Barry McKinley

I left San Francisco for India and Nepal in August 1974, my second journey to the East. Nepal was such a small country, nestled in the highest of the Himalayas, bordered by India to the south and China to the north. It only had one consulate, and it was attached to the UN mission at the United Nations in New York City. I had no idea that New York would seduce me into its wild, exciting, captivating, and bewitching world.

I'd contacted Richard, a friend in New York, and asked if I could stay in his apartment while I waited for my visas to be issued. He was a nice guy. We'd met through mutual friends in San Francisco. Richard said I could stay for the week; he had an invite to Fire Island and wouldn't be at the apartment. I had the place all to myself.

A few nights passed, and he called me up. He said one of their guests hadn't come out for the weekend and asked if I'd be interested.

"Sure," I said, "but where's Fire Island?"

He chuckled. "I'll give you directions."

I'm sure when he got off the phone, everyone had a good laugh at my expense. Anyone who was gay knew where Fire Island was. You must understand that I'd only just come out the year before. I was still green.

"Well," Richard said, "you take the A train down to Penn Station, buy a ticket for Sayville, change at Jamaica for the train to Sayville, get out at the station, and take a minibus to the ferry landing for Fire Island, buy a ticket on the ferry, and you've arrived.

"We're on Ozone Walk, so when you get to the dock, find the little red truck to carry your gear to the house. It's got a rusted handle, it's not locked, and it has the house number eleven on it. Wheel it down Fire Island Boulevard three or four blocks, and then it's halfway up on the right-hand side. You can't miss it. If you get to Ocean Boulevard, you've gone too far."

I had no idea what he was talking about. I just hoped I'd find people to help me along the way. Who the hell lives on Ozone Walk anyway? It was all starting to sound a little farfetched, but I was game. I just hoped I could find it.

What I wasn't prepared for as I arrived at the Pines around four in the afternoon was the tea dance at the Botel, which was a hotel, bar, and discotheque right on the harbor. As the ferry arrived at the dock, the sheer number of gorgeous men in spandex bathing suits parading down the dock took my breath away. They'd come straight from the beach, on their way to the Botel's afternoon tea dance. The bronzed bodies in multicolored swimsuits represented New York City's finest. I'd never seen more exquisite men anywhere than on that ferry to Fire Island. *Where the hell did you say I was again? Heaven?* This place was every gay man's dream.

I got off the ferry and realized the island was more like a sand dune. There were no cars. The only transportation was your own two feet. Instead of streets, there were boardwalks, elevated three to four feet off the dunes, in some cases even higher. I was thankful I'd arrived when there was still light. Traversing it in the dark could be a little tricky, as I'd later find out.

I took a right turn onto Fire Island Boulevard, which was the wrong way, and wound up at Tuna Walk on the bay side of the island. I decided to head toward the sea and ran into Ocean Walk and backtracked down Ocean until I found Ozone.

All along the way, gorgeous men gave me directions, and the eye. When I asked one gent where Ozone was, he said, "I'll show you where the Ozone is, honey. Just step inside."

I was cracking up at how loose everybody was. I definitely needed more time at the beach to loosen up. "Eleven Ozone Walk. Ah, this is it."

It was a small walk full of shade trees. The house seemed ordinary, but some of the houses were enormous and right on the beach, with marvelous architecture that spanned from the '40s to the present. Richard's friends were cordial, and it was a pleasant night. We all helped put dinner together. It was nice to contribute and be a part of things.

The next day, I went to the beach—it was playboy at the beach. I'd never seen such a collection of good-looking gay men. They were awesome. There were groups of guys talking on the beach, groups of guys walking down the beach, and groups of guys swimming.

"Does everybody know everyone?" I asked.

Richard, my housemate, explained that everyone in the houses rented for the summer, so a lot of people knew one another. Let's say it was a small community, and word traveled fast.

"You're a new face," Richard said as he looked up at me and winked. "I'll give you a few days."

"A few days for what?"

"Before they're talking."

"About me?"

"Well, yeah."

I smiled in disbelief. I was a nobody from San Francisco. These guys were all artists, designers, models, and big-time executives. What was I, a Spanish teacher of unknown origin?

That night, Richard asked me if I'd go to the butcher shop on the harbor and get some steaks to barbecue. We'd just returned from the tea dance, and I was still in my bathing suit, so I threw on a tank top and some shorts and left.

I walked down Ozone onto Fire Island Boulevard, past the two gorgeous straight cops from Sayville who patrolled the Island, one blond and the other dark-haired. What a job. They were cruised day and night by all the gay men and straight women on the island. Their egos were so inflated. They tried to put on a front of authority, but they were ready to play unless somebody really got out of order. Fire Island was just like the city. We had domestic disputes, occasional robberies, medical emergencies, and illegal drug deals. One guy, who turned out to be a friend of mine from San Francisco, overdosed and had to be airlifted out.

I walked by the harbor as the sun was setting. The light was beautiful that time of day. It cast a warm glow over the bay and the island. A summer's day was coming to an end. People passed me, still coming back from the beach in their swimsuits. You couldn't walk down Fifth Avenue or Fifty-Ninth Street in New York in your bathing suit. This kind of freedom only existed on the island. There was a ferry bringing another load of people eager to taste this liberty. I looked down at my watch and realized I had to get going. The grocery store closed at 7:00 p.m.

The store was crammed with people buying their last-minute items for dinner. When the grocery store (which was the only one on the island) closed, that was it—no twenty-four-hour market at midnight when you were hankering for a snack. I went to the butcher shop. Wow, the butcher's son was hot, and the butcher wasn't bad either. They'd run their family business for some thirty-odd years, separate from the store.

"What ya have? You're next," shouted the butcher in his deep, Long Island accent.

"Four New York steaks, please," I answered.

"There ya go. Anything else for you today?"

I wanted to say, "Yes, your son, please." But I thought better of it. "No, that will be it."

He handed me the steaks, and I got into line and waited for the clerk to ring me up. It wasn't your normal grocery line like it is in the city either. These weren't the usual crazies, you know, the little old lady in black platforms with the shopping cart or the Jewish lady with two out-of-control kids, screaming, "No, you cannot have that.

Put that back! Gerald, your father's gonna hear about this tonight." This grocery line was almost entirely made up of gorgeous men in their twenties, most still in their bathing suits or shorts.

While standing in line, I checked out the clientele. In front of me was a tanned, handsome, auburn-haired guy with sparkling hazel eyes and a hint of freckles. He was wearing army fatigue shorts and a light denim shirt, open at the front so you could see he was well-built. He looked up at me while he paid the cashier. Our eyes met.

Cute, I thought.

His eyes said: *Come here. I'll lick you all over like an ice cream.*

The feeling was intense, and I finally broke the glance. I looked up again, and he just grinned. I smiled back. I was excited and nervous at the same time. It felt like it was love at first sight, if you believe in that sort of thing. As I look back on it now, that's exactly what it was. I was young and not that confident. Would he be waiting for me out there?

Wouldn't you know, he *was* waiting for me outside. *Now what do I say?*

He stood at the bottom of the stairs with a friend. "Hello, there," he said matter-of-factly in an Australian accent.

"Hi," I said and nodded at his friend.

"What are you doing for dinner tonight, mate?" he asked.

"I'm actually just taking dinner home. Why do you ask?"

"I'd like to invite you to my house for dinner tonight. Can you come? My name is Barry McKinley, and this is my friend Ken."

"Hi, I'm Michael," I said. "About dinner, I really don't know what to say . . ."

"Say yes you'll come and have dinner with me tonight."

His friend Ken smiled coyly in the distance.

"Yes, I'll come," I said. "I'll have to drop this off at the house first. Where do you live?"

"We're at Fisherman and Atlantic. You can't miss it. There's an Australian flag by the front door."

"So you're Australian?" I asked.

"Yes, well, New Zealand, to be exact. I went to boarding school in Australia. What about you?"

"San Francisco," I replied. "What time is dinner?"

"Eight p.m.," he said confidently.

"I'll see you then. It's nice meeting you, Ken."

As we walked off, Barry turned around and called out, "See you later, Michael from San Francisco."

I flew back to Ozone Walk. I hadn't even showered yet. I was giddy with excitement. Things were moving quickly. I hadn't expected this. I was so excited. I opened the door and said, "Guys, I have an invitation to dinner, and I've accepted. Is that okay?"

"Oh, sure," they chimed.

Richard said, "Whose house is it?"

"He said his name was Barry McKinley."

"You have an invitation to Barry McKinley's house?"

"Yes. Why?"

"He's a pretty famous fashion photographer in New York."

Great, I thought. *It's only dinner. If it doesn't work out, nothing gained, nothing lost.*

I showered and threw on a pair of khaki Girbaud shorts that I'd bought at Bloomingdale's earlier in the week and the tightest tank top I could find, black to go with my sandals. I slicked back my hair, looked in the mirror, and frowned. Then I shrugged my shoulders and walked out the door.

"Have a good time," my housemates called.

As I walked along the boardwalk, I felt a high. Love was in the air. I found the flag in front of Barry's house and walked down the narrow pathway to the front door. I rang the doorbell and waited.

A few moments later, Barry answered the door. He was barefoot, wearing a colorful Hawaiian shirt open to the navel, and white pants. I gave him the bottle of wine I'd brought. I quickly glanced around, noticing the house was one of those modern constructions with lots of wood and glass. There was a beautiful pool and deck right off the living room, which had a huge stone fireplace and a walkway all the way out to the beach. I could see the waves crashing from where I was standing. What beautiful architecture. It combined the natural beauty of the island, the dunes, and tall grass, with the wood, stone, and glass.

"Hi, handsome," he said, and we hugged.

"Hi," I said as I stepped inside. "What a great house you have."

"You met Ken earlier."

"Hey, Ken," I said as he smiled back at me.

Ken was drop-dead gorgeous. He had black hair, blue eyes, and a body to beat the band. You could see his nipples poking against his tight white T-shirt, and his biceps bulging through his sleeves. He had an airbrushed look to him, perfect. Barry and he had met in Manhattan, where Ken was working at the Australian embassy. Ken would wind up stabbing me in the back later on. I was so naïve that I never saw it coming.

"And this is Baby Bob," Barry continued.

"Nice to meet you," I said as we shook hands.

"You're tall," Bob said.

"Six foot two," I said, without a hint of ego.

Baby Bob was a top model with the Eileen Ford Agency, and straight. Barry's friends were always falling for him. He was dark-haired, about five foot eight, with beautiful green eyes, easygoing, and really sweet. He got his nickname because even though he was the picture of masculinity, he had a baby face. We'd become good friends.

"And this is Louic."

"Nice to meet you," he said in a heavy French accent. "Barry has good taste."

I nodded politely. I was beginning to feel like I was in a receiving line.

Louic was one of the top ten models in New York, and one of Barry's best friends. Very French, he had thick blond hair, blue eyes, and high cheekbones. He and Barry had worked together in Milan. We would tolerate one another.

"This is Erik, and his lover Sam," Barry continued.

I recognized Erik immediately. He graced the Smirnoff advertisements on every subway in New York.

"Hi," I said. "You're a popular guy. Haven't I seen you on every train in New York?"

We all started to laugh. Erik was Dutch and probably the most sought-after model on the planet. We'd wind up being good friends, too, and he'd turn out to be a lifesaver.

Barry moved down the line of people he'd introduced to me already. "And this is Giorgio Sant'Angelo."

He said it as though I should know him, but I didn't. "Are you Italian?" I asked.

"Yes, I am," he said.

"*Io parlo Italiano un po,*" I said. "I speak a little Italian."

We began to converse and he told me he was from Florence. He asked me where I learned Italian. I told him it was a long story, but he wanted to hear it anyway. "India," I said.

Giorgio was Count Giorgio di Sant'Angelo, a famous fashion designer from Florence, but I was clueless when it came to the fashion industry. He could have been Giorgio the pizza maker for all I knew. Giorgio was a hoot, a hilarious guy. We'd run into one another from time to time in the city and on the island.

"*Mangiamo tutti,*" Barry said in Italian. "Everybody, let's eat." He placed the rack of lamb neatly in the center of the table.

By the time dinner was finished, everybody had heard about my journey to the East, which I could tell had captured their curiosity, coming from one so young. In return, I'd learned a lot about the ruthless fashion industry.

They talked about the Ford Modeling Agency and Eileen Ford, unanimous in their distaste for her personality. Baby Bob said she was quoted as saying, "It's all about the money." According to her, nothing else mattered. He said she was touted as the Jekyll of Jekyll and Hyde. She was a fiend, totally obsessed, and treated her models in a condescending manner, then had to have the last word.

Louie said that John Casablanca had broken away from Eileen and founded his own agency, the Elite Model Management. Furious, she felt he'd betrayed her, so she tried to sue him.

Then there was Angelica, a model who showed up for a shoot high on cocaine. Barry was so angry with her, he told her, "Just get out!"

I was getting all the dirt about drugs, sex, and betrayal, the models and the magazines, the agencies, the photographers, and everyone who was in bed with one another.

When all the guests had left except for Ken and Louie, who were guests for the weekend, Barry invited me to his room. It was filled with picture after picture pinned to the wall of friends he'd photographed, all in black and white. The photographs were works of art, without a doubt. I was so impressed. I fell in love with the photography before I fell in love with the photographer.

I could feel something of each person he photographed, something deep and personal, or something silly. His photographs were powerful images, like the one he took in the middle of Columbus Circle with a model wearing an evening gown with tiger stripes, walking a real tiger across the path. His photos grabbed your attention and held you there, quite naturally, the way they were meant to. Sometime later, I posed for him myself. He poured everything he had into each shot. He was a master.

He told me about coming from New Zealand to go to boarding school in Australia. Even though he didn't say so, it sounded as though it may have been a tough time for him growing up. He told me how his career had taken off on the runways of Milan. We talked about his friends and his enemies. Then he offered me my first taste of cocaine, sweet cocaine.

We talked late into the night. He wanted to know everything about me. He asked me about my life in San Francisco, growing up, about my socialist upbringing, my teaching career destroyed by a drug bust, my brother's suicide, being marooned in India. He asked me when I came out, and was surprised to learn it was so recently. It turned out that he knew a girlfriend of mine, Roberta, from Milan.

What were the chances of that? She worked the runways doing the makeup for all the models, and they'd worked together. Talk about six degrees of separation.

Then he motioned me toward the bed, which was in the middle of the room. Overhead was mosquito netting, hanging down like an exotic tent in Africa. The roar of waves breaking on the beach made it so romantic. Barry, his friends, his house, the photographs, the see-through netting, the cocaine—I'd been seduced by all the images of Barry and his world. He took off his clothes without saying a word, climbed onto the bed, and drew back the netting. Then he beckoned me to come to him, and everything in me said yes.

We made love all night. It was like waves of ecstasy with the roar of the sea as the background music. I watched as if I was an observer, yet I knew I was a part of an intense romance that was bursting forth effortlessly, his mouth inside of mine, our legs entwined like the tentacles of an octopus. When it was over, I rolled off him, my body drenched with our sweat, as we lay there ecstatic, waves crashing on the beach, the sounds of a new love affair.

The next morning, everyone was smiling over coffee and sweet Danishes. Ken, who was Barry's roommate, was smiling, as were Barry's other two roommates, Andy and Louic.

"Did you have a good time last night, Michael?" Ken asked in his heavy Sydney accent. He knew I had, but he had to tease me.

"Yes, very nice, and you?"

"Wonderful," he replied as a half-naked blond bombshell walked from Ken's bedroom to the bathroom wearing nothing but a towel.

"Oh, so I see," I said.

Everyone at the table laughed. Ken backed down from being such a tease when he realized it could go both ways. Though I was young, I had a certain maturity that wouldn't allow him to walk all over me without taking some licks himself. Each one at the table was giving me some kind of seal of approval in their own way, it seemed, about being with Barry. It felt encouraging, if not a little presumptuous on their part.

When Barry asked me to join them at the pool that afternoon, I said yes, but first I had to get back to my roommates and tell them where I'd be. I left for Ozone Walk, my mind in the ozone too. As I pondered the night's events, I was excited about the possibility of love. Then it dawned on me that I hadn't told Barry I was only there for a week. I knew I was in love, but it had never happened so fast for me before. I think we both thought it might only last the night, but our feelings ran deeper than that.

After a phenomenal weekend, I flew back with Barry to the Twenty-Third Street Pier on the East River in a seaplane. What would have been a three-hour trip for me back into the city became thirty minutes. We waded out to the seaplane with our pant legs rolled up over our knees and our bags on our heads. The pilot came out on the wing, helped us with the baggage, and gave us a hand on board.

The plane took off, giving us an aerial view of the island. As we began to climb, I could see the surf pounding the beach that ran along the entire island. Then we were airborne over the bay that separated the island from Long Island. I saw all the neatly rowed houses with their summer pools gleaming in the sun, their motorboats tied up on the numerous canals that led out to the bay. Suddenly, we were over JFK, looking down on the busiest airport in the world. That was a bit scary. Then the skyline of Manhattan appeared, and I saw the Empire State Building and the Twin Towers. Fantastic. We flew in down the East River below the Brooklyn Bridge. What a thrilling view of the city. Right down the river, past the UN building, the pontoons of the plane splashed down near Twenty-Third Street. We pulled into a wharf, and we were home, just like a fairy tale.

My relationship with Barry was beginning to feel like one too. He asked if I could stay overnight at his apartment in the city. I told him I'd have to go uptown for some fresh clothes.

"Okay," he said. "Here's the address: Five West Jones Street, apartment five. It's at Jones and West Fourth. Don't be long."

I met Richard uptown, and we chatted as I filled my bag with a few fresh things.

Michael Rossum

Fire Island, sunning around Barry's pool, Barry in the middle and model "Baby Bob" taken from my journal 1974

"I never thought inviting you to Fire Island could be so dangerous," Richard said.

"What do you mean?" I asked. "You did tell me to come out and have a good time."

"True, but you're really young, and he's at least ten years your senior," he said, chiding me.

"He's thirteen years my senior, but what does that have to do with it? I'm pretty mature for twenty-three."

"What about India?" he asked.

"Yes, I know, we've only just met, but if I leave now without finding out if there's more to us than mere infatuation, I'll miss out on a chance at love."

He agreed, smiling.

On the Seventh Avenue local, I thought about my conversation with Richard. Maybe he was right, but Barry already knew why I was in New York. I was sure it hadn't escaped him that I was leaving. Maybe I should just enjoy the time we had left. Yes, that's what I'd do. My mind drifted. *Oh shit, here it is, my stop, Sheridan Square and Christopher Street.* I found West Jones. *What a neat little street.* It was tucked away in Greenwich Village, off West Fourth. "Ah, here it is," I said to myself. "Number five." I rang the bell, and he buzzed me in.

When I got to the top, the door was open, and he was waiting for me with that little sexy grin. "You found it all right?"

"Yeah, no problem."

We kissed and then he helped me with my bag. As we walked down the hallway that led into the small, utilitarian kitchen, I saw more of his photographs. Eleven-by-fourteen black-and-whites covered the wall. I was mesmerized by them. He pointed out the different people as we passed. The hall and kitchen opened into a marvelous living room/dining room with twenty-foot ceilings and windows that occupied one whole wall facing east. There was a zebra-skin rug in front of the fireplace and a few pieces of African art. The furniture came from a scuttled luxury liner. It consisted of several overstuffed chairs covered in maroon leather and a sofa to match. Behind the sofa was a palm tree that practically touched the ceiling. To the left were some stairs leading to the loft bedroom. From the bedroom, you could look out the windows and see the whole city. It was such a fantastic space that he used it as a studio sometimes.

Barry was in the middle of making dinner and asked me for a favor. "Can you run down to the liquor store on the corner of Seventh and Bleecker and get a bottle of *Pouilly-Fuissé*?"

"What is Pouilly-Fuissé?"

He looked at me kind of funny, as though to say, "You poor innocent man—you really are ignorant," and explained that it was an expensive French wine.

"Oh."

"Michael, I'm going to open you to a whole other world," he said. He handed me twenty dollars, which at the time I thought was a lot for a bottle of wine, and I left.

I didn't have much experience with fine wines, but I was learning. I'd learn more in New York City in the short time I lived there than the four years I'd spent at SF State.

That evening, we had a romantic dinner of salmon, green salad, rice pilaf, and a bottle of Pouilly-Fuissé for two, with a view of Manhattan. Barry was a charming guy. He'd been just about everywhere. We could talk about anything—sex, politics, religion, art, travel, you name it. He always had a cheeky remark. I guess it was that dry British humor, but I loved it. We laughed as he told me about growing up in Australia in a strict boarding school and how they'd torment the professors. I love a good storyteller. He made me laugh, and he was also good in the sack.

When we'd finished dinner, we went up to the loft.

"When are you leaving for India?" he asked.

I told him honestly that I didn't know for sure.

"You know I'm hot for you," he said in that sexy Australian accent. "Would you consider living here with me?"

"Barry, I can't do that," I said. "I don't even have a job."

"You could get one."

"Yes, but I could never afford your lifestyle—this apartment, flying in and out of Fire Island in a seaplane, bottles of Pouilly-Fuissé."

"Well, you could just pay for your share, and I'll fill in the gaps."

"Barry, I'm falling in love with you, but we come from different worlds."

He put his hand over my mouth. "I've been there. You think I don't know what it's like to not have enough for cab fare or to pay the rent? I've been down and out. Michael, I love you. You make me laugh. You're like a breath of fresh air, with your charming naiveté, good looks, and your California accent. It's so West Coast and carefree."

"Charm and good looks won't pay the rent. Anyway, I don't know, Barry. I've fallen in love with you, too, but I don't want to be kept. What will your friends think?"

"It's none of their business," he said.

"You'll start to feel resentment, and it will tear us apart," I said. "I want us to be happy. I couldn't stay if that happened."

"It won't. I can make you a star in New York, Michael. Don't you know that?"

"I don't want to be a star."

He was stunned. "Well, what do you want to do?"

"I'd like to be a photographer like you," I said.

"The business of modeling is more than just standing in front of a camera," he said. "It's an art, it's exciting, and there's nowhere else on the planet to do it like New York."

"Fuck, Barry, we've only just met!" I cried out.

"Do you believe in love at first sight?" he asked.

"Yes."

"Well then, we should go for it." He came over and wrapped his big arms around me. "Say okay. We'll try it for a couple of months. What do you think? Are we good?"

I caved. "Yeah, but I get the right side of the bed."

We started laughing, then fell asleep. We just held one another all night.

251

Did I just say yes? I must be delusional. Love is powerful. One minute you're going to Asia on a spiritual fact-finding mission, and the next you're falling in love with an Australian in NYC. *Well, the tickets are good for a year*, I mused. I banked all the money for the trip at Emigrant Savings around the block on Sixth Avenue. Then if things fell apart, I'd return to India.

Five West Jones Street, Penthouse Five

When I moved into the Jones Street apartment with Barry, it was early summer, 1974. The street was full of sycamore trees in full foliage. We were flying in and out of Fire Island all summer and spending long weekends at the beach house. The weekends were incredibly peaceful. We'd walk the length of the beach, stopping along the way at the houses of people Barry knew, and they'd invite us in for drinks.

I met a lot of Barry's friends: Calvin Klein, Egon Von Furstenberg, Cristina Ferrari, Marisa Berenson, and Elizabeth Ashley. I met Francois Lano, the owner of Paris Planning, the largest modeling agency in Paris. I met the art editor of GQ, Jean-Paul Gaultier the designer, and Patti Hansen, the wife of Keith Richards of the Rolling Stones. The list went on, just some of the many guests Barry entertained for dinner at the beach house.

What amazed me was how friendly, open, and relaxed they were on the island, and the way they treated me with a respect reserved for naïve babes in the woods. When we'd see them in New York, their attitude was slightly different. They were much more guarded. Out on the island, everything was different.

Back at Five West Fourth Street, I'd have to try to find a job that paid enough to support my new lifestyle of the rich and famous, paying for the seaplane and bottles of Pouilly-Fuissé. I'd studied for five years to be a teacher, and that was pretty much all I knew. But with a federal offense on my record, I couldn't teach anywhere. I was washed up, kaput. I went to NYC in search of myself and found what

I wanted to do: photography. Isn't it strange how life can just point you in the right direction? It was Barry's work that inspired me.

Barry wasn't too keen on me being a photographer. I guess he didn't want a protégé who might be an upstart. But he tried to give me some tips, and we'd go over his proof sheets when they came back from the lab. He knew naturally which of the thirty-six shots he'd taken were flawless. He circled them, and then I'd study why he chose those over all the others.

I began taking my own shots in between shifts at an uptown clothing store called Wrangler Ranch.

Summer came to an end, and we went out to close down the house in the middle of October. It was sad that summer was over. It had been such a spectacular season. We walked the beach, now empty of crowds, the houses deserted. Fire Island in autumn had gray clouds and rough seas. Everyone had fled back to the city.

The month before, I'd been on my way to work one day and realized everyone was wearing winter jackets. Coming from California, I was used to seasons that weren't quite so pronounced. I wasn't prepared for New York winters. One night, I came out of a restaurant, opened the front door, and landed on my proverbial ass. The streets had iced over in a matter of seconds. My advice: don't wear cowboy boots on the ice. It's a killer.

In October, Barry's friend Erik and his lover Sam invited us out to a B&B in Bucks County, Pennsylvania, on the Delaware River, to see the fall colors. I'd never seen the leaves change before, and it was a rare treat for a boy whose only change of season was an umbrella. Barry and I walked along the Delaware hand in hand, our noses red from the cold.

My life had never been so romantic. I thought I was living in the pages of *GQ* and *Vogue:* pictures of a dining room set for two, with the Manhattan skyline out the penthouse windows and a bottle of champagne in ice on the table. I'd been thrust into this lifestyle on my own accord, and I was moving with the flow as I learned about Barry's life and the world of fashion.

The next morning, we came down for breakfast. Erik was already seated and sipping his first cup of coffee. "So glad you could both make it down. Did you have fun last night?"

"Well, yes, as a matter of fact," I said.

"Come sit by me," he said.

He was such a warm soul. I think the Dutch are like that. He kissed me on the cheek as I sat down, which was his way, but this hadn't escaped the horrified look of the matron of the B&B. When she left to go into the kitchen, we couldn't hold back our laughter any longer. It was almost as if we all had a secret. Back in those days, it was better kept that way.

We had a wonderful time, and I got a chance to get to know Erik better. It was almost Halloween, and I'd taken a picture of him in front of some huge pumpkins while he leaned on an old hay wagon. Barry developed it and surprised me. Impressed, he told me it was good. I knew he was just being kind, but it felt great that he liked the picture. Maybe I actually had talent.

Barry called me one afternoon and told me we'd been invited to a fabulous party at Francois Lano's house. He moved between Paris and New York and owned a beautiful brownstone on the Upper East Side.

When I arrived home, I asked Barry, "What's the attire for the party?" I didn't own anything formal.

"It's a cocktail party for the end of the movie *Fortune* with Jack Nicholson and Warren Beatty," he called out from the upstairs bedroom. "It'll be casual. You know, blue jeans and a flannel shirt."

Perfect, I thought. I had plenty of those. I put on a denim shirt, blue jeans, and some loafers. I was good to go. Barry showed up in army fatigues and a flannel shirt. We hailed a cab and were off. It was the first big party of the season since we'd left the island, and I was excited and nervous, but mostly nervous about being in unfamiliar territory. I mean, who was I, after all? A school teacher, not even? All summer, I'd been introduced as Barry's lover, and I was beginning to feel like an extension of Barry, wondering what had happened to Michael.

We arrived late, and the party was in full swing. The brownstone was a mansion with a winding staircase from the first floor to the fourth. There was no one on the first floor as we entered except one butler taking coats and another offering champagne. The real party was on the second floor. As we climbed the spiral staircase, we could look all the way up to the fourth floor. The place was massive.

I glanced around when we finally reached the second floor. To my amazement and chagrin, everyone was dressed to the nines. It was black suit and tie. Not only was I petrified that I was a nobody, now I was a nobody in blue jeans, surrounded by some of the biggest Hollywood stars one could ever hope to be in the same room with.

"Barry, you said blue jeans and flannel shirts," I said in a panic.

He whispered apologetically, "Yes, I know." But he was a master of the schmooze. He could have shown up in his birthday suit, and everyone would have been okay. Then he started pointing out people to me. "Oh look, there's Julie Christie."

There she was, all in black, with a black waistcoat, a black pillbox hat with a rose on it, and a sexy black veil pulled down under her chin. All legs, she was stunning. I watched her saunter through the crowd, so seductive, so classy. Every head turned in her wake.

Before Barry could say another word, I started moving down the steps.

"Where are you going?" he asked.

"Home," I said. "I can't go in there looking like this. I'm uncomfortable already."

"Well, look at me. I'm in army fatigues, for Christ's sake! C'mon."

As I regained my composure, I joined him.

"Look over there," he said, pointing his finger. "Mick Jagger."

This is crazy, I thought. I was in the same room with one of my idols from the Rolling Stones. I'd gone to the concert at Altamont to see him. His hair was cut short, and he was in a drab gray suit. If it hadn't been for his lips, I never would have recognized him.

"And there's Warren Beatty and Jack Nicholson."

I forgot for a brief second that I was still in blue jeans and a denim shirt and allowed my eyes to drift over the crowd—amazing, frightening.

"Oh Michael, look, there's Francois. Let's go say hello."

"You go," I said.

"Come with me," he pleaded.

"Thank you for the invitation, Francois," I said.

He looked down on me and smiled. What else could he do?

After that snub, I made my way through the crowd as Barry met people he knew. I fled to a corner, far from the madding crowd, sipping my champagne.

A woman also standing in the corner looked over toward me and whispered, "I see you got the wrong invitation too."

I looked up, and it was Lauren Hutton, with that big split between her teeth, grinning at me over her champagne glass. She, too, was wearing a denim shirt and blue jeans.

We started laughing. What a hoot. She told me she was hiding out, too, and asked where I came from.

I told her California.

"Me too," she said. Then she told me about her house in Baja California where she liked to go riding. After a while, she asked, "Did you come here tonight with someone?"

"I'm here with Barry McKinley."

"Oh, I've worked with Barry," she said. "He's great."

I asked her if she wanted another glass of champagne.

"Yes, that would be nice."

I walked to the bar to get the drinks. As I waited, I turned around to see the crowd, and there was Warren Beatty in a white suit and white shoes, his thick black hair slicked back '30s-style. He was walking toward me in slow motion as I tried to take it all in. I'd never been that close to a movie star of his stature, and he had the total aura of a big star. Graceful, six foot two, handsome, he put his hand through his hair midway to the bar. He had the air of movie star, but a no-nonsense feel to him, like he didn't take himself too seriously. He was shining in the light, but maybe it was the glare off the white suit. But wow, what a striking man. Now he was right in front of me and speaking to me. *Why me?*

"Hi, my name is Warren Beatty."

Oh boy, here goes. "My name is Michael Roussssumm," I said, half covering my mouth with my drink as I slurred my last name, hoping he wouldn't remember it.

He sized me up. "Where are you from?" he asked politely.

"California."

"What part?"

"San Francisco." I looked into his eyes and then had to look down, it was so intense.

"I love San Francisco. That's one of my favorite cities. I thought you might be from out of town."

"Really?" I asked playfully. "Is it that obvious that I'm not a native New Yorker?"

"No, it's obvious you're not from New York because you smile too much. That's what gives it away. I hope you never lose that."

"Thank you," I said, completely taken aback by his amazing down-to-earth attitude and his warmth. I congratulated him on his new movie, and he turned around with that sexy Warren Beatty grin and smiled as he raised his glass to me with a half wink.

I'd totally forgotten about Lauren and the champagne.

~~~

Barry and I used to eat at a little dive around the corner from his apartment on West Fourth called the Bagel. The manager there was Mario, an effeminate and animated Puerto Rican man who made the place so much fun.

He'd sing the orders out as he brought them to the table. "Bagel and eggs over easy for you, my dear."

A few months after the party at Francois Lano's, I was alone having a late breakfast when Lauren Hutton came in for lunch. I started to say hello but stopped, thinking she probably wouldn't remember me, and then it would feel uncomfortable. After all, she had a right to her privacy. That's what New York was all about.

As I leaned over to borrow the salt for my eggs, she asked, "Don't we know each other?"

"Yes we do," I said. "I met you at Warren Beatty's party for the end of the movie *Fortune*."

"Oh, yes, now I remember. You came in blue jeans and a denim shirt too. You're Barry's lover."

"Good to see you again," I said. "Isn't this place great? Nobody knows about it, and the food is so good."

She agreed, and we chitchatted a little longer. *New York really is a small town when you get to know people*, I thought. But would I ever be known for myself and not merely as an extension of Barry McKinley?

I really had to pinch myself occasionally. So much was going on in my life. Truly it was *Lifestyles of the Rich and Famous*, though that show came about later. But I still didn't fit in. I don't know why, but I didn't have the drive or the desire. When I was stranded in Goa, I'd realized I was a free spirit. I'd known true freedom, and somehow this was beginning to feel like a trap. Life with Barry was exciting, but on so many levels, it seemed superficial. I wasn't sure that I could live with him, but knew I loved him, and I wanted to at least follow my heart.

It was late fall. Patti LaBelle and the Bluebelles were playing at Lincoln Center. It was a big show. Everybody was going. Now that Fire Island was over, the city became insular. The party scene had moved back into the city too. Flamingo and 12 West were the hot new discos. Patti LaBelle's show at Lincoln Center was attracting literally all the paparazzi, and the big-name designers and Barry and I were invited to the opening. The costumes that Patti and the Belles wore were gold, silver, bronze, sapphire blue, and ruby red lamé. They looked like astronauts in their one-piece zip-up suits and hoodies. They came off the stage into the audience.

Everyone was on their feet singing, *"Voulez-vous coucher avec moi-ce soir? Voulez-vous coucher avec moi?"*

They were hot, hot, hot. All the designers who'd sewn their costumes were in the audience and were standing and taking bows. It was quite the event.

Meanwhile, on the evening of the performance, a limo pulled up in front of the apartment. Louic and a few of Barry's friends, Ken included, were already inside. One of the models who'd been invited was passing a mirror with coke on it, so the party was in full swing.

The performance was fantastic. At the intermission, we stood on the balcony overlooking Columbus Circle. I leaned over and kissed Barry and thanked him for the lovely evening and for teaching me so much about New York.

As I walked away, he grabbed me back. "I love you, Boop," he said.

It was nights like that when New York was magical.

Fall Fashion Season

Fall was a big time for the fashion industry. All the designers came out with their new creations, and all of Paris, New York, and Milan were atwitter. *GQ* was looking to Barry to provide the cover for its September issue. Barry and I were having some trouble, instigated by Ken, who had blackmailed Barry into putting him on the *GQ* cover. Their friendship hung in the balance.

I didn't know that Ken was trying to drive a wedge between us, but Barry had been acting oddly. One cloudy, cold September day, we were walking arm in arm down Christopher Street, and Ken was with us. It was a Sunday, and we'd just finished brunch at the nearby Pot Belly.

Barry saw me staring at a group of men standing outside Ty's Bar. "You like them, do ya, baby?" he blurted out. "Well, why don't you go over there and just ask one of them to go home with ya?"

He was so sarcastic, I was flabbergasted. Here I was walking hand in hand with the love of my life, and this nightmare of a question, full of innuendo, took me totally by surprise. What the hell was wrong with him? Did he not notice that my hand was locked in his? What kind of question was that, but one of insecurity? He knew I'd do anything for him. Perhaps he didn't realize the depth of my love. But how could he not? When did this breach of our love affair occur in his mind? My heart was broken. Somehow, I knew Ken had a hand in the whole thing.

Shortly thereafter, I was walking home from work at the Wrangler Ranch, uptown on Forty-Second Street and Madison. As I headed for the subway, I stopped dead in my tracks, frozen. *GQ* had just hit the newsstands. On the cover was Ken Farmn in an Armani tux and the beautiful Marisa Berenson of *Cabaret* (she played the Jewish countess, and happened to be a real heiress) in some gorgeous gown by Halston. It was hot. I bought a copy immediately and moved on toward the subway entrance

I was numb. He'd done it. Ken had put his friendship up for sale, and Barry bought it. It hit me like a ton of bricks. Here was this wannabe telling Barry that their friendship hinged on this edition. And all Barry had to do was take this embassy paper-pusher and make him into a star. Which was exactly what he'd done. Did I wish it were me? Absolutely not. Was I pissed off at Ken for manipulating Barry in such a way? Yes.

My boss was a great guy. When I told him the story, he gave me some sound advice. "Don't say anything more about it. Give him a chance to apologize."

"Australian men don't do apologies," I said with a sarcastic quip.

"Maybe this one will," he said.

Still, I was convinced I had to confront Barry about his suspicions—I had some of my own as well. When I got home, I said, "I saw your cover of *GQ* on the way home from work. It was great. I guess Ken finally got you to agree. I'm curious, though. Didn't the magazine wonder where this model was coming from, having no history or work-related experience?"

"It was a deadline, and the model who was supposed to show up for the shoot didn't, so Ken stood in for him. He was right there, so we used him."

"Wow," I said. "It'll launch his career."

"Possibly," Barry said.

"So I take it you're still friends?"

"Yeah, sure we are."

I left it there but moved on to another topic. "Barry, what's wrong? The other day in the street, you practically told me to find a new boyfriend. Is that what you want? Do you really think I'm interested in someone else?"

"No, I know you love me, but your eyes were straying a bit."

I'd never realized Barry was jealous. He certainly had no reason to feel that way, even though many of his "good friends" were playing footsie under the table with me. Even Calvin Klein and his good buddy Egon von Furstenberg had made moves that I'd rejected. The truth was, I'd really fallen in love with Barry. He just couldn't believe that anyone could fall in love with him for who he was, not for what he was, or who he knew, or how much money and power he wielded. It was that simple.

One day I was cleaning the apartment. We had a maid, but I was just straightening up before Barry got home for dinner. He was on a shoot for *Harper's Bazaar*.

He walked in mad as hell. "Those idiots!" he fumed.

"What idiots?"

"The models, Ken, and the editor from *Harper's*. They all walked off the set. They just don't do what I tell them. I told them three times, 'I want your face and hands like this,' and they just couldn't get it. They just couldn't get it. And Ken's the worst. He's clueless."

I was beginning to see a pattern I hadn't noticed when first we got together. Barry's angry streak was starting to reveal itself.

Even Ken was complaining to me about Barry, how he'd bossed around everyone on the set, including the female models, Angelica and Patti, who happened to be his friends.

"He was acting in a condescending manner, like he was God, dictating how they should interact," he told me. "When we didn't get the shot right first time, he flew off the handle. Well, we all had just about enough, and we walked off. He can't treat people like that. They're just not going to work for him. I don't care how sought after he is, he's going to lose clients. I know you guys do coke from time to time. Has he been doing a lot of it?"

"Frankly, I don't know, Ken, but why don't you ask him yourself?"

"Well, I thought, you know, being his lover, you'd have access to that information."

"If I did, what makes you think I'd give it to you?"

"Well, you don't have to get all in a huff, baby."

"The truth is you don't give a shit about Barry or me," I said. "I know you won't tell Barry because you don't have the balls, but you can tell me. I know you've been driving a wedge between us for some time. But I'd just like to ask you why. Why would you do this to your best friend? Why would you break up what little happiness Barry has in his life outside of his work, when it's obvious to everyone around us how happy he's been since he fell in love with me?"

"Well, darling," he said in his obnoxious campy Australian accent, "you know, you were taking a large bite out of my piece of pie."

"Your piece of pie!" I exclaimed.

"Well, yeah, baby," he said. "You were getting too close to him. You were taking up all his free time."

"So it was you who decided to plant this evil shit in his mind, so he'd leave me. You told him I was unfaithful, didn't you? Because you knew he was vulnerable, and you knew he'd surrender to whatever you said even if it wasn't true, to avoid looking weak to himself or others. You know for a fact I've never gone out with anyone and have no desire to. It must have made it so easy for you to deceive me. After all, I'm nothing to you, just a dumb kid in love whose only wish was to follow his heart. Damn you, Ken Framn. Damn you. You are not my friend."

"Well, baby, I guess you're right. I'm not. But I do fancy shagging you."

"Not a chance in the world, but I guess you knew that already," I said sarcastically.

The world of models, magazines, photographers, and agencies was becoming oppressive. I wasn't really a part of it, and yet, it was all around me. Barry's life had become my life.

Barry and I ran into Ivan Wells, Damien, and Keith on Christopher Street one Sunday afternoon in November. They all worked together with Ken at the Australian embassy and were friends of Barry's. Damien's lover Doug and I were beginning to develop our own relationship, apart from the Australians, even though the two of us were romantically involved with them. We began to refer to all of them as the "Australian contingent" while we became known as the "American slags." It was playful, but there was a note of discontent on Doug's part.

Let me paint a picture of the Village bar scene. Ty's had a particularly nice crowd of men and was popular. Keller's was down on West Street. On any Sunday afternoon, the beer bust could have three hundred men standing out on West Street across from the piers down by the Hudson. There was a rather phenomenal drag queen by the name of Rollerena, who wore a white wedding dress complete with tiara and roller skates. She used to skate all over the neighborhood, carrying a white wand by night and wearing a plaid suit by day. She carried her skates to work in the morning on the Seventh Avenue line.

One cold Sunday afternoon, three hundred men were standing out in front of Keller's, drinking beers. A Puerto Rican wedding party got out of a limo at the pier, and Rollerena flew across the street on her skates to welcome the wedding party to the neighborhood. She skated right into the bridesmaids and could be seen chatting up all the other colorful girls in taffeta. A roar came up from the hoard of men standing outside Keller's as they looked on in disbelief. She waved her gay wand, crowning the bride and groom with a touch of it on their heads as if she was the good fairy. The wedding party cheered in response.

Up from Keller's were the Anvil, the Eagle, and the Spike, which were heavy leather bars. Rollerena could be seen skating through the Spike as two S&M guys acted out their master/slave relationship. It was supposed to be a serious high exhibition for the bar clientele, but when she "bonked" the master with her wand, the place went wild, cheering and laughing at the master's humiliation. But Ty's was innocent, just a place to meet and be seen. Being relatively new to New York, for me, the Village was the epicenter of gay life on the East Coast.

As the weeks passed, my relationship with Barry deteriorated. He grew intolerably jealous. Again, we were strolling down Christopher Street when I happened to notice some men hanging out at Ty's. Again, he became insanely jealous. That was when he pushed me too far.

Referring to a very hot man in white Levi's leaning against the wall and smiling at me, he said in his heavy Australian accent, "You slag. Like that one, do you? Well, go get him."

That's exactly what I did. I walked across the street, knowing that it probably would end our relationship forever, and chatted up the handsome man. He asked me to go home with him. I struck out at Barry's heart. I was so angry, I wanted to hurt him the way he'd hurt me. I shocked myself. I didn't think I was capable of doing such an awful thing to someone I loved. I'd never done anything like that before because I took love seriously. Of course, in hindsight I know it was terribly immature. Barry's jealousy sucked the life out of us. There was no hope that we could survive. I knew I had to leave.

The next day, I began packing. Barry wasn't home, so that made it a little easier. I left a note on the mantel. I said I was sorry I'd hurt him but that I had to go. I told him I'd be leaving the following night on an Air France flight bound for Bombay. I asked him to forward any mail to me care of Poste Restante, Bombay, India. I told him I still loved him.

I looked back through the apartment, and in a flash, all the wonderful evenings we'd shared together came alive again. Then I locked the door and slid my key underneath it.

Chapter Seventeen

India

I was torn up emotionally when the plane touched down in Bombay, but I knew I'd made the correct decision. I wouldn't have time to dwell on self-pity. I was going back for something of myself I'd lost in New York and thought I could find again in Goa.

When I went to the post office, there was a card from Barry. It was dated November 1975, just two weeks after I'd left.

> *Tried to catch your flight minutes before you left JFK. I have a photo shoot in Morocco. Have a villa in Tangier. Ten big bedrooms. Are you interested? Love, Barry.*

As far as I was concerned, he'd chosen Ken and his friendship over our love affair. No, I wasn't going back.

I decided to return to Goa on the boat. It was like déjà vu. I wondered if any of my friends were still there, Maria and Eduardo or maybe Umberto. I also wondered if I was running after an illusion. I knew I'd experienced freedom and consciousness there. Could I find it again? Or was freedom in me, and I didn't need to find it at all? There was tremendous peace and tranquility in Goa, which was why it was a good place for me to recover. I was going back. Would things be different now that I had a choice of whether to stay or leave?

Calangute Beach

The whole journey began to feel like a pilgrimage. I crossed the river at Panjim and caught the boat to the northern beaches, then the bus to

Calangute Beach. As I walked through the village into the noonday market, still full of fresh fish from the morning catch, it was like I'd woken up from a dream.

"Saab!" an old woman yelled out from one of the stalls. It was Maya. "You come back." She jumped up from peeling her papayas and came over to me. In true Indian friendship, she held my hands, shaking them together one on top of the other. Then she clasped her own together and bowed, giving me the traditional welcome. "Namaste. How are you?"

She and the others were genuinely happy to see me again. I walked past my barber, and he immediately took me in for a shave.

"Raj," I said, "I have money to pay you," and we laughed. I used to pay him in fish.

"We will make you look very handsome, saab. You look healthy, not so skinny like before. There are many girls here this year. Maybe you will settle down with one?"

What he didn't know wouldn't hurt him.

"Do you rent a house?" he asked.

"No, Raj. Maybe this time I'll just rent a room."

"I know a woman on the beach. She is renting rooms. There is one Western man living there now from Italy."

"Can you take me to her today?" I asked.

"*Accha, baba*, I will take you."

I met the woman, Chandra, a fisherman's wife from the village. She recognized me from before and I her.

"Oh, saab, will you stay for a long time?" she asked.

"I don't know."

Her boarder turned out to be an Englishman, not an Italian. He was a nice guy from Dover who loved to go surfing every day.

"The room comes with meals," Chandra said. "Two hundred fifty rupees."

"I'll take it for a month."

I immediately undressed and got into the *lungi* I'd purchased in Bombay. Eagerly, I put on a T-shirt and sandals and headed for the beach. I couldn't wait to climb the point and see my friends at Anjuna Beach. A year and a half had passed since I'd left. I waded across the Vaga River again and started to climb the rocky cliff to the point, past the blooming cashew trees, everything delightfully familiar.

Yet I noticed something had changed. It wasn't the landscape. It was me. I realized I was trying to recreate the beautiful freedom I'd found there. But freedom wasn't a place. It was something inside me.

I was sadly disappointed. Goa wasn't the same. There were a few tepees still on the beach, but most were gone. The Indian government had moved out all the vagabonds. It was such a shame to see it deserted. It was over. It had been a beautiful experiment, but realistically, how long could it have lasted?

What I found instead was an imitation of the village at Anjuna Beach: young people from Western Europe and the Americas trying to resurrect what proved a unique experiment in freedom.

We'd lived in a community built on love, this small fishing village, Anjuna, this lotus on the ocean. Anjuna, where in the winter of 1973, freedom reigned unchecked by the rest of society. Where for a brief period in my life, there was no yesterday and no tomorrow, but only today. It was an international commune built on the edge of the Indian Ocean that housed people who searched for the truth and wanted to become an instrument of it. Goa had been an international "free zone" for the world's hippies, an experiment in freedom. Now it was commercialized, sold as a tourist destination.

Patrick Trinier

Still, it was beautiful beyond words, and so I settled back to just taste its wonders again. I wandered down the beach, deep in nostalgia about Barry, rethinking how it all went down and dissecting each point at which it failed. The breakup hit hard. I was only twenty-five, so there would be other Barrys, I thought, or at least, I tried to convince myself. Our meeting was pivotal, and I knew that when

I returned to the States, I'd have to be serious about exactly what I wanted to do with my life. For the moment, I was content to wander the beaches of South Asia. Who knew when this opportunity would come again?

That was when I met Patrick Trinier.

He was six foot four, with silver hair and the most electric blue eyes you could imagine, the kind that make you stop and take notice. The mixture of premature gray and handsome young looks—high cheekbones, square jaw, and swimmer's physique—was irresistible. What was even more unbelievable, he was gay.

We were the only gay men on the northern beaches. How amazing was that? Most gay men didn't think of India as a destination but rather a blurb in the newspaper describing a horrible drought, typhoon, or famine, a place to be avoided. Palms Springs was a more likely destination.

The two of us were befuddled at our good fortune, and blinded by our chemistry. What were the chances we'd find a mate in India? We explored one another slowly. He was living in a house, and I had my rented room. As the relationship grew, I realized he was either very quiet or very cautious. There was something he wasn't telling me, and I could feel it.

I told him all about Barry and New York, and he told me about Gibsons Landing in British Columbia, where he bartended at a resort. He was French and from Canada. The details were sketchy, and I had to keep asking questions until he finally revealed why he'd really come to India. He was trying his hand at smuggling, since bartending wasn't going to advance him into the landed gentry in the form of a house with a white picket fence.

I laughed and told him about my near catastrophe in Turkey. It seemed nothing I could do or say would dissuade him. He was sure he'd get through. Who was I to tell him no? After all, I'd done the same thing.

After wandering the beach for about a month, I told him I was going back to Bombay, and invited him along. I had it in my mind that I was ready to go back to New York and try my hand at photography. It would be less profitable than smuggling, and a lot safer. But I had to admit to myself that I had a thing for Patrick. We'd been together every day for a month and a half. We were, for all intents and purposes, living together. He was kind and soft-spoken, not at all the type to smuggle hashish. He also was a take-charge kind of guy and a real gentleman. Women adored him, and I'm not sure, but I think he was bisexual. His darker habits made him a bad boy and a rebel. I secretly liked it. There was some juice around it.

We took a room in my old stomping grounds at the Rex Hotel in the Colaba district, near the Gateway of India. The room was on the third floor and had a view of the Indian Ocean from the Victorian wrought iron balcony. We'd have our breakfast brought up while we were dressed in nothing but loincloths. He smoked Gitanes, like every good French-Canadian did back then.

The waiter arrived and put down the breakfast tray, holding eggs, bacon, and strong Indian tea. Patrick paid him, the cigarette hanging from his mouth while he searched for some change, sticking the remainder inside his rolled-up sarong.

"Sandeep?"

"Yes, saab?"

"Can you bring me the *Times*?" Patrick asked, referring to the London paper. "I like to read it with my meal."

"Yes, of course, saab," the waiter sang out in that pedantic Indian accent, swaying his neck like a snake. "Right away, saab. Hurry, hurry. No problem, just five minutes."

Sometimes we didn't get out of bed until noon. It was a steamy, laid-back, and exotic love affair. The man was an animal. That day, he asked me if I'd ever tried snorting morphine.

"Honestly, no, and I don't think I will."

"Why not? It's like every other experience. For some, it's good, and for some . . . Try it and see for yourself. You've got an open mind."

"Yeah, but Patrick, it's dangerous. You can get hooked."

"Not when you snort it. Just try it. If you don't like it, don't do it."

"You want to do it now?"

"Why not?"

"Because it's too early. It's barely noon."

"Perfect time."

"Okay, so how do you do it?"

Instantly, he produced all the paraphernalia. Out came the hand mirror and a razor blade. He quickly went about the job of refining the powder. Chop, chop chop, chop chop atop the mirror. He pulled from his sarong a fifty-rupee note and rolled it up like a cigarette for a straw.

"Okay, get those hot buns of yours over here," he said, making some lines on the mirror with the blade like a lightning bolt in a long, continuous line.

"Where do I start?"

"Pick your end," he said. "It doesn't matter."

I took a sniff. "Oh baby, it burns. That's not nice."

"Well, honey, it's going to get a lot nicer soon."

As the morphine hit, a feeling of euphoria spread through me. "Wow, that's intense!"

He began kissing me and rubbing his hands over my chest, and before I knew it we were making love, seamlessly, with no beginning and no end.

A few days later, I told him I had to go back to the States. I told him that if he wanted to contact me, he could write care of Barry McKinley, the only address I knew by heart. I told him it was time for me to return to the Big Apple and then I hoped to find a job in San Francisco.

He said he'd come visit me in San Francisco when he returned. I thought he was in love, but I wasn't sure, and I figured time would tell. If he showed up on my doorstep, I'd see then if we were meant to be together.

Chapter Eighteen

New York, New York

It was March 1976, cold and bitter, when I arrived. I almost wondered why I'd returned, but I knew it was time to move on with my life. I called Erik and Sam, old friends of Barry's, for help. I told them I'd just arrived in New York, and without me even asking, they invited me to stay with them. I sat in a dive of a diner on Forty-Second Street, waiting for Erik to pick me up. My hair was damp, and I had no umbrella. My denim jacket wasn't nearly warm enough for a New York winter. As I cupped the hot coffee mug with both my frozen hands, Erik walked in.

"Oh, Michael, you look absolutely frozen. How are you?"

"Cold," I said. "You look terrific. Thanks so much for picking me up. You're a doll."

"You know you've been missed." He smiled.

"By whom?"

"I think you know the answer to that."

"Oh, no, Erik, I can't. I can't see him for a while. It's really over."

He told me how upset Barry was after I left, and how he blamed himself for everything. I told him it would be impossible for me to go back to Barry's, and asked if I could stay with him for a few days until I could organize myself and start looking for a job.

"Of course," Erik said. "You can stay as long as you need."

I breathed in deeply, so glad I was home. Erik was like family.

New York wasn't new to me. I'd first come to the city the summer I was thirteen. It was so hot you could fry an egg on the sidewalk. My uncle Milton lived on West 105th Street. We'd take a cab up there from my aunt Anna's at West 80th Street and Columbus. It was a rough neighborhood in those days. They called it Spanish Harlem. Some Puerto Rican kids were playing baseball in the street, and as our cab passed, they struck it with a baseball bat. The driver was pissed, screaming at them in Spanish. I was shocked. It reminded me of *West Side Story*.

All my relatives, except for my immediate family, lived in Manhattan when I met Barry, and I wanted to visit them.

I saw my great-aunt, Anna, a spinster and a little conservative but a sweet lady. Her life had stopped sometime in the '30s when the love of her life died of cancer a few months prior to their marriage. She'd lived in the same building for forty years, on the third floor, overlooking Planetarium Park on Columbus Avenue, and she was probably the building's oldest tenant.

I confided in her about everything—Barry, the trip to India, that I was ready to stop traveling and work on what I wanted to do. But first, I needed an apartment and a job. I convinced her to put in a good word with the superintendent of her building, which was how apartments were rented back then. You needed to know someone. Usually someone had to die before you could find a nice place in a good neighborhood with a view, but Anna worked miracles. She set up an interview with the superintendent, and I convinced him to give me an apartment with no money down, saying that within two weeks I'd pay for the whole month. Anna had a lot of clout. Now I only had to figure out how I'd pay for the apartment.

It was a ninth-floor studio, with two floor-to-ceiling windows overlooking the most expensive real estate in Manhattan, the Upper East Side. I had a view of practically all of Central Park and even the East River, Queens, and Brooklyn. What a find. At $185 a month, it was perfect.

When I returned to Erik's, he was on the phone with Barry, letting him know I was back and staying with them. He hung up.

"Michael, Barry's pissed off. He thinks you should have called him first, and he wants you to come down to Jones Street and stay with him."

"Does he now?" I cried out sarcastically. "Erik, this is never going to work."

"But he loves you, and it's so obvious."

"He doesn't love me. He loves the idea of me. And if anyone gets too close, he becomes insanely jealous. I think there's a part of Barry that truly loves me, but his ego rules, and it speaks through him with unloving actions, which separate and estrange us by judgments on whether I'm loyal. If I go back for a trial run, I'll be walking on eggshells."

"No, he told me that whenever you want to go, he won't stand in your way."

"He said that?" I questioned, smiling. "Okay, where's his phone number?" I called, expecting him to be rude and arrogant, but he wasn't. He was the sweet man I'd first met a year and a half ago, charming and funny. He caught me off guard, and I felt bad for thinking the worst. "Hi, Barry" I said. "How are you?"

"I've missed you something awful, Boop. Why don't you come down and stay with me for a while and just see if we can make a go of it again? Michael, I've changed. I really do love you, and I know I acted like such a fool before you left for India. Let me make it up to you."

"On one condition," I said. "I have a new apartment, and I'd like to keep it. That way I won't feel like I'm burdening you, or that you're taking care of me, okay?"

"Okay, but can you come and stay with me tonight?" he begged.

"Okay, see you in forty-five minutes."

I had no idea what I was doing. My feelings still ran deep, even though he'd really hurt me. And what about Patrick? I was apprehensive. At the same time, if it didn't get awkward, I'd try it. Maybe there was a chance again that something was calling me. I needed to find out for sure. I hadn't told him I'd stay.

When we met again, it was like the first time. There was a sparkle, a glimmer, maybe of something to be. That night turned into intimate dinners, evenings at the theater, invitations to parties, and wonderful sex. It was going well. I thought maybe he'd really understood that I was the one person in his life who didn't want anything from him. A week passed, and I was looking for work every day.

Then it began again, the jealousy, and I realized Barry hadn't changed. I told him I couldn't go through it again. He was furious. We had a big argument, and I stormed out of the apartment. We struggled through the next week. I consulted his friends, and all of them agreed he was stressed out. His parents were coming for a visit from Australia. We agreed I should move back to Erik's for a week before my apartment was ready, while Barry's parents were visiting. It would give me some time to reassess whether I'd been too hasty in returning to him. I began to see the picture of an unhappy genius, a frustration not uncommon in gifted people. It's almost like the fatal flaw that keeps them from being fulfilled.

I left Erik's after a week and took possession of my apartment.

Meanwhile, I received a letter from Patrick. Barry gave it to me. He asked who it was from, and I replied, "Just a friend."

I read it later. It said: "Am sending you candy in a magazine."

I couldn't believe Patrick would have the audacity to send something illegal, most likely hashish, in the mail, to a fictitious name, care of Barry McKinley. I called Barry and told him Patrick was sending something illegal in a package to the Jones Street address, and by no means should he accept it.

The next day, Barry invited me for dinner and introduced me to his parents as his friend. I knew he hadn't told them yet that he was gay, which was another reason I had to leave the apartment. His parents were conservative, but very nice folks. At dinner, he leaned over and told me he'd received a notice that the mailman had tried to deliver a package, and he'd have to go down to the post office to sign for it.

"Don't go. Don't try to pick it up. It's dangerous."

He agreed he wouldn't.

I said good night and went back to Erik's while Barry entertained his parents.

A couple of nights passed when I received a call from him. He was completely undone, his voice shaking.

"What's up, honey?" I asked. "You sound terrible."

"I went down to the post office to pick up the package, and they said that they'd deliver it the next day."

"What happened?"

"They delivered the package," he sobbed.

"Yes, and what happened?"

"I accepted it and closed the door. Then they practically broke down the door, threw me on the living room rug, and handcuffed me, right in front of my parents."

"Who was it?" I asked in angst.

"It was the FBI."

"Oh, Barry, I'm so sorry. Why on earth did you ask them to redeliver the package?"

"I don't know," he cried. "Can you help me?"

"Of course. What can I do?"

"I need you to tell them I didn't know what was in the package."

"Well, what was in the package?" I asked. "Hashish?"

"No, Michael, it was heroin. They want to deport me. It's a felony, and I only have a green card to work here."

"Oh my God! Sure, I can tell them that you didn't know what was in it."

I was livid with Patrick. I never wanted to see him again. I couldn't imagine he was capable of this. What's more, the damage he'd done was inconceivable. Now I was responsible for my lover's possible deportation. It would ruin him and his reputation. I wondered how I could possibly make this right.

While Barry's bust went down, I got a call from David Cohen, Robin's cousin, who was the lawyer handling my claim with the insurance agency for the broken elbow. He told me they were ready to settle and he'd like to see me in his office in Brooklyn the following day. Since David was a lawyer, I wanted to ask him about what was going on with Barry and see if legally I had any culpability.

Then Barry called to say he'd failed the polygraph. They knew he was lying when he said he had no knowledge of what was in the package. The truth was he knew it held drugs, just not heroin. He was extremely upset, and again, he asked me to lie and tell the authorities that he knew nothing of the contents. When I hesitated and asked him how I could really be of help when he'd failed the lie detector test, he said he'd show the authorities the letters I wrote to him talking about taking acid on the beach in Goa under the full moon. He was blackmailing me.

His vengeance flared. "If I'm going down, you're going down with me," he said.

I couldn't see how, unless guilt by association. I knew he was desperate, and if there had been anything that I could do to help him, I would have done it. But he'd betrayed himself, and if I lied under oath, I'd only be perjuring myself.

I went to see David and discuss everything. I told him I still loved Barry, but I was seeing a different side of him, one I'd only glimpsed earlier. David said Barry would try to take me down with him, but there was no evidence I'd done anything illegal. He told me that if Barry was willing to blackmail me, what else would he be willing to do? David advised me to have no contact with Barry, and all future contact should be through him. He made it clear I must agree.

"Barry is scared, and he's going after you," he said.

Barry called and told me that if I didn't help him, he'd never speak to me again. This would be one of the last times I'd communicate directly with him for the remainder of our lives, and it was heartbreaking that it ended like that.

I couldn't believe that Patrick's complete lack of maturity could have caused so much pain and suffering. Barry's parents were devastated. The government wanted to deport him. He lost friends, who distanced themselves lest their own drug problems surface. He was scorned by the editor of *Vogue*. But worst of all was his lover, who wouldn't lie to the police about what he knew or didn't know. There wasn't a soft place for him to land. I felt so sorry for him. I felt guilty that I'd given Patrick Barry's address. I didn't think I'd ever be able to forgive Patrick.

When the paparazzi and the newspapers got the story, the headline read: *Top Fashion Photographer Barry McKinley Arrested for Heroin.*

I was depressed. I still hadn't found work with all that going on, and I only had another week to pay the superintendent the month's rent. I was looking in earnest. I had interviews every day—overqualified, underqualified, not enough experience, too young. With the felony on my record, a teaching job was out of the question.

It's every gay man's dream to live and work in Manhattan, and we're all obsessed with the idea, but after Barry and the high-flying life I'd led, I was seeing Manhattan from the bottom up, just scrimping by.

Then one day, when I'd given up all hope, I was walking down Twenty-Eighth Street in the garment district. Everywhere back then you'd see Puerto Rican men pushing large racks of clothing on wheels that the latest designers had just finished, ready for mass-marketing in the surrounding warehouses.

In between the troves of clothes were Jewish delicatessens. I'd been looking for work nonstop since the breakup, and I just had to get a job. I was so tired of pounding the pavement that I took refuge in one of those diners. I ordered a bowl of matzo ball soup, some comfort food, and watched as the district's buyers and sellers kibitzed over their borscht and brisket lunches.

After I caught my breath, I looked up, and there was a familiar face. "Richard!" I yelled.

"Hey, Michael," he said, remembering the circumstances of our meeting out on Fire Island earlier that summer.

"Richard," I said. "I've been looking for a job for weeks, and I can't find anything. Do you know anyone who's hiring?"

He pulled from his jacket a pen and business card and scribbled something on the back of it. "Call this guy. He'll help you out."

"Thanks" I said, in total amazement.

"Good seeing you again," he said as we parted.

My God, maybe I just might get a job after all.

I called the name on the card, and he agreed to see me that night for what I assumed was an interview. He told me to meet him on Twenty-Third Street near the Chelsea Hotel. I arrived at the apartment and knocked. The door opened, and a man in his mid-thirties appeared. I walked in and saw black shag rugs, a glass-and-chrome coffee table, and a black leather sofa and side chair. This didn't seem at all like a proper interview, but I was penniless, so what did I have to lose?

"Hi, come on in. My name is Jack, and you must be Michael."

I nodded politely.

"I suppose Richard told you what this was all about, right?"

"Not really," I said, clueless.

"Well, you'll be expected to work weekends, as that's when most of our clients come to New York. If they want you for the whole weekend, it'll be seven hundred dollars. If they just want an hour, it's seventy-five. We split fifty-fifty."

"Okay," I said, finally realizing what I'd agreed to do. I was about to become a call boy, an escort, or whatever the term was.

He asked with some angst, "Is it a deal?"

"Deal," I said, and we shook hands. At least it was a handshake and not a blow job.

I walked to the Seventh Avenue Line at Twenty-Third with a grin on my face and descended the long, dirty, urine-stained stairwell into the bowels of the city that I loved so much. I was going to make it in New York on my own no matter what it took.

I met my first John at the Twenty-Third Street apartment, and I spent the weekend with him. He was from Columbus, Ohio. I don't think I'd ever met someone from Ohio before. It wasn't terrible, but I felt like I'd betrayed myself. He was a nice enough man, but the whole weekend? I was so over that job before it began. But that was just how I had to look at it, as a job. In two weeks, I paid my rent and had enough money left for food.

I decorated my apartment with used furniture from the best neighborhoods in Manhattan. I found a radio from the '40s with the speaker still in good condition, and an abandoned cactus five foot tall. Oh, what else could you find in New York? A nice old bureau to fit the nice old radio, two stuffed chairs, an old Persian rug, a coffee table that served as my dining table, and cushions from India that served as chairs. I was rockin' and rollin' in my studio in Manhattan.

The kitchen was so small that if I had the oven door down, I couldn't open the front door. But I didn't care. I had two huge glorious windows looking out at the most fantastic city in the world, with a view right down Central Park to the East Side. Across the street was Planetarium Park, and the Museum of Natural History.

I was still looking in earnest for honest employment, and found a job with Foremost-McKesson, packing bean sprouts on Canal Street. My neighbor down the hall in 9A, Martin Esterson, turned me on to the job. I guess he'd started out there before he got into selling art. I didn't know what I wanted to do. It seemed like packing bean sprouts was a step down from packing johns. The finale came on my last night of employment with Jack.

He called me up about eight-thirty. "I've got a job for you—a Louis Stein on East Seventy-Fifth Street, Apartment 1A. He's expecting you in an hour."

"Jack, I was just getting ready for bed."

"Think of it as dessert," he said.

"Okay, I'll go," I said reluctantly.

I arrived at nine-thirty at East Seventy-Fifth Street and rang the doorbell. A portly, middle-aged Jewish man in the shape of a pear greeted me. The smell of Chanel No. 5 was overpowering, and a little yappy French poodle was nipping at my feet. As I looked down the hall of mirrors, I saw nothing but French provincial everywhere and paintings with huge gold-gilded frames. The element that most repulsed me was his high voice. It sounded like a woman. I felt sorry for him because he was obviously successful, but he seemed so needy and lonely.

"Please come in," he said.

After the door closed behind me, I looked at him and knew he'd be my last. "Sir," I said, "I just can't do this."

"I understand," he said. "Just come in and talk to me for a little while, and I'll pay you when you leave."

It was refreshing. We talked, and I realized everybody in the Big Apple has a story worth listening to, and everybody wants to be heard. In the end, we left on good terms, and he taught me a lesson in judgment, for it was my initial impression that created all the negative angst. He turned out to be a violinist with the New York Symphony. Like I said, in New York I grew more open-minded, as if anything could happen there. No more black and white, but shades of gray. There was no realm the mind could imagine that couldn't exist in the Apple, and it was all okay. That's what made New York special.

I called Jack and stopped by the Twenty-Third Street bachelor pad to tell him it was over and to pick up my last easy check. From then on, it would be packing bean sprouts with the Chinese down on Canal Street, and that was okay by me. I'd keep my eyes open for other opportunities. Hopefully, they'd come. God knows I'd hit the bottom of the barrel and was coming up slowly. If my mom could have seen me then, I would have made her proud, turning down lucrative money in prostitution for an honest day's wage. I'd joined the working class.

My studio at 101 West Eightieth, apartment 9C, was my little portal to the greatest city since Roman times. I was making a living and living to go out in New York, to taste its pleasures. It was exciting and glamorous and frightening—sometimes cold, sometimes hot and steamy, but always thrilling—because anything was possible there. I was on my own.

When I rode the subway, I'd look over the packed car and know there was a universal consciousness running underneath all of us, and we weren't separate. What happened in that subway car happened to all my fellow New Yorkers. Once at rush hour coming home from work, the train was so packed there were five people hanging off each hand grip. A crazy black man approached our section of the car, screaming racial epithets. He was one of the many sad and sorry passengers who lived on the subways. I was still green from California and hadn't learned all the ways of city life, but I was about to learn a good lesson in eye contact. Don't look at anyone who's crazy, and don't hold their gaze. They'll be in your face by the time you exhale.

So it was with this crazy man. I saw him, really saw him, and I felt genuinely sorry for his circumstance. I wasn't prepared for what happened next.

He flew into my space and began screaming, "You motherfucking honky, you motherfucking white-trash honky."

I looked at the ground as everyone around me moved away, and suddenly there was space all around this guy. I was still holding the hand grip, standing my ground, as the man's spittle from his drunken speech flew past my face. It was then that I looked at the crowd around me and realized that collectively, we all knew what was going on, and they were genuinely sorry for me, sorry that I was the one caught in the crossfire. That was when I realized collective consciousness was all around me. We're New Yorkers. I finally moved away like everyone else, and the man became an island in a sea of humanity, cursed by his disease and tolerated by us all.

I was discovering myself in New York. I'd never lived alone. I'd always had roommates. I was making new friends, and they ran the gamut from the party boys in the Village to a Revlon executive and everyone in between. I was high on the Big Apple. I had invites to the Hamptons and weekends at Fire Island. I went to the openings of artists and to poetry readings, saw Broadway shows and had evenings out at Carnegie Hall.

I was living the life of a rock star on a beer income, and every now and then when things got tight, I'd call Mom.

One night stands out. It was cold and rainy, and the luster of the big city was wearing off. I walked for blocks to find a phone booth that hadn't been jimmied or didn't just have a cord dangling like some corpse where the phone once hung. Finally, across the street from Nathan's Famous Hot Dogs on Thirty-Third Street, I found an intact booth.

"Hey, Mom, how are you?"

"Hi, sweetie," she said. "How are things in New York?"

"I'm a little glum, actually," I said, not wanting to let her know how down I really was.

"What's wrong?"

"I'm short on money, Mom." I grew sarcastic. "All you have to do is walk out your front door and there's twenty dollars missing from your wallet by the time you get back."

"How much do you need?" she asked. "Would a hundred tide you over?"

"That would be great," I said. "Can you do that?"

"As long as you don't tell your father. He thinks you should come home. Remember San Francisco, the City by the Bay?"

At that moment, as I stared out the booth at Nathan's flashing neon hot dog, I felt a pang of homesickness. Then a huge black woman wearing her best Sunday hat tried to force her way into the booth. She had an umbrella, and she'd nudged it between the doors, trying to pry them open. "I've got to make me a call," she bellowed.

The sky opened, releasing a torrent of rain.

"Lady, I'm talking to my mom!" I shouted.

But she was on a mission. She probably couldn't find a working phone either. We fought for a few minutes while I leaned against the doors to prevent her entry and she kept whacking the doors with her umbrella.

"Mom, there's a crazy lady outside the booth, and she's trying to hit me with her umbrella," I cried out hysterically, laughing in between my words. I was completely dumbfounded, realizing once again that anything was possible in New York.

Mom began laughing uncontrollably. Being a native New Yorker, she knew all too well the pitfalls of the mean streets she'd grown up on.

It was then that the notion of returning home entered my mind. As the rain pelted my little booth and I glared out through the cold, wet neon lights, I was warmed by my mother's love and the laughter of hearth and home.

My friends all told me New York was a dangerous town and to always look out the peephole when anyone knocked. I was sure they knew what they were talking about.

One night I got a call from Doug, Damien's ex. He wasn't flying for American that weekend and he invited me out for dinner to hook up with the guys, Bob and Louie, on Seventy-Second Street. "How about coming out with us tonight for dinner, and later we can go to 12 West to go dancing?"

The truth was I was broke. I had a yam cooking in the oven and a pork chop on the stove. "That sounds great, but I've got a date tonight," I replied, lying through my teeth.

"Maybe Sunday brunch in the Village then?"

"Okay, I'll call you Sunday," I said with some hesitancy. There was silence as I replayed the conversation in my head. *You're broke, my friend. You can't continue to live this kind of lifestyle on your income. Something's gotta give.*

Just then the doorbell rang. Thinking it was my neighbor down the hall and forgetting all that I'd been told, I opened the door.

Bang, bang, bang went the front door against the oven door. I'd left it down while checking the yams as I was talking to Doug.

A black man's hand and foot became wedged between the door and the jam. I was being robbed. I threw myself against the door with all my might, but he still kept pushing his way through. I wedged my foot against the oven and pushed with every bit of strength within me. The adrenalin rushed through my veins like a river of fear. There was no time to think, just push. I caught his hand, then his foot in the door. He screamed out in pain. Then I had the advantage. I was crushing his foot with the entire sub-primal force of my survival at stake. He screamed and tried to get out, but I wouldn't let up.

285

He finally tore his foot from the jam, the door banged shut, and I slammed the bolt across it.

I stood there in shock, my jugular vein pounding in my neck. I looked out the peephole to see a black man in his late twenties or early thirties in a hooded sweatshirt and blue jeans—disoriented and limping horribly down the corridor, trying to find his way to the stairwell. He looked so pathetic that I started to laugh. It was a brutal reminder that I wasn't in Oz anymore.

Paul Meyers

As the summer of 1976 slipped into fall, I found myself dating a wonderful man I'd met on Fire Island. His name was Paul Meyers. He lived in a modest house on the bay side and was an executive at Revlon. He was one of the most unpretentious, unassuming, and down-to-earth gentlemen I ever knew. I say gentleman because he was just that. He was mature, he knew who he was, and he was spiritual. Not the church-slapping kind of spiritual, but when I woke up with him, I could feel the connection to the planet, to everything. He was mild-mannered, with a great sense of humor and an intellect that made me want to stay with him, and an oh-so-sexy smile. And I wasn't alone in that assessment. He was like Michael Caine in *Alfie*. The boys were lined up for Paul.

Touchstones *A Survivor's Story*

Paul Meyers

Why he took a shining to me, I'll never know for sure. He always used to say that sex with me wasn't too shabby, his roundabout way of telling me that he liked me a lot. I was twenty-five, and he was in his mid-thirties. A real sage, he'd seen the world. We'd sit up in bed, and I'd recount my journey to the Middle East and Asia. We'd talk into the wee hours of the morning, never tiring of the mystery of our lives in Manhattan. We both felt that the sun rose and set on that sliver of an island.

We'd make love all night and wake to a glorious morning, and he'd make me brunch. We'd sit outside on the deck with only the birds to keep us company. Then we'd swim at the beach, come home, light a fire, and make love all afternoon. At night, we'd take a water taxi from the Pines to the Ice Palace in the Grove and dance high on ecstasy until sunrise. Then we'd walk the beach back to his place through the warm surf.

Paul lived uptown on Seventy-Fifth Street, between Madison and Lexington, in a beautiful brownstone. He designed the whole interior of the place. Everything had a function as well as being beautiful. He was a class act.

By December of that year, I was still working downtown, waiting tables and packing bean sprouts, not very glamorous gigs for a guy who had such fine friends and such an upbeat lifestyle. It seemed what I wanted to do, which was become a photographer, wasn't something I could do in New York. I couldn't find even an entry-level position in photo development. I'd have to go back to school.

Then one winter night after work, a week before Christmas, I was walking down Broadway from the Seventy-Ninth Street station. There was sleet pelting me in the face and a wind chill factor of minus seventeen degrees. My nose and ears were frozen. Suddenly, New York, the city I'd come to love like a lover, was showing signs of disillusionment. Sure, I'd survived, but I wanted more than that. I wanted to thrive. I wanted to be a photographer like Barry. Maybe it wasn't realistic, but that's where my passion was.

I knew it was time to leave. Everybody in New York knows when it's time to leave, when things haven't worked out like they should. I'd seen it with so many people who came and went. I just didn't think I'd be one of them. Maybe I was just holding onto a dream, not reality.

I dialed the phone. "Paul, I'm leaving," I said.

"Where are you going?" he asked innocently. "To the Hamptons for Christmas?"

"I'm leaving New York. I'm going back to San Francisco. I can't do it anymore, Paul. It's always a struggle here, and I can't do what I really want to do if I don't go back to school. You know what I'm saying?"

"What about NYU, and studying photography here?" I could hear the disappointment in his voice.

"You know I couldn't afford the tuition with what I make at my job," I protested, sadness in my words.

He knew I'd never ask him for money, so he never offered it. He knew me well enough to know better. "When are you leaving?"

"December twenty-third," I said.

"That's in four days!"

"Yes, I know," I replied remorsefully.

"I'll take you to the airport," he said, trying to sound upbeat.

"You don't have to do that," I said. "I can take a cab. I only have a few boxes."

"I'll come by and pick you up," he insisted.

"All right then. Thank you. I'd love to see you and say goodbye." When I hung up, I felt such mixed emotions. I was torn apart, feeling like maybe I was making a mistake. I knew Paul loved me, might even be in love with me, but it wasn't mutual. I loved him. I just wasn't in love with him, which made leaving a little easier but just as emotional. My love affairs with New York and with Barry were over.

I said goodbye to my family, my uncle Milton, my great-aunt Anna, and a few of my cousins. With Anna, a spinster living on her own, I had second thoughts, but she'd been living that way for fifty years in that same apartment, so she'd get on. We were close by then, and I knew I'd miss popping down to her apartment for breakfast on a Saturday with her fresh coffee grinder and her bagels with cream cheese and raspberry jam. And dear Uncle Milton. A sweet old soul, he embodied everything that was loyal and good in our family. He was always there, lending a helping hand with whatever he could. I'd miss him.

I called Barry to say I was leaving and how sorry I was that everything had gone so badly. I really don't know what I was expecting.

"Well, goodbye then," he said. "Don't call me again. I want to try to forget you forever."

"Goodbye, Barry," I said sadly.

Barry influenced me more than he'd ever know, and I'll always be grateful for that rendezvous with destiny, for he and New York changed my life. My experiences there prepared me for much tougher things to come. My appreciation for photography has been a lifelong pursuit. Surely, there are no accidents in life, only bad choices. I've been extremely lucky.

All my buds were totally miffed that I was leaving. I asked why, but I knew. We had a party, dancing at 12 West until dawn, and then they walked me to the Sheridan Square subway station. They all waved as I boarded the Seventh Avenue for the trip uptown. We'd shared something special in New York at a special time in its history—the early '70s. They all promised to come to San Francisco, but none ever did. By 1982, all of them were dead except for Barry.

I left my huge cactus plant with Martin, my friend who lived down the hall in 9A, along with the antique radio he admired. I packed my things from India and my clothes inside two medium boxes, tied them with hemp and handles to carry, and that was it. I took one last look out my windows. It was gray, but I could see Central Park as it stretched uptown, all brown from winter, the East River, and Brooklyn. It was time to close that chapter of my life.

I called Paul.

"Are you ready to leave?" he asked.

"No, I'm looking at the view. Just honk. I can see you from here, and I'll come down."

"Okay, see you in about twenty minutes."

I was expecting a cab, but instead, a black limousine pulled up. Paul got out and waved me down from the ninth floor. When I reached the car, the chauffeur took my boxes without a glance, as though they were Louis Vuitton, and put them safely in the trunk. I jumped in, so happy to see Paul. He gave me his sexy, excited smile, but I could still see his disappointment. We kissed.

"Driver, JFK as fast as you can," he said. "Champagne?"

"Sure, why not?" I said, feeling wonderfully familiar and warm in his presence.

There in the limo was a bar all set up. *I Love Lucy* was playing on the television. The bottle of champagne was chilling in a bucket of ice.

He poured me a glass and then one for himself. "To the future," he announced.

Our glasses clinked. Then from the cabinet, he pulled out a mirror full of cocaine. I laughed. It was unbelievable. I took a snort, then he did, and we began to talk about New York as we sipped our champagne. We laughed and talked and smooched across the Brooklyn Bridge. I always must look back at this point to realize what I was leaving behind. It's my ritual.

We talked about our affair. "I love you, Paul. You're one of a kind. You have no idea how hard this is for me." I invited him to come stay with me in San Francisco, as I knew he'd be out there for work from time to time.

Just as I started to get comfortable with him again and contemplated not leaving, he said, "Well, here we are. It's time for you to go."

I was so high that the last thing I wanted to do was leave, and he was aware of it. He was trying to let me know what I'd be missing.

"Goodbye, Paul. Thanks for everything."

It was the end, the class act, the limousine, champagne on ice, cocaine, and *I Love Lucy*. I had tears in my eyes as I kissed him goodbye. One last hug, and I was standing in front of American

Michael Rossum

Limousine leaving New York with Paul Meyers, 1976

Airlines, carrying my cardboard boxes, one in each hand, on my way back home.

I always had a heavy heart when it came to Barry. Some years ago, in 1992, while Adrian and I were visiting my relatives in New York, I took him down to my old haunts in the Village. I don't know, maybe I thought Barry might walk in. We sat in the Bagel having breakfast the way Barry and I had done so many times before. Mario, the Puerto Rican manager of the place, was still there, and he came up and said hello.

"How is he doing?" I asked. "Do you see him?"

Mario knew exactly who I was talking about and shook his head. "Not too good."

"What do you mean?" I asked.

"Barry has AIDS. He doesn't look so good. He has a new lover, you know."

"Is he happy?" I asked.

"I don't know, really," he replied. "You should call him."

Poor Barry. Maybe it was time I made the call. Maybe he'd be ready to put the past behind him and let me apologize for what happened.

I dialed, and a young guy answered the phone.

"Who are you?" the young man asked.

"My name is Michael Rossum, and Barry and I were good friends once. I was hoping to reach him. Is he available?"

"No, he's on a shoot, but I'll let him know that you called."

I left my number, but he kept his promise never to speak to me again. On advice from a therapist, sometime after the call, I wrote him a letter and told him everything that was going on and how much he'd meant to me and that he'd changed my life. I made my amends with him in the letter and told him I'd always regret what happened to him and that I loved him.

I never heard from him again. He died a year later, in 1993.

Michael Rossum

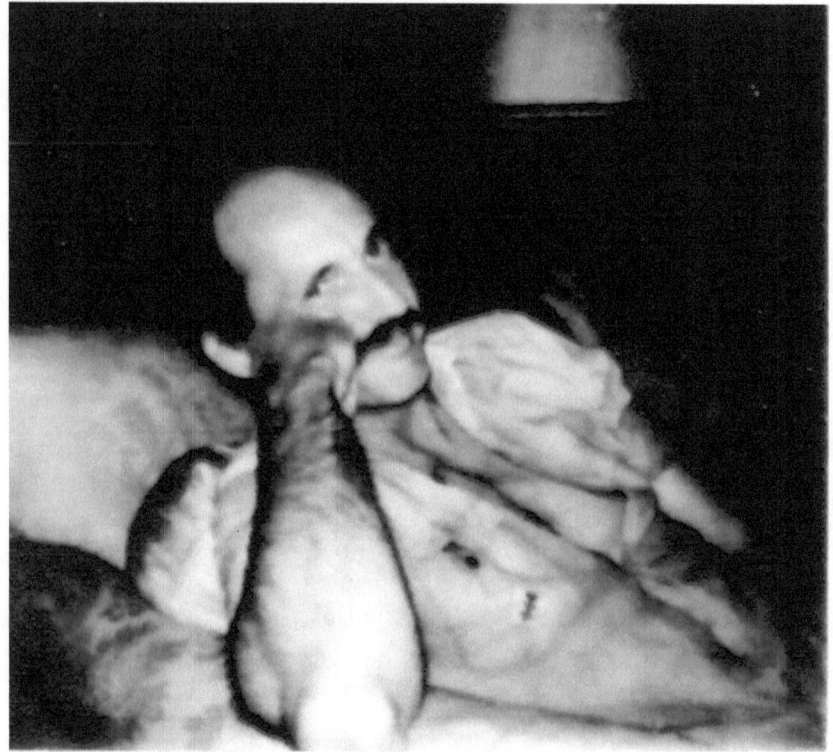

Michael Strater

Chapter Nineteen

Michael Strater

It was 1976 when I met Michael. He was friends with my landlord, Donald Lipper. My landlord was the Anna Madrigal of Waller Street in the Haight-Ashbury. Just like in *Tales of the City*, he lived in a grand Victorian next door to our apartment house, which was on the corner, linked by a walkway. However, unlike Anna, the landlady in the book, he was the male version of the mystical, pot-smoking landlady without the sex change.

Don was a real character with a lot of charisma, and I believe he spent as much time in my apartment as he did his own. In fact, he was friendly with all his tenants. We'd all take the sun and have picnics on the roof deck, which spanned the entire roof and could only be accessed by the side staircase on Ashbury Street or from my apartment. Our communal life took place on the roof. That was where we could get away from it all, catch a breeze coming off the ocean, and socialize after the day's work was done.

Besides me, there were Marilyn Galinsky and Richard Chamberlin, my roommates. Downstairs was a good-looking gay boy by the name of Tim, a construction worker. Marie and her dark-haired prince Jacque from France lived on the Waller side of the building. He and she crafted beautiful silver and semiprecious stones into jewelry, which they sold to tourists at Ghirardelli Square. And then above them were Bobby and James, two brothers, one gay and one straight. Bobby was a waiter, and his brother worked at Bank of America as a teller. They rounded out the eccentric apartment house at Waller and Ashbury.

One beautiful day in May, Marilyn, Tim, and I were sunning on the deck when Donald brought Michael Strater up to meet his wild and crazy tenants and take in the view. Michael looked to be in his early forties, with a receding hairline and a prominent Roman nose that made him look like a patrician. When he became animated, he drew people to him as if he was a wizard. Michael was a teller of stories, and he had many. He was a worldly man of substantial education and privilege, a masculine man with a handsome physique.

They sat on the edge of the blanket, and I offered them some wine. Donald pulled out a joint. We got to talking, and then Donald said to Michael Strater, "Michael has just come back from India. You should see the way he's decorated his place downstairs. It's like a pasha's palace with all these saris he brought back and bronze statues."

Michael said he was interested in Asian art. "I went to Asia and to Borneo," he said. "It was on a rich bitch tour to see the indigenous tribes, but we wound up in the middle of a war between two tribes, and our guide was incompetent and completely unprepared to handle it. One of the tribesmen had killed the son of the chief of the rival tribe. As our air rafts floated upstream toward the ensuing turmoil, we saw a man carrying a dead body in his arms. He laid it down on the river bank just as our crafts landed. They became enraged at the killing and suddenly turned on us. As the guides tried to unhitch the boats from their moorings, they started shooting arrows. I mean, we're talking about overweight middle-aged white people scrambling for their lives. As we made our escape back to the cruise ship, one of the arrows pierced the raft, and it began to sink. We rescued the others in our boat as the waves washed the scuttled raft to the rocky shore."

Michael had us all mesmerized, and we were cracking up over the poor rich white folks who almost met an untimely death at the hands of a people who were completely unpredictable and living in another millennium. He was a fascinating storyteller, and he commanded our attention just with his presence.

I invited him down to the apartment, and we sat in the tent room, made with all the saris, as I told him the saga of my journey to the East and the long, unintended stay in Goa, my life in the village in Kathmandu Valley, and my interest in Buddhism. I could see we had chemistry and similar interests, and I was mildly attracted to him. We talked for a long while, and then he pulled from his jacket a plastic bag of cocaine with a rock in it the size of a lemon.

Everything Michael did, he did in a big way. There was no such thing as mediocrity. He was rich, eccentric, talented, and compassionate. I was fortunate to have made his acquaintance. He came into my life when I needed direction and some financial aid to make progress. He helped me get my photography business started by lending me his own lighting equipment, which was top-of-the-line, and sending me for one semester to the Art Institute of San Francisco to learn my trade. It was exactly what I needed, and I was thankful for his generosity.

I knew Michael was in love with me, but unfortunately, the feelings weren't mutual.

Even my father thought us a good match. He said in private after meeting Michael, "I like him. He's an intelligent man, he's well-off, and he's a socialist. He'd be a good match for you."

"Yeah, but Dad, there's one little problem. I'm not in love with him."

"Well, I hadn't thought about that," he said. "You're right."

I continued to see Michael, and though there was an understanding that I could never be his lover, I'd gladly count him as a friend. He began to mentor me, not just about photography, about which he was considerably knowledgeable, but also the arts, opera, literature, and history. We'd sit in my living room and talk for hours. I never tired of his stories or his innate wisdom.

One day he asked if I'd like to go to the opera for a season as his guest. I hated the opera as a kid, but here was an opportunity to open my horizons. Did I want to go?

"I have nothing to wear to the opera," I said.

"We can remedy that."

He took me to Wilkes Bashford on a buying spree. Wilkes Bashford was the first all-gay men's high-end clothing store to open in San Francisco. I'd only window-shopped there. Now I'd be on the inside looking out.

We walked in and were immediately met by a man who asked us if we'd like some champagne while we shopped. I felt like Audrey Hepburn as Eliza Doolittle in *My Fair Lady*, as she's completely made over by Professor Higgins so she can pass at the ball. Michael didn't want me to be embarrassed.

The sales clerk gave us each a glass, and I sipped.

"A chocolate, perhaps?" The young man passed a bowl full of Godiva chocolates.

Oh yes, I was feeling right at home.

Then another salesman greeted us. "How can I serve you today, gentlemen?"

"Well," Michael said, "I'd like a tweed sports coat for this gentleman here, some light gabardine pants to go with it, some dress shoes, and a tie."

"Right this way," the salesman said. He started putting jackets on me.

Each time I'd turn around to show Michael, he'd say, "No, not that one."

Finally, they settled on an Italian wool tweed full-length sports coat, gabardine slacks, Italian slip-ons that felt like gloves, and a beautiful tie.

Now I was making my first-ever entrance to the Opera House, all spiffed up in my new wardrobe. We walked up the front steps. The crowd was milling about, but all I could notice at first were the coffered ceilings in gold leaf, the bronze lighting, and the crystal chandeliers. It was like a royal place. Everyone was dressed up, some of the men in tuxes, and the women in fine jewelry and flowing gowns. Michael took me downstairs for a cocktail before the curtain rose. Suddenly I started seeing men from the neighborhood, my gym, the grocery store. In all the time I'd lived in the city, I'd had no idea there was a culture of gay men who loved the opera.

The bells rang three times, and then they rang again a few minutes later, announcing the opera was about to begin. We took our seats. Michael told me that the best view of any performance was from the thirteenth row—a side of his eccentricity I'd grow to love and despise—so that was where we found our seats. As we sat down, people were saying hello to Michael and nodding at me courteously. Then I realized they all had season tickets too and they all saw one another at every performance.

The orchestra began to play the prelude to *Aida* by Verdi. Leontyne Price had the starring role as the slave girl taken by the Egyptian pharaoh Ramses from the Nubian king, his enemy. But the slave girl turns out to be the Nubian king's daughter, though she doesn't reveal it until the end. Ramses professes his love for Aida and saves her from the Egyptians, who pursued her after her escape, and the two are condemned by the court to be buried alive in a tomb together.

I was stunned. At intermission, we went for another drink. I confessed to Michael that although I'd held no real love for the opera prior to the performance, I'd fallen in love with the music and the story. I told him how grateful I was for all his generosity and for showing me the beauty of the opera. Suddenly from the bar I heard my name.

"Michael, Michael, over here." It was Bill Tester and his lover Jeffery. "I didn't know you liked the opera."

I looked up at Michael and said, "I do now." I introduced him to my friends.

The bells rang again. As we sat down for the second act, Michael said with an impish smile, "Small world, isn't it?"

Thanks to Michael, I'd discovered a whole new world. As Ramses and Aida were lowered into the tomb, and the last of the light hit their eyes, I noticed some moisture dripping down my face. The performance had moved me to tears, and as I looked around, I realized that I wasn't alone.

Michael took me to Mexico to see Monte Albán in Oaxaca, the site of ruins of the Mixtec and Zapotec Indian cultures. We stayed in one of the Parador hotels, which used to be a convent, then became a jail, and then a five-star resort.

The closer I got to Michael, the more I learned that underneath his masculine exterior was a tortured man. When we returned from Mexico, he began to open up. He told me about his abusive, alcoholic mother and his absent father, the famous painter Henry Strater. He told me he'd grown up in a wealthy family from New York, then moved to Maine and New England, where he spent his formative years. In conservative New England communities, fags were never discussed, just denigrated. His mother threw lavish dinner parties, then grew sufficiently drunk to tell all her guests around the table that her son was "a faggot, a pansy, and a puff."

I can't imagine the pain she caused him. She sounded brutal.

Michael dealt with her abuse for years, until his feelings turned to rage. At night after she'd passed out drunk, he'd take all the gin bottles she'd consumed and throw them in the garbage, after which, in a rage, he'd grab her by her "piano legs" as he described them, and drag her upstairs. "Making sure that her head hit every step," he said coldly.

He told me he was seeing a psychiatrist named Dr. Andersen, and that he was making much progress. He said Dr. Andersen worked mostly with frigid women, so he was glad to spend time with Michael. It gave him a diversion. He described him as a gorgeous man with long dark hair and glasses, typically dressed in a flannel shirt, cowboy boots, blue jeans, and a silver cowboy belt. For all his kidding, it sounded like this doctor knew his problems intimately.

The more I got to know Michael, the more his illness presented itself. One weekend, he invited me and my roommates and Bill Tester to his estate in the Santa Cruz Mountains. Michael grew more and more attached to Bill, and vice versa, as they had so many things in common. They loved the opera, they both came from wealthy families, and they both enjoyed horticulture.

Surrounded by live oaks, the octagon house was situated along the coastal mountains, right at one of their peaks. A private road ended at his property. It had a spectacular panoramic view of the Pacific Ocean, and its coastline stretched for as long as one could see as it glistened over the large expanse. I was awestruck by the beauty.

Bill had come up without Jeffery, so he wasn't sure about how far to go with Michael, in terms of keeping his distance. He was terribly polite, and they got on well. They both possessed a humorous side, and laughter filled the kitchen. I was happy to see Michael so animated. He'd been so depressed. His taking a liking to Bill was a joy and a relief for me.

Later that day as we sat around the pool, Michael brought out a plate of peyote buttons that he'd purchased from some Native Americans in Arizona. All of us looked in wonder at the odd-shaped cacti buttons with furry centers. We'd heard about the Indians' great respect for this potent medicine, and we were curious to try it.

"First," Michael said, "you must take a sharp knife and cut out the furry part. It's strychnine and it's poisonous. It can kill you."

We looked at one another like maybe this wasn't such a good idea, but curiosity got the better of us, and we all dug out the centers, determined to try it.

After we took them, we waited and waited. We thought maybe we didn't take enough, but then one by one, we started to feel nauseated, each wondering whether we'd cleaned them properly. Then we began to laugh. We felt giddy and light-headed, and as the strength of the peyote increased, we began to trip. Then it was no laughing matter.

No longer attached to our egos, we felt things that prior to taking the peyote we hadn't noticed. Little things, like the breeze brushing our cheeks and hair, the heat of the sun, the hawks circling overhead, the sound of the leaves rustling. Our minds were expanding, too, not only taking in the natural beauty but also the beauty inside each of us. This continued for some time, and we didn't speak. We just experienced the world from a different perspective than we were used to, which had been veiled until then.

I stared at Bill. He bit his lip, raised his eyebrow, and stared back with a look of complete understanding, as if reading my mind. The same was true with Michael and Richard. This was powerful medicine. I'd never experienced any of them in the same way as I saw them that day, and that connection with each would last until the day they died.

When we started to come down hours later, we were finally able to speak and share our experiences and our visions. In the same way, this truly powerful medicine must have helped the young Navajo and Zuni adolescents see their visions and be welcomed into the brotherhood of the tribe as adults, being at one with each other. I know that what we shared there was sacred.

Michael invited us up to the house several times that summer, and I watched how Richard and Michael began to dislike one another. Michael was from old money, and Richard was jealous because Michael represented everything in life that Richard wanted. Rather than tell him openly that he was envious, he did it surreptitiously, by pretending that Michael's extravagances were over-the-top, and ridiculing him for his wealth. Michael, in turn, despised Richard as nouveau riche, someone who put on airs and wasn't completely authentic.

One night, Michael made us a sumptuous chicken cordon bleu dinner. We took our places around the dinner table, overlooking the Pacific, as he prepared to serve.

Richard turned his plate over. "My, my, my," he said. "Limoges china. We are dining in style tonight."

From the kitchen, Michael retorted, "Fit for a queen, Richard. Perhaps you'd like to take inventory."

We all laughed. Michael always had the upper hand in these banters, and was the last to thrust the dagger.

After dinner, he invited us to look at his 1937 Duesenberg. He'd been refurbishing it for years and had just finished painting. We walked out to the garage to take a peek. The vehicle filled the garage, a marvelous burgundy color with a tan interior, complete with running boards.

"Oh wow!" I exclaimed.

Michael asked me if I wanted to drive it.

"Yes!" As I drove down the road that led to the house, it felt awkward—no power steering in those days. I turned around and drove it back. It really was a museum piece.

When I returned, Richard had just come out of the house and wandered over to the garage. "A Duesenberg," he said, in a condescending manner. "Well, of course. What else would you have in your garage on the top of the Santa Cruz Mountains overlooking the Pacific Ocean?"

"Oh, Richard," Michael retorted, "perhaps a red Honda Civic like the one you're driving?"

Shaking it off and trying to change the subject, Richard said, "I understand from Michael you're going to Antarctica in the fall. How does one get to Antarctica?"

"You go south," Michael replied.

There was silence. The duel was over.

As time passed, Michael began to write again. He was a prolific writer and wrote hundreds of poems. Some were good, but some were dark, a reflection of what was going on in his head and the heavy pain that he bore: a mother who'd berated him and damaged him, and now, just as he was entering middle age and in a good place, having embraced gay life, he'd come down with erectile dysfunction.

He began to indulge in cocaine. He started having hallucinations, and became paranoid. He'd call me at all hours of the day and night and tell me he couldn't take it anymore. He said he wanted to end his miserable life.

He had a key to the apartment and often let himself in. He'd write at my desk in front of the bay windows that looked out onto Waller Street. One day when I returned home, I found an envelope with a typed note inside that read *I can't take it anymore. I'm going home to kill myself.*

I knew—at least I thought I knew—he'd never go through with it. I called him.

In a frightened voice, he said, "Michael, people are watching me. I see their shadows as they cross the doorway."

"What people?"

"You know," he muttered, "the ones who want to hurt me, the ones who think I'm crazy."

"Michael, no one wants to hurt you. It's the drugs talking. You need to get off them completely. You know I love you and would do anything for you."

"But as a friend," he said sadly.

"Yes, as a friend. You know that. You know I can't be your lover, but I'll always be there for you as a friend."

"It's not the same thing, is it?"

"It is, in that I admire you, love you, and hold you in high esteem. I just cannot go to bed with you. Michael, you need help. Make an appointment to go see Dr. Andersen, for pity's sake."

"I suppose you're right," he said. "I do need to get off this shit."

I told him how talented he was, a great writer, painter, and photographer. "Why waste it on drugs? They don't love you back. They just numb the pain, and when you wake in the morning, the problems are still there." I finally convinced him to go see the good Dr. Andersen.

I had problems of my own, which I shared with Michael. I'd never gotten over my brother's suicide, and I was conflicted with my father. My girlfriend had been murdered in Paris, and I had a tendency to drown my own tears in substance abuse.

Michael made me an offer: he'd pay for me to see Dr. Andersen for four months to see if he could help me, and he'd continue to see him too. It was so generous that I almost refused, but I knew I needed to talk to a professional.

Michael's kindness and mentorship were most appreciated. At that time in life, I never could have afforded to go to the San Francisco Art Institute or engage an expensive psychiatrist like Dr. Andersen, buy clothes at Wilkes Bashford, attend the opera for a season, or see the temples of Monte Albán. I was indebted to him.

My experience with Dr. Andersen was positive. At the end of it, I had a crush on him, which is expected with a doctor who does a good job. More than that, I'd resolved some of the problems plaguing me. I brought him some exotic flowers to thank him during our last session, and he was taken off guard.

As we sat across from one another, he said, "Your therapy is over. I believe these last months have shown you that you're a healthy young man. Just remember to use your charm in a positive way, not to manipulate, but to show your warmth."

I thanked him for his kind words, then added, "You know, I could just as easily be sitting in your chair asking you these same questions."

He laughed. "Yes, you could, but you'd be bored. You need to be on stage."

We both laughed, and then I thanked him once more, in all earnestness. Finally, we parted, never to see one another again.

Michael, too, had gotten some help and announced that he'd be leaving for London in two weeks to get away from San Francisco, the cocaine, and most likely me, though he didn't say that. I was the one guy he couldn't have, and with an ocean to separate us, it made sense. He wouldn't be tempted by cocaine, or longing for me. At dinner I wished him well and thanked him for his generosity. He said he'd write, which he did—almost a letter a week. I was genuinely sorry to see him leave, but he had to for his own survival. I supported him completely.

Then he wrote that he was leaving for all the places I'd told him about in my travels to Asia. He was flying to India and would see Rajasthan and the Taj Mahal, Jaipur, Varanasi on the Ganges, and fly to Tibet and the temples of Bangkok. I was happy for him. He wrote during his travels, but I could read between the lines. The sites offered an escape from reality, but underneath each letter remained a current of sadness.

He came home two years later. I'd opened my own recruiting business and had a new lover. He presented me with two gifts to choose from, both from a monastery in Tibet. One was the bone of a *lama* (a monk of high standing in Buddhism) encrusted with silver, turquoise, and coral. The other was an antique prayer wheel of ivory and silver. I chose the prayer wheel, which to this day, I'm glad to say, I'm still the custodian of. It was a true gesture of friendship. He'd grown up since I'd last seen him, and he was ready to take up life again in San Francisco.

We saw one another from time to time, and then one day he came over with a suitcase.

"Are you going somewhere?" I asked.

"No, these are some poems I haven't published, and I wanted you to have them in case something happens to me."

He handed me a stack of poems, at least 150 deep. I took them gratefully and told him that they'd be safe with me. I put them in a trunk with my other important possessions. I never actually counted them, and still haven't read them.

I thought Michael's actions a little odd, but not completely out of character. He was beginning to spiral down again into his cocaine addiction and his dark notions of suicide, but there was little I could do but witness the fall.

A few days later, a mutual friend called to say that Michael had been found dead in his apartment.

"How did he die?" I asked.

"They found him in the bedroom, completely nude, on his hands and knees over a mirror filled with cocaine," Bill said. "The straw was still in his nostril, so it must have been instantaneous."

"Thank you for letting me know." I hung up and cried. Poor Michael, my mentor, my friend. Now he, too, was dead. *What does it matter?* I thought. *He's finally at peace. His demons can no longer rob him of his sleep and destroy his waking hours.*

Thus ended another chapter of my life, with the death of my beloved friend Michael. By the time Michael died, my losses had mounted. I'd already buried my father and brother, Robin, Richard Chamberlin, and Bill Tester. Death was no stranger.

Michael Rossum

Mark

Chapter Twenty

Mark

As his lifeless body lay at the California Pacific Medical Center, Davies Campus, shriveled and gaunt, his beautiful blue eyes looked up at me wide open, his mouth agape, his thick blond hair matted and wet. The life had been wrung out of him like some used dish towel. He'd given everything in those last few moments of his life. He looked like a man who'd seen seventy and seven rather than a young man of twenty-seven.

I closed the lids of his eyes, never to see them again, as my tears fell upon his face. I kissed him and hung on to him, sobbing as Adele hugged me. The fight was over. He was finally at peace, leaving Mom and me to struggle with the void he'd left behind.

I had met Mark as I was crossing Eighteenth and Castro streets in San Francisco one sunny day in May 1983. I got a glimpse of him from behind and blurted out, "Don't I know you?" Of course, when he turned around, I didn't recognize him at all. It wasn't a come-on or a one-liner. I really thought I knew him.

"I don't think so," he said, lifting his sunglasses.

"I guess maybe I don't," I said. "I thought you were a friend of mine." I wondered if he believed me, seeing how handsome he was. *He must get lines like that thrown at him all the time*, I thought. "Are you visiting?"

"Yes, as a matter of fact."

"Where from?" I asked.

"Laguna Beach."

I'd never been to Laguna Beach, but I'd heard it described as a resort town in Southern California with a reputation for beautiful beaches and beautiful men. "Hey," I said, "how would you like to have dinner tonight?"

"What about lunch?"

He took me by surprise. "I'm on my way back up to my apartment to let a new maid into the house, since she doesn't have a key."

"Maybe we could occupy the bedroom while she cleans downstairs," he said brazenly.

"Oh, I see, that kind of lunch," I said. "Well, it is noon. Why not? We'll just keep it down to a low roar when she comes in. What do you say?"

"Sounds perfect," he said.

We eyed one another up one side and down the other. By the time we got to my front door, we were excited with anticipation. I couldn't get the key in the door fast enough, and kept having trouble. "Damn lock," I said.

As soon as we stepped inside, we began to rip off one another's clothes. There was a trail of them leading up the stairs, ending with underwear and socks on the landing. *What will my new maid think when she arrives?* I wondered. A soft-spoken Japanese woman by the name of Michiko, she'd been referred to me by my friend Olaf. *Ah hell.* I threw caution to the wind and hoped for the best outcome, sex with this gorgeous man.

I met the maid and Mark on the same day. It was the tenth of May, 1983. The two of them would form a special relationship I only began to touch on years later, when I discovered that she was a wisdom teacher. A Buddhist from Japan, she'd teach me one of the most powerful lessons in life: to let go. Later, I'd ponder the heart-to-heart discussions we'd have.

"You know," she'd say in her broken English, "people work very, very hard all time, no rest. This very bad. You must take time, enjoy your life. Oh yes, people, they get cancer, all type ailments, not take care of their spiritual needs. Oh, yes, you must let go and breathe the air. It is so good for you. And when death comes, you must let go of everything, so do it now."

You never know who will touch you, or who will be your teacher. Sometimes it might be the cleaning lady.

Buddhism was all new for Mark. He lived in a world in which to get somewhere, you had to know somebody. He started working in West Hollywood restaurants right out of high school. He was a smart man, and he had street smarts from growing up in Los Angeles in the '70s. He did the whole gay scene in West Hollywood and wasn't impressed by it. He told me it felt shallow, and at times it could be.

He knew someone at the Surf and Sand where he worked in Laguna, a ritzy restaurant right on the beach. He worked hard, and the owners saw in him a possible partner at twenty-four years old. He was great with the customers, remembered their names and what they drank, and he could schmooze. He had a charming personality that was hard to ignore, so if the kitchen was backed up, he'd entertain the customers.

There was a pianist who played everything, so the lounge was hopping. The restaurant was on one of the prime sections of the beach, close enough to the shoreline that the mirrored ceiling of the posh dining room caught the waves crashing on the beach. It was a first-class place. Little Mark Domen from Buena Park was rubbing noses with the likes of Barbara Streisand, Frank Sinatra, Bob Hope, Dean Martin, Donna Summer, Shirley MacLaine, and her brother, Warren Beatty. I was impressed. They'd call to make a reservation and request Mark specifically because they had such great rapport with him, and they knew he'd take care of them. I had the opportunity to watch him in action one night when he invited me for dinner.

He saved me a romantic seat in the back right by the windows, so I could see the beach. This was our second date since that afternoon when we met in San Francisco the week before. He wanted to show me his world. Sitting in my smart sports coat and bow tie, I looked out at Laguna Beach as the waves crashed. I've never been comfortable eating alone in a fancy place. Mark's roommate, Richard, stopped by to say hello. He was a nice guy, handsome and witty. He was the head waiter. They'd worked together at the Surf and Sand for years. Mark introduced me to the entire staff, right down to the dishwasher. They were like a family, and he wanted them to get to know me.

In between seating people, he'd come by to talk, and he'd introduce me to more people. Then he'd have to go back to being his charming self, the maître d'. The food was exceptional, and I totally understood why people flew in and dropped a few hundred for a meal there.

That was the beginning of falling in love with this young man—days spent on the beach, rides along the Pacific Coast Highway, intimate dinners. When he came home from work at night, I'd be waiting to tear off his sexy tuxedo and run my hands over his hairy blond chest. We liked one another, but it was more than that, and we both knew it while it was unfolding. We were having a romantic affair that felt much deeper.

The following week, Mark was to come to San Francisco, but then a little doubt started to sink in. I thought, *He lives so far away. How can this work?* He loved his work and his friends. How could I ask him to give up his life in Laguna, drop it all, and come live with me?

That weekend, I took him for Chinese at the Hong Kong on Eighteenth Street. It was an old place, built in the '30s. There were cubicles carved out of mahogany with curtains for privacy and a bell to call the waiter.

The waiter, named Bill, was a real character. He knew I could speak a little Cantonese, so he'd make jokes with us, because we were gay. "*Ni sei ham sat lo*," he'd say. "You are dirty old man." With the other customers, he was mild mannered and spoke softly.

"Bill, this is Mark," I said.

"Oh, you ham sat lo too?"

We all had a good laugh. He understood gay people. He just didn't have any tact. With us, he felt he could be himself. I'm telling you about the Hong Kong because it was part of the mix of the gay village we lived in called the Castro.

Mark was a natural. Everybody loved him. He had a warm personality and drew people to him. He had an infectious laugh, too, not to mention a rock-hard body and a six-pack to match.

Aside from the good looks, he had a big heart. He was generous, and he always saw the glass as half-full. He doted on me, cooking breakfast on Saturday morning and making sure I wasn't lacking anything.

It goes without saying that we had a remarkable relationship. About two months into dating and flying back and forth, he told me he wanted to move to San Francisco and live with me. Immediately, I felt like we were moving too quickly. I also realized that if I didn't take the chance at love, I might not have another one. I agreed.

That was when I discovered our age difference. "You know, Mark, I never asked you how old you were when we met. How old are you?"

"I never told you, did I? I'm twenty-four years old."

"You're what?" I cried in dismay.

"I'm nine years your junior," he said matter-of-factly, like he'd worked it out on a calculator.

"Well, I'm in shock," I said quite frankly. "Why didn't you tell me this before?"

"Because you never asked," he said. "It's not that big a deal, is it? We still love each other. Explain to me how our difference in age would hurt the relationship."

"Well," I said, "for one, I thought you were around thirty, a little closer to my age. You're so mature, I guess I'm just a little shocked. At twenty-four, you're so young, and you don't know what you want."

"Actually, I do. I've been around, and I know a good thing when I see one. You're a handsome, successful, mature man who knows what he wants, and I'm in love with you. Listen, Michael, I'm not moving to San Francisco on a whim. I've done my homework and I have a job interview with the Mark Hopkins Hotel next week. If I get it, I want to come up and move in with you and make you happy for the rest of your life."

I stood silently. I was giving up bachelorhood just when I was getting used to living on my own. But I knew it was right. I loved him and wanted to be in a committed relationship.

Mark moved up in August 1983, and I was one of the happiest guys in the world. I was terrified at the same time, but I knew the chemistry was right. I just had to let our relationship blossom.

～～

Mark got the job at the Mark Hopkins Hotel, and I was waking up to his first morning of work. He stood there in our bedroom while I watched him iron and starch his tux shirt, making sure every line was perfect. Then he put on his slacks and shirt, then the black studs for the shirt, and last, his black bow tie. He turned to me for some encouragement, as he was a little nervous, being his first day and all.

"You look so handsome," I said. And he did, like a movie star. "Come here, stud, and give me a kiss."

Then he was gone. One moment I was living alone, and the next I was telling my husband, "Have a nice day, babe," as he walked out the door. He'd come home after work, and we'd make dinner together.

I was excited. I quickly got dressed for my own job. I thought about him all day. I knew I was embarking on another journey, and there would be someone to share it with. I was in love.

Mark told his mother and his eleven siblings that he wouldn't be going back to LA, that he'd met someone special, a guy. That didn't go over too well with his Roman Catholic family. Amelia, Mark's mother, said he could stay in the relationship as long as he remained celibate. Like that was going to happen. That would have been torture. I can't imagine a mother wishing that kind of unhappiness on her offspring, but she was as serious as a heart attack.

Mark was my other half. We fulfilled one another. I thought I was gregarious, but by the second week, he knew half the people on the block by name. I'd been there for two years and only knew my next-door neighbor.

When I introduced him to my mates at the gym, they immediately liked his warmth and accessibility. They also wanted to jump his bones, but they tried to disguise how much so by acting completely charming. I just watched while they fussed over him. It made me feel good that my friends liked him because I knew at the end of the day, he was coming home with me.

We began to forge a beautiful love affair that went much deeper than the physical attraction. He'd get up first, and I'd hear him downstairs. The sounds of the coffee grinder and then singing wafted upstairs. He'd meet me with a kiss and a cup of fresh brew. We'd open the back door of the kitchen and sit on the steps, with a 180-degree view of San Francisco, looking right down Market Street to the Ferry Building.

The lover I had prior to Mark had introduced me to a new business. I'd come to understand that I couldn't realize what I loved doing most, photography. I cut costs and did my own developing, but there just wasn't enough business in the city. I began working as a software engineering recruiter, finding jobs for executives and professionals in Silicon Valley. It was a profitable business, and I excelled. I was the top recruiter at my firm. My boss wanted to get me involved in real estate, but I realized his motives. He wanted me to invest my earnings in real estate because he was afraid I'd go out on my own and start my own recruiting firm. I'd already made that decision, and I left after one year to do just that.

When I opened the business, I asked Mark if he'd like to come on board as a recruiter. He could keep his evening shift at the restaurant and work days in my office, recruiting. He was a born salesman, and he took to recruiting like a duck to water. We were making enough money to afford to take off a month for Christmas and New Year's, when business was slow. We'd forged a beautiful love affair, and now he'd become a great business partner.

In the winter of 1984, we went to Hong Kong. We spent Christmas in Canton, China, New Year's in Bangkok, Thailand, and took a train to the Golden Triangle where Burma, Laos, and Thailand meet at the

Saigon River. After Thailand, we had two marvelous weeks in Bali, Indonesia, and fell in love all over again.

Mark had never been out of California, so it was a big trip for him. Not only was he far from home, he was way out of his comfort zone.

To prepare for the trip, I'd enrolled us in a Chinese class at the YMCA in Chinatown to learn Cantonese. Nixon had just opened relations with Communist China in 1983, paving the way for American travel. No one in China spoke English back in those days. They'd been learning Russian in school and traveling to the Soviet Bloc. Twice a week, we had lessons with our teacher, Jueng Sin Sang, or Mr. Jueng.

I'd studied Spanish and spoke it fluently, and with all my travels, I was ready to tackle Cantonese. Mark, however, though enthusiastic, was less able to wrap his mouth around some of the sounds that rose and fell in the singsong manner of Cantonese. I must say, though, he stuck with it, and by the end of our lessons three months later, he could order food and ask for directions. This all came in very handy when we finally left the safety of Hong Kong, where English was spoken, for the interior of mainland China.

After we left the glitzy lights of British Hong Kong, the train ride to Canton was beautiful, like something from a movie. We went through a large tunnel that brought us out from Hong Kong into mainland China. The train passed small villages, where creeks flowed under arched stone bridges and women in traditional garb carried water from the river using a bamboo rod across their back with buckets hanging from each end. Water oxen plowed the fields for the next crop of rice, the lifeblood of China. Little children on their way to school through the rice paddies waved at us, welcoming us to their unseen landscape.

It was a land where cone-shaped mountains of limestone rose from green rivers, and a few pine trees managed to take root in their crevices. It was a land where fishermen sat on rafts of five or six large bamboo stalks lashed together, using cormorants to catch the fish. The birds had rings around their necks to ensure they couldn't swallow the catch, which they deposited so willingly into their masters' straw baskets. It was scenery as ancient as the people, but for us, it was something rare, like a jewel.

We arrived at our destination, Canton, a city of fifteen million people. The sheer size boggled the mind. We came to a stoplight, and instead of hundreds of cars, we were met by thousands of bicyclists, who lined the breadth of the street. When the light changed, the wave of cyclists made the Tour de France seem miniscule.

Everywhere we went, something took our breath away. A few days prior to Christmas, we arrived at the White Swan Hotel, the same hotel that had hosted President Nixon. That was the year he lifted the travel ban for the first time since the communists took over. Built on an island in the middle of the gigantic Pearl River, whose delta empties into Hong Kong, it stands as a testament to the modernity of the Chinese republic. Its causeway the only connection with the mainland, it seemed like it would have been private, but upon waking early Christmas Eve, we found the causeway full of hundreds of people practicing the ancient martial art of Tai Chi by the river's edge. Their unified movements spoke of the harmony of body and mind. We sat watching, our noses pressed against the window in awe, as the sun rose over the river.

We decided we'd go sightseeing and Christmas shopping. Since we were so far from home, we'd make our own Christmas celebration in our hotel room. After seeing the Sun Yat-sen Memorial, we went to the government's Friendship Store. It was an arcade of room after room of Chinese art, from jade carvings and bowls to cloisonné vases and carved ivory. The items were all handmade in the ancient style of craftsmanship. It was difficult to choose among them. I found a beautiful large jade ginger jar and silk pajamas for Mark. Mark purchased a beautiful ivory carving of Quan Yin, the goddess of mercy. He also bought a cloisonné vase of exquisite style and color, depicting birds, butterflies, and chrysanthemums on a blue-sky background. Later, I found a pair of silk pajamas under the Christmas tree for me as well.

On our way back, we realized we were lost, and far from our hotel. I thought our Chinese paid off when we could ask, "Where is the hotel?" but we didn't know how to say "swan," which was the qualifying factor and most important.

They just looked at us and asked which hotel.

I started flapping my arms like the wings of a bird, but that only confused them. I asked in Chinese, "*Ni gong Yingman*? Does anyone understand English?"

Everyone in the crowd of people we'd attracted shook their heads in unison.

Here we are lost in a city of fifteen million people, and I'm just short of one word to get us home, I thought.

Then, miraculously, Mark produced a room key. Its Chinese characters saved the day.

That night was Christmas Eve. Back at the hotel, we looked out over the Pearl River, the lights of the mysterious country before us. We popped open a bottle of champagne, then exchanged gifts. This would be one Christmas Mark and I would never forget. He was feeling homesick, and he wanted to call his family and wish them a Merry Christmas.

He called, and his oldest brother picked up. "Hey, Mark, how's it going?" he asked. "Are you having sweet and sour turkey with chopsticks?"

I knew then that his family had no idea where he really was, and this was all they could say in the face of the marvels Mark was experiencing in this mysterious land. There was Mark Domen, who grew up in Buena Park in south suburban Los Angeles, who'd never been out of the city, now the head waiter at the Mark Hopkins Hotel, seeing China. Most Americans, including Mark's brother, had no idea what we'd been missing: the opportunity to see an enormous and historic nation like China at that moment, before it would change dramatically as it opened up to Western culture. We were in another world, in another time. There were little villages that came out of fairy tales, rice paddies that stretched the river banks, vast green rivers with Buddhist temples, limestone mountains, and the imperial cities of Suzhou and Wuxi with their emperors' palaces and magnificent sculpted gardens.

We traveled extensively for a month, leaving China for Thailand, Singapore, and Bali, Indonesia. While in Bali, we took a cabana on the beach in Kuta, with its famous stretch of white sand. For a week, we wore nothing more than sarongs and bathing suits. We could get massages on the beach for two dollars. We became friendly with a masseuse named Surea, who was so delightful and funny and gave a great massage. She wore a sarong and a conical straw hat with the number five on it. She was working to get back to her home in Sumatra. She was a wealth of information, and she helped us immensely in understanding the two cultures of Indonesia.

We rode motorcycles to the temples in Ubud and were attacked by monkeys in the jungle. It was almost a mental overload for Mark. He'd seen so much in such a short time, such a range of culture and religion. He loved it, but was homesick, I could tell. After Bali, we headed home.

We'd been back around six months when things began to go terribly wrong. Mark woke one morning with no vision in his right eye. We rushed him to our ophthalmologist and learned that his retina had detached from the back of his eye. The doctor was dumbfounded. We hadn't tested positive for the AIDS virus because there was no test yet. The doctor questioned why the retina had suddenly, without trauma, detached. His only idea was that it was HIV-related.

Mark was operated on a week later, and the retina was sewn onto the back of the eye. To hold it in place, he was made to lie facedown on a pillow so that the air bubble that was forced into his eye would hold the retina in place while it healed. This process took ten agonizing days. It was torture. I took off from work to care for him. The only time he could get up was to relieve himself or to eat, but always with his face down. What courage and strength he exhibited in the face of such suffering.

I tried to put myself in his place, and I couldn't. It was unbearable to see him suffering so. But as a testimony to his stamina and good nature, if I was there, he never complained.

As if this debilitating process hadn't been agonizing enough for a man of twenty-five, three months later the whole process began again, only this time with his left eye. It was a nightmare, and this young pup took the process to task again without complaint. Had he complained, I don't think I could have consoled either of us.

After the eye surgeries, there was a lull, and we began to feel like we'd gotten past the worst of it. We went to parties. I took him to Puerto Vallarta. He was working out hard at the gym, and it was paying off. He had the body of an Adonis, and we were more in love than ever. But underneath that layer of calmness was a volcano about to erupt.

When the AIDS test came out in late 1984, we both got tested. The only organization working on our behalf was the Centers for Disease Control, which had developed the test.

We went to see Dr. Ainesworth, a kind, older gay man who was on the frontlines of the epidemic. "Your test results have come back, and I wanted to discuss them with you," he told us. "You are both positive for the virus that causes AIDS."

I think we'd both expected the results, but the confirmation felt like something had died within us. We were devastated, numb to the core.

As time passed, Mark began to lose weight, followed by drenching night sweats. I'd have to change all of our bed linens by the middle of the night. He'd have fevers that suddenly spiked to 104 degrees, and then it was one opportunistic infection after another. The volcano had erupted. Mark was diagnosed with full-blown AIDS in 1985, with no cure in sight and with nothing to fight it. We were at the mercy of God. The thought of losing Mark was unimaginable.

Mark decided that he wanted to spend Christmas 1985 with his family in Los Angeles. I completely understood. He was worried he might never have another one with them. It gave me some time to think about my own family, my mother. What about me? I could be next.

I decided to take my mom to China for Christmas, like I'd taken Mark the year before. From the time I was a babe, all I ever heard her say was, "Someday, I'd love to go to China." Not Paris or London, but China.

I took her that Christmas, and though it was tough being away from Mark for two weeks, I knew he needed to be with his family. Later, I regretted the decision, though. Two weeks is a lifetime when you have AIDS. I wondered how he was doing, and worried for his safety. The trip was wonderful, but underneath it lay an uneasy feeling. I couldn't wait to return to Mark's smiling face.

Things seemed to level out over the winter and spring of 1986. Though he never regained the weight, Mark was doing well. We were taking small vacations, and both of us were working full time. He was succeeding in our business, and life was good.

We had constant reminders of the holocaust taking place all around us. Our close friends were dying, and one couldn't turn a blind eye to the men on crutches or in wheelchairs on Castro Street. The obituary column in the *Bay Area Reporter* filled two pages, then three, sometimes four. The signs were everywhere. One of Mark's roommates in LA got sick and died within two weeks. We went down for the funeral and learned more of his friends had died in his absence.

We thought maybe the worst was behind us when we heard of a new drug called AZT. It was having some success in prolonging life in research studies, but wouldn't be available until the trials were over. Meanwhile, people continued to die while waiting for FDA approval.

Mark continued to work from home, closing deal after deal, until the summer of 1986. He was so weak he could barely get up in the morning. He began to look fragile, but I never gave up hope that soon we'd have AZT and we could save him. I never believed for a moment that he'd die. I decided to work from home and take care of him until we got the new drug. That was August, and the drug was to become available to all who needed it by September. I thought surely we could hold out a few more weeks.

The night sweats became more frequent, and I stopped working altogether. It was all I could do to stay on top of his needs. I had to change the bed linens, sometimes twice in a night, attend to his fevers, help him to the bathroom downstairs, and make sure he ate three meals a day. I'd feed him pancakes and bacon, grilled cheese sandwiches for lunch, and hearty soups at night—whatever he wanted, trying to keep up his appetite.

I took him to the emergency room one day in October, after he complained of a stomach ache. Dr. Ainesworth had died some months earlier, and we'd scrambled to find another doctor. I'd finally met a new young doc at my gym by the name of Steve Mahalko. Steve came in to see us at Davies Hospital and ordered an MRI.

When the images came back, Steve told us they showed a Kaposi sarcoma tumor the size of a grapefruit in Mark's liver. "We have to hospitalize him immediately," he said.

We agreed, thinking they could do radiation or chemotherapy. We were frightened, but we still held out hope for AZT.

I called my mom from the second floor of the hospital, the de facto AIDS ward, and explained what was happening. She came down to sit with me.

I helped Mark to the bathroom. As he stood there relieving himself, he caught a glimpse of the mirror. "My God, I look like an eighty-year-old man," he said, beginning to cry.

I began to cry as well as I helped him back to the bed.

The doctor came in and gave him a shot of morphine. "This will help with his pain."

"He's going to be all right, isn't he?" I asked.

The doctor took me aside. "No, Michael, he's not. Mark has about twenty-four hours to live."

The impossible was staring me in the face. I'd brought my lover to the hospital, and he was never going to leave. I was going to lose

Mark forever. I told my mom in the hallway outside his hospital room.

"Oh no, Michael," she said.

We just wept.

When Steve tried to console us, I told him, "He doesn't want to die here, Steve. He wants to go home." Tears fell from my cheeks.

"But Michael, he'll be much better off here. He's going to start having difficulty breathing because the tumor is so large. We can offer him oxygen and pain medication to make it easier on him, so he doesn't suffer so much."

I stared and nodded while my mother held me in her arms. I kept saying repeatedly, as if shell-shocked, "I thought we had more time. I thought we had more time."

We returned to the room and looked at Mark in his hospital bed, a shriveled-up little man of twenty-seven. He looked back at us and managed a raised eyebrow of contempt for what was happening. We smiled back to ease his fears.

I called his mother, Amelia, and told her she had to come right away if she wanted to see Mark again. Her reply sent chills down my spine.

"I have to go to work tomorrow. I'll come on Friday."

I hung up in disbelief. My mother was there for Mark, but his own had to work. They brought in a cot so I could stay with him through the night. My mother asked for one, too, as she wasn't leaving either one of us. My mother was one of the finest human beings I've ever known, and her compassion and love for us both was enormous. We would spend the night together, the three of us. We were Mark's family.

That night was one of the longest I'd known as that boy struggled and clung to life. He began to have trouble breathing, just as Steve said he would. He gasped for air, and the nurses gave him oxygen, then he slept again, unencumbered by this world. Changes in his breathing came and went, and with each episode, I jumped from my cot to his bed.

Then, in the middle of the night, he woke from a deep sleep and sat up. "Michael, Mommy, come quick. I think I'm dying, and I'm afraid."

I held him, and he grew calm again. I told him how much I loved him, and that I was right there and I'd be with him. Adele rose and held him too. He looked up into our eyes, too weak and drugged to cry, but I could see it in his face. I was suddenly terrified of him leaving me alone and looked up into my mother's grief-stricken face. She sobbed quietly for all of us as I held him. He lay back down again.

The nurses heard the commotion and brought in more morphine. He slept but again awoke suddenly from his labored breathing. Each time, he lay back down. This went on for hours until, out of exhaustion, we all fell asleep.

Then early in the morning, Mark rose once again and called out, "Mommy! Michael!"

I ran to him and grabbed his hands, tears streaming down my face.

"Get me a priest!" he cried.

For a moment I dropped his hands to run to the nurses' station to ask for a priest, but my instincts thought better of it and I ran back and held him. The veins in his neck bulged, he turned red for a second, and his beautiful blue eyes widened as if he, too, was in shock, as the massive coronary ended his life, and part of mine.

It was over. There was silence. He was finally at peace.

Mark was like a shooting star that lights up the heavens for a moment, then burns out. He came into my life and gave me the kind of unconditional love I'd always been looking for in a mate and never found. He showed me there were so many possibilities in life, and then he left.

Mark, 1983, Laguna Beach our first weekend together

Chapter Twenty-One

The Epidemic

We flocked to "Mecca" from small towns and big cities, longing to come out of the closet, longing for freedom and to escape the closed-minded families and communities where we grew up. We'd never again feel the stigma of being unworthy or unwanted. This was the powerful draw San Francisco had on us. We came by the thousands from all over the world to the city we called Oz, a little speck three miles wide and seven miles long. The Castro became ground zero, and the gay men and women in it became our family. We found safety here, a place to call home.

I am a warrior from the front lines of a catastrophe, a battle to survive the AIDS epidemic. These are my accounts of the first grim days of the epidemic. Most of my friends have long since passed from this scourge. The fact that I'm here telling their stories is a testimony to my longevity. The gay community in San Francisco in 1981 was about to be wiped out. We'd lose an entire generation in less than ten years. I lost all my friends that I grew up with from my teens to my late twenties. These are the bonds that should last a lifetime. Even the doctors who were treating me died. This was a plague the likes of which we'd rarely seen before. By the end of Ronald Reagan's second term of silence, 200,000 Americans had died.

When people began dying from blood transfusions, doctors knew that the blood supplies were unreliable and they'd have to work quickly to find a test. The CDC, with the help of Dr. Don Francis, discovered early on that the test for hepatitis B could factor out infections of potential blood donors by 88 percent.

Around that time, five major clinics in the US were conducting studies of hepatitis B. Dr. Francis believed that if they could contact the thirty thousand participants in the studies from 1978 to 1981, they'd have a blueprint for how the AIDS epidemic began.

I was one of those people they were looking for. When I read an article in the local gay newspaper that they were looking for four thousand men in San Francisco who'd taken part in the hepatitis B study, I called the clinic immediately. They thanked me for my help and sent the results back. I wasn't positive for the AIDS virus in 1979, but by 1981, there was a darkness that hovered over the gay community. I and many others like me believed we were infected. The only proof we had was that we'd been intimate with a large number of people who were dying.

San Francisco's gay life changed dramatically. Bars were open one day and suddenly shuttered the next. Restaurants and after-hours dance clubs in the South of Market area closed. Once thriving, these areas began to be taken over by the straight community as we abandoned the heart of where we'd socialized. Since so little information was available, people thought they could catch the virus like one catches the flu. Fear was rampant. The party was over.

In those dark, early days, fear spread precipitously. Terror gripped us. There was no support from any organization. The government was silent. We were on our own. What happened afterward could have been prevented, but even the CDC was under pressure from the White House not to let the gay community know that AIDS was a sexually transmitted disease. So we continued to have sex, infecting one another and dying in the darkness of ignorance.

News traveled by word of mouth, in a whisper. "Did you hear that Mike Maleta died?" someone asked me in a hushed voice. "He died of AIDS."

I sat there, numb. I'd slept with Michael just months earlier. If Michael had died, I thought surely I'd be next. We were friends and casual lovers. Michael was a party boy, handsome, with just enough charm and good karma to make himself irresistible.

I first heard about the disease in the local newspaper one morning. The July 3, 1981, headline read *Rare Cancer Seen in 41 Homosexuals*. It was the HIV virus. The gay community was taken by surprise, just like the rest of the world, and we felt fear in our hearts. No one knew if they had it, but anyone who was sexually active suspected they did, and figured that was probably how it was contracted. Everyone was talking about GRIDS—gay-related immune deficiency syndrome. Nothing had shaken the community quite like that headline and the subsequent articles.

In the summer of 1981, my closest friends were falling ill, one after another. I saw my friend Reed on the corner of Eighteenth and Castro, and as we embraced, I noticed a purplish lesion next to his nose.

"Michael, I've got AIDS."

"Reed, I'm so sorry. How long have you had the lesion?"

It was obvious when you had Kaposi sarcoma. It was like the plague. There was no hiding from it, and the stigma so great that some didn't want to venture out of their homes for fear they'd be shunned. There was nothing for us to do but watch them die. Helpless, they grew weak and feeble until they withered away. Some were afraid to die, and others begged for it. All the while, we tried to support them with our love and wondered when we'd be next.

Not everyone who died knew everyone else, but we knew who they were, or we knew someone who knew them. We were a small community. It hit us like a tsunami. Everywhere it struck, there was devastation. People suddenly lost their eyesight for no apparent reason. Their legs became weak with neuropathy, and before long, it was common to see young men hobbling down Castro Street using canes or riding in wheelchairs.

They were men in their twenties, guys we knew from the gym, the bank teller, a bartender, a photographer, a violinist, a ballet dancer, friends and lovers, doctors, lawyers, artists. Within a year, they were dying. Helplessly, I watched the disease squeeze the life out of some of my closest friends. Their parents were so afraid they could catch the virus from just touching their sons that some died without ever being held or caressed by their parents again.

When the AIDS crisis was just one year old, more than a thousand people had already died in San Francisco. There was such condemnation coming from the born-again Christian right and the Republican president, who never once uttered the word "AIDS" during his two terms in office. We deserved what we were getting, the Rev. Pat Robertson said. It was God's wrath. That's how they justified their complete lack of Christian compassion.

Finally, in 1983, the scientific community told us AIDS was transmitted sexually and that you couldn't just get it from kissing someone or from handling their utensils. Then we began to overcome our own fears.

"We must tell your family," I told my friend Christian Ashman. "Especially Ingrid, your twin sister. You two are so close."

"No, Michael, I'm not telling any of them," he said. "It would kill them, especially my mother and sister."

"Christian, wouldn't it be better that they know the truth? Then they can make their own informed decision. Then if they want to come here, they can stay in the apartment."

"No, I've made up my mind. I don't want them to see me like this with purple lesions all over my face like a monster."

I said no more on the subject until he was on his deathbed, and then we called them.

My mother loved Christian like a son and visited with him, as his family was so far away in Stuttgart. None of them had known, not even Ingrid, whom I'd met a few times when she visited San Francisco. The truth was, I thought they were better off not having seen him. His face had become distorted with huge lesions. His beautiful blue eyes stuck out of a hideous purple mask. That's how AIDS left my friend. I'll never forget going to the hospital that day and finding his empty bed. It was as if I'd been punched in the gut so hard I was breathless. He died alone, without family or friends. A more courageous spirit you couldn't find.

Ingrid came from Germany. I met her at the airport and drove her to Christian's apartment. The last time we were all there together had been several years prior. We'd dressed in costumes for a Halloween party at the Galleria, laughing and carrying on as we smoked a joint and listened to the Rolling Stones.

She walked into the empty apartment, hugged me, and refused to let go until she'd cried her last tear. During the Cold War in Berlin, his mother smuggled Christian in one suitcase and Ingrid in another past the East German border guards to safety in West Berlin, risking their lives for freedom. He'd survived the border crossing, but he couldn't survive AIDS.

Paul Merar was a hulk of a man. He was one of my Jewish buddies from my gym, the Muscle Systems on Market Street. That man was handsome, with dark hair and eyes and a thick mustache. He stood six foot three inches tall and weighed about 240 pounds. His shoulders were as wide as a truck. Then there was Phil Goldberg, who was short and stocky with a sly, sexy smile and bedroom eyes. George Ash was a part owner in the gym. We were more intimate, sharing our deepest desires and fears with one another. Paul was tough, and never showed how fearful he was. When I tried to broach the subject, he'd change it. When Paul died, he weighed about 140 pounds.

All of them died. I was the only survivor.

I began to ask myself, *Why me? Am I just here to be a witness to the destruction of everyone dear to me?* Then while visiting my doctor, I ran into my cousin Jeff. We'd grown up together. One look, and I knew he had it too. AIDS was even killing my family.

Jeff grew up with two sisters and was considered the prince of the family by his mother, Klara. That instilled in him a sense of superiority that he held over his sisters relentlessly for most of their lives. Jeff was sarcastic, biting, brilliant, and hilarious. He also had a spiritual side that he didn't share as much, but he was wise and always called a spade a spade.

One of the last times I saw him still relatively happy after his diagnosis was right after he'd gone out and bought a yellow Porsche. Adrian and I had come to a stop at the intersection of Market and Castro, and he pulled up next to us, wearing his rainbow-colored woolen hat (because my cousin was gay to the bone). We exchanged pleasantries, and then with a grin from ear to ear, he sped off, realizing the incredible power of his new toy. With a wave out the window, he was gone, a yellow dot on the horizon of Castro Street. He died six months later.

Kevin—what a looker. Northern Italian, with fair skin and fabulous blue eyes that could take your breath away, he had a heart of gold. He could have had any man he wanted, and he did. He loved the outdoors, and we used to ride motorcycles to Point Reyes National Park on the north coast of Marin County. His Harley-Davidson was bigger than he was. Once while we were both parked on a steep hill, he got on to start his bike, lost control, and wound up underneath it. His leg was pinned under its weight. I don't know how I managed it, but I was able to lift his bike up enough for him to free his leg.

Later while in the hospital for an AIDS-related infection, he said, "Michael, I never could have imagined that at thirty-four, I would die from making love."

We'd been friends for years, and I loved him. He died in his home in the Oakland Hills, surrounded by his three gay brothers and one lesbian sister, with his trusted friend Evelyn, a cocker spaniel, by his side.

Richard Chamberlin, my roommate from my Haight-Ashbury days, was a consummate host who knew how to throw a party and how to find one. A divorce lawyer by trade, he told me after each of his failed love affairs, "Never get married, Michael. Take it from me. It just doesn't work. I know. Look at the business I'm in."

I'd attended so many funerals by the time Richard died that when I pulled into the parking lot of the Unitarian church on Van Ness where his service was taking place, I parked the car and didn't move. I cried and cried, then pulled out of the lot and drove home.

Alex Desy was one of my inner circle. We had such plans for the future. He's the one who opened the salon on Castro Street called Prima Facie and asked me to show my photographs there, a plan he devised on Fire Island when we were high on ecstasy. The salon opened with much fanfare and is still there today.

Two years later he came down with Guillain-Barre, a horrible, disabling nerve disease that left him crippled. He died of pneumocystis. I went to see him days before he died.

We just looked at one another. "All our dreams for each other's futures," he finally said. "How could they come tumbling down like a house of cards before we ever had a chance to realize them?"

He seemed resigned to his fate, but I'm not sure he ever fully accepted it—it was unimaginable at thirty-eight.

On that same visit to Fire Island in the summer of 1977, when Alex devised his plan to open Prima Facie, I'd met Bob Lomonto. We were dancing to Donna Summer's disco hit "Last Dance." "Last dance, last dance for love . . . last chance for romance tonight." So the lyrics go.

It was our last chance, as the evening was ending and neither of us had a date. He was a beautiful boy of just nineteen years, visiting from Philadelphia, Pennsylvania. He'd just come out into gay society that weekend on Fire Island. After the disco closed around six in the morning, we walked along the empty beach, barefoot in just our jeans. The Atlantic surf pounded the beach, and the sunrise looked crimson as it rose on the horizon. He walked me back to where I was staying, the rays of the sun warming our backs, and then I asked him if he'd like to come in. Just one beautiful morning, and I'd never see him again. At least, that was what I thought.

A few years later, I met the boy from Philadelphia again in San Francisco. By then, he'd matured into a man, and like so many others, had been drawn to San Francisco, to the freedom and a place he could call home.

We grew up together in the city, worked out at the same gym, had the same friends, and went to the same parties. He was a sweet man, no games, just a handsome, honest Joe, and sharp as a whip, with a deadly sense of humor to match.

Years later in the early '90s, when he was almost unable to walk from AIDS wasting, I found him and his lover David at a barbecue on a rooftop on Mars Street, a small street with a panoramic view of San Francisco and the bay. He was leaning against the railing, looking out at the city that would become his resting place. I walked up and gave him a big hug, and we smiled.

"Beautiful, isn't it?" he asked.

"Yes, you are," I said.

He began to laugh. "We go back a long time, don't we, Michael?"

"Yes, we do, my friend," I said, my arm still around his shoulders.

"Did you know you were the first man I'd ever gone to bed with?" he asked.

"Yes," I replied. "I kinda gathered that from our conversation when we met back on Fire Island. I was so flattered that you chose me, and I'll never forget that morning walking barefoot down the beach."

"Wasn't it grand?"

That was the last time I saw him alive. I received an invitation from David a month later to a memorial for Bob, to be held at the Conservatory of Flowers in Golden Gate Park, a grand 1880s white wrought iron and glass Victorian conservatory. It was a beautiful memorial. Bob would have been proud to see how much he was loved by the gay community of San Francisco.

As we left the conservatory, his brokenhearted lover gave each of us a redwood sapling. Adrian and I planted ours in a large cement planter. By the time we left our home on Grove Street ten years later, the tree was ten feet tall and had equally large branches. We couldn't keep moving it, so we gave it to Sue Ann, a girlfriend of ours in Bolinas up the coast from San Francisco some thirty miles. We planted it on her property, and now it's part of the coast redwoods on the mesa overlooking the Pacific Ocean. It will be there for thousands of years.

Jerry Alvarnez cast me a life raft in the midst of a sea of grief. My lover Mark had just passed away at twenty-seven, and if the grief of his passing wasn't enough, the second mortgage on my house, which was a balloon payment of $17,000, was due two weeks after he died, and I didn't have it. It meant I'd lose my house as well as the love of my life at the same time.

When Jerry heard about it, he told his lover, "Allen, we're going to have to loan Michael the money for the second."

"What?" Allen asked incredulously.

Allen was such a tightwad, but Jerry, he had a heart of gold. "Well, of course we'll charge him interest, just like a bank," he said, soothing Allen's troubled mind.

I was speechless. Allen agreed, and I was able to save my house and slowly pay them back. If it weren't for Jerry's generosity, I don't know where I'd be today.

Jerry came with my mom and me on a trip around the world after Mark died. When we were in India, he came down with HIV meningitis. After weeks of recovery, he was able to travel again, and we completed the trip.

When we got home, he said, "Thank you, Michael."

"What for?" I asked.

"I've always wanted to see the world, and now I have, thanks to you."

Jerry died six months later of pneumocystis. He was forty years old. He was one of my best friends. After Jerry passed, Allen gave me a beautiful hand-carved Buddhist altar made from an extraordinary red soapstone, with a drawer in the middle of it. It was so large that it weighed at least fifty pounds, and it told the story of the Buddha in three individual carved panels that fit into the altar. I was pleased that Jerry remembered how much I loved the altar. As the years passed, the drawer in the center became a depository for pictures of all my friends who died of AIDS. I would take photos out every once in a while, and just cry. There were so many. In this way, they'd always be remembered.

Paul Meyers and I had a summer love affair on Fire Island. Paul was a brilliant PR executive for Revlon on Fifth Avenue. The man was one of the most interesting, enthusiastic, and talented people I ever met. He was a photographer, an interior designer, and an inventor. When I told him I was leaving New York, he was crushed. But he came and stayed with me in San Francisco on several visits, and he had a key to my apartment.

One day he mysteriously sent the key back in an envelope with a note that said, "I love you, sweet man. Goodbye for now."

The note disturbed me. After several weeks passed pondering it, I called to see if everything was all right. His brother answered. He told me Paul had died of AIDS the week before, and he was there to execute his will. Was I a friend of Paul's?

"Yes, I was a very good friend," I said, trying to hold back the tears. "I will miss him terribly. I didn't even know he was sick."

"Yes, I know," the brother said. "No one knew. He wanted it to be kept a secret."

When I got off the phone, I cried like a baby, knowing full well this was exactly how Paul would have wanted it—no pity and no goodbyes. That was Paul. I have a photograph of him on my desk, and it inspires me every day to try to be compassionate toward others and to be the best human being I can be.

Loy Taylor was a competitive bodybuilder. He looked like the Hulk and was as sweet as they come. He'd been in the closet for years, because gay bodybuilders would never be taken seriously in the sport. Mark and Loy were old boyfriends, even though he remained in the closet. But slowly, Mark and I coaxed him out into gay life, and the first guy he met, Tony, became his lover. We met Tony at a dance club in San Diego. Loy wanted to meet him, but just didn't have the wherewithal to go about it. He kept eyeing him, and Tony kept eyeing him back. He motioned to me from afar to make contact with Tony, so he could come up and be introduced.

What happened next could only be called fate. I turned to my right and started to take a sip of my drink when Tony began to take a sip of his cocktail, and we ran right into one another, clinking our glasses. It was a perfect setup for Loy. I apologized, and Loy came up and introduced himself. They were together from that moment until he died. When Mark became ill with AIDS, Loy refused to see us because he was afraid he'd get AIDS from Mark. Mark passed away without ever seeing Loy again.

Loy called a few years later and told me how sorry he was for the way he'd treated Mark. He confided that he was sick too. He asked to see me, but I was leaving for Asia with Adrian the next day. Loy thought I hadn't forgiven him for the way he'd treated Mark, but I told him that I loved him like a brother. I never got a chance to say goodbye in person. Tony wrote me a card when I returned, letting me know that Loy had passed.

Clive Cohen came from South Africa and escaped apartheid's brutal suppression of gays and colored people, but he couldn't escape the epidemic that was unfolding. We used to go up to the Russian River in the late '70s and go rafting. He was one of my mates. We shared a lot in common apart from being Jewish.

He taught me about his life in South Africa and apartheid. "I fell in love with an Indian boy from Durban," he said, "and one day while we were swimming on a secluded beach nude, the police came down and arrested the two of us. I never saw him again." He was discriminated against because he was a Jew, too, and told me of the degradation he had to endure at the hands of the police and skinheads before he fled to the safety of San Francisco. A year later, he'd fall victim to an even greater threat than apartheid.

Larry Layden was a former lover of the man I'm currently married to. I say married because in 2008, Adrian and I were married legally in San Francisco. We never thought we'd live to see the day. I knew Larry from the Pump Room, one of the city's first gay gyms back in the mid-'70s. The owners went on to open Muscle Systems. Larry and a group of our friends used to go dancing at the I-Beam, one of the first large discotheques on Haight Street. By the time they were playing Gloria Gaynor's "I Will Survive," we were stripped to our jeans and dripping wet.

Larry used to tell me that he wasn't going to get AIDS, that he was going to beat it. But in the end, even he succumbed to what we all felt was our fate but couldn't bear for a moment to believe. Why should he? He was only forty years old. He had his whole life ahead of him. Larry had an AIDS-related brain tumor that ended his suffering. Adrian helped him let go with dignity and love, which is all any of us can ask for.

Dr. Steve Mahalko was my friend and our doctor. When Dr. Ainesworth, our first doctor, died early in the epidemic, Mark and I found Steve. Dr. Mahalko showed such bravery and courage as he fought tirelessly to meet the needs of his patients, knowing that most would never survive. He was the one who told us when we took Mark to the hospital that he wouldn't be leaving. Steve fought tirelessly in the trenches of the war on AIDS, spending late nights in the hospital trying to save us all, but in the end, he couldn't save himself. Two years later, he was dead too.

Ray Hailey was an architect by day and a professional homosexual by night. He threw the most awesome margarita parties the city had ever seen. They became annual events in his backyard on Gay Pride. After each event, he'd have to replace all the turf, because the sheer amount of people crammed onto the lawn trampled it. He was one of the sweetest men San Francisco could order up. His memorial was attended by many. It was at the height of the epidemic, and he was so loved by his family and the friends he'd made in San Francisco that we sent him off with a party in his honor.

I was walking down Castro Street one day in 1982 when I saw Carmine Allesio, my first boyfriend from back in 1973. One look at his sunken cheeks told it all. I approached him, gave him a big hug, and reminded him that he was my first love.

He smiled with his beautiful blue eyes. "I love you, Michael."

We parted, but I turned around to watch him walk down the street. One more glance, and he was gone too.

Sylvester was a famous R&B singer, and what a career he had. He became a sensation overnight with his hit "Mighty Real." The lyrics went: "You make me feel mighty real." I worked with Syl at the Cabaret After Dark. He performed there, and I ran the lights and sound for his show. We became friends. He was a fantastic performer, as everyone knows, but what most people don't know was that underneath all that big black girl thing was a shy boy who had seen a lot of pain.

We put on some fabulous shows at the cabaret. During rehearsals one day, as I was climbing down a ladder, he said, "Michael, sugar, did I ever tell you, you sure got some fabulous-looking legs and ass? Could you ever fall for a black girl like me?"

"Sly," I said, "I think you're an incredible performer, but I already have a boyfriend."

We remained friends. I used to see him every once in a while, riding his Italian Vespa down Market Street in his full-length mink coat. I'd think, "You go, girl."

On Gay Day in 1988, as the crowd was on its way back to the Castro, where Sylvester lived just up the street from the intersection, there was a stage set up and a band began playing "Mighty Real."

The lead singer told us what we already knew. He said, "Sylvester is dying, but he can hear you from his house up on Sates Street, so let's let him hear how much we love him."

As the band continued to play his song, the crowd let out a roar you could have heard in Kalamazoo so that he'd know that all of San Francisco was with him at the end.

Gene Davis, George Ash, and Ron Holt were friends of mine from the gym whom I'd photographed for the cover of the *Advocate*, the local gay newspaper. I positioned the three of them on the Smith rack, a large piece of equipment in the middle of the gym. I had them at varying levels, with no shirts on, reading gay books by gay authors. It was the lead-in to a story headlined: *Gay books muscling into the mainstream*. I was looking through my old portfolio one day and found the cover. As I stared at all the guys hanging from the equipment, I realized I was the only one still alive.

Jeff Kowalski was a psychiatrist and had perhaps the saddest story of all. When Jeff found out he was sick, he took the news hard. He'd already been depressed about the lonely life he was living and worried that he'd never have a meaningful relationship. With his diagnosis, he was sure it was impossible. I spoke to him one day and told him that Adrian and I were there for him if he ever needed us, that he wasn't alone. I guess it wasn't enough.

"At least the two of you have each other," he'd said. "I can't do this by myself." He promptly went home and killed himself.

Michael Rossum

~~~

I'm seventy years old at the time of this writing. I've been positive for thirty-nine years, and I've witnessed a kind of genocide. My country, known for its ideas of justice and compassion, watched and waited and did nothing to help us when the need was so great. There were huge fundraisers for famine-ravaged Africa, but the epidemic killing tens of thousands of Americans went unnoticed.

I can only think that we were left alone in the dark for one reason, and that was that good Christians believed we were sinners. What we'd done was so abominable that we should be cast out of the Garden because we loved the wrong people.

These men were my confidants, and I loved them. We were tied together by a common thread. We shared life at a pivotal time in the history of gay America. I thought we would grow old together. But this was not to be.

I don't know how I've survived them all, but as I write these lines, I'm keenly aware that they are absent, and that my life is immensely diminished by their passing. They were my link to another time and space. I am an old warrior on the battlefield of a global catastrophe. I've survived to tell their story, which is my own.

~~~

In memory of Jeff Evanson, Christian Ashman, Mike Maleta, Paul Merar, Ron Vulk, Don Singer, Richard Chamberlin, George Ash, Larry Layden, Jeff Kowalski, Blake Lane, Bob Lomonto, Phil Goldberg, Michael Anthony, Steve Sordelli, Ron Holt, Jerry Alvarnez, Loy Taylor, Dr. Ainesworth, Dr. Charlie Williamson, Dr. Steve Mahalko, Barry Colburn, Steve Matejka, Alex Desy, Ray Hailey, Ken Fletcher, Bob Dougherty, Tommy D'Mato, Carmine Allesio, Clive Cohen, Noel Walsh, David Abbott, Barry McKinley, Mark Domen, Sylvester, Bob Walton, Paul Meyers, and the millions who have died since.

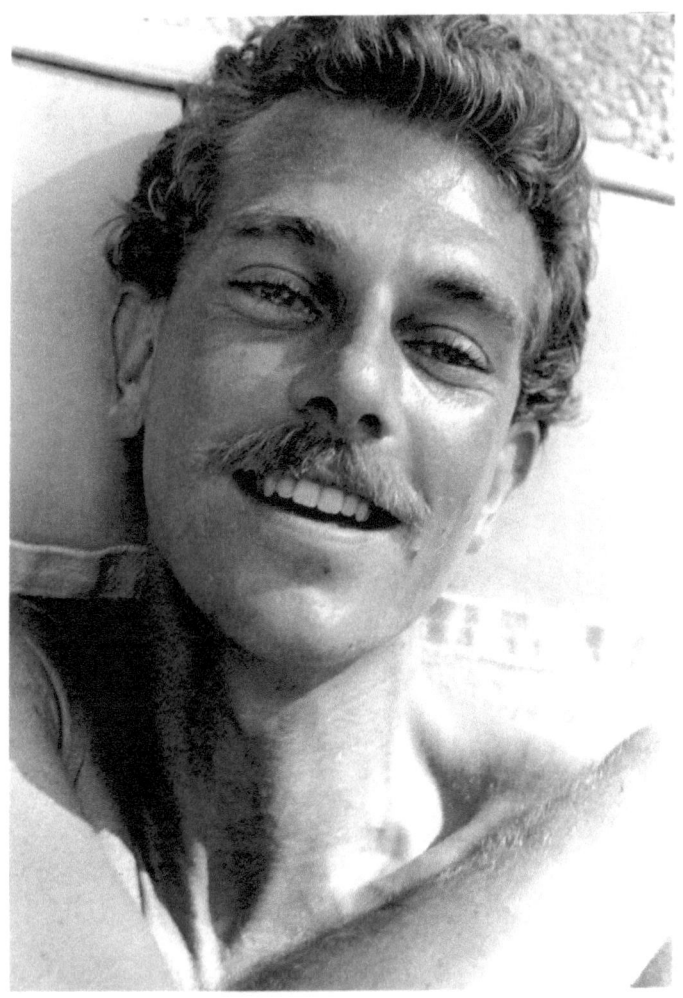

Richard Chamberlin

Michael Rossum

Loy, professional bodybuilder

Touchstones *A Survivor's Story*

Jerry Alvarnez

Michael Rossum

Ad for publication, on Gay Men's books;
Muscling into the Mainstream Gay Books

Alex Desy, owner of Prima Facie Salon on Castro Street; I had my first exhibition of photographs at his opening that launched my career, and he created his dream of opening the salon.

Christian Ashman center with twin sister Ingrid, their mother smuggled them out of East Berlin to West Berlin in 1948 each in a suitcase. Christian escaped Communism but he couldn't escape AIDS.

The AIDS Quilt tells the story of the immense loss of life from the Epidemic. This massive collection, each square quilt represents 6 people who died of AIDS and whose lovers or family members quilted them with love,

"Lest they be forgotten."

Michael Rossum

Steve Matejka

Chapter Twenty-Two

Steve Matejka

Steve Matejka was a joyous soul. I feel so much pain as I tell his story. Steve was my best friend. Most of my friends were already gone by the time we met. I was sure I'd never have a close friend again—a confidant, someone who always had my back, someone who loved me unconditionally. It wasn't for lack of trying, but friendships like that don't happen every day. Sometimes you can lose friends and never find the likes of them in a lifetime. I was lucky.

I walked into my gym, Muscle Systems on Hayes Street, one morning and saw a beautiful man working out. Deep in thought, as though he were alone, he was dedicated to his workout.

"Who's that hot man over there doing biceps?" I asked Ray, a friend of mine who was working the front desk.

"Oh, he's new to the gym. He's from Los Angeles, and his name is Steve Matejka."

"Thanks."

As I began my workout, I watched him from afar. I don't know what it was. I guess I thought he was sexy. He was anything but ordinary. I just stood and watched, and he paid absolutely no attention to me. A week went by, and I saw him every day at the gym. It was a bit uncanny, but not unusual. Again, he never looked up or caught my glance. I went about my workout, then asked him in passing if I might borrow the bench he'd been working on.

"Sure, no problem," he said in a friendly way.

"You're new here, aren't you?" I asked.

"Yes, I'm from LA. Have you been here long?"

I told him I grew up in the Bay Area. We chatted some more, and he told me he was going to Palm Springs over the weekend to the White Party, which was a big gay venue every spring. It was April 1993.

"What about you?" he asked.

"That's funny. My partner Adrian and I are going too. You'll have to look for us."

"For sure," he replied. "We fly into Orange County, and then we've rented a car and will drive from there."

"That's great," I said. "I'll see you there."

"Have fun," he said. "It's supposed to be gorgeous weather."

I smiled, grabbed my gym bag, and said goodbye.

When I got home, I told Adrian I'd met a nice guy at the gym, and he was going to Palm Springs this weekend as well.

"That's great," Adrian replied. "I guess all of San Francisco will be there, and of course, LA and San Diego."

"It should be fun," I said. "I'd like you to meet him."

"Well, we'd better get packing," he replied. "It's an early flight."

The next morning we left for Palm Springs. I was so excited to get away. We arrived at LAX and went directly to pick up our rental car. While I waited for Adrian at the Hertz counter, Steve walked by with his luggage.

"Hey, Steve," I called out. "I told you we'd see you down here."

He didn't recognize me at first but then chuckled and came over and gave me a big hug. "Are you alone?"

"No, my partner's at the desk getting us a rental car. What about you?"

"I'm waiting for a friend to pick me up."

"What a coincidence," I said. "Oh, here's Adrian now. Hey, Adrian, this is the man I was telling you about the other day. He's from our gym. Steve, this is Adrian."

"Well, this is just fine," Steve said. "Here I'm single and new to San Francisco, and I meet the two hottest men and in town, and of course, they're married to one another."

We all laughed. He was so frank and open. We grew to be best friends, the Three Musketeers. We grew so close that Steve became an integral part of our lives. He filled a void for both of us. He was my best friend, the guy I could talk to about everything, including Adrian. Adrian saw his relationship with Steve as one where he could let go, and if he didn't want to join us, he was content that Steve was with me. He, too, sought his confidence, and the three of us were harmonious.

When we went out to the bars, we were, as Steve was, engaged with someone and therefore approachable, but always with a way out. When things got too hot for the two of us with other men, we could introduce them to our third party, thereby leaving us free to take leave if we wished, or have a new date for our friend. In any case, it worked out with few exceptions.

Steve was a waiter at one of the most prestigious digs in town, the Ritz-Carlton on California Street. A bit stuffy, old money, but we always had an invitation. Nick was the maître d'. He was a classy guy, as charming as they come, with a knack for giving people exactly what they wanted.

Nick was the nicest guy. Steve would invite me for my birthday to come dine with them at the Ritz, and Nick would find us the best seats in the house, usually near Boris, who played a gold harpsichord. All the waiters—John and Art, Dean, and of course, Steve, who was the head waiter or captain—kept the champagne flowing and brought endless rounds of hors d'oeuvres, then sumptuous entrées. Then came the sommelier with bottles of wine and port, and then the cart with cheeses and fruit. It was like an orgy. After that, a waiter served dessert. It had a taste of every dessert on the menu with *Happy Birthday, Michael* written in script over the entire rim of the plate in chocolate. Needless to say, we stuffed ourselves.

Nick had elevated the restaurant's status to five stars by introducing cheeses and unusual desserts and entrées as a part of the dining experience. He taught the staff to be charming yet aloof, to give the client the space to feel comfortable, yet always be available. It was first class. Most people left with a bill of $300 or $400 and smiles on their faces, thanking Nick for the lovely experience. Our bill was never what it should have been, and we thanked Nick profusely, too, just not from the bottom of our pocketbooks, thanks to Steve.

Steve was a first-class captain. He had about five waiters under him and a sommelier, but the guy was a real charmer. Flattery rolled off his lips like wine into an empty glass. He filled us with joy and made us feel special, and the truth was we were special because Steve held us in high esteem and made us feel that way. He made us laugh with inside stories of the upper echelons of San Francisco, the rich and powerful and their peculiar behavior due to status, money, and ego and how the staff at the Ritz-Carlton soothed and caressed their fragile egos.

I watched in amazement at how much Steve was in his element when he was on the floor of the dining room, in charge. Charming, funny, and willful, he could get away with anything. Serve someone the wrong dinner, and he'd compensate with a beautiful dessert. If reservations were tight, if they were a good customer, he'd fit them in. Everyone in the dining room, from the chefs to the busboys, loved him.

Not long after we got to know one another, I found cheap tickets to a continent I'd never visited and always wanted to go to. I asked Steve if he'd like to join us.

He looked at his calendar and said, "Hell, yes."

It was Mardi Gras in February 1994, the hottest gay parade in the world. Not only was he able to travel with us, he was able to reserve rooms at the Ritz-Carlton for our stay as part of his employee benefits. We stayed in one of the finest hotels in Sydney. We were on Club Level, which meant a continental breakfast, drinks and sandwiches for lunch, and drinks and cocktails before dinner. We were "puttin' on the Ritz."

We flew out of San Francisco about February 1, ten days before Mardi Gras, on a seventeen-hour flight to Sydney via Auckland, New Zealand. Fortunately, the three bodybuilders got first dibs on the emergency-exit seats so we could stretch our legs. About three hours into the trip, I laid my blanket on the floor in front of the emergency exit and went to sleep for seven hours. When I woke up, I asked Adrian how much more time we had, and he told me seven more hours. I was shocked at how far away Australia really was. I looked up at Steve, who was still asleep from the sleeping pill he downed over the Pacific. His head was slumped to one side, chin to chest, and he was drooling. "That's it," I said to myself, and I lay back down for another five hours, not wanting to succumb to Steve's fate.

Awakened by Adrian, who told me we were landing in Auckland, I got up, sat in my seat, and fastened my seat belt as we taxied in. I looked out the window at the green mountains and thought, *Wow, New Zealand.* I'd always wanted to go there. Then the purser announced, when we were down on the ground, that we'd be making a temporary stop to let passengers off, and that all those going on to Sydney should stay in their seats. I was most disappointed, as I wanted to walk and stretch my legs.

The three of us just sat in our seats, silent and numb from the number of hours in flight. Steve had by this time cleaned himself up. Suddenly the purser announced that they'd be spraying the plane for insects that might have taken a ride with us from the West Coast. Evidently, they had strict environmental laws. The exit door opened, and men in uniforms, wearing gas masks, boarded the plane and started spraying us with insecticide down both aisles. The three of us looked at each other and just lost it. We were laughing so hard I thought Steve would split his gut. We thought they'd be spraying the outside of the plane. There we sat, my first official stop in Auckland, in a fog of insecticide—not exactly how I'd romanticized it.

We arrived in Sydney a couple of hours later and went straight to the Ritz. Steve had reserved a suite with two queen beds and a balcony overlooking the harbor, with views of the Sydney Bridge and the Opera House. Fantastic. It was way beyond our expectations.

We immediately threw ourselves in the shower while Steve called his friend David Biegle from LA, who was staying with an Australian friend by the name of Dave McMahon in the Paddington district of Sydney.

An hour later, David and Dave rolled up in a BMW and whisked us off to Oxford Street, the gay area of Sydney. We went directly to the Oxford Hotel for drinks, then across the street to the Aubrey, where the drag show was taking place on top of the bar where the guests sat. We met so many people through Dave McMahan. He knew everyone. He was the Perle Nestor of Sydney, a man-about-town. Then Dave took us back to his wonderful Victorian in Paddington for a late-night dinner. It was like a whirlwind tour of Sydney.

The Australian men, aside from being gorgeous, were friendly, funny, and gregarious. There was a feeling of confidence and assuredness, even brazenness, in the manner in which they carried themselves. They reminded me of cosmopolitan cowboys. Later in our stay, we realized some of them were a little egotistical and a bit conceited about being "down under," without ever having seen the world outside of their isolated island continent.

Adrian and I were the first to bed, and the next morning we wondered if Steve had even made it back to the hotel, being the single man. As we slowly awoke, we looked over to the other bed to see if it had been slept in.

"Look," I said to Adrian. "That's not Steve's ass sticking out from under the covers."

So whose was it? As we mused on that, the cutest blond pulled his head from the covers, showing us his gorgeous blue eyes.

"G'day, mate," he said. "I'm Malcolm."

Our dear friend had gotten laid the night before as we slept.

"Well, I knew that ass didn't belong to Steve," I said.

Malcolm sheepishly smiled and pulled the sheet over his naked butt.

"It's a fine ass, understand me. It just doesn't belong to my friend."

Both beds began giggling. "What's all the noise about?" came from under the sheets of one, as Steve's head finally appeared.

"They're talking about my ass," Malcolm said.

"And rightly they should," Steve said. "It's a fine ass."

"We didn't even hear you come in last night," I said. "You were as quiet as mice."

"We did it in the bathroom," Steve said. "I'm getting used to the bathroom. If I'm not fucking on a cold marble slab, it's just not sex."

We all laughed. That was Steve. He could make a party even out of the morning after.

Malcolm would be just the first to see the inside of the gray marble bathroom at the Ritz, which was almost as large as our room. There would be a succession of men, ending with Ranger Rick, Steve's date on Mardi Gras night.

By that time, we had an invitation to go sailing on Dave's boat in the harbor to Obelisk Beach, a secluded nude beach. The boat included a somewhat motley crew and Captain Dave, who had one too many gin and tonics under his belt by the time we got there, and some magic mushrooms that I'd brought from San Francisco. We anchored about a half mile off the beach—not far, or so it seemed, high on mushrooms.

I dove off the back of the boat and started swimming for shore. The boat was getting a little claustrophobic, and I needed to connect with Mother Earth. The water was delightful, and I egged Adrian on to join me, which he did. Steve was content talking to Dave Biegle and nursing his cocktail. As we swam toward shore, we both began to tire, probably a combination of the cocktails and our mushroom adventure. I'm a fairly strong swimmer, but I found myself gasping for air and crawling up onto the beach like an amphibian taking its first breaths on land, Adrian not far behind. As I pulled myself up, all I could see were nude men. When we caught our breaths, I turned back to the boat. All eyes were on our daring escape.

"Steve, join us," I yelled. "The water is beautiful."

Steve put down his cocktail and dove off the ship. We waited on the shore as the natives grew restless and became interested in our landing. When Steve joined us, we all decided to investigate Obelisk Beach and see if there were any available men who could satisfy our friend's passions. The rocky beach felt a little like Darwin's Galápagos, filled with older men whose lizard-like skin had seen a bit too much of the Australian sun.

The three of us talked and sat on the rugged rocks and reminisced about how we'd all gotten to Australia together and that it wasn't just a chance meeting. We talked about the magic and chemistry we shared. Then we swam back to the party. It was still in full swing, but the three of us were far beyond it. We'd shared something special, and you could see it in our smiles. As Adrian hugged me, we smiled and then kissed. We were having the time of our lives with Steve, and Australia was the perfect backdrop.

Back at the hotel, we showered for what would be the first of one eventful evening after another, and we'd only just arrived. Adrian was in the shower, and Steve and I were drying off on the balcony when we looked out the window to see an entire floor of an office building across the street full of men with their faces pushed against the windows, watching us.

"Steve, can you believe this? Is this whole town gay?"

He let out that infectious laugh. "If they want to see us nude, let's give them a real show."

We dropped our towels and bent over. We thought they'd be put off, but no, they were jumping up and down and egging us on for more. Sydney had an air of anything goes. It was more like the Barbary Coast.

We decided to go out on our own and investigate the world of gay leather bars. We were given directions to the hottest one, but we didn't understand them and found ourselves walking through the shadows of what looked like the outback—small hotels and bars with wooden sidewalks and porches held up by overhangs of corrugated metal to keep the rainwater off. It was in one of these seedy bars that we took refuge from a torrential downpour that came from nowhere, as the skies suddenly darkened, opened, and unloaded.

We were completely drenched when we walked in and sauntered up to the bar.

The barmaid was a rather unattractive, heavyset woman with a big wart on her nose and three very long hairs growing out of it. "What ya have?" she asked in a heavy Australian accent that obviously lacked education and was hard on the ears, not to mention attitude.

I looked at the boys, soaking wet, and said, "Three Harveys Bristol Creams, please."

Somewhere in the back of the room, I heard someone say, "Puffters."

She flashed a dimwitted smile. "Up or on the rocks?"

"On the rocks, please."

Then from the back of the bar, we heard, "Well, if it isn't the doll boys."

We turned halfway to see where the words were coming from. Against the back wall sat four old curmudgeons wearing Aussie cowboy hats in varying degrees of deterioration. The three of us looked at one another and couldn't hold it back. We were beside ourselves with laughter, and from that day on we became the "Doll Boys."

When we related the story later to our Aussie friends, they were delighted that we'd had a real outback experience while in cosmopolitan Sydney. They started to call us the Three Doll Boys from California. News travels fast in a small town, even one as large as Sydney. The next time we went to the Oxford Hotel to dance, the DJ up above us looked down, smiled, then played "California Dreamin'" by the Mamas and the Papas on our behalf.

Sydney was a nonstop party, and we were definitely on the circuit. The next day, Dave McMahan took us to "Glamoramma Beach," actually Tamarama Beach, which got its nickname from all the gorgeous gay men who frequented it. Within a few hours, Dave had introduced us to everyone on it. It turned into a big party, then half the beach headed to Dave's for a barbecue.

We were lucky to have taken the trip with Steve and met his friends. If not, I don't think we'd have had half the fun we had. But one never knows. We were pretty gregarious ourselves.

I told the boys I was tired of partying and wanted to see something of Sydney, so a friend of Steve's organized an outing to the Blue Mountains just outside the city. It was a marvelous getaway. The mountains, full of gum trees of all varieties, gave off a gas that turned the whole range a blue hue. It was magical. We hiked to the creek below, and it was nice to commune with nature after all that partying in Sydney.

The weekend before Mardi Gras, Dave took the three of us to his house in the countryside up the coast from Sydney, a beautiful place called Wollongong. When we woke the next day, I heard the strangest sound. When I went to the window, I found the entire deck had been taken over by wildlife during the night. We had koala bears and kookaburras. Who needed to go to the outback, when the outback came to you?

As we neared Mardi Gras, Oxford Street began to swell with thousands of tourists, mostly gay, from all over Australia and the world, who descended on Sydney for three incredible days. We began to see familiar faces from San Francisco, Los Angeles, and New York, and the street at night had a carnival atmosphere, with people in groups stopping to catch up.

Saturday night was the parade, and the big party. Some of the five pavilions that were having parties would host some thirty thousand people. We chose a smaller venue with just five thousand of our closest friends. Everyone was there—all the people we'd met over the course of the ten-day stay. We were like a big family. It felt good, and I was glad we'd come early to be able to share the Australian experience in the way that we did.

The Doll Boys drove with Dave in his BMW to within a few blocks of the pavilion, arriving around nine-thirty. It was an all-night affair. To aid our longevity, Dave gave us some ecstasy. The pill enhanced awareness and sensitivity to everything around us. It was like our senses were amplified, so if we felt joy, it was tenfold. Love, sensuality—all would be enhanced beyond our normal senses. The crowd danced to the music in undulating waves of ecstasy.

Around midnight, the Australian Gay Men's Chorus paraded out onto the stage in pink Speedos and matching Aussie swim caps, each an Adonis unto himself. They began to sing lines from "Somewhere," a song from the Broadway musical *West Side Story*. "There's a place for us, somewhere a place for us . . ." It hit a chord with the crowd, and we could see the joy emanating from the idea that yes, indeed, as gay people on the planet, we did have a place in the world, and that night, it was Sydney. We cheered them, for they represented all of us.

It was around that time that a broad-shouldered, six-foot-four-inch blond man of Herculean proportions approached me on the dance floor and told me straight out that he wanted to go home with me. I introduced myself, and he told me he was visiting from Namibia, Africa, which is a long way off from just about everywhere.

I was struck by his frankness. "I'm already taken," I said, and I pointed to Adrian, who was now acknowledging us.

Though he spoke with an accent, perhaps Dutch, he understood me. "Oh, I see," he said. "But couldn't he give you up for one night? That's all I ask."

"No," I said. "I can't give him up."

"Ask him if it is all right, just for one night."

"Sure," I said. "I'll ask him."

Of course, Adrian said no, and I told the African his answer. I thanked him for his interest, gave him a hug, and then went back to dancing with Adrian.

Then things got mucky. The African's friend, an Aussie wearing an Australian Army hat pinned to one side of his head and no shirt, revealing rippling abdominals, tapped Adrian's shoulder. He asked him if his friend could take me home for the night. Again, Adrian refused.

We were both a little shocked at how insistent his friend was, so I asked poor Steve over and introduced him to the fellow with the hat, thinking he might be able to defuse the situation. Low and behold, that was the last time we'd see Steve the whole night. As we danced the night away into the morning hours, dripping wet, with our tank tops stuck in our Levi's at the waist, we asked one another, "Where's Steve?"

As the music continued, the huge doors of the pavilion began to open to the light of day—a very bright one at that—and threw streaming beams onto the dance floor. The party was over. It was time to go home. For those of us fortunate to have remembered that the dawning of the day would come, our sunglasses gave us a welcome respite from the harsh light. The majority of the crowd, who hadn't thought they'd see the sunrise, exited, hands over their eyes, like bats departing a darkened cave.

We found Dave McMahan, and he corralled those he'd brought with him, minus Steve, in his BMW, which by that time of the morning was a welcome sight. We drove off as though escaping, as thousands of people streamed past our moving car.

We had a wonderful time on the way back to our hotel, singing all the way. Dave was in mini shorts and a black vest, and everyone else was shirtless—it seemed pointless to put on our dripping wet tank tops. Dave pulled up in front of the Ritz-Carlton to drop us off. It was Sunday morning.

Adrian and I were in shock. There in front of us was a huge wedding party dressed in tuxes and white gowns, waiting for the bride and groom to arrive. Instead, they got our motley crew. Bare-chested as we were, how could we act nonchalant as we found our way to the elevators through this crowd? All the bellboys knew us well, and our reputation preceded us with the other staffers. After all, we were the Doll Boys.

"How was it?" they asked as we poured out of every door, dripping wet, in front of all the ladies-in-waiting.

"Fantastic," I said. "Just fantastic!"

Then we said goodbye to Dave, and he reminded us, "Don't forget the recovery party down at Finnegan's later."

All we could think about was getting to the elevators without being seen half-nude at nine in the morning. After all, the hotel had a reputation to uphold. We ran for the elevator banks with our wet, naked backs to the wedding party. We heard some commotion behind us, but we waited until we got into the lift before we looked back at the crowd. All eyes were on us as we pressed the buttons frantically to close the doors.

All we could think of was a shower—and where Steve was. Our flight home would leave the next day at noon. We showered and made love. Then Steve rolled in, alone and in a new tank top. Being an employee, he had the sense to buy a fresh shirt, which hadn't even occurred to us.

"What did you do when you came back?" he asked. "The whole hotel is all abuzz about the two guys who walked into the Ritz half-naked. Was that you two?"

We nodded and bowed our heads.

"Well, that's a fine how-do-you-do," he said. "One of the managers is complaining about our behavior, and of course, now I understand why."

We apologized profusely, but he was a little shaken.

Then he said, "Ah, fuck 'em If they can't handle a little excitement on Mardi Gras . . ."

"Steve, what happened to you?" I asked. "We missed you for most of the evening. Where did you go? You missed an incredible party."

"Well," he said, "Ranger Rick wanted to go for a walk and smoke a joint. You know, the guy you introduced me to with the ranger's hat."

"Yes," I said.

"So we started walking to his car, but it was so far away from the pavilion, we wound up going to his house. After we got to his place, he filled the bathtub, and then he took off his clothes. He had a beautiful body, but when he removed his hat, he was bald and the whole image I'd conjured up crumbled. I wondered what I was doing there and why I'd agreed to leave you and Adrian and the party. I was totally depressed, but I made the best of a bad situation."

"I'm so sorry," I said.

"I'm going out to the recovery party at Finnegan's. Do you guys want to come?"

"Not now," I said. "Maybe later. We both want to take a nap."

"Well then, I'll see you down there later," he said and left.

When we awoke from our nap, we remembered we'd be leaving the next day and decided to trot down to Finnegan's to pay our respects.

On our way out of the hotel, one of the bellmen approached us. "You guys were brilliant when you rode in here in the BMW this morning in the middle of that stuffy wedding reception. The driver in mini shorts and no shirt, and all of you buffed without your shirts—you should have seen the looks. It was positively brilliant."

We thanked him, but I don't think *brilliant* was what we were feeling.

Down at Finnegan's, the recovery party was in full swing, and we found Steve there with Dave McMahan and David Biegle, Malcolm, and all the Australians we'd met over our stay. We laughed and reminisced that the Doll Boys had taken Sydney by surprise. It was a fitting end to our journey down under.

We shared the next four years with Steve. We journeyed to New Orleans, Provincetown, and Puerto Vallarta, Mexico, sharing most holidays, birthdays, Christmases, New Years, and Thanksgivings with him, either at the Ritz or at home.

We all became so close that some people asked if he was our lover. Steve would just call me up and say, "Let's get together for lunch or brunch after the gym." Since he worked nights, his days were free, and we spent an unusual amount of time together, as my days were my own.

Then just after Christmas 1993, he began complaining of a pain in his stomach. Since he was HIV positive, we urged him to see his doctor. We went with him on several occasions. He took one test after another, but none could pinpoint the problem. All were inconclusive.

The pains worsened, and yet Steve still went to work and put on his charming face and met the public. Adrian and I were concerned.

We didn't think his doctor was doing enough to get to the bottom of the pains. His doctor finally tested for bacterial organisms and found that Steve had a massive infection. It could have been taken care of months earlier with simple antibiotics, but by then it was out of control and had lowered his immune system so gravely that we had to feed him via a tube inserted directly into his stomach.

We sat with him in his bedroom on Divisadero Street and fed him a milky mixture with syringes. Each day he lost more strength, until he had to be admitted to the hospital. He languished as friends and family visited, saying goodbye. Steve finally lost the battle, and we lost our best friend. We were the Three Musketeers no more.

I fell into a deep depression after Steve died in 1996. Part of me died in that bed at Davies Hospital too. We stopped going out, the phone stopped ringing, and a dark cloud loomed over us for years. It took that long for me to say goodbye. Even today, there's a void next to me where he once stood, and I'm acutely aware that he's gone.

Michael Rossum

The Three Musketeers; Doll Boys, Australia, 1993

Michael Rossum

Adrian

Chapter Twenty-Three

Adrian

I met Adrian on Castro and Eighteenth streets in San Francisco. The streets intersected at the crossroads of mecca in a city called Oz. For a moment, they intersected the two of us, too, and would change our lives forever, though we didn't know it. Call it fate. Adrian would one day be my soul mate, the one I'd end my journey with, the mature love of my life.

It was 1982, a year after the plague began, and while people died, life continued. People still made passes at one another, got hitched, and fell in love. We were mostly in denial since there were no drugs to help us, no cure, and a government that had stuck its head in the sand.

Adrian was a lawyer who had come to San Francisco to work on a case and decided to stay for the weekend. We met on a Friday. My business associate Rick Williams and I had come down to the Castro to begin our weekend early with a banker's lunch, which included a martini and more time off from work than prudent.

As we passed Eighteenth and Castro, I saw a hulk of a man crossing the street. Tanned and built like a tank, he was blond with wavy hair. As he stood on the corner, I noticed he was talking with someone. I couldn't take my eyes off him. I stopped Rick. "Hold up a minute."

Rick urged me to go on, but I stayed long enough for him to see me staring at him. Our eyes met, the light changed to green, and we began walking toward one another. I noticed every detail about him as he made his way closer to me. His arms and chest were poured into a yellow tank top and blue jeans. As he strode closer, I saw a red college ring on his finger. He began to smile, a little shy at first, but it grew wider by the time he'd almost reached me. I caught his steely blue eyes. He was a blond god, and he was coming for me.

We met in the middle of the street and extended our hands. He grasped mine, and we shook.

What a man, I thought. "Michael," I said, still feeling his strong grip.

"Adrian," he replied.

"That's a beautiful name. Where are you from?"

"Los Angeles," he replied. Of course, he was one of those Adonises from down south, plucked right off a beach in Santa Monica or Malibu, I thought.

"We're going to get killed if we stand here much longer," I said. We headed back to the side of the street, where his friend was waiting for him.

We could feel the electricity between us. "Do you have any dinner plans?" I asked.

"Actually, I'm going with a friend I met up here to Beach Blanket Babylon."

"Oh, who's your friend?" I asked, casing him out. San Francisco's a small town. Maybe I could figure out if it was a romantic date or just a cordial one.

"His name is Max Platt Rayfield the Third, Esquire."

Yes, I did know him. A bit pretentious, like his name. But who was I to say? Maybe he saw something in him. I was sure it wasn't the same thing we saw in one another. "How about tomorrow night?" I asked.

Disappointed, as I was, too, he said he was leaving for Los Angeles the next day.

"Well," I said, "it was nice meeting you. Very nice."

"Hey, listen, here's my card," he said. "Call me sometime. Maybe you could come down for a visit."

The card read *Adrian Fredric Barrow, Attorney at Law, Woodland Hills, California.*

"Well, you are one handsome man," I whispered in his ear as we embraced.

"You too," he said.

"See ya, Adrian."

"See you, Michael. Call me."

He left me standing dazed on the corner, clutching his card. I watched him walk up Eighteenth until the street devoured him. I stuck his card safely inside my wallet, where it remained for four years.

I never called. I figured guys from LA never moved to San Francisco. They hated the weather. I didn't want a fling, or an affair, either. I wanted true love, and I'd wait until it came.

A few months later, I met Mark. Two years after Mark and I were married, at least in our hearts, if not on paper, we ran into Adrian and a friend of mine from San Francisco at a party. I saw him moving through the crowd. All eyes were on him. I flashed back two years and remembered our meeting. I realized I was still carrying his card in my wallet. I told Mark I'd met Adrian a year before we'd met. When he passed by me with Larry, I said hello, and he remembered me. I introduced him to Mark, and he introduced me to Larry as his lover, then passed by again and was lost in the crowd. I can tell you to this day what he was wearing.

I was truly in love with Mark, and was happy for Adrian that he'd found love. I knew my friend Larry was a lucky guy. The next year passed, and we saw them out at parties and dances. It was all casual. We traveled in the same circles, and I was always glad to see him. Then toward the end of 1985, Mark, the love of my life, came down with the plague. Things started to spiral down into what I saw as a "Dante's Inferno." AIDS was a living hell.

I began running into Adrian at the supermarket in Diamond Heights, where we both lived. We'd stand in an aisle and talk for an hour or more, while people dodged us trying to find whatever it was we were blocking. I told him that Mark was sick, and he was supportive. It was uncanny how many times we ran into one another at the market, and every time my story grew worse. We got to know one another through those talks in the dark days of the epidemic.

Mark died in October 1986. I was heartbroken. The next time I ran into Adrian was months later. I told him that Mark was gone, and he could tell that part of me was too. We talked for a bit, then said goodbye and hugged one another tightly. That's all I can remember. That time was a blur.

We saw one another on and off, and then one day when I ran into him at the supermarket, he told me Larry was sick too. Tears came to his eyes as he recounted his own despair, now our mutual nightmare. I wanted to comfort him, but it was impossible. I could give kind, sympathetic words of encouragement, but that was all. I knew all too well what was happening in the silence of his mind at night.

They'd been working on the new drug AZT. We all had high hopes that it would hold the virus at bay. Larry was on it, but it seemed like the drug was killing more people than it was saving.

We saw one another again when the AIDS Quilt was first shown at the Moscone Center. The Quilt Project, as it was called, was devised by Cleve Jones, one of Harvey Milk's protégés. It was a plan to help the people left behind, the walking wounded grieving loved ones. It gave us a way to deal with their loss—although I didn't believe there was anything that could help me deal with mine.

Then one day I found myself in front of the window on Market Street where people were busy making quilts. The next moment I found myself inside, talking to a sweet girl by the name of Christie. "My lover died," I said. "I want to make a quilt for him."

I was still numb, but she took me by the hand and gave me a quilting cloth, and I began to make a quilt for Mark.

"It can be about a special moment you shared," she said. "You can sew pictures and personal articles onto it, or names, or just do anything you feel like doing."

I thought about it for a time as I sat there staring at the blank cloth. Then it came to me. It was like Zen, simple, one mind and present—present for the life Mark and I had shared. I began to pick up the scraps of cloth on the table in front of me, and fashion a quilt that he'd be proud of. I tried to remember when we were the happiest together. It was in Bali, Indonesia, on the beach, wrapped in sarongs in the humid early morning, quiet and serene.

The island appeared, and the palm trees were sewn with the sun rising over the volcano and the seabirds overhead. I put Mark's name below everything, and the day that he died, all of it sewn with love and tears. Then one day, weeks after I started, it was finished, and I felt joy.

At the opening of the AIDS Quilt's first display at Moscone Center, I brought my mom, as she'd never seen it, and ran into Adrian and Larry. I could see Larry was ill. He'd lost weight, and his face was gaunt. They could see I was disturbed.

The entire convention floor was covered with quilts. They were everywhere, including hanging from the rafters. The scope of how many San Franciscans had died was overwhelming.

I found Christie and said, "I've been looking all over for Mark's quilt, but I can't find it."

"I don't know how you could have missed it," she said. "It's in the front window when you first walk in."

I took Mom back up the escalator to the main entrance of the exhibition. We walked outside, and sure enough, there it was.

My mother put her arm around me and cried, as did I. "Oh Michael, it's beautiful."

I'd finally found Mark's quilt, out of the thousands that lay everywhere, and there it was, prominently displayed.

I didn't see Adrian for a long time after that, not at the gym, nor the supermarket.

Almost three years had passed since Mark was gone. I'd just started dating a few months prior and just getting over a perfectly disastrous affair. I thought I'd probably never fall in love again, or have something even close to what Mark and I had shared. I was still measuring other people by my relationship with Mark, which I knew wasn't fair.

I went down to the Detour, a pub in the Castro, for a drink one night. I was lonely and wanted some attention from afar, somewhere I could be safe and in control. Just one drink, I told myself, but as I walked in, I saw Adrian at the bar with a man I didn't know. I was glad to see him again. He said things were bad at home, and he was taking a break from caring for Larry and needed to get out. He said there was someone at home watching him. He told me Larry had a fatal brain tumor. I felt bad for him. I tried to support him, but I knew all too well that his was a solo journey. He'd have to go through it on his own. I knew Larry well. I'd met him long before I met Adrian, and my heart went out to both of them. Larry and I had grown up together during the evolution of gay life in San Francisco.

I finished my drink, set the glass on the bar, and went home.

A few days later, I got a call from Adrian asking me if we could meet.

"Yes, of course," I said. I asked if he'd like to have lunch at the community pool where my mom lived in Diamond Heights.

He said yes.

"How about eleven a.m.?" I asked.

He came by, and we went up to the pool. We sat there for hours, just talking, and then I invited him in for a swim. There were other people around. In fact, the complex was quite gay. Mom had made friends with two lovers down the hall from her, Ira and Bob.

The discussion we had was intense, but what was even more remarkable was how the energy we shared suddenly became physical for me, and I lost all self-control. I found myself swimming up to him and kissing him. It was like my emotions just took over, and all I could do was follow my heart. The next thing I knew, I was feeling him up in the pool in front of all of those people. And what's worse is that I didn't care.

He finally stopped me and suggested, "Maybe we should go back to your house."

As a matter of fact, I really hadn't expected any of it. Things were happening beyond our control, his and mine. What was going on? I knew he must be thinking of Larry and how this must look to the outside world. That crossed my mind too. Did we know what we were doing?

Yes. When we got back to the house, we couldn't take our clothes off fast enough. I knew then that I was falling in love with him. There we were, naked, and we kissed and embraced and just held one another for a time. Not moving, I caressed his head, knowing the pain he was enduring and wishing I could make it better. Maybe that was what this was all about.

He responded in kind. I knew he was the one. But how could that be? What a predicament we were in. It was so complicated. But for the moment, all of that fell by the wayside, and we were making love. It felt good.

I think he felt the same, but he was wrestling with his conscience. Before we'd finished, he looked at the clock and told me he had to get back. I understood. As we dressed, I could tell that he wanted me, too, but I didn't want to get hurt either. Knowing what lay ahead for him, I knew it was too soon for us. He told me that he couldn't make commitments and that I should see other people. It was painful for both of us. But I figured he had to know what was best for him. I'd resigned myself to not thinking there was any hope we'd get together. Yet I knew already that he was where my heart was.

~~~

I got an invitation to Fire Island from my good friend Kenny Gutterman, from the days of the Five Towns and Far Rockaway. He had a house on the island, not fancy, but it worked as long as you didn't mind sleeping with strangers. The house had four bedrooms and eight people in them. If you found an empty bed, it was yours, all except one room, which only had one bed for two people.

I tried to forget about San Francisco, though wondering what was happening with Adrian and Larry lay heavy on my mind. But Adrian didn't want me in his life at this moment, and I could understand perfectly, so I tried to have fun and keep my heart open.

On my first night, I came home at five in the morning, high and exhausted, and found that the only bed available had someone in it already. I'd have to slip under the covers and join whoever it was. It turned out to be Jerry, a twenty-three-year-old from New York, six feet, four inches tall and gorgeous. I was surprised he hadn't connected, but such was Fire Island. Sometimes the chemistry just wasn't happening. As I curled up in the fetal position and pulled the covers up, Jerry snuggled up behind me and put his arms around me.

I said, "Jerry, it's Michael."

"Yeah, I know," he said. "I thought you'd never come home."

It was hot and steamy, and we made love until we were exhausted. Our ecstasy was still running through us when we finally fell asleep in one another's arms.

When I woke up, he was still there. *What are you doing?* I thought. *You're old enough to be his father.* I took one last look at his awesome body and his youth and snuck out of bed.

I found Kenny and a few others around the kitchen table, having a late breakfast and gossiping. "So it was you who wound up with Jerry last night. Tell us all about it."

"There's nothing to tell," I said. "It was late when I got in, and he was already asleep."

"There's something you're leaving out," Kenny said. "These walls are thin."

"He's a nice guy," I said. "I like him." I grabbed a piece of toast from the table of wolves as they dished about their nights and mine.

The door to the bedroom opened, and Jerry appeared, hair all tussled and his underwear halfway off his hips.

I jumped into the shower, and he cornered me there.

"That was fantastic last night," he said.

"Yes, it was," I said, but I didn't want to tell him that I was thinking about Adrian and that what we'd had was just a one-night stand. He was gorgeous, but I had no long-term interest.

I made my way to the beach. It was a hot August day and the surf was up. I threw myself into the Atlantic.

When I came up, there was a handsome man with a square jaw, high cheekbones, and big, sensual lips bobbing in front of me. "Hi, my name is Heinz," he said in a rather heavy German accent. "What's yours?"

"Michael," I said.

"I was watching you from the beach, and I wanted to meet you," he said matter-of-factly.

Nobody in NYC fucks around. They just don't have a whole lot of time to waste. They get right to the point.

He was the dominant type who had to make it clear who was in control. I know this sounds weird, but while we were having sex, he kept reminding me of the Jewish boy being seduced by a Nazi SS storm trooper. It was totally off the wall. But this was no fantasy of mine. Afterward, I had real Jewish guilt and reservations about my judgment as I exited his apartment.

The next weekend, I met a nice guy by the name of Steve Meyers, a good-looking Jewish boy who fell in love with me overnight. I spent a couple of days with him, hanging out on the beach and meeting his friends. I could tell he really liked me, but as we talked, something wasn't quite right. He was a married man, unhappily so, and evidently, I was the one who showed him how unhappy he really was. He asked if he could come out to San Francisco and visit me for Halloween, which is a major party for San Francisco. All those closeted drag queens get to come out for a night, donning their thirteen-inch heels. I told him the truth: I was in love with someone else in San Francisco, even though I had no idea if the man I was in love with felt the same way.

He was disappointed, but there it was. I'd said the *L* word out loud. Then I called home for messages, and there was one from Adrian telling me that he wanted to see me. I was so jazzed. I couldn't wait to get home.

Adrian and I saw one another briefly a few times in August 1989, and then the inevitable happened: Larry passed away in mid-September. We saw one another afterward, but his grief had consumed him, and he told me he needed more time. I knew all too well how much time he might need, so I gave it to him.

Then on October 17, I woke up and realized it had been exactly three years since Mark's death. I was filled with sadness as I sipped my coffee on the back porch of our apartment, where he and I had sat on many a San Francisco morning, looking out over the city. The view from Upper Market was spectacular, but there was no one to share it with. I always remembered the day Mark died because a few years afterward on the exact day, we had one of the worst earthquakes to hit this region, the Loma Prieta.

I was working as a software engineering recruiter for major companies in Silicon Valley. I had my own company on the corner of Gough and Lily, which found super-talented software geniuses for technology giants in San Jose. In 1989, business was booming. The dot-com IPOs were being announced almost weekly. I was making six figures.

I never thought I'd wind up in sales. My father's story was like *Death of a Salesman*, and I promised myself I'd never end up like him. I was proud of having built the business from nothing. Still, if I had my druthers, I'd have walked away had the money not been so good. It allowed me to take care of my mom, so no complaints. I just knew this was part of the journey, but something was missing, and I could feel it. My thoughts were on Mark. He would have been thirty years old. I was lonely. I missed not having someone in my life. The chances of getting together with Adrian seemed nominal, as he'd only been grieving for a month.

After work, I went to the Muscle Systems, the gym I've mentioned before. Around the corner on Hayes Street, it was in a carriage house from the 1800s and was made of brick and mortar, with skylights in the ceilings. Its two floors were supported by huge wooden beams. It was the premier gym in town, and gay.

I was working out with my best friend, Steven Clark, and we were just finishing up on the exercise bikes when suddenly, the twelve-by-twelve-inch beam over my head began to shake.

"Michael, an earthquake!" Steven shouted.

As I struggled to get off the stationary bike, my foot got caught on the pedal strap. I lost my balance and fell. It was pandemonium. It was five o'clock and the gym was packed. Everyone ran toward the stairs to get to the first floor. I quickly got up, and Steve and I ran with the rest of them. As we ran up the stairs, I looked down and saw tennis shoes scrambling for the next step. Then the anchors at the bottom of the stairs broke loose, and we swayed back and forth as we gripped the rails to keep from falling. Once we reached the main floor, I looked up and saw the overhead lighting fixtures swinging back and forth. In just a few short seconds, I saw the brick walls swaying, and because of the friction, there was mortar coming out from between the bricks in the form of dust and smoke. I knew the building was on the verge of collapsing. We all ran for it, into the middle of Hayes Street.

There we were, 175 queens standing shirtless, in spandex shorts, in the middle of Hayes Street. It was eerie. There were no other people around. As the ground continued to shake, we watched the power of the San Andreas as the earth moved back and forth along the fault under our feet.

Then came the sound of glass shattering everywhere, and in a few seconds, the up-and-coming neighborhood had been reduced to shards of broken glass and brick. Whole chimneys had been rocked off their foundations and fell to the streets below from three stories up. Then all was quiet, save for police sirens and the fire engines that were beginning to respond to calls. Otherwise you could have heard a pin drop.

We stared at one another in complete disbelief, hands over our mouths. Then from nowhere, like something out of a safety drill when people were given the all clear, people came piling out of stores and office buildings. We must have looked a total fright, a hundred-plus pretty boys, half-nude, in tight spandex, in the middle of Hayes Street. But nothing phased these hearty souls. They were so quiet. They were frightened and worried about their loved ones, and they didn't know how they'd get home. Our clothes were still in our lockers inside the gym. Now, with the aftershocks, we were scared to go back inside.

I looked up to a beautiful blue sky with big puffy clouds passing over us. There was a soft, warm October breeze, and an uneasy evening was approaching.

When we thought it was safe, Steve and I went in to get our clothes from the locker. We walked through the smoky gym's first floor all the way back to the men's locker room, trying to move as quickly as possible, as we were still feeling the aftershocks.

"We better make a run for it while we can," I said.

We grabbed our clothes and ran outside to the street, then put them on.

By then, the streets were full of people, and the traffic was backed up for miles. Everyone just started walking, hundreds of thousands of people silently plodding home. Some people were trapped in the city and stood on the corners away from buildings in a stupor. The two main arteries, the Bay Bridge to the East Bay and the Golden Gate Bridge north to Marin County, had been cut off.

As we walked along, I asked people what was going on. They said the train that went under the bay was closed, and there were people inside. The subways had stopped, and people found themselves walking along the train tracks to the next station. There was even some talk of fires burning. I told Steve I was going to try to make it home and check on my mom, but I was really thinking about Adrian. He only lived a block away from me. I knew he was alone, and I wanted to make sure he was okay. As the electricity was off and the lights out, I needed to ask him if he could give me a ride on his motorcycle to Twin Peaks, where my mother lived.

I got in my car and drove up the main artery of the city, Market Street. The stoplights weren't working and the street was backed up all the way to the Ferry Building eastward. Westward, traffic reached to the top of Twin Peaks and beyond. The street also was filled with people, five abreast, walking in silence up both sides. As we looked down Market Street, lines that looked like ants stretched from downtown to Twin Peaks, heading over the hill all the way to the beaches.

It took me almost two hours to get home. Normally, it took ten minutes. I parked and walked the rest of the way to Adrian's house. I rang the doorbell, and he answered, already on his way out.

"Hi," I said and gave him a big hug. "Are you all right? I was thinking about you here all alone."

"Yes, I'm fine," he said. "But a friend of mine called from Castro Street and asked if I'd come by and see him."

"I hope this won't be an inconvenience," I said. "But can you give me a lift on your motorcycle to my mom's house? The traffic on the street is bumper to bumper, and the lights are out. She's all alone, and I need to find out how things are up there."

He said of course, so we hopped on his fiery red Yamaha V-Max and drove through the middle of all that mayhem, in between the rows of cars, to my mom's house.

We were there in no time. She was well, though a little frightened, as the power was still out and it was getting dark. We made her comfortable, found some candles, and got her settled in with some leftovers to eat. That was the first time Adrian and my mom had met. Later, they'd forge a close relationship.

We left my mom and headed down to Castro Street to see Adrian's friend Blair. When we got there, he was outside, as were most of the residents. The bar on the corner, Harvey's, was filled with people partying. The owners were giving away free beer, since there was no refrigeration to keep the draft from spoiling. Broken glass and piles of bricks from the toppled chimneys littered the street, but otherwise it was calm, almost a party atmosphere.

We said goodbye to Blair, who was in good hands, and drove back to my house. We raided the refrigerator, finding half a turkey breast, cranberry sauce, and a carton of milk. We returned to Adrian's condo, which overlooked most of the city and had a view straight down Market Street to the Ferry Building and the bay. As we looked out over the panorama, we saw what looked like fire in the Marina District. Buena Vista Park had an orange glow high over its peak, and we knew there must be buildings on fire there. With no news, we were in the dark.

As darkness set in, San Francisco was black. There were a few lights from cars on the Bay Bridge, but then they stopped too. It was eerie to look out over the darkness and the hundreds of thousands of people below, not knowing how bad things really were. All we could hear in the silence were the sirens of fire trucks, ambulances, and police cars. Before long, the rooftops filled with everyone from below, trying to assess what was happening.

Adrian's neighbors came out with a small, battery-operated TV, and we huddled around it. We heard Dan Rather say parts of the Bay Bridge had fallen and part of the freeway had collapsed, and we all gasped. That was our first inkling of how serious things were.

There was nothing to do but watch, so we made some turkey sandwiches and stared at the glow as the marina burned. I like to think it was the earthquake that brought us together. It certainly speeded things up, for from that time on, the two of us have never been parted.

Chapter Twenty-Four

Christmas 1989

Our first Christmas together after the earthquake, and I scored big-time.

I wanted to give Adrian something that screamed, "I want you for all time." He'd mentioned earlier when we got together that he used to love playing with toy trains as a kid, but I could see that he wasn't done yet, especially at Christmas. He told me how when he was a kid, he always wanted the Santa Fe line, especially the piggyback locomotives. So that was what I decided to get him.

I searched and searched until I found a shop that specialized in antique trains. They had the locomotive I was looking for, and the shopkeeper showed me the engine, made in 1953 and in mint condition. Even the horn still worked, as well as the smokestack, which was controlled at the transformer site. This was all new to me, but toy train hobbyists are really into them. I told him I had a conductor at home who put up a freight train every year at Christmas underneath the tree, and boy, was he going to be excited when he saw the Santa Fe *Chief*. The salespeople asked me how old my son was, and I told them thirty-six. They smiled politely.

"So how much does one of the engines cost?" I asked. I wasn't prepared for the answer.

"Six hundred and eighty dollars."

I repeated it in my head. *They're just toys*, I thought.

The shopkeeper said it was another $200 for the piggyback locomotive without the motor.

"That's a lot for a toy," I said, still in shock.

"These aren't toys. They're antiques. They don't make them anymore. They were made in 1953. They're collectors' items."

"I'll take them both." *Well*, I thought to myself, *he'll be completely jazzed when he sees this.*

We spent Christmas at the condo on Corbet Avenue that Adrian had shared with Larry. It was his first Christmas without Larry, which was why I wanted to make it special. We sat near the Christmas tree while he played conductor with his transformer and freight train. He was so fixated on the train, and it gave him solace.

"Well, let's have a little Christmas," I said, pointing at a large box with a red bow. "Open that one, but don't shake it or turn it right side up."

As he lifted the box, the horn blew, and I thought my cover had been blown as well. But as he unwrapped it, the box remained silent, and he didn't seem to have a clue. Then he pulled back the tissue paper and exclaimed in surprise, "It's the Santa Fe *Chief*! I've wanted this train ever since I was a kid." Amazed, he smiled ear to ear. For a moment, he was happy.

It was just what I'd been hoping for.

"How did you know?" he asked.

"You told me when we first met."

"And you remembered?"

"Yes, I did."

He came over, kissed me, and gave me a big hug. "You devil," he said.

He looked like a little kid as he returned to the two locomotives, investigating how they were connected and the horn and the smoke that came from the engine. He immediately put the train on the track, and the little red Santa Fe began to circle the Christmas tree. His face lit up, and for a few moments he'd forgotten the sad year that had preceded Larry's passing.

It was a difficult time for both of us. I'd lost Mark only a few years earlier, so I knew I'd have to give Adrian the space he still required to recover. At the same time, of course, I was excited about the two of us making our own life together. It wasn't like the other times I'd fallen in love, joyous and overwhelmingly happy. There was little of that in our beginning. It was a somber romance that slowly developed and flowered like no other I'd ever had.

I knew Adrian loved me, but I couldn't tell when he fell in love with me. It took him some time to let go of his life with Larry. Our lives slowly merged until they caught up to our hearts.

Through no effort of our own, we became an item in the gay world. We met people easily, and were invited to parties and dance clubs, and a little getaway outside the city in the Russian River area. Everyone knew us as Michael and Adrian, or as some of our friends called us, the "M and A Show."

We used to love going to Club Universe, where, high on ecstasy, we danced in the crowd, completely absorbed with one another. There was only the music and the love between us swirling on the dance floor. We looked into one another's eyes, and we were madly in love, as our bodies, dripping with perspiration, touched and swayed together like cobras.

Other men on the dance floor picked up on the energy and would dance with us. Some were single and wanted a three-way, some were coupled and wanted a four-way, and others just wanted to dance because the energy was so good. That was the kind of energy we gave off, and a lot of people wanted a piece of it. If we'd been insecure, we wouldn't have been able to handle it, but because we knew who we were, we took their advances as compliments.

I think the change in Adrian, and our relationship, happened in Spain on our second anniversary. I took a month and a half off from work, and we spent five weeks in Spain and one in Morocco. I noticed Adrian was taking the initiative physically, and there was more warmth and laughter, replacing the melancholia. He was coming out of it, but not just from Larry's death. He was beginning to flower.

I encouraged him to believe in himself. He began to tell me what he wanted, what he liked and didn't like. We grew together. It was exciting to see us as a couple in our own right. Adrian had let go of the pain of Larry's death, and I had let go of Mark's passing, enough to let ourselves forge a new relationship together. Perhaps this was the beginning of our love affair. I'll never know for sure, but it's when I first noticed a change.

I wanted to show him Spain. I'd been there once as a young man when Franco was in power. Now we found a country in which gay people had torn the closet doors right off their hinges, and the people had reinstated a king. We traveled everywhere—Madrid, Toledo, Barcelona, Ibiza, Granada, Cordoba, Seville—and then we crossed the Strait of Gibraltar to Tangier, Casablanca, Marrakesh, and Fez.

Our flight touched down in Madrid, and as we disembarked, the gay steward who had attended us in business class, knowing it was our anniversary trip, handed us a bottle of champagne nicely wrapped in a serviette. We were delighted, but the bottle was so heavy, and our anniversary was two weeks away. Needless to say, we dragged that bottle all over Spain.

Our cab sailed to Hotel Carlos V, near the Plaza del Sol. It was a four-star hotel from the late 1800s, nestled on a quiet walking street near the plaza. The next day it was nice to step onto our balcony and see no cars, just people on their way to work, stopping at the cafés for their morning espresso and pan dulce.

We walked along La Gran Via and stopped at a large outside café for lunch. The older couple sitting next to us took an interest, knowing we were tourists. The woman spoke to me in Spanish, as she'd heard me speaking to the waiter earlier. It was a genial conversation at first, but turned negative when I brought up the changes that had taken place after Franco left: the king back on the throne, gay liberation in the face of the Catholic Church, and abortion rights.

The couple soon said they wished Franco was back in power. When I asked why, I learned they were *franquistas*, people who backed Franco's policies. I realized in that moment there were many

Spaniards unhappy about the changes in Spain. Though not widespread, there remained support for Franco, especially in Madrid.

We decided we'd check out the gay scene, and found a bar with a rooftop deck. The neighborhood looked a lot like the Castro. Its little shops sold clothing, a variety of memorabilia, and the usual rainbow flags. We walked upstairs and were seated at a large table with wicker chairs. The room was filled with deaf gay people, both male and female. It was unusual to see how much the women were integrated into the gay community, compared to the States. We sat next to them, and I acknowledged them with a nod. They looked at us with intense smiles, which I believe was solely because of our size. We were both bodybuilders.

I got up and went to the bathroom. On my way back to my seat, they smiled at me again, and I smiled back. Adrian and I started discussing where we'd go that night when suddenly we began to hear the wicker chairs rapidly creaking. I turned around and spoke to the group in Spanish and learned they could read lips. One of them replied in Spanish, in a strained voice, telling me they were delighted to meet us. I told Adrian, and he smiled at them. We continued to discuss our plans for the evening, then started to hear the creaking wicker again, slowly at first, until it reached a fevered pitch.

Ee-ee-ee-ee.

We looked toward the group and realized the noise was a result of their hand signing and the movement of their bodies in the wicker chairs. The increase in the wicker creaking was due to us—they were talking about us!

We laughed, as it was something we'd never experienced before. They looked at us, grinning shyly as they realized we were on to them. Then they began to laugh too. We went around the table and introduced ourselves. Smiles and grins of joy permeated the table.

When we returned to our hotel for siesta each day around three in the afternoon, we'd find a quartet playing several floors beneath our balcony. They were a fine group that played classical and Spanish music, which wafted up to our room while we made love. It was magical.

Ibiza was one of the most fascinating places I've ever been. Part of the Baleares chain, Ibiza is an island off the coast of southern Spain inside the Mediterranean. The necropolis, which was built on the top of the island, has been the center of its history since the Phoenicians. The walls were built out on the rock outcropping, and the fortress had a 360-degree view of the sea and the island. It was invincible, with a drawbridge and moat to defend it. Everyone who goes to Ibiza wants to find lodgings inside its eleventh-century walls. Aside from lodgings, inside the fortress were several plazas and some fine restaurants.

We had no idea where the gay area of town was located, but Ibiza was one of the hubs of gay life. It was around sunset when everyone went out for drinks and tapas. We saw a man dressed in a black lace shirt walking toward the drawbridge that exits the old city. We followed him, hoping that in this stereotype, we might find what we were looking for. He led us to an area just outside the walls. The streets were lined with gay boys cruising. It was a panorama of gay life. As we walked down the street, our size alone brought *saludos* from the Spaniards.

"How are you tonight, my friends? Can I buy you a drink?"

I finally stopped the man in the lace shirt and thanked him for bringing us to the right spot. He introduced himself as Jose. It turned out Jose worked in one of the bars, and he introduced us to half of Ibiza. After the first night, we were referred to as *Los Americanos*. We danced for four nights straight and recovered on the beaches during the day. We were having the time of our lives, coming back at night to our room that overlooked the necropolis, the city, and the ocean. It was romantic, and our love affair was blossoming.

We spent our anniversary in Cordoba, where our balcony looked out on the grand mosque. I was finally able to open the bottle of French champagne I'd been dragging around since landing in Madrid.

I poured, and we toasted our second anniversary. "To love and to Cordoba."

The rich history of Cordoba, a city that in the twelfth century may have had as many as a million residents, was everywhere. We learned so much as we traipsed through Seville and the Alhambra in Granada, in complete awe of Moorish beauty and architecture. When we reached Seville in Andalucía, we'd already seen Toledo and Barcelona and Sitges. The five-week stay had given us a real understanding of Spain's diversity and its undeniable beauty. We were more in love than ever.

I'd always wanted to go to Morocco, and when I realized how close we were, we took the ferry to Tangier. Names like Marrakesh and Casablanca conjured exotic images of camels, palm trees, and men in turbans. On the ferry, I read my guidebook's account of what not to say upon entering the old casbah when approached by young men eager to be our guide. We passed the Rock of Gibraltar to pick up passengers and in a few hours disembarked in Tangier.

The next day our taxi dropped us at the arched entrance to the casbah. The streets were too small for cars, as it was built in the first century.

As soon as we got out, I was approached by a man in his thirties who said, "Would you like a guide, sir? I can show you the casbah." He was drunk and stumbling toward us.

On the ferry, I'd learned to say "No thank you" in Arabic. "No *shukria*," I said.

The would-be guide replied, "What the hell does that mean?"

"No thanks," I said.

"Listen, man, I take you everywhere."

I had to push him away as he fell into me.

"What the hell you mean, 'No shukria,'?" he said again.

"Get the hell away from me," I said in a loud voice.

At that point, he pulled out a knife and thrust it in my face. Adrian grabbed my shoulders and drew me backward.

"I said I'm not interested, okay?"

Suddenly, a young man came between us and slowly moved us away from the man with the knife. We hired the one who intervened, realizing how dangerous Tangier was.

Fez was a jewel. Our train arrived near the city, and we could see it from a distance. Ancient and mysterious, it lay upon a hilltop surrounded by walls. As we entered the city, we passed the *mellah*. Like Fez, the mellah was built in the first century but outside the city gates. It was historically intact, showing how the Jews in ancient times were separated and forced to live outside the city walls. The place had a profound impact on the two of us, especially Adrian, who'd never been to an Arab country where the history and architecture was so intact.

As we walked along the city streets, I saw official guides who wore long robes and medallions around their necks, which signified they were sanctioned to give tours. I told Adrian to get us a guide, but not one with the robes. I didn't want to be so noticeable. They screamed "tourist" to everyone, shopkeepers and hawkers alike, and I wanted to blend in.

I met back up with Adrian, and he introduced me to the guide he'd found. I looked at his robes and the medallion around his neck that seemed the size of a grapefruit. I was disappointed, and Adrian could tell. Our guide took us to the casbah and then to a tannery that dated to the first century. I told Adrian again how I wished he hadn't hired the guide, and the man must have overheard us. Shortly after the visit to the tannery, he took us to a café to have mint tea and a pastry, then left us there, saying he'd be right back.

As we finished our tea, he reappeared, this time wearing blue jeans, a shirt, and a tweed coat. The medallion was gone. He also produced a chunk of hashish the size of a silver dollar, much to our delight and my embarrassment. We broke out laughing. I apologized profusely for what I'd said about him wearing the *jellaba* and the medallion.

He refused my apology and told me he hated wearing the medallion, but he had no choice. It was a government edict. We continued the tour, which was fascinating. His name was Ibrahim, and he really was an expert on the history of the region.

Ibrahim invited us to his mother's house for tea and lunch, which we accepted. The house was on one of the many streets where the buildings arched above both sides of the street, with windows that looked out onto them. More than a thousand years old, the home was constructed of wood and brick, then the walls were plastered. In the main room was a dome that let in light, and a staircase in the middle spiraled up to the second floor. A walkway crossed the street below us to the other side. In the middle of the walkway was an arched window from which one could see the street in both directions. There were hand-carved wooden shutters with a beautiful geometric design. The walkway continued well above the street, which was where most of the bedrooms were. Below them on the other side of the street were shops.

Ibrahim then invited us up to his room, where he produced a hookah pipe and the hash he'd shown us earlier. He mixed it with some tobacco, lit it, and we each took a hit. It was wonderful to feel so euphoric in such a mysterious country and in a marvelous city so far from home, so exotic. Just then there was a knock on the door, and his mother entered with a tray of mint tea and baklava, followed by a plate of fresh vegetables, olives, hummus, and pita bread.

As we talked, I told Ibrahim I hadn't worked out at the gym since Madrid and how much I missed it.

"There is a gym across the street," he said. "Would you like to go?"

"Yes, I would," I replied without hesitation.

"Then I will take you."

I thanked his mother, in the little Arabic I knew, for her hospitality and generosity. Then we walked across the narrow street to the gym. Ibrahim opened a door that must have seen twenty generations pass through it, and inside this one-room gym must have been at least that many men working out. The manager sat at a desk in one corner, and the opposite corner had a shower and a torn plastic curtain. The walls were papered with posters of Sylvester Stallone, Bruce Lee, and Arnold Schwarzenegger.

Ibrahim introduced us to the manager, and he was delighted that I wanted to work out with them. At the time, I was six feet, two inches tall and weighed 230 pounds. I greeted them all in Arabic: "*Salam Alaikum.*"

They all smiled, and I heard several whisper, "Rambo." I asked in English if I could work out with them, and they gave me the bench to do some flat bench presses. I lay down on it in my black T shirt and white walking shorts.

As I began to lift the bar and press it to my chest, I looked up to see a perfect circle of eyes all looking down on me, almost like a kaleidoscope. I felt like such a curiosity. As time passed, they went back to working out.

The Moroccan men were built like tanks, even the smallest of them. They were so serious about the sport, they were quite inspirational. I asked Adrian if he'd join me, but he was having too much fun enjoying them watching me. It was so hot in the room, I asked if I could shower when I finished, and the manager showed me to the opposite corner. I took off my shirt and tried to turn on the shower. Three of the guys helped me out with that, one pulling the curtain back, and the others adjusting the water and the showerhead. I was so impressed. Slightly uncomfortable about taking off my shorts, I did anyway and jumped in. When I looked out from behind the torn curtain, there were twenty faces staring at me sideways.

Days afterward, we were greeted all over the casbah whenever we reached an intersection. "Hey, Rambo, Rambo," they shouted. "Hello, California!"

We began to feel like we were a part of the community instead of just tourists, especially Adrian. It was so nice to see him excited, and it was gratifying. It was everything I'd hoped he'd take away from the experience.

One night my curiosity got the best of me, and I asked Adrian if he wanted to go to the *hamam*. The baths were as old as the mellah, as most of the houses didn't have showers. The proprietor took us in, and we were assigned attendants who took us to a room to disrobe. We were given towels to put on, and taken to a steam room, where we sat on cement floors while our masseuses gave us sponge baths. Then my attendant took me to another room, where he began to stretch my limbs and give me a massage. It felt good to relax after a long day. My attendant continued to stretch my aching body in ways I wasn't used to, but it felt good.

Then I heard distressing screams coming from Adrian's room. "Ow, ow!" he screamed over and over again. He was so loud, they could hear him all over the mellah. The Jews probably thought it was the beginning of another Inquisition.

"What's going on?" I shouted.

"He's killing me. He's stretching my muscles beyond what they're used to."

This continued for some time, and laughter erupted through the baths and from the other men in Adrian's room.

Then Adrian's attendant brought him into my room, laid him on his stomach, and, straddling him, began to massage him, his oiled hands sliding the length of his tortured back. There were moans of euphoric pleasure, and there was finally peace in the kingdom of Fez.

Our love had blossomed in Spain, and we were making our own story together.

Upon returning to San Francisco, we sold Adrian's condo and my house in the Russian River area in May 1990 and bought a beautiful Victorian on Grove Street that needed a lot of work. We refurbished the house, installing a winding staircase to the attic, where we built a master bedroom and bath with window seats and dormers that looked out over downtown. French doors led out to an enormous deck that overlooked Buena Vista Park and the city. We replaced the front stairs with an elegant staircase and a balcony over the first-floor window, which in those days was called the fainting room, a place where ladies whose corsets were too tight could lie down for a few minutes in between dinner and walking through to meet the men. Adrian and I designed, painted, and restored all the Victorian wood detailing and plaster work that had been taken off in the '60s. Then we gold-gilded all the detailing until it looked like one of the many Victorian Painted Ladies that one sees throughout the city.

During our restoration, we found out from a chimney flue pipe that the house dated to 1885, a nice discovery since all the files had burned in the earthquake and fire of 1906, and most people don't know exactly how old their homes are.

While working on one of our two double gables—which happens to be an unusual design in San Franciscan Victorians, most only have one—we found a penciled note underneath the metal siding that was plastered over the original, incredible, hand-carved wood wainscoting. Left by the installers, it read: *We knew you'd find it.*

We both almost lost our lives on that fourth-floor gable when we lost our balance gold-gilding the ornamentation. Restoring the home to its original state and leaving our mark on San Francisco was an act of blood, sweat, and tears.

~~~

Adrian and I were lucky to have found one another after our lovers died. I made it a point to live life to the fullest after losing Mark and all my friends. I wanted Adrian and I to take a bite out of whatever was left. One thing that a terminal illness teaches you is that tomorrow could be your last day, and to make good use of the precious time you have.

I worked hard as a software engineering recruiter so we could travel. During the winter, when business was slow, we'd take a whole month off. Our first trip was to Asia. I wanted Adrian to see it because I was so connected to it culturally and spiritually. He was no longer working as a landlord-tenant attorney. He was more interested in constitutional law, but his HIV disability and his mental fatigue kept him from working such a vigorous schedule, and that allowed him time for travel as well. We flew to Japan and then to Hong Kong. I took him to the temples in Bangkok and the island of Bali in Indonesia.

I also took Adrian to Paris, and we met my cousin Alfred, whom I'd never met before. While there, we fell in love with the city, and with one another all over again. We were living a fairy-tale life. We were happily married, went to the opera, the symphony, lived in a beautiful Victorian in San Francisco, had good friends, and our health was holding. We traveled to some of the most distant, troubled, and exotic places—Burma, the Palestinian West Bank and Jerusalem, Egypt, Jordan, and Vietnam. I was always afraid I was going to lose him on one of those no-frills trips, like Burma, where we had fifteen-year-olds pointing machine guns in our faces and slept on straw mattresses. But he appeared to thrive on these trips, and they opened him up to a world he never could have imagined.

While in Rangoon, we met another couple in the reservations office at the train station. In their mid-thirties, Sue and Stuart had just recently married and were from Washington, DC. Burma was run by a ruthless military dictatorship, and traveling alone could be dangerous. I overheard them talking about buying tickets to Mandalay, a beautiful city in the north. We introduced ourselves, and I asked if they'd like to travel with us. We agreed to take the train that night for Mandalay.

Sue had been a cheerleader when she was younger. She looked and acted the part—blond ponytail, makeup, and effervescent personality. Stuart was an easygoing and handsome computer geek. They were the perfect companions, and we got on famously. We agreed to meet back at the station at six o'clock.

When we returned, they were already waiting for us. We boarded the RangoonMandalay Express. It was an old British passenger coach from the days when Burma was a British colony. We sat opposite our spouses, Sue next to me. The seats were plush and swiveled. They were just close enough and wide enough that we could stick our legs on one side of our partner and vice versa and go to sleep, as it was a ten-hour journey.

As the train gained speed, we began to hit bumps in the poorly maintained track. The four of us would fly up out of our seats and land back exactly where we'd been. It was hysterical. We bonded on that journey and would remain together through the whole trip.

Mandalay was magnificent, and we got to see the old temples and monasteries that gave the city its name. From the mountaintops, we had panoramic views of the lush vegetation and beautiful white and gold-gilded temples rising out of the jungle. We were having a great time together and decided to go on to Pagan, a valley with five thousand temples in it, some of them as tall as five or six stories. This was the religious and spiritual center of Burma and is a UNESCO World Heritage site.

We boarded a river barge on the Irrawaddy River, a leftover from the period of British rule. At five in the morning, it was still dark, and a low fog hung over the river. The sound of natives carrying all their belongings on their heads was drowned out momentarily by our Rollaboards hitting the pegged plank of the gangway: *buh-bump, buh-bump, buh-bump*. Our first-class accommodations for the twelve-hour journey consisted of some sling-back beach chairs on a deck. A thin cord separated first class from second. Once we got settled, Stuart and I got off in search of food for the long trip. I found hard-boiled eggs and bread for our breakfast, and Stuart came up with some bananas, oranges, cheese, and biscuits.

As the barge sounded its last call before departure, the second- and third-class passengers rolled out their blankets and mats on the other side of the cord, while we settled into our beach chairs. We pulled away through the mist, and the fog began to lift, exposing the temples of Mandalay, ancient and beautiful. We were in another world completely.

Fog lifted from the Irrawaddy displaying majestic Burmese temples

I looked at Adrian as we admired the view. "Not exactly what you were expecting for first class, eh?"

"Not at all."

We laughed.

"You all right?" I asked.

"Yeah, this is kind of exciting."

"Look at the temples," I said. "Have you ever seen anything like them?"

"No, never."

We'd been advised before our visit to bring items for trade and barter, as the economy was so bad. People were desperate for American and European products, from the most mundane to luxury items, which they were unable to obtain. We filled our knapsacks with Marlboro cigarettes, toothpaste, perfumes, soap, and cosmetics.

One hour into the journey and I was already bargaining with the natives for beautiful handmade blankets of cotton and natural dyes. "*Ne kaundala*," I said in perfect Burmese to the woman selling the blankets. I'd studied Burmese before we left, and it was amazingly helpful.

"*Ne kaunde*," she replied with a wonderful smile, as though she hadn't expected to hear Burmese coming from the lips of someone like me.

"How much for the blankets?" I asked, pulling from my sack a pack of Marlboros. We had no idea it would be so cold on the river, and we weren't prepared.

"Yes, yes," the woman said to me as I held up the pack.

"We trade one for one?" I motioned.

"Yes, yes." The woman smiled.

My first transaction was four blankets for four packs of cigarettes. As I passed a blanket to Sue, I could hear her teeth chattering.

"Wow, that was unreal," she said.

The four of us settled in for the passage and dozed until dawn, wrapped in our new blankets.

Later, Adrian and I met a monk on deck who spoke perfect English. I wanted to ask him all about Burma.

"Be very careful," the monk said. "People will want to talk to you, but you will endanger them. It is against the law for us to speak with you. The junta doesn't want you to know what's really going on."

I told him I was a practicing Buddhist, and we went to the observation deck to meditate. It was a humbling experience. If we couldn't talk, then we could at least sit together in solidarity.

Sometime that evening, we arrived in Pagan. It was pitch-black. Horse-drawn carts came to pick us up to take us to the government hotel—which, by the way, was the only way you could stay in Burma, by paying the government. They wanted the tourist dollar funneled directly into the hands of the regime that repressed the very people it claimed to represent. There was no freedom in Burma. Aung San Suu Kyi, the pro-democracy leader, was still under house arrest while we were there, locked up for twenty-one years.

In the morning, we woke to massive temples all around us, some two thousand years old. We visited many of them. One day as the sun set, all four of us climbed one all the way to the spire. We sat looking out over the vast valley, all the temples protruding like mountains. We sat in silence, we were so in the moment, taking in the view in the warmth of the setting sun.

I turned to Adrian. "Glad you came to Burma?" I asked.

He just smiled.

The four of us had become inseparable, and when it was time to leave Pagan, we had to figure out a way to get back to Rangoon, and eventually Bangkok. The infrastructure was so bad that there were no buses, just the boat, which took so long. We decided to rent a car and driver, which was difficult because gasoline was rationed there. We had to find someone willing to take the chance to drive us all the way to Rangoon, seventeen hours by car.

Michael Rossum

Travelling companions Sue and Stewart on
top of temple in Pagan valley at sunset

We finally found a driver. It's all about survival in Burma and weighing the risks. He was a nice man, but he ate betel nut leaf the whole way, which turned his teeth blood red. When he smiled, it was scary. Then he'd spit it out and start chewing some more.

The car was a Toyota Corolla station wagon. Sue, Stuart, and Adrian sat scrunched in the back seat, and I sat shotgun with the console between me and the driver, who sat on the right side, British style. My seat had to be pushed all the way forward, so for my six-foot-two-inch frame to be comfortable, I had to stick my left leg out the window. I almost lost it to several cars and lorries in the opposite lane, which was barely wide enough for a vehicle.

We took bathroom breaks on the side of the road, and all of us tried to pull ourselves out of the pretzel positions we'd been locked in for hours. It was brutal, with the driver spitting his betel nut out, coasting down hills to avoid using his brakes, and driving without his lights at night to conserve his battery. When night fell and he was running low on gas, he turned his lights on and off whenever we came into a village, signaling to anyone that he was looking for black market petrol. Whoever had gasoline to sell would signal in the dark with a lantern, swinging it back and forth. This was life in totalitarian Burma.

When we finally reached Rangoon, it was after midnight. The streets were deserted because of the curfew, and the only lights were streetlights. Teenage soldiers toted AKA machine guns. We were lost. The driver didn't know Rangoon, or where the hotel was. He was driving so slowly that we must have looked suspicious. One of the soldiers, no more than a boy of fifteen, stopped us. I asked him in English where the Strand Hotel was. He aimed his flashlight at our faces, moving from one to the other. His other hand held the gun, still pointed at us, his finger still on the trigger. For a few moments, we weren't sure what he was going to do. Then he spoke to the driver and gave him some directions that got us to the hotel.

After a few experiences like that, the four of us were ready to leave Burma early. At that point, we just wanted out. The following day we went to a Thai Airways office to try to get an earlier flight. When we arrived, it was closed, and an iron grate covered the door. We were the first ones there, and I clung to the grating until they opened.

Some other Westerners arrived after us and asked, "Are you trying to get out too?"

I thought the phrasing was golden. That was exactly what we were doing.

All four of us got tickets out that night. While we waited in the terminal for the plane, they called us to board. Just as Adrian and I passed through the gateway, officials stopped Sue and Stuart and held them back. I think we were all frightened right down to the eleventh hour, and then that happened. What was going on? Was this the last flight out? The airline officials didn't know what was happening either, but they prodded us forward.

I looked back at Stuart and Sue and called, "Do you want us to stay?"

They yelled back, "Go on ahead. We'll meet you in Bangkok at the Ambassador Hotel."

I could tell they were anxious, and who could blame them? This was the first time we'd been apart from one another since we'd met, and it felt ominous.

The next day we waited for them, and in the afternoon, they checked in to the hotel. We'd become good friends through our travels, and as it turned out, we've continued the friendship all these years.

Cambodia

Adrian and I left the two of them in Thailand, for our journey was not over. The next day we flew out to Phnom Penh, capital of Cambodia. We wanted to see the magnificence of Angkor Wat and Angkor Tom, two ancient Hindu cities built in the twelfth century, a UNESCO site.

Upon our arrival in the capital, it was impossible to escape the catastrophic holocaust that had taken place there. We went to the museum, and one of the photographs out of many that left me with a gut-wrenching feeling was the one of Phnom Penh, the city completely emptied of the two million in habitants. Newspapers tumbled through the dusty streets, with hundreds of bicycles left behind, and no sign of life. The museum is in a converted elementary school, because that was where the terror death squads interrogated the population of the city. The walls were covered with the faces of the dead, as they kept records on everyone they killed. The faces of these men, women, and children were horrifying mug shots before they were tortured, starved, limbs amputated, and beaten to death with bamboo canes as they were less expensive than bullets. We were shown the jail cells and the torture chambers. Adrian and I walked out onto the front lawn where people gathered. We just hugged each other. I don't think there was a dry eye anywhere.

We went to the "Killing Fields," a memorial to the two million victims who died there. We drove over a dusty, potholed road that led to the memorial. It took your breath away. We covered our mouths in disbelief; a building three stories high made of glass was filled with thousands of skulls plucked from their grave sites just feet away. *Shocking*, I think, would put it mildly. I'm still haunted by the imagery, having taken a picture of it. What disturbed me the most was that no one had come to their aid until it was too late. This was personal, as one human to another, and we cried. We thought that Auschwitz was the end of man's inhumanity to man, and now Cambodia.

As we flew to Angkor Wat, I kept looking down at the fields, some of which had rice growing and other kinds of agriculture, but then there would be huge swaths of red dirt that covered tens of thousands of acres, and they were devoid of everything. This was the landscape left by Pol Pot, who had cut down the huge teak forests of Cambodia in exchange for money from the Chinese to prop up

Thousands of skulls piled three stories high in memorial to 2 million murdered in the Killing Fields, Cambodia

their totalitarian state. Seventy-five percent of Cambodia's rain forests were destroyed—astronomical when you think of the size of the country, how much the planet needed those forests, the loss to the Cambodian people economically, the destruction of rare animal habitats, and the list goes on. Viewing it from the air had a huge impact seeing it firsthand.

As we neared Angkor Wat, the swaths of red dirt finally gave way to the jungle and the teak rain forest. It was beautiful and lush and very humid.

Our driver met us there and took us to Angkor Tom first. It was older than Angkor Wat and had been damaged by the huge roots and trees that grew back after it was abandoned. The Architecture was spectacular, like out of a science fiction movie, the magnificent carvings of the god Shiva and goddess Kali, and others carved and chiseled into its face. The roots had invaded its beautiful halls and broke its pillars. At one time there were over a million people living there—hard to imagine.

A path through the jungle led to Angkor Wat. The shade of the jungle was like an umbrella, giving us relief from the relentless, searing heat. I met a monk in passing. He smiled at me, and we stopped to talk. A kinder people you could not want for. He told me that Pol Pot deliberately had taken the beautiful statues of Buddha from many of the temples and threw them into the Mekong River in an attempt to crush the spirit of the Cambodian people. I stood there talking to him in disbelief. We really knew nothing of what had happened here, except for the stories we read in the newspapers and reports on TV.

We left the monk and continued our walk along the path, when suddenly we heard music wafting through the jungle. I thought I was back in the twelfth century. This gave life to Angkor Tom; one could imagine what life must have been like in this magical place. As we got closer to the source of the music, we came across a quintet of musicians, men who had been tortured and mutilated by the Pol Pot regime, playing traditional classical Cambodian music. They were smiling at us, and we were struck by their amazing resilience in the

Michael Rossum

Tortured and mutilated Cambodians strive to live after Pol Pot Regime's terror

Adrian and Michael in Angkor Tom, Cambodia, 1994

face of such atrocities. We parted with some of our money, leaving it on their prayer bowls. It was so hard to look at their mutilated bodies, and yet their smiles showed us so much love.

After seeing the beauty of Angkor Wat, completely intact as it was back in the twelfth century and cleared of the jungle around it, with its long, majestic entrance way with two reflecting pools on either side, one had to just stop to take it all in. It was a large complex with living space for many people inside its walls. The architecture was Hindu, and there were gods everywhere along the long hallways, carved into the walls. They decorated every edifice. On our way out, I could not stop taking pictures; it was a photographer's dream. We met our driver, who was waiting patiently for us, and drove back to the airport.

I wondered if Adrian would be okay. This trip was filled with such sadness and such joy, the duality of life presents itself. The Journey had been very hard, but it was all worth it, for now we had a better understanding of what took place here. It left us with an education you cannot get from a book.

We headed back to the capital, then Bangkok and home.

Although I knew this trip had been hard on Adrian, it was our trip to Russia in December 1997—the middle of the winter—that would test Adrian's judgment at having fallen in love with a wandering Jew like me, a gypsy.

St. Petersburg— December 29, 1997

A blanket of snow covered the city. On the outskirts, there were forests, black against the white background, tree limbs laden with snow. We'd never been that far north. Everything seemed frozen as the taxi wound through the roundabout. Suddenly, army trucks came into view, then factories with spewing black smokestacks. Long lines of workers bundled in fur coats and hats crisscrossed the frozen, well-packed paths that wound from the street to the buildings.

It was just like I'd always pictured Russia.

Crossing the frozen Neva River, St. Petersburg, Russia

Our car turned after what seemed like miles of workers and factories in the cold. We could understand why the revolution was fought. And then we could see the Neva River, the heart of the city. Huge frozen ice sheets stood at angles, as though a glass had been shattered. The pieces sticking up from the river were screaming frozen, cold and white.

We traveled along the banks of the river for a long time. There were fewer and fewer factories. Huge square blocks of housing had replaced them, dark and gloomy against the white snow. Suddenly in the distance, the spires of the Nevsky Monastery, Smolny Cathedral, and the Admiralty rose from the thick mist like a fairy tale. The Hotel Okhtinskaya, where we stayed, was a Russian venture that looked like it was held together by a thread.

To my amazement, Adrian was holding up rather well. It would be one of the most fascinating trips we'd ever take. One day we stood in the freezing cold on Revolution Bridge, bundled in our mouton coats and fur hats. He looked up and smiled. "Only you could bring us to Russia in the middle of winter," he said. Then he hugged me, and all was well in St. Petersburg.

We went out on New Year's Eve to see how the Russians celebrated. St. Petersburg was a fascinating city. Because we were so far north, the sun didn't rise until ten in the morning, and it was dark by four in the afternoon. The city was colorful. The buildings dated to the 1600s and were painted in pastels—yellow, robin's-egg blue, mauve, green, pink, rose, and so on—mostly because everything was so gray because of the weather. The Four Horse Bridge crossed over the many canals that wound through the city. The horses were bronze with an exquisite green patina.

Along the canals were magnificent buildings in which two Hercules statues over a story tall held up a portico of an apartment house. The architecture was amazing, and the onion dome churches so unusual. It was a city like no other, all of it dripping in a thick covering of winter snow. It was a fairy-tale city, called "Venice of the North."

We left our hotel for the center of St. Petersburg around 7:00 p.m. to watch the New Year's celebrations. There were people in the streets already partying by the time we reached the center. Music was playing, and people were dancing. There were groups of people drinking from a flask of vodka three feet high that they passed around in a circle, probably to keep warm as well as to get high. Around 10:00 p.m., the flask could be heard breaking and the Russians becoming loud and boisterous. That was our signal that the party was over.

We woke the next morning to a city that had been abandoned. There were no footprints in the snow anywhere, and no tire tracks. I loved photography and was using a Nikon with black-and-white film. All morning, I explored the city. It was a photographer's dream. Photographing the snow and the architecture was like capturing the soul of St. Petersburg. That was how we spent our New Year's Day, and Adrian was ecstatic.

As we wandered the empty streets, we passed the statue of the Four Sisters and Czar Nicolas the First in Saint Isaac Square across from the Astoria Hotel. It was magnificent, commanding the roundabout. Snow dripped off the ball gowns of all the sisters as they waltzed around their father. It was something straight out of *War and Peace.*

The Astoria Hotel is the premier hotel in the city and has a long history, especially during the siege of St. Petersburg by the Nazis. Hitler had his eye on celebrating his capture of the city at the Astoria, and had already printed out invitations to a victory ball. He was terribly disappointed as the brave people of what was then called Leningrad held out for two years, eating rats to survive rather than surrender to the Nazis.

"Let's go in and have some lunch," I said to Adrian.

We were starving, and wanted to warm up with a hot cup of tea. We were met at the front door by a gorgeous blond, blue-eyed doorman dressed in Victorian clothing and a top hat. We traipsed into the checkered black-and-white tiled lobby straight to the bathroom

Michael Rossum

New Year's Eve shoppers line up at Kiosks, St. Petersburg

Park between Admiralty and Neva River, St. Petersburg, New Year's Day

Adrian and Michael frozen on the Palace Bridge with the Winter Palace and the Neva River in the background

Street Vendors, Man selling hot roasted garlic

after the long morning's trek through the city. Our boots were full of snow, and we shook our pant legs. Then we opened the bathroom door to exit and find the restaurant. To our horror, we saw the mud of two pairs of shoes crisscrossing the otherwise pristine lobby all the way to the bathroom to where we stood. We gasped, laughed, and ran like hell. All we could think about was getting out of the hotel before we were found out.

We went on to take the midnight train to Moscow. The train was filled to capacity. We shared our compartment with an old babushka and her grandson. They took the bunks on the bottom, and we took the two above. We changed into our pajamas and climbed underneath the sheets. Lace curtains covered the windows. I pulled them apart as the train passed through the frozen landscape of Mother Russia. Lying there in my bunk, as town after town passed by, all I could think of was *Dr. Zhivago*. I looked over at Adrian, and he smiled, as he, too, was watching the snowy little villages.

In Moscow, we saw the opera *Aida* at the Bolshoi. What luck to be able to get box seats at one of the world's premier opera houses. It had been recently restored to the elegance it knew during the period of the czars. The Soviet hammer and sickle were replaced on the box seat of the czar and czarina with the two-headed eagle of the czars. The only evidence of the former Soviet Union was in the gold curtains, where one could still see the hammer-and-sickle pattern embroidered into the fabric.

We stayed at the Radisson on the Moscow River with a view of Moscow University and the Kremlin, which is a monument to Stalin. While at the Radisson, we discovered it was the headquarters for a segment of the Russian mafia. The room next to ours, occupied by the hotel manager, was being used for making pornographic movies, and the lights were still set up over the bed as we passed down the hall on our way to breakfast. The lobby was where the mafia met.

While having lunch, we were almost taken out by some hit men who mistook us for a rival mafia group. A mafia boss with long, stringy hair who wore a black overcoat, entered the lobby, followed by a dozen or more bodyguards who looked like the Dallas Cowboys on steroids. They all wore black leather coats, black turtlenecks, and black Armani "duck" shoes. The Associated Press, which had offices in the lobby, had reported on another mafia boss who had been murdered there just the week before our arrival.

They swarmed around the mafia boss like a school of fish to protect him should it happen again. Everywhere he moved, they moved. He stopped in front of where Adrian and I were eating lunch and stared at us. The goons he was with did the same thing.

The two of us looked at one another as if to say, "Is this for real?" It was like something out of a bad movie.

Then the chef in the open-air restaurant where we were eating rushed out. His neck was the size of a football player's and he wore an earpiece. He signaled to the boss that we were just tourists. Unbelievable. Our lives intact, and Adrian still not planning to divorce me, we left Russia soon after on a Finnair flight to Helsinki and the West.

In the years that followed, we led charmed lives. Adrian worked with me as a recruiter, so it was easy to take time off together. He said that had it not been for me, he never would have seen as much of the world as he did, especially places like Burma, Vietnam, Thailand, and Bali. As many doubts and reservations as he had, each time I'd say, "What do you think about going to Thailand and Bali for Christmas?" he always responded with: "That sounds good."

Well, he was turning fifty, and I said, "How about Bali for your fiftieth? I had spoken to the girls in Montreal, Gina and Sylvie, and they said they'd love to come. He said, "Yes," and I began to make plans.

His birthday was on the 22nd of January, so I decided to arrive in Bali for Christmas in December. Then it happened. Terrorists in Java, the large Muslim island west of Bali, had infiltrated the island and had set off a bomb in one of the many discotheques frequented by Australians. Just as we were sitting down to dinner, the breaking news came on that extremists had blown up a major discotheque in Kuta, Bali, with live, horrifying video of people on fire running from the disco. It was October 12, 2002, a little over a year after the Twin Towers fell in New York. The headlines read *250 dead*—mostly Australian tourists in their twenty's and thirty's. The pictures of them running on fire were imbedded in my mind.

Then the phone rang, and it was Sylvie. "Michael, you heard about the bombing?"

"Yes, unbelievable," I said.

"It could have been us, you know," she said.

I replied, "Yes, I know."

"Gina is frightened, and so am I. We've decided to cancel the trip."

I said, "I totally understand your fears. Those poor kids. I will let Adrian know."

"I'm so sorry, Michael," she said.

"Sylvie, I understand. Are your tickets refundable?"

"Yes."

"Well, that's good."

We said goodbye and I hung up the phone. I was completely numb. No words . . .nothing.

Adrian and I discussed the trip and its dangers, and our non-refundable tickets. What were the chances they would do this again with all the security around the island? We were sorry the girls would not be joining us. Bali was so beautiful, and there was still so much we hadn't seen. We felt that if we cancelled the trip we'd be giving in to the terrorists' aim, which was to bankrupt the island by depriving it of its enormous tourist trade. So, we decided to go.

When we arrived in Denpasar, the capital, we caught a taxi to Legian, where we had rented a room that was all-inclusive: meals, the bar, and beach chairs and pool. Our room and verandah looked right on to the ocean and through groves of palm trees.

The first thing we noticed that was odd was the lack of people. We met a couple from Australia and went to dinner with them. The restaurant in the middle of town was empty. The maître d' sat us at a table with a view of the ocean. It was eerie. Upon finishing our meal, we went outside to call for a taxi, and there must have been twenty five empty taxi's at the stand. It was then that we realized how deadly the bomb really was. The taxi driver greeted us with a smile and thanked us for coming to Bali and told us that we were courageous. But I knew that the Balinese were the courageous ones. The terrorists had destroyed their entire economy, judging by the taxi stand.

The next day, I employed a driver who took us in the subsequent days all over Bali. I took amazing photographs that chronicled the grieving of the Balinese over the destruction of their economy and their efforts, spiritually, to repair the damage.

The driver took me to what the Balinese call the Mother Temple. It is where their creation story began. The temple is built at the base of the volcano, one of three on the island. It is active, so you take your chances. People from all over the island had come by the truckload. This had been happening ever since the bombing. They were coming village after village in rented lorries, leaving offerings to Shiva and Ganesh and many more deities. It was a steady stream of people going up the steps and down with their offerings gracefully balanced on their heads as they ascended and descended. There were no other Western tourists outside of me there that day. For a photographer, it was as authentic as it gets, and they acknowledged me. I clasped my hands together and bowed. I was so honored.

Here are a few e-mails I sent back home to describe our experience.

E-mails from Bali

Selemat Sore, Good Evening.

All is good with us. Bali is a fascinating place. It is exotic, and it carries a mysticism that one could truly describe as, "The Island of the Gods." It has been a voyage of mixed emotions. The bombing of October 12th has laid an indelible mark on the peace and tranquility that is so pervasive here.

Yesterday while we were on the beach, a village from Kerobakn came to the sea some 30 kilometers from their home to make a ceremony on the beach to drive away the evil forces that have invaded their island. A group of about 100 people meandered down the white

Michael Rossum

Hindu priest driving out evil spirits on beach in
Bali after September nightclub terrorist bombing

sand. Leading them was a Hindu priest preceded by a huge gong and a band of gamelan players. Following them were the women of the village with offerings of flowers and fruit and incense piled high on their heads moving through the sand like waves of cobras balancing their gifts with beauty and elegance and a sense of purpose. I was dressed in only my sarong and a baseball hat, but they allowed my entrance into their space. I clasped my hands together in prayer towards them, which is how all Balinese address one another, and they did the same in response. Then I started to photograph them. They smiled at me as if I was no intrusion, and they went on with what they had come there for: to drive out the pal of evil that was hanging over Bali and restore the harmony between "Heaven and Earth." Meanwhile, all the time the elusive Adrian remained behind me in support and respect to avoid invading their space.

We rented motorcycles a few nights ago. We entered the Kuta area looking for some sandals for Adrian, and just before we found them, as Adrian was looking for shops, we drove past the bombsight which I was trying to avoid. It was more painful than I ever could have imagined. I was so choked-up I couldn't control my bike. We stopped and just held each other and cried. I think like you, we too felt we had put it behind us, but then the reality of the pain and suffering that emanated from the site was huge. The restaurants are practically empty. The Australians are gone, as are the Americans, and there is desperation in the air. The Balinese people have been hit hard.

Fortunately, once out of the Kuta area, Balinese life goes on as it must. Elaborate weddings and funerals and ceremonies are a daily experience here and a reminder that we are only here for a short time. So make the best of it . . .

Love, Michael and Adrian

~~~

Slemat Jalan, Good Afternoon.

Michael Rossum

Thanks for the e-mails. From what you've written, we aren't missing much, I guess. We are so very far from home, but sometimes when we are feeling a little groundless and long for some news we are reminded by CNN that not all is well back home. We are surrounded by Europe here at our hotel Resor Seminyak. We are, I think, the only Americans in Bali at the moment. There are French, Italians, Germans, a smattering of Czechs, Austrians, and a very nice couple from Australia. We have befriended all of them, but as usual they don't talk to each other much. There are no Americans here and no Australians. For obvious reasons, only the fearless are here.

Our hotel is beautiful, flanked between two ancient Hindu temples, and our room is fifty meters from the beach. The sunsets are magnificent. We have hired a local driver for the long trips up into the volcanoes. Bali has five of them. Yesterday we went to Lake Batur. Our journey took us past terraced rice paddies, along river valleys filled with rain forests, rice farmers planting rice, women in the village markets, children at play, temples filled with people making offerings to the gods, a cock fight, and preparations for funeral rites.

There is no end to the simple beauty that is Bali, and if that were not enough, we arrived in the village of Kintamani on the crater rim of the second largest volcano to find that the cinder cone is a lake, and rising from the middle of it is another new cinder cone, one thousand feet high! "Spectacular" would be putting it mildly.

We are spending some quality time together, and we both realize how precious it is. Apart from the heat, with which we are both prone to suffer, we are well.

Love, Michael

~~~

Selemat Pagi, Good Morning.

Offerings at the Mother Temple after the Bali Bombings.

Michael Rossum

I awoke today and looked out our window to find war ships in Kuta Harbor. Indonesian destroyers lay off the beach. It looked like we were being attacked by the Japanese. Everyone was lining the beach to get a glimpse. People were wondering if there had been another terrorist plot as had been promised by Indonesian terrorists last week, or if these were maneuvers related to Iraq. No one here seems to know.

Last night we heard about the *Columbia*. What a sad day for the space program. No one here seems to be touched by those events, and we feel sadly, alone in our isolation regarding this.

So, it looks like Bush will have his way in Iraq. Has everyone gone mad? What's the take from the home front?

Tuesday we have been invited to a wedding ceremony in a small village north of here. We befriended the manager of our hotel, Resor Seminyak, and one of his relatives, a cousin, is getting married. He has been married for 15 years, but they could not afford the cost of a wedding ceremony so they are having it now.

The people are so kind and open here and the villages so quiet and peaceful, you'd never know that a war was brewing.

Love, Michael and Adrian

~~~

As always, I tried to learn some of the language before we went on a trip. In this case we were leaving Bali for Java, where they spoke a combination of Indonesian and Arabic. Adrian had help me, thereby learning some of it himself. I wanted to get as close to the people as I could so that we'd have authentic experiences. There were many times I'd greet someone in their language and they'd invite us into their homes, or in some cases into, say, a Buddhist monastery, or show us a part of their culture that we never would have seen had it not been for that initial opening. Had I not taken the initiative, we would have missed out on a lot. I was so touched by some of the people I met, and vice versa. The memories are as vivid as if they'd happened yesterday.

Touchstones *A Survivor's Story*

My mother passed away in 1994 in our home on Grove Street near the Panhandle of Golden Gate Park. Adrian and I were devastated, and I wanted us to go to Jerusalem so I could say Kaddish, a prayer for the dead, and to leave a message for Adele at the Wailing Wall. Adrian was like a son to her, and she was like a mother to him, since his own mother wasn't in the picture.

Some years passed, and then we lost our best friend, Steve Matejka, to the AIDS epidemic. Losing Steve was one of the biggest losses for both of us, and we were inconsolable.

Our health had been holding all these years, so when it suddenly began to deteriorate, neither of us was prepared for the relentless decline from injuries and lengthy illnesses, on top of numerous surgeries and a cancer diagnosis. But neither of us had expected to live this long, so it was all icing on the cake anyway.

While in Bali in 2002, we both came down with a serious bronchial infection akin to SARS. We were hospitalized in the main hospital in Denpasar, the capital, then had to leave the island. We suffered multiple attacks due to the fungal infections we got in Bali, which left us asthmatics. Then Adrian had sinus infections. We got sick a lot, and each time, it took months to heal. It seemed like it was one thing after another. Then I tore a rotator cuff that took two operations to repair.

There was a lull, and we thought things might be leveling off. But in 2006, I had to have back surgery and a hip replacement within one month of each other. I was horribly depressed afterward. It took so long to recover, and my back has never quite been the same.

I was taking painkillers to dull the pain, just to maintain an ordinary life—shopping for food, going to the bank, the gym, or the pharmacy. Meanwhile, Adrian had taken on all our bills and managing our rental properties while he took care of his elderly mother and his handicapped brother. Sadly, he was born with his umbilical cord wrapped around his neck, which had cut off the air supply to his brain. They lived down in LA, which meant travel was involved. On top of that, Adrian had me.

Later in 2006, I tried to relieve the pain in my back with a cortisone shot to my lower lumbar spine, only to have it aggravate the nerve root and wind up giving me permanent neuropathy, pain, and numbness in both legs from the waist down.

Every time I got up and brushed myself off, something else would knock me back down. Then I came down with HIV-related cancer, and I had to undergo chemotherapy in 2008.

It was no wonder that in 2009, I had a mental breakdown. My health problems had become so overwhelming that I couldn't cope. It was one of the darkest periods of my life, next to my brother's suicide. I wanted out.

I'd become riddled with anxiety and had even lost sight of what the anxiety was about. I was either too hot or too cold. I was unable to watch TV because the images moved too fast. I wanted to be inside. I wanted to be outside. I had no appetite. If Adrian had to go to the store, I became fearful of being alone, yet I couldn't leave the house. Being in public made me even more anxious. I was so frightened that I was going to land in an insane asylum, yet I knew I needed help. All I wanted to do was leave. I wanted to commit suicide, but didn't have the balls to do it myself, so I begged Adrian to help me. Of course, he refused.

We tried to get help and delved into the mental health provider list given to us by our health insurance company. It was a phantom list of doctors who didn't exist or who weren't taking new patients. It was sad to see the state of our country's mental health system. People like me, on the verge of doing something terrible, couldn't find a hospital or any psychiatric facility that wasn't full, or a doctor who would help.

The more dead ends I reached, the more desperate we became. Neither of us was working. We were both on disability, which was a blessing in disguise, since neither of us could concentrate enough to hold down a job.

I finally spoke to a psychiatrist on the phone who agreed to meet with me. But as soon as I walked in, I knew he didn't have the resources to help me. He'd been in the profession for twenty years. We talked for an hour, and he didn't have a clue how to help me or direct me to someone who could. When I got back in the car, I said to Adrian, "Take me to the hospital."

We went to the emergency room, which was only a quick fix. They gave me a shot of Valium and sent us home.

Had it not been for Adrian's unconditional love and his ability to give me space and show me nothing but kindness, I don't think I would have survived. I was so frightened. I'd never experienced anything like that before, and I asked Adrian, "Am I going to wind up committing suicide like my brother? Do you think this is hereditary?"

"No, sweetie," he said, comforting me. "You're just going through a really rough time of it. I'm not exactly sure I could handle everything you're going through and keep my own sanity."

I was so unsure of myself, and he was so reassuring.

We finally found help with a psychiatrist from SF General. I saw him once, and my symptoms went away in a week. The guy was brilliant.

After talking to me for an hour, he said, "You're not depressed, are you?"

"No, not really."

"That's what I thought. You don't seem depressed to me. I think you're having anxiety about having another anxiety attack."

He made me write down my thoughts every time I had an anxiety attack. In a way, it was a little like the Buddhist doctrine of confronting your demons directly. Instead of running away from them, run toward them. It worked.

I tell everyone that Adrian is my rock, but he's really a saint. No matter how difficult things were or how unsolvable they may have seemed, he always stayed constant, my touchstone, my beautiful soulmate.

Chapter Twenty-Five

Eli—Path to Freedom

I'd met many people along my journey to freedom. All my touchstones had been pointing me in that direction, but no one showed me I could free myself from myself until I met Eli Jaxon-Bear. My friend Sue Ann gave me a book called *The Enneagram of Liberation: From Fixation to Freedom* back in 2003. It sat on my nightstand for a year before I picked it up. She kept telling me what an awakened spirit Eli was, a wise man. I began reading it. It was about egos and ego fixations that were numbered. I thought, *This is crap. Where's the spiritualism in that?*

I was suffering physically, my body was in a lot of pain, and all I wanted to do was escape. I'd studied Buddhism all through my youth. All the years I'd spent traveling in India and the Himalayas were part of my journey toward freedom. I'd found it in Big Sur on acid when I was young, and during the Summer of Love. I saw it in Nepal with Robin. I found it on a beach in Goa, India, and with an adopted Mexican family and all the friends I'd lost to the AIDS epidemic. Then there were Bill, Mark, Barry, Steve, Michael, and, of course, Adrian, all pointing me toward love and compassion.

I'd found freedom in Zen meditation, but the idea of freedom and living it day to day escaped me. The older I got and the more serious my medical conditions became, the more I felt trapped. Trapped in a body that no longer functioned harmoniously, I felt betrayed, as my world became more limited. However, no matter how long I practiced meditation, the glimpses of freedom and moments of bliss were fleeting. I knew that above all else, what I really wanted was peace and freedom, but how? Hours of meditation, though relaxing, didn't keep me from suffering. It didn't stop the super ego from thrashing me about for not being more compassionate or more loving. I knew there was nothing that could stop the chronic physical pain I was going through except for pain medication, when it worked.

But what about the mental suffering attached to it? It was like a huge weight hanging over me. I could do something about that. Through the chronic pain, there were moments in which I "smelled the coffee," watched a beautiful sunrise, made love, and wasn't caught up in the story of "me." They say that it's usually suffering of one kind or another that brings people to a spiritual awakening, and so it was for me. My pain became my path to freedom.

I picked up Sue Ann's book, and I began to reread it. The Enneagram was originally a Sufi text depicting the nine different ego fixations of the human being. Eli took the Sufi text and translated it with his own understanding of what the Sufi intent was in writing it. The Sufis were a mystical religious sect that aimed to bring us closer to ourselves by developing a tool, if you will, a mirror image used as a type of medicine to heal the suffering of mankind and point us toward our true nature.

As I delved deeper into the book and read about understanding the nature of ego, I began to realize that maybe this was what was holding me back from finding my way home. One of the first questions Eli has us ask is: Who am I and what is my true nature? Suddenly I couldn't put the book down. I read it front page to back several times.

I was confused when I tried to find my own ego fixation out of the nine, that place where you're tied in a knot and have been ever since you can remember. As I flipped back and forth through the book, the binding suddenly broke at No. 3: The Magician. As I read the chief characteristic of the fixation (efficiency), I realized I was looking into a mirror. I could multitask. I could juggle shaving while being on the toilet or talk on the phone while brushing my teeth.

The more I read, the more I realized that knowing how my fixation operated was essential to finding freedom. I read on. I was needy for love but didn't think I could be loved. I was okay with just being validated. I broke down and cried, because just being validated was all I thought I was worth. I'd been running from that feeling all my life. As a No. 3 ego, I was successful, and my avoidance was failure. Failure was not in my vocabulary. If something didn't work out, I just moved on to something that did. But when my body started to fail me, I realized this wasn't going to be something I could be successful at. I could take care of myself as best I could, but I had a shelf life, and there was no getting around that diagnosis.

Most people don't ever think of inquiring into how their ego fixation functions, or for that matter, whether they even have one. The truth is that most of us are asleep. We know something is wrong, but we can't hone in on it. You've been telling yourself the story of you ever since you can remember. Eli asked, "When you drop the story of 'you,' what's there?" Emptiness, space, silence, that's what's there. Consciousness comes before any thought.

We've been conditioned for so long to believe our story is real that it becomes solid in our minds. We fall into the trance of what the Hindus call *maya,* or the veil. It's the veiling by the fixation that hides our true nature, which is conscious love.

What I learned through Eli's book was that the story and all the conversations we're having in our heads aren't trustworthy. Love is the only thing that's trustworthy.

My chronic pain had become overwhelming. Knowing that I'd have to rely on heavy pain medication for the rest of my life, I spiraled into a deep depression, suffering physically and mentally. It was the story of Michael's pain, and it played like a broken record inside my head for most of my waking hours. I could be distracted, but the story kept pulling me into its trance.

It was some months after I finished his book that Sue Ann invited me to hear Eli speak. The event was called a *satsang* at a college in Marin County. Satsang is made up of two Sanskrit words: *sat,* which means "truth," and *sang*, which means "seekers," or "community of truth seekers." We came in late, and the group of about fifty people was meditating already. Just as I began to sit down, Eli looked up and smiled at me. That was my first glimpse of the man who would become my teacher.

Adrian and I delved deeper into the quest for freedom. We went to a retreat to study the Enneagram, hosted by Eli and his wife, Gangaji. We studied in depth about the ego and ego fixations, and saw videos of people who represented the nine ego fixations of the human being.

Both of us had breakthroughs. Adrian realized that he was a No. 9, the Saint, an anger point on the Enneagram. He was angry about being born in a physical body he couldn't escape. This finally made sense to the two of us. Because he felt that expressing anger wasn't loving, he stuffed his anger rather than show it. His fixation was trapped, as Eli put it, "between obedience and defiance, vacillating between compliance, which produces rage, and noncompliance, which produces fear, thereby staying in the middle, showing no anger." He went along with everything I suggested. He avoided conflict, but beneath the cool exterior was rage.

When we were talking and I could feel the anger, I'd ask, "Are you angry with me?"

Raising his voice, he'd exclaim, "No, I'm not angry with you!"

But clearly, he was angry—not with me, but rather with the way things were in the world. For him, nothing flowed the way it was supposed to. So rather than show anger, Adrian would just fall asleep. I don't mean literally. I mean he wouldn't participate fully. This was his way of numbing out.

The two of us got a chance to see one another's fixations, mine coming from the emotional body, and his coming from the physical body. Through our entire relationship, I'd wanted Adrian to be more emotional like me, and to talk about his feelings. Meanwhile, he was angry that I wanted to make him more emotional, and would dig in his heels or just fall asleep. I couldn't even get a good argument out of him. I always felt like the bad guy because when the relationship was stale, I was the one who had to bring it up.

Suddenly, everything made sense. We understood that our habitual ego fixations were coming from different places. Now I could let go of wanting him to change. I knew he wasn't wired that way. I'd ask myself when we'd argue, "Am I coming from Love?" If the answer was no, I'd stop. After so many realizations like this, we started to change the way we saw one another, and Eli made it possible.

When we attended a couples retreat in Ashland, Oregon, we opened up to one another even further. There were one hundred couples taking part in the event. By the end of the week, some broke up after a lifetime together. When they saw the truth—that they were only holding on for security, or that they had nothing but contempt for one another—they broke up. The retreat gave them the opportunity to move on with their lives, and not to stay trapped in a loveless marriage of convenience. This was huge. Others, like Adrian and me, grew even closer.

Eli and Gangaji gave the group twenty-five questions. Each time one partner would ask the question—for example, in our case, "How have I hurt you?" He'd ask the question repeatedly for five minutes. The one asking the question would play the friend who listened without judgment, while the other told him just how he'd hurt him. Every time the question was asked, the other partner would describe another way in which he'd hurt or emotionally damaged him.

I heard the sound of a hundred couples asking the question repeatedly in the background, as I asked Adrian the same question: "How have I hurt you?" I could only listen to him, not console him, but just listen as a friend would listen.

"I'm so sorry, Michael, that all these years I haven't participated fully in our relationship." He began to cry. "I'm sorry I hurt you when you were trying to bring us closer to each other."

When it was my turn, he asked me the same question. I told him, "I'm sorry I wanted you to be something you couldn't be, and for pushing you to be more open, when you weren't wired to be like that. I'm sorry for getting so angry when you weren't there for me."

Then we broke down and collapsed in one another's arms. Asking those questions was a little like having someone pour vinegar over your heart. We were so wounded. In that moment, we held one another tightly and cried for the pain we'd inflicted unknowingly for more than twenty years.

After the retreat, our relationship changed dramatically. Now we had a choice, whereas before we'd been acting out our habitual fixations, not even aware of how they functioned, or how much pain they inflicted. Now we could recognize the trance, and we could either choose to continue in it, causing pain and suffering, or we could choose love. We chose love because we were knotted at the heart and loved one another so deeply that we could no longer consciously hurt each other.

We'd still slip back into ego trance, telling our individual stories of us, but the difference was now we knew it, and we recognized it in one another. We used Eli's Enneagram as a tool, a mirror image of what and how our fixations operate. The most important thing the Enneagram taught us was that these fixations weren't who we really were; they were merely pointing a finger to what they veiled—love.

Had it not been for Eli, we still might be in the dark and wondering how to get home. Eli brought us to the path of freedom, but he could only point the way. We had to want freedom so bad, bad enough that we were willing to die for it.

When I think about that chance meeting at the intersection of Eighteenth and Castro in the city of Oz in 1982, I'm filled with gratitude and joy that we've come this far together, that Adrian and I will finish out our journey together. I've led a blessed life full of incredible people, like Eli, who touched me and whose journeys intersected mine, and who gave of themselves and whose love guided me.

The End

My Teachers, Eli and Gangaji

Epilogue

As I look over my shoulder at Adrian, he's reading by the light of the bed lamp. His face silhouetted by the light, he looks content, though a little tired, perhaps. The wrinkles under his eyes betray his age. We were once strong and healthy, but the years and the disease have taken their toll. I silently tell myself how lucky we are to have found one another. Do you believe in fate, like kismet, that it's all laid out, just waiting to happen? I often wonder about fate, if everything didn't happen just the way it was supposed to. If the earthquake hadn't occurred, if I'd been five minutes later when I knocked on his door, would we be here in bed together now?

No man knows his destiny. Whether it was fate or chance, I must thank the universe for all the people who passed through my life and changed it. They were beautiful, talented, with unique insight, incredibly brilliant beings who showed me something unique about the universe and myself, something I may have missed had we not met. Some teach us what it means to be brave, courageous, and joyous. Others teach us what it is to love unconditionally, to be a best friend, or how to dream. These connections show us the heights of happiness and the depths of sorrow. They are our spiritual connections. Some we meet for a brief moment and others for a lifetime; but each brings their gift, that which is beyond words. Words can describe them, but their essence is indescribable: they are our "touchstones."

www.ingramcontent.com/pod-product-compliance
Lightning Source LLC
Chambersburg PA
CBHW021050080526
44587CB00010B/199